Prosodic Phonology

Studies in Generative Grammar 28

Editors

Harry van der Hulst
Jan Koster
Henk van Riemsdijk

Mouton de Gruyter
Berlin · New York

Prosodic Phonology

With a new foreword

by

Marina Nespor and Irene Vogel

Mouton de Gruyter
Berlin · New York

Mouton de Gruyter (formerly Mouton, The Hague)
is a Division of Walter de Gruyter GmbH & Co. KG, Berlin.

The series Studies in Generative Grammar was formerly published by
Foris Publications Holland.

♾ Printed on acid-free paper which falls within the guidelines
of the ANSI to ensure permanence and durability.

Library of Congress Cataloging-in-Publication Data

Nespor, Marina.
    Prosodic phonology : with a new foreword / by Marina Nespor
and Irene Vogel.
      p. cm. − (Studies in generative grammar ; 28)
    Includes bibliographical references and index.
    ISBN 978-3-11-019789-1 (cloth : alk. paper)
    ISBN 978-3-11-019790-7 (pbk. : alk. paper)
    1. Grammar, Comparative and general − Phonology.   2. Pro-
sodic analysis (Linguistics)   I. Vogel, Irene, 1952−   II. Title.
    P217.3.N47   2007
    414'.6−dc22
                                2007039632

Bibliographic information published by the Deutsche Nationalbibliothek

The Deutsche Nationalbibliothek lists this publication in the Deutsche Nationalbibliografie;
detailed bibliographic data are available in the Internet at http://dnb.d-nb.de.

ISBN 978-3-11-019789-1 (hb)
ISBN 978-3-11-019790-7 (pb)
ISSN 0167-4331

ὄσα εἴδομεν καὶ ελάβομεν,
ταῦτα απολείπομεν
ὄσα δὲ οὔτε εἴδομεν οὔτ᾿ ελάβομεν,
ταῦτα φέρομεν.

'what we have seen and caught,
we have left behind us
what we have neither seen nor caught,
we are carrying with us.'
(Heraclitus, from Hippolytus, Confutation 9,9,6)

Contents

Preface

This book is the result of a series of discussions, disputes, and reconciliations that we have had over the last five years in different – most often beautiful – places in Europe: *Anche l'occhio vuole la sua parte* (an Italian saying meaning 'The eye, too, needs its share').

As the title suggests, *Prosodic Phonology* is primarily a book on phonological theory. It deals with domains in phonology and the interactions between phonology and the other components of the grammar, as well as with such related issues as perception and poetic meter. We have done our best to render the book accessible not only to phonologists but also to linguists working in other fields, as well as to scholars with a basic knowledge of generative grammar involved in research in neighboring disciplines.

As the reader will immediately notice, certain languages have a privileged position in this book. This is not by chance: they are our native languages – Italian and English – and some other languages we have learned for necessity or pleasure – Dutch, Greek, French, and Spanish. We have not, however, limited our attention to these languages. Instead, we have attempted to provide a broader basis for our claims and thus have examined phenomena in over twenty-five languages, making use of grammars, previous linguistic analyses, and, whenever possible, intuitions of native speakers.

Many people have contributed to the development of the ideas presented in this book, and several institutions have made its realization possible. The Dutch phonological community has been particularly important for having provided us with a stimulating and encouraging environment. In particular, we would like to thank Geert Booij, Harry van der Hulst, and Mieke Trommelen for having carefully read the entire manuscript in a short period of time and for having made valuable comments and suggestions. We are grateful to Sergio Scalise, who, besides reading and commenting on the entire manuscript, has offered us his time and insights during all stages of the preparation of this book. Ivonne Bordelois and Mauro Scorretti were always available for stimulating and pleasant discussions and gave us valuable comments on the chapters most related to syntax. Pietro Beltrami, Pieter de Meijer, Costanzo Di Girolamo, Karijn

Helsloot, and Helen van Hoorn made useful remarks on matters of meter. We thank all of them. Thanks also to Kostas Dimadis, Giorgio Graffi, and Enzo Lo Cascio for helpful discussions at various critical moments.

The chapter on poetic meter owes much to the students of the University of Amsterdam who participated in the course on Dante and who refused to recognize that the semester was over. Karijn Helsloot has been a valuable help both for her enthusiasm and for her somewhat more material work of scanning many verses of Dante and of preparing the indexes.

We would like to thank the many native speakers of different languages who patiently talked into a tape recorder or offered their intuitions about large numbers of sentences, and Berber van Onck, who provided relief by graciously offering to type parts of the manuscript in moments of need. Thanks also to Luca Bruyning, who helped interpret some of the mysterious messages that came out of the computer.

We are grateful to the University of Amsterdam for the financial support which allowed us to spend several weeks in Italy, during which most of the tape recordings were made, and to the Nederlandse Organisatie voor Zuiver-Wetenschappelijk Onderzoek and the Consiglio Nazionale delle Ricerche for grants which allowed us to spend time together either in Italy or in Holland once we were no longer working in the same country. That time was essential. In addition, we wish to thank the University of Venice for having made available space and other facilities during several periods over the last few years.

Last but not least, we thank each other for going on in periods in which the geographic distance made the end seem progressively farther rather than nearer.

As the riddle we have chosen for the first page of this book suggests, what we have not found we are still carrying with us. We will leave it somewhere else if and when we find it. The content of this book is what we have found up until now and we leave it with the reader.

Foreword to the second edition

We are glad that *Prosodic Phonology* is now available again after over 20 years from its original appearance.

For years, we have been contacted by students and researchers looking for copies of our book, which has been out of print for quite some time. Given this continued interest in *Prosodic Phonology*, we believe it is important to publish the book again, in its original form, as this has served – and continues to serve – as an inspiration for scholars interested in a wide variety of issues.[1] Over the years, *Prosodic Phonology* has been the impetus for a large body of research in diverse areas of inquiry. We have seen investigations of numerous languages and types of phonological phenomena based on the fundamental concepts of the prosodic hierarchy and its constituents. We have also seen extensions of the theory into more recent linguistic frameworks such as Optimality Theory. In addition, *Prosodic Phonology* has stimulated research in a variety of areas of psycholinguistics and cognitive science.

It is beyond the scope of this brief introduction to discuss the wealth of research that has followed the original publication of *Prosodic Phonology (PP)*. In the sections that follow, we briefly mention some paths in which *PP* has taken us in recent years. Our own work has led us, on the one hand, to a strengthening of our commitment to the theory, and on the other hand, to an understanding of some ways in which the theory has needed to evolve. Furthermore, it has provided information regarding the roles that the constituents defined in *PP* play in the processing and acquisition of language. It is our hope that these observations, in combination with the original text, will continue to provide stimulation for those reading *Prosodic Phonology* for the first time, as well as for those who are already familiar with the first edition.

1. Introduction

Prosodic Phonology, familiarly known as N&V86, has inspired much inquiry into basic theoretical aspects of the prosodic hierarchy, in particular, the inventory of constituents and their definition as well as the geometry of the hierarchy itself. Linguists working on languages spoken throughout the world, including relatively understudied languages, have brought to light additional fascinating information about phonology and its interfaces in the context of the proposals in N&V86. In addition, N&V86 has inspired inquiry into other related areas of research including language acquisition, linguistic perception and production and language processing.

As with any area of research, available information and views change over time. One interesting aspect of such change has come in the area of syntactic theory. The model we assumed originally was a relatively early version of X' theory, but this has been replaced by different versions of the theory, or by other theories in some cases. As a general interface theory, *Prosodic Phonology* must of course be able to interface with the fundamental principles of syntax and other components in all human languages, regardless of the representation of these principles. We believe that the fact that *PP* has weathered developments in other areas of grammar, and still provides a basis for intensive research on phonological interfaces with these other areas, attests to the fundamental nature of its insights and value as a theory of language.

Any well constructed theory provides clearly testable hypotheses. As such, *PP* has been tested over the years. What is important in evaluating such "tests" is to determine whether any findings that appear to be in conflict with the theory indicate language-specific deviations or more fundamental issues related to the architecture of the theory itself. In some cases the findings have supported the original proposals, and in others they have indicated the need for certain modifications. In both cases, however, we find that the overall outcome is to strengthen the original theory.

Despite the challenges, since there has been no subsequent systematic theory of phonological interfaces with the other components of grammar, we can only conclude that *Prosodic Phonology* still constitutes a robust starting point for interface and related research. Indeed, in recent years, each of us has gone in rather different research directions, nevertheless deriving our impetus from original aspects of *PP*.

While we have primarily focused on different levels of the prosodic hierarchy, Nespor on the Phonological Phrase and, partly, the Intonational Phrase, and Vogel on the Phonological Word and Clitic Group, our work shares a common theme. Although we have also at times examined other constituents, the constituents we have focused our attention on are precisely those that exhibit the most intimate connections with morpho-syntactic structures. We outline below some of the core issues relating to these constituents.

We leave for further research and discussion the smaller constituents (i.e. the mora, syllable and foot), those that we have defined as being "purely phonological", that is, not involving an interface with other components of grammar. We also leave for further research and discussion the largest constituent (i.e. the Phonological Utterance), since it appears to involve more variable types of considerations including semantics and pragmatics.

At the very core of linguistic theory is the claim that an appropriate theory should be able to account for the psychological reality of language. It is noteworthy that the constituent structures of *PP* in fact provide insightful accounts of psycholinguistic phenomena. As will be shown, this is true with regard to the Clitic Group as well as the Phonological Phrase and the Intonational Phrase, and with regard to both language acquisition and adult linguistic behavior.

In the following sections, we first address the interface of phonology with the morpho-syntax. In particular, the Phonological Word and Clitic Group are discussed. Subsequently, we consider the interface with syntax, specifically in relation to the Phonological Phrase and Intonational Phrase. General conclusions follow.

2. The Morpho-syntactic Interface:
The Phonological Word and the Clitic Group

2.1. Constituent Structure
The part of the prosodic hierarchy that probably has received most attention in the past twenty years involves the smaller interface constituents – the Phonological Word (PW)[2] and the Clitic Group (CG), the topics of Chapters 4 and 5 of *PP*, respectively.[3] It would appear that the reasons for this attention are two-fold. The first, positive, reason is that the elements involved in these constituents - words, affixes, clitics - are relatively accessible, and tend to be described at least to some extent in all grammars. While there is certainly some controversy regarding morphological structure and the analysis of clitics, it is not necessary to have as thorough an analysis of the syntax of a language and an understanding of potentially complex phrase structures in order to examine the PW and CG, as opposed to the larger constituents.

The second, negative, reason is that the original proposal in *Prosodic Phonology* can be seen to involve a problematic analysis of certain structures relating to the PW and the CG. This problem can be summed up in regard to an Italian sentence such as the following:

(1)

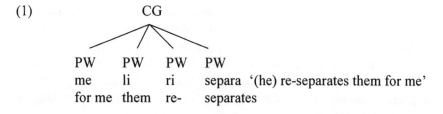

As can be seen in (1), the clitics (*me*, *li*) and a prefix (*ri-*) are attributed PW status, although in reality they do not share the properties of a typical PWs such as *separa* (e.g. satisfying the two mora minimality constraint and exhibiting a primary word stress). The assignment of PW status to such items in N&V86 was a direct consequence of the Strict Layer Hypothesis (SLH), which permits a given constituent to dominate only those constituents of the immediately lower prosodic level.

As mentioned above, in testing a theory, it is important to carefully evaluate potential challenges as well as their proposed remedies. In cases such as (1), it does appear that the PW has been over-assigned by the SLH. If we completely abandon the SLH, however, this would leave the geometry of the prosodic hierarchy unconstrained, and if any type of structure becomes permissible, we no longer have a testable (and falsifiable) theory. Instead, attempts have been made to weaken the SLH without abandoning it completely.[4] Frequently, a combination of remedies is adopted together involving a) the elimination of the requirement that a constituent only dominate constituents of the directly lower level (i.e. the skipping of prosodic levels), b) the introduction of recursive structures such that a constituent may dominate constituents of its same level, and c) the elimination of the CG as a constituent of the prosodic hierarchy. These can be illustrated with the sentence in (1), as shown in (2a-b). Both structures further involve the absence of the CG, when it is assumed that the PW level is dominated, instead, by the Phonological Phrase.[5]

(2)

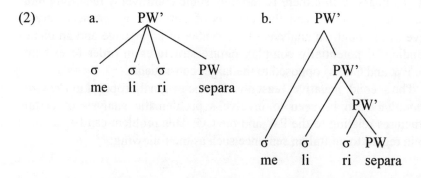

In both cases, we observe a PW constituent dominating another PW, as well as elements at a lower level of the hierarchy, the syllable. The CG is essentially replaced by PW' in the above structures. The "prime" diacritic distinguishes this constituent from the usual PW, although the difference is sometimes simply identified as the "outermost" vs. the "innermost" PW. This type of analysis avoids the problem of labeling clitics and affixes as PWs, however, it introduces problems of a different nature.

While it may at first glance appear that the prosodic hierarchy is simplified by excluding the CG from the inventory of constituents, in fact, such a reduction is only illusory. The fact that recursive PW structures must distinguish at least two levels or types of PW is an indication that there are at least two distinct phonological patterns and thus domains that must be accounted for. The innermost PW exhibits the properties associated with the PW in N&V86, while the outermost PW (PW') exhibits the properties associated with the CG. By labeling both constituents as varieties of PW, rather than PW and CG as in *Prosodic Phonology*, we do not escape the need for two distinct levels, but only obscure the distinction with overlapping names. In fact, such an arrangement actually compromises the definition of linguistic constituent as a particular type of string with clearly and uniquely identifiable properties. If PWs sometimes exhibit one set of properties and at other times exhibit a different set of properties, there is no longer an unambiguously defined PW constituent.[6]

Indeed, such a problem can also be seen with compounds, which are frequently analyzed as recursive PWs (e.g. *[[water]$_{PW}$ [bottle]$_{PW}$]$_{PW'}$*). As is well-known, there are distinct stress patterns associated with a) lexical stress, b) compound stress, and c) phrasal stress. If individual lexical items and compounds are assigned the same phonological status as PWs, it is no longer possible to account for their different stress properties. In this case, too, it has been argued that the CG provides the necessary constituent between the PW and the Phonological Phrase,[7] leading to the proposal that a more appropriate name for the CG is "Composite Group", since this is more adequately encompasses structures with affixes and clitics as well as compounds.

It should be noted that an additional type of problem is introduced by structures such as those in (2). Although the SLH is not completely abandoned, a consequence of permitting such structures is that the theory becomes substantially more permissible. This in turn makes it less clear what would constitute a falsification of the theory, and the theory is thus significantly weakened. While it might still be possible to invoke a modified SLH to exclude structures in which a constituent dominates larger constituents than itself, there no longer appears to be a principled way to determine other aspects of the geometry of prosodic structure. Specifically, if we introduce the possibility of a constituent dominating items more than one level lower in the hierarchy, questions arise as to a) whether all constituents of the prosodic hierarchy are permitted to dominate material more than one level lower, and b) how many lower levels in the hierarchy a constituent may dominate. Furthermore, the introduction of recursivity into the prosodic hierarchy raises additional questions as to whether a) all constituents permit recursivity and b) if recursivity is permitted, whether there is some limit on the increased depth of the resulting constituent structures, for example do we only add one additional level of depth for a given constituent as in (2a), or do we permit any number of levels as in (2b)?[8]

Independently of the answer to these last questions, the introduction of recursivity blurs what has been considered a fundamental difference between morpho-syntactic structure and phonological structure. While the former is widely viewed as permitting indefinite depth via recursivity, the latter was argued to be crucially flatter in this regard, an issue that has recently been brought into focus again.[9]

Returning to the issue raised by structures such as (1), it remains clear that some solution is still required. Indeed, there appears to be a relatively simple modification that both resolves the problem at hand and at the same time offers a restrictive and falsifiable alternative. Rather than introducing the combination of three alterations mentioned above, we propose that the only change needed is for the SLH to permit a constituent to dominate material more than one level lower in the prosodic hierarchy.[10] This is illustrated in (3), where the CG dominates items that are not PWs, but simply syllables.

(3)

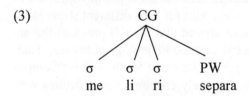

Such a structure continues to capture the original difference in phonological behavior between PWs and larger CGs. This in turn allows us to maintain the concept of constituent as a uniquely defined linguistic string for both the PW and CG.

The issue of restricting the theory must still be addressed, and we propose that this be can be done by strictly limiting the applicability of the proposed innovation. Specifically, we permit a constituent to dominate material more than one level lower in the hierarchy only within the CG, including the PW. Even in cases where phonological clitics may be introduced in positions related to larger constituents, either phonological or syntactic, it appears that their phonological behavior is nevertheless strictly local. That is, they exhibit phonological interactions only with the linearly adjacent material, either the PW that serves as their host, or other elements also associated with the host in longer strings. For example, the "auxiliary s" or "possessive s" in English in *The scare crow's falling* is pronounced as [z] due to the immediately preceding vowel, despite the fact that it is otherwise associated with the entire NP.

It is interesting that the increased structural flexibility appears to be limited to the CG - and the PW. In fact, both of these constituents also appear to exhibit some degree of idiosyncrasy in their rules. Indeed, it has been suggested that this is not a coincidence, but rather a reflection of the fact that these are the two constituents that involve interfaces with morphology, the component of grammar that is associated with exceptions.[11]

With regard to how many levels may be skipped, it appears that this can be restricted as well. In the Italian structure seen above, the CG dominates syllables, thus permitting a skipping of two levels: the PW and the Foot. Although not shown here, it is also possible that only a single level may be skipped. This situation may arise with function words that are more substantial than single syllables, but nevertheless cannot be considered PWs. Assuming that such items constitute Feet, the CG would thus only dominate material involving the skipping of a single level, the PW. Similarly, if a PW includes a stray syllable in addition to Feet, a single level, this time the Foot, would be skipped.

The result is still a very restrictive model, and one that is clearly testable and falsifiable. It continues to express the fundamental concept of linguistic constituent, and it maintains the crucial difference in recursivity and depth of structure between morpho-syntax and phonology.

2.2. Psycholinguistic Evidence

In two recent studies, Wheeldon and Lahiri (W&L) have proposed that the basic unit of speech production is a prosodic constituent rather than a morpho-syntactic one.[12] On the basis of speech production of Dutch speakers, they demonstrate that the number of (grammatical) words fails to predict the response time latency when subjects are required to supply a specified answer in response to a stimulus question. A potential phonological candidate, the number of syllables, also fails to make the correct predictions. Instead, it is proposed that the crucial unit in predicting the response latencies is the PW.

Crucially, W&L include clitics in the PW, so in a sentence like *[Ik zoek het]$_{PW}$* 'I seek the' *[water]$_{PW}$* 'water', the bracketed strings are both considered the same type of structure with regard to speech production. Indeed, such items exhibit equivalent speech production latencies. W&L encountered an unexpected finding with compounds, which they originally analyzed as consisting of two PWs, the usual analysis of such items. Instead of exhibiting response latencies consistent with other structures with two PWs, however, the compounds behaved as single PWs. It was thus proposed that only the highest PW, indicated here as PW', was relevant for determining speech latencies, as in *[[oog]$_{PW}$ [lid]$_{PW}$]$_{PW'}$* 'eye lid'. As mentioned above, if distinct properties are associated with different types of linguistic strings, but the strings are labeled in the same way, we forfeit the concept of constituent as a string defined by a specific set of properties.

The alternative is to explicitly recognize distinct constituents with their own properties. While W&L implicitly introduce a distinction between two types of constituents into the system, this difference is masked by their use of the term PW for both structures. Closer examination of the set of various structures that behave in the same way with respect to response latencies reveals that it coincides with the CG as described above. That is, it includes individual lexical items without associated clitics, items with clitics, and compounds – precisely those structures subsumed under the proposed modifications of the CG (i.e. Composite Group). This, furthermore, leaves the PW constituent available as the domain of its own phonological properties (i.e. stress, phonological rules, and phonotactic constraints).

Thus, the response latency experiments provide independent psycholinguistic evidence for the CG constituent. Furthermore, since response latency is taken as an indication of structural complexity in language processing, we can conclude that the CG is the appropriate constituent for determining this complexity. That is, instead of considering the PW to be the crucial structure for speech encoding, we have evidence that the CG is the crucial structure.

3. The Syntactic Interface:
   The Phonological Phrase and the Intonational Phrase

3.1. The Phonological Phrase
In *Prosodic Phonology*, the Phonological Phrase (ϕ) is the most crucial constituent for the interface between syntax and phonology, in that it is proposed to reflect the relative order of heads and complements and thus also of most subordinate clauses with respect to main clauses (Green-

berg 1963, Hawkins 1983).[13] Both the φ domain and the location of main prominence within it change according to whether in a language complements follow their head, as in English or Italian, or precede it, as in Turkish or Japanese. As established in Chapter 6 of the present volume, the Phonological Phrase extends from the left edge of a phrase to the right edge of its head in head - complement languages, and from the left edge of a head to the right edge of its minimal phrase in complement – head languages. An optional restructuring includes the first non-branching complement or modifier that follows the head in the first type of languages or precedes the head in the second type of languages. Word order is also signaled by main prominence which is located at the right edge of φ in head-complement languages and at its left edge in complement-head languages.

One question that has been addressed in the last 10 years is whether the φ constituent is used on-line in language perception and processing. It has been shown, for example, that the φ constrains lexical access both in adults and in infants of 10 and 13 months of age. Specifically, lexical access is delayed in adults if a local ambiguity is contained within a φ, but not if it straddles two Phonological Phrases. For example, in the French φ [*chat grin*cheux] (cat - grumbling = 'grumbling cat'), the syllable *chat* and the first syllable of the following word - *grin* - are homophonous with the word *chagrin* 'affliction'. The same two-syllable sequence may also be found across φ boundaries, for example in [son grand *chat*][*grim*pait...] ('his/her big cat climbed...'). On the basis of these and similar examples, it has been shown that lexical access is delayed in the first but not in the second case. That is, syllable sequences that are contained within a φ, but not syllable sequences that straddle two φs, are hypothesized by the listener to constitute words.[14]

A subsequent experiment was designed to test whether the Phonological Phrase also constrains lexical access during language acquisition. Infants of 10 and 13 months of age, familiarized with bisyllabic words of English, were tested with bisyllabic items either constituting the same words e.g. [*paper*] or homophonous bisyllables taken from two Phonological Phrases, e.g. [...*pay*] [*per*suades...]. The results showed that they prefer the real target words to the bisyllables straddling two Phonological Phrases. It can thus be concluded that φs also constrain lexical access in infants.[15]

A second question concerning the role of the φ for language acquisition that has been addressed by different scholars is whether it is feasible to think that some aspects of phonology can be exploited to acquire other components of grammar, in particular morphosyntax. This is known as the prosodic bootstrapping hypothesis.[16] The question is: given infants' sensitivity to the smallest differences in linguistic sounds, and given the theory of interfaces in which some aspects of syntax are projected onto prosodic constituents, can the patterns of sound inform infants about the syntax of their language of exposure? The two constituents that have played a major role in this line of investigation are the φ and the Intonational Phrase (IP).

In one of the first works appealing to prosodic bootstrapping for the acquisition of syntax, it was proposed that the main syntactic parameter responsible for word order, the head – complement parameter, may be set at the prelexical stage, i.e. before children know the meaning of words. Notice, in fact, that if children already know some words (e.g. they know that in a sentence like *drink milk*, *drink* means "drink" and *milk* means "milk"), they also know that the verb precedes the object and no word order parameter is left to set.[17] Prelexical setting of word order would account for the fact that when children start combining two words, they do not make mistakes in their relative order.[18]

Specifically, on the basis of Japanese, Mazuka proposes that the head – complement parameter may be set on the basis of intonation breaks between main and subordinate clauses. She further assumes that once infants hear intonation breaks, they are also able to deduce the relative order of heads and complements. This assumption is based on the observation that in rigid word order languages the two orders tend to be related.

In the same line of research, Nespor, Guasti and Christophe (1996) propose an alternative way to set the head – complement parameter. This proposal is based on the observation in Nespor and Vogel (1982), elaborated in *Prosodic Phonology*, that in head – complement languages φ prominence is final, while in complement – head languages, it is initial, as mentioned above. The head-complement parameter may thus be set on the basis of the location of prominence within φs. That is, if prominence is leftmost, the complements precede their head; if it is rightmost, the complements follow their head. Thus if rhythm at the Phonological Phrase level is iambic, as in English [The oldest **boys**] [are **invited**] [to **come**] [to the **pool**] [every **Monday**], infants might realize that in their language of exposure heads precede their complements. If it is trochaic, as in Turkish [**eski** antrenörüm] [**Cumartesi'nden** sonra] [**Istanbul'a** gelecek], ([my old coach] [Saturday after] [Istanbul-to will come] = 'My old coach will come to Istanbul after Saturday') they may conclude that in their language of exposure heads follow their complements. For the same reason used by Mazuka, i.e. that the relative order of head and complements is correlated with the relative order of main and subordinate clauses, in this proposal, it is the relative order of heads and complements that would lead infants to expect a certain relative order of main and subordinate clauses.

The main motivation for the new proposal, based on the Phonological Phrase, rather than the previous one, based on the Intonational Phrase, is that in infant directed speech, to which infants pay particular attention, complex sentences are very rare. It is thus desirable that the smallest phonological constituent that represents the interface with syntax be involved in the bootstrapping of the basic word order parameter. In addition, motivation for the ϕ as the relevant constituent used in the bootstrapping of word order comes from mixed word order languages, such as German or Dutch. In these languages, if a head and its complement are contained in the same ϕ, its prominence varies according to whether the head precedes or follows its complement, thus indicating for each phrase the word order that characterizes it.

Psychological plausibility regarding the bootstrapping of word order on the basis of the relative prominence within Phonological Phrases comes from the proposal that the physical realization of ϕ prominence varies depending on whether it is initial or final. Specifically, it has been proposed that the "iambic-trochaic law" determines the phonetic realization of main prominence within ϕs that contain more than one word. That is, prominence is realized more through pitch and intensity in stress-initial ϕs, and more through lengthening in stress-final ϕs. Since ϕ prominence is initial in complement – head structures and final in head – complement structures, as proposed in *PP*, a trochaic grouping indicates a complement-head structure while an iambic grouping indicates a head-complement structure. Since the perception of grouping as established by the iambic trochaic law applies also to nonlinguistic sounds,[19] the conclusion can be drawn that one of the basic properties of syntax could be learned in the prelexical stage through a general mechanism of perception.

We have supported the hypothesis that the phonetic realization of prominence within the ϕ varies according to its position with interlinguistic data (French and Turkish), as well as with intralinguistic data (German).[20] On the basis of delexicalized French and Turkish sentences,[21] it has been shown, furthermore, that at only a few weeks of age, infants discriminate the two languages only on the basis of prominence at the level of the Phonological Phrase, thus lending plausibility to the proposed bootstrapping mechanism.[22] As to intralinguistic evidence, it has been shown that 14-month-old German infants are sensitive to the prosodic content of phrases that differ only in their ordering of heads and complements.[23]

This is not to say that prominence within φs is the only cue to the relative order of words. Distributional cues appear to be exploited as well: it has been proposed that a frequency-based bootstrapping mechanism is based on infants' ability to track the order of functors and content words, identified through their different frequency distributions, functors being much more frequent than content words. Indeed, 7-month-old Japanese and Italian infants have opposite order preferences in an artificial grammar experiment, mirroring the opposite word orders of their respective native languages.[24]

3.2. The Intonational Phrase

The Intonational Phrase (IP) is proposed in Chapter 7 of this volume to offer cues to the constituency of phrases within sentences, rather than, as is the case for the Phonological Phrase, to the relative order of words within phrases. Main IP prominence universally falls on the rightmost Phonological Phrase in broad focus sentences, otherwise on the constituent that is interpreted as bearing narrow focus.[25] The location of IP prominence in narrow focus sentences has been proposed to give a cue to the possibility a language might have to move or delete subject and object noun phrases and thus to play a role in the bootstrapping of the relevant syntactic parameters.[26] The reasoning goes as follows. Prominence on the last φ not only leads to a broad focus interpretation, it also corresponds to interpretations in which either the last word, or all constituents that dominate it, have narrow focus. If, for discourse reasons, narrow focus must be placed on a different constituent, languages vary as to their behavior.[27] Languages whose syntax allows constituent movement, move the focused noun phrase to the stressed position; languages that do not allow a particular movement in syntax, move stress to the focused noun phrase. Thus in an English sentence like *I gave a book to John*, if narrow focus is on the direct object *a book*, main IP stress is on it. In the Italian sentence with the same meaning, *Ho dato un libro a Giovanni*, if narrow focus is on the direct object, the requirement that new information and stress coincide is obtained by moving the direct object to the right edge of the sentence, yielding *Ho dato a Giovanni un libro*. On the basis of these data, it is thus proposed that fixed stress at the right edge of Intonational Phrases, as in Italian, gives a cue to the possibility of having different word orders; stress in different positions within an IP, as in English, instead, gives cues to rigid word order. The next step would be to investigate this proposal on the basis of psycho-linguistic experiments.

Intonational phrases also have a function in speech segmentation, since the edges of IPs are always aligned to the edges of words, and since edges have a privileged position in speech processing.[28] Prosodic cues, however, are not the only cues to speech segmentation and thus to the identification of words: transitional probabilities between syllables have been shown to allow word segmentation both in adults and in infants. That is, participants habituated with artificial streams of speech in which tri-syllabic words are defined exclusively on the statistical coherence of their syllables (the first syllable predicts the second syllable with certainty and the second predicts the third with certainty) choose words over part-words (i.e. items that contain a dip in transition probabilities).[29] Recent experiments investigate the interaction of statistical and prosodic cues to extract words from the speech stream. These show that, while transitional probabilities are computed independently of prosody, IPs filter words that contain an IP boundary, while words that are entirely contained in an IP are stored in memory. It can thus be concluded that sensitivity to IPs constrains the lexical search process.[30]

4. Conclusions

In sum, our own work has taken us in a variety of directions with relation to the original proposals to *Prosodic Phonology*, and in each case we have continued to find evidence and support for the original proposals. In some cases, certain modifications appear to be needed, but the basic architecture of the system, including the nature of its interfaces with other components of grammar, continues to be reinforced by our research – both theoretical and experimental.

Beyond our own work, a great deal of additional research has been conducted on the basis of *Prosodic Phonology* from many perspectives, too numerous to mention here. It is our hope that the basic concepts proposed in the present book will continue to stimulate research in a variety of fields both in theoretical linguistics and in the cognitive neurosciences. In the former, we look forward to deepening our understanding of phonological theory in general, as well as the relationship between the phonological component and other components of grammar. In the latter, we anticipate gaining further insight into issues of language perception, language acquisition, and the study of language deficits.

NOTES

1.   We apologize for any typos and inaccuracies in the original text. A factual inconsistency regarding Yidiɲ has been corrected in the present version. We are very grateful to Ursula Kleinhenz for producing this second edition of *Prosodic Phonology*, and for her help with the practical matters involved in this process. We extend our thanks to Harry van der Hulst and Baris Kabak for their helpful comments on this introduction.

2.   The symbol "ω" was originally used for the Phonological Word; however, we use "PW" here to be consistent with more recent representations of this constituent.

3.   Recently two entire volumes have been devoted to investigation of the Phonological Word: Hall and Kleinhenz (1999); Dixon and Aikhenvald (2002). The PW is also the focus of a large scale typological study by B. Bickel and colleagues at the University of Leipzig, although the approach is rather different from that of N&V86.

4.   See among others Itô and Mester (1992); Vogel (1994, 1999, in press a); Selkirk (1996).

5.   This approach is taken by Booij (1996); Selkirk (1996), Peperkamp (1997), Hall (1999), among others.

6.   See Vogel (in press b; to appear).

7.   Kabak and Vogel (2001) for Turkish; Vogel and Raimy (2002) for English; Vogel (in press a, b; to appear).

8.   It should be noted that Ladd 1997 has proposed that the Intonational Phrase is recursive. His ips, however, serve only to align intonational contours, as opposed to delimiting the domains of phonological rules, and would appear to be distinct from the constituents of the prosodic hierarchy in N&V86.

9.   Jackendoff and Pinker (2005); Pinker and Jackendoff (2005); Neeleman and van de Koot (2006).

10.   Vogel (in press b; to appear).

11.   Vogel (to appear).

12.   Wheeldon and Lahiri (1997, 2002).

13.   From a different perspective, the Phonological Phrase has also received attention within the Optimality Theory framework (e.g. Selkirk 2000; Truckenbrodt 1999).

14.   Christophe et al. (2004).

15.   Gout et al. (2004).

16.   Gleitman and Wanner (1992).

17.   Mazuka (1996).

18.   Brown (1973).

19.   Bolton (1984); Woodrow (1951); Cooper and Meyer (1960).

20.   Nespor, Shukla, Avesani, van de Vijver, Donati and Schraudolf (submitted).

21.   That is, all sentences contained the same phones, taken from Dutch. In addition, vowels were reduced to schwa, stops to [p], fricatives to [s], nasals to

[m], liquids to [l] and glides to [y]. The languages could thus not be identified on the basis of their phones.

22. Christophe, Nespor, Dupoux, Guasti, van Ooyen (2003).
23. Bion, Hoehle, and Schmitz (2007).
24. Gervain, Nespor, Mazuka, Horie, and Mehler (in press).
25. Hayes and Lahiri (1991).
26. Nespor and Guasti (2002); Donati and Nespor (2003).
27. Nespor and Guasti (2002).
28. Endress, Scholl and Mehler (2005); Mehler and Endress (2007); Endress and Mehler (submitted).
29. Saffran, Aslin and Newport (1996), Peña, Bonatti, Nespor and Mehler (2002).
30. Shukla, Nespor and Mehler (2007).

References

Bion, R. A. H., B. Höhle and M. Schmitz (2007). The role of prosody on the perception of word-order differences by 14-month-old German infants. *Proceedings of ICPhS 2007.* 1537-1540.
Bolton, T.L. (1894) Rhythm. *American Journal of Psychology.* 6:145-238.
Booij, G. (1996). Cliticization as prosodic integration: the case of Dutch. *The Linguistic Review.* 13:219-242.
Brown, R. (1973). *A First Language: the Early Stages.* Cambridge, Mass.: Harvard University Press.
Christophe, A., M. Nespor, E. Dupoux, M.-T. Guasti and B. v. Ooyen (2003) Reflexions on prosodic bootstrapping: its role for lexical and syntactic acquisition. *Developmental Science.* 6.2:213-222.
Christophe, A., S. Peperkamp, C. Pallier, E. Block and J. Mehler (2004). Phonological phrase boundaries constrain lexical access: I. Adult data. *Journal of Memory and Language.* 51:523-547.
Cooper, G. and L. Meyer (1960) *The Rhythmic Structure of Music.* Chicago. University of Chicago Press.
Dixon, R.M.W. and A.Y Aikhenvald (eds.) (2002). *Word.* Cambridge: University Press.
Donati, C. and M. Nespor (2003). From focus to syntax. *Lingua.* 113.11:1119-1142.
Endress, A.D., Scholl, B.J. and Mehler, J. (2005). The role of salience in the extraction of algebraic rules. *Journal of Experimental Psychology: General,* 134(3): 406 - 419.

Endress, A.D. and J. Mehler (submitted). Perceptual Constraints in Pho-
    notactic Learning.
Gervain, J., M. Nespor, R. Mazuka, R. Horie and J. Mehler (in press).
    Bootstrapping word order in prelexical infants: A Japanese-Italian
    crosslinguistic study. *Cognitive Psychology*.
Gleitman, L. and E. Wanner (1982). The State of the State of the Art. In:
    E. Wanner and L. Gleitman (eds.) *Language Acquisition: The State
    of the Art*. Cambridge, MA: CUP. 3-48.
Gout, A., A. Christophe, and J. Morgan (2004). Phonological phrase
    boundaries constrain lexical access: II. Infant data. *Journal of Memo-
    ry and* Language. 5:547-567.
Greenberg, J. (1963). Some universals of grammar with particular refer-
    ence to the order of meaningful elements. In *Universals of Language*.
    Cambridge, Mass. MIT Press. 73–113.
Guasti, M.-T., M. Nespor, A. Christophe and B. van Ooyen (2000). Pre-
    lexical setting of the head - complement parameter through prosody.
    in J. Weissenborn, and B. Hoehle (eds.) *How to get into Language
    Approaches to Bootstrapping in Early Language Development*. John
    Benjamins. Amsterdam. 231-248.
Hall, T. A. (1999). The phonological word: a review. In T.A. Hall and
    U. Kleinhenz (eds.) *Studies on the Phonological Word*. Philadelphia:
    John Benjamins. 1-22.
Hall, T. A. and U. Kleinhenz (eds.) (1999). *Studies on the Phonological
    Word*. Philadelphia: John Benjamins.
Hawkins, J.A. (1983). *Word Order Universals*. New York, Academic
    Press.
Hayes, B. and A. Lahiri, 1991. Bengali intonational phonology. *Natural
    Language and Linguistic Theory*. 9:47-96.
Itô, J. and A. Mester (1992). Weak layering and word binarity. Ms, Uni-
    versity of California at Santa Cruz. Updated version 2003.
Jackendoff, R. and S. Pinker (2005). The nature of the language faculty
    and its implications for the evolution of language. (Reply to Fitch,
    Hauser, and Chomsky). *Cognition*. 97: 211-225.
Kabak, B. and I. Vogel (2001). The Phonological Word and stress as-
    signment in Turkish. *Phonology*. 18:315-360.
Mazuka, R. (1996). Can a grammatical parameter be set before the first
    word? Prosodic contributions to early setting of a grammatical para-
    meter. In J. Morgan and K. Demuth (eds.) *Signal to Syntax*.
    Hillsdale, New Jersey. Laurence Erlbaum Associates. 313-330.
Mehler, J., A. Endress, J. Gervain, and M. Nespor (2007). From Percep-
    tion to Grammar. In A.D. Friederici and G. Thierry (eds.): *Early
    Language Development: Bridging Brain and Behaviour*. Trends in

Language Acquisition Research (TiLAR), Volume 5. Amsterdam, John Benjamins.191-213.

Neeleman, A. and J. van de Koot (2006). On syntactic and phonological representations. *Lingua.* 116:1524-1552.

Nespor, M. and I. Vogel (1982) Prosodic domains of external sanghi rules. In H. van der Hulst and N. Smith (eds.) *The Structure of Phonological Representations.* Part I. Dordrecht. Foris. 225-255.

Nespor, M. and M.-T. Guasti (2002). Focus-stress alignment and its consequences for acquisition. *Lingue e Linguaggio.* 1:79-106.

Nespor, M., M.-T. Guasti and A. Christophe (1996). Selecting word order: the rhythmic Activation Principle. In U. Kleinhenz (ed.) *Interfaces in Phonology.* Berlin. Akademie Verlag. 1-26.

Nespor, M., M. Shukla, R. van de Vijver, C. Avesani, H. Schraudolf and C. Donati (submitted). Different phrasal prominence realization in VO and OV languages.

Peña, M. L.L. Bonatti, M. Nespor and J. Mehler (2002). Signal-driven computations in speech processing. *Science.* 298:604-607.

Peperkamp, S. (1997). *Prosodic Words.* The Hague: Holland Academic Graphics.

Pinker, S and R. Jackendoff (2005). The faculty of language: What's special about it? *Cognition.* 95: 201-236.

Saffran, J., R. Aslin, & E. Newport (1996). Statistical learning by 8-month-old infants. *Science,* 274:1926–1928.

Selkirk, E. (1996). The prosodic structure of function words. In J. Morgan and K. Demuth (eds.) *Signal to Syntax: bootstrapping from syntax to grammar in early acquisition.* Mahwah, NJ: Erlbaum. 187-213.

Selkirk, E. (2000). The interaction of constraints on prosodic phrasing. In M. Horne (ed.) *Prosody: Theory and Experiments.* Dordrecht: Kluwer. 231-261.

Shukla, M., M. Nespor and J. Mehler (2007). Interaction between prosody and statistics in the segmentation of fluent speech. *Cognitive Psychology.* 54.1:1-32.

Truckenbrodt, H. (1999). On the relation between syntactic phrases and Phonological Phrases. *Linguistic Inquiry.* 30:219-255.

Vogel, I. (1994). Phonological interfaces in Italian. In M .Mazzola (ed.) *Issues and Theory in Romance Linguistics: Selected Papers from the Linguistic Symposium on Romance Languages XXIII.* Washington, DC: Georgetown University Press. 109-125.

Vogel, I. (1999). Subminimal constituents in prosodic phonology. In S. Hannahs and M. Davenport (eds.) *Issues in phonological structure.* Amsterdam: Benjamins. 249-267.

Vogel, I. (in press a). The Morphology-Phonology Interface: isolating to polysynthetic languages". In F. Kiefer and P. Siptar (eds.) *Selected Papers from the 12th International Morphology Meeting*. Special Issue of *Acta Linguistica Hungarica* . Volume 54:2. Budapest, Hungary.

Vogel, I. (in press b). Universals of prosodic structure. In S.Scalise, E.Magni, E.Vineis, A.Bisetto (eds.) *With more than Chance Frequency. Forty Years of Universals of Language*. Amsterdam, Springer.

Vogel, I. (to appear). The status of the Clitic Group. In J. Grijzenhout and B. Kabak (eds.) *Phonological Domains: Universals and Deviations*. Berlin/ New York: Mouton de Gruyter.

Vogel, I. and E. Raimy (2002). The acquisition of compound vs. phrasal stress: the role of prosodic constituents. *Journal of Child Language*. 29:225-250.

Wheeldon, L and A. Lahiri (1997). Prosodic units in speech production. *Journal of Memory and Language*. 37: 356-381.

Wheeldon, L and A. Lahiri (2002). The minimal unit of phonological encoding: prosodic or lexical word. *Cognition*. 85: B31-B41.

Woodrow, H. (1951). Time perception. In S.S. Stevens (ed.) *Handbook of Experimental Psychology*. New York. Wiley. 1224-1236.

List of Abbreviations and Symbols

A	adjective
	adverb
abl.	ablative
abs.	absolutive
acc.	accusative
ant	anterior
AP	adjective/adverb phrase
ART	article
asp	aspirated
AUX	auxiliary
C	clitic group
	consonant
CL	clitic
cons	consonantal
cont	continuant
cor	coronal
dat.	dative
DCL	directional clitic
del rel	delayed release
dim.	diminutive
DTE	designated terminal element
[e]	empty category
fem.	feminine
G	glide
gen.	genitive
ger.	gerund
I	intonational phrase
imp.	imperative
inch.	inchoative
inf.	infinitive
L	liquid
lat	lateral
LF	logical form
loc.	locative

masc.	masculine
N	nasal
	noun
nas	nasal
nom.	nominative
NP	noun phrase
obstr	obstruent
P	preposition
ϕ	phonological phrase
Pe	person
pl.	plural
PP	prepositional phrase
PRE	prefix
pres.	present
PRON	pronoun
purp.	purposive
Q	terminal syntactic node
R	rhyme
RP	Received Pronunciation
s	strong
S	sentence
σ	syllable
Σ	foot
sg.	singular
son	sonorant
strid	strident
SUF	suffix
syll	syllabic
t	trace
U	phonological utterance
V	verb
	vowel
vce	voice
w	weak
	word
ω	phonological word
W*	word star
[+W]	diacritic feature
WFC	well-formedness condition
$\overline{X}$	X-bar

Chapter 1

Preliminaries

1.0. Introduction

In early generative theory, phonology was characterized by a linear organization of segments and a set of phonological rules whose domains of application were implicitly defined in terms of the boundaries of the surface morpho-syntactic constituent structure (see Chomsky and Halle, 1968, henceforth referred to as SPE). Thus, the interaction of phonology with the rest of the grammar was limited to an interface with syntax such that the output of the syntactic component constituted the input to the phonological component with the possible intervention of Readjustment Rules. While such a model is appealing for its simplicity and has, indeed, yielded many interesting results, it is our contention that this view of phonology is fundamentally inadequate. That is, on the basis of developments in phonological theory over the past decade, it seems that the phonological component cannot be considered a homogeneous system, but rather must be seen as a set of interacting subsystems, each governed by its own principles, such as the theories of the metrical grid, lexical phonology, autosegmental phonology, and prosodic phonology.

The subsystem we will be concerned with in the present study is the prosodic subsystem, and in particular, the theory of domains. According to prosodic theory, the mental representation of speech is divided into hierarchically arranged chunks. In the typically continuous flow of speech, such mental chunks, the prosodic constituents of the grammar, are signaled by different types of cues ranging from actual segmental modifications to more subtle phonetic changes. That is, each prosodic constituent serves as the domain of application of specific phonological rules and phonetic processes. The development of a theory that accounts for such domains thus represents a change of focus in the study of phonology similar to the change that has taken place in the study of syntax in the last twenty years. That is, there is a shift away from the study of systems of rules in the direction of the study of the principles that govern the application of grammatical processes.

Within the model of prosodic phonology proposed in this book, not only is each prosodic constituent characterized by the different rules that apply in relation to it, but also by the different principles on the basis of which it is defined. That is, each constituent of the prosodic hierarchy draws on different types of phonological and nonphonological information in the definition of its domain. While the principles that define the various prosodic constituents make reference to nonphonological notions, it is of crucial importance that the resulting prosodic constituents are not necessarily isomorphic to any constituents found elsewhere in the grammar. Specifically, the prosodic constituents built on the basis of information contained in the morphological and syntactic components are not necessarily in a one-to-one relation with any of the constituents of the morphology or syntax. Since prosodic structure above the word level reflects certain syntactic notions and relations, it can be used in certain cases as a diagnostic tool in relation to problems of syntactic analysis. That is, if it has been determined that a phonological rule applies within a particular prosodic constituent, in the case that more than one syntactic analysis of a given construction is possible, the application or nonapplication of this phonological rule between two crucial words may provide evidence in favor of one analysis or another (see also Nespor, 1977).

In relation to the difference between the morpho-syntactic and prosodic hierarchies, it should be noted, furthermore, that the two differ not only in the way they divide a given string into constituents. They also differ with respect to depth. That is, since the rules that construct the phonological hierarchy are not recursive in nature, while the rules that construct the syntactic hierarchy are, the depth of phonological structure is finite, while the depth of syntactic structure is, in principle, not finite.

A relation between the phonological and semantic components of the grammar is also necessary in that certain types of information contained in the semantic component must be made available to the phonology at the highest levels of the prosodic hierarchy. Thus, the overall model of the grammar must be such that there is an interaction between the two interpretive components, as opposed to the more traditional model in which the syntactic component generates structures that are separately interpreted by the phonological and semantic components.

The remainder of this chapter is dedicated to a description of the general theoretical framework we will assume and the material that forms the empirical basis of this book. The inadequacy of the constituents of the morpho-syntactic hierarchy as domains of application of prosodic rules will be systematically demonstrated in Chapter 2. We will then discuss the different constituents of the phonological hierarchy, providing for each of them both the principles that account for the mapping of notions found in other parts of the grammar onto phonological structure, and examples of phonological rules that apply in the domains thus defined. Specifically, the two units below the word level, that is, the syllable and the foot, will be presented in Chapter 3, while the phonological word will be treated in Chapter 4. The four phonological units above the word level – the clitic group, the phonological phrase, the intonational phrase, and the phonological utterance – are the topics of Chapters 5, 6, 7, and 8, respectively.

The fact that prosodic theory provides a unique set of grammatical constituents, each of which may be signaled in the speech chain by specific phonetic cues, suggests that it is precisely the set of prosodic constituents, rather than other types of constituents, that accounts for the first level of processing in speech perception. The relevance of prosodic phrasing for perception is borne out by the results of a test discussed in Chapter 9, in which the possibility of disambiguating ambiguous sentences was correctly predicted by the prosodic rather than by the syntactic structure of the sentences involved.

The relevance of prosodic constituent structure is also seen in another area of language, that is, in verse, where prosodic categories can be seen to provide the appropriate domains in the description of metrical conventions. This will be discussed in Chapter 10, in relation to Dante's *Divina Commedia*. The last chapter contains some concluding remarks and the outline of a model of phonology that represents the interface between the units of the phonological hierarchy and the other components of the grammar.

1.1. Interface between phonology and the other components of the grammar

Without looking very far for evidence, it is clear that a totally autonomous phonological component is implausible. In fact, in traditional generative phonology there are many cases in which the application of phonological rules depends crucially on other than purely phonological information.[1] Such information, however, was typically encoded in pseudo-phonological terms by means of different types of boundary symbols. For example, in order to account for the pronunciation of the sequence [ŋg] before *er* in words such as *finger* and *longer*, as opposed to the single segment [ŋ] before *er* in *singer* and at the end of the word *sing*, Chomsky and Halle (1968:85) make crucial use of the distinction between word boundaries (#) and morpheme boundaries (+). The following representations are thus posited for each of the words in question: /fɪngər/, /lɔng+ər/, /sɪng#ər/, /sɪng#/. The deletion of /g/ in the third and fourth words, but not in the first and second words, can now be accounted for by a simple rule that operates only before word boundaries: $g \rightarrow \emptyset$ / [+nas]__ #. According to this formulation, *g*-Deletion appears to be a purely pho-

nological process, although this rule, in fact, encodes information of a somewhat different nature. That is, the specification of # in the structural
description of the rule provides more than phonological information; it
allows the rule to apply in specific morphological contexts but not in
others, even when the segmental phonological environments are the
same, for example before the *-er* of the agentive (*si[ŋ]er*) but not before
the *-er* of the comparative (*lo[ŋg]er*).

The nonphonological information required to account for phonological
processes is not only morphological in nature; there are also phonological
rules that are sensitive to information relating to syntactic structure. The
interface between phonology and syntax has in large part been treated in
traditional generative phonology in an analogous way to the interface
between phonology and morphology, that is, in terms of different types
of boundary symbols. For example, in the case of phonological phenomena that operate across words, external sandhi processes in the Classical
Indian tradition, the application of a rule depends crucially on the syntactic relation between the words in question. The way in which such information was encoded in phonological terms was in terms of the distinction
between a single and a double word boundary, as illustrated by Selkirk's
(1972) analysis of Liaison in French. Thus the application of Liaison in
a sentence such as *Il y a encore deux après-midi* 'There are still two
afternoons' and its lack of application in the same segmental environment
in the sentence *Il y en a encore deux / après lui* 'There are still two of
them after him' was accounted for by specifying that the rule applies
freely across a single word boundary found, for example, between a
specifier and its head (. . . *deux#après-midi*), but is blocked across a
double word boundary found, for example, between two phrases
(. . . *deux##après lui*).

Since in standard generative theory the input to the phonology consisted solely of the output of the syntax, the implicit claim was made that
information of any type not contained in surface syntactic structure
could not affect the application of phonological rules. There are, however,
phonological rules that demonstrate that such a position is untenable.
One such rule is Linking-*r* in the RP (Received Pronunciation) style
of British English, a rule that applies not only across words within a sentence, but also across words that belong to different sentences, as in
There's my mothe[r]. I've got to go. Aside from the fact that there is
no syntactic constituent that groups two such sentences together, an
additional problem arises in accounting for the observation that Link-
ing-*r* does not apply between just any two sentences, as illustrated by its
failure to apply in *There's my mothe[∅]. I've got two cats*, where the
segmental context is identical to the one in which the rule was seen to
apply above. While the two sentences in the second example are not relat-

ed in any way, the sentences of the first example are crucially related by the implicit semantic relation that holds between them, specifically, 'sentence$_1$ THEREFORE sentence$_2$', an issue that will be discussed more extensively in Chapter 8 (see also Vogel, 1986). Since such semantic relations do not fall within the realm of the logical form component, that is, they are not interpretations of structural syntactic relations, this suggests that an interface between phonology and semantics must be allowed in the theory of grammar.

The position taken in the present study is thus that an adequate theory of phonology must provide a way of making reference not only to the morpho-syntactic bracketings of the surface syntactic structure, but also to other syntactic as well as semantic notions. This is achieved in the model presented in this book by means of the mapping rules that group the terminal elements of a string in a way that creates units that are not necessarily in a one-to-one relation with the constituents of the morpho-syntactic hierarchy. Such phonological units constitute the domains of application of phonological rules and, to the extent that they are not isomorphic to the morpho-syntactic constituents, they make a theory of boundaries impossible to maintain. It is precisely the set of mapping rules that provides the interface between the phonology and the other components of the grammar, since the rules that define the various prosodic constituents make use of different types of grammatical notions for each level of the hierarchy. The specific relations between the levels of the prosodic hierarchy and the other components of the grammar, furthermore, are highly constrained. That is, whether a given mapping rule makes use of a specific type of morphological, syntactic, or semantic information is not a free choice. In particular, the lower constituents that make use of nonphonological information take into consideration notions present at the lower levels of the morpho-syntactic hierarchy. Higher constituents in the prosodic hierarchy depend on notions incorporated at higher levels of the syntactic tree, and the uppermost levels also make reference to semantic notions. In addition, the generality of the type of nonphonological notions used in the mapping rules increases as we proceed to larger prosodic categories. Each prosodic category thus has a degree of variability across languages which is greater than that of the category directly above it in the hierarchy; the last two categories, in fact, are those that are the most universal in nature.

1.2. Theoretical framework

Since the theory of prosodic phonology advanced in this book is a formal representation of the phonological interpretation of the linguistic material generated by the morpho-syntactic component and interpreted by the semantic component, it is important to clarify at the outset the positions we take with respect to a number of theoretical issues regarding the organization of the grammar in general. We will first present our view of the structure of the phonological component, and in particular, the prosodic subsystem. We will then briefly discuss the aspects of the other components that are relevant to the interaction of these components with the phonology.

1.2.1.   The phonological component
In recent years, the field of phonology has witnessed the development of a number of new theories, including autosegmental theory, the theory of the metrical grid, lexical phonology, and prosodic phonology. The model developed in the present study falls under the general heading of prosodic phonology in the sense of Selkirk's germinal proposal in 'On prosodic structure and its relation to syntactic structure' (1978b) and an extension of this proposal found in Nespor and Vogel (1982). As we mentioned earlier, the model presented here is a theory of phonological domains, that is, a theory that organizes a given string of language into a series of hierarchically arranged phonological constituents that in turn form the contexts within which phonological rules apply. It is our contention that such a prosodic theory forms a subsystem of the phonological component of the grammar and interacts in interesting ways with other subsystems represented by the different theories mentioned above. For example, the most appropriate analysis of a number of harmony rules seems to require an interaction between autosegmental theory, which accounts for the way in which the rules operate, and prosodic theory, which accounts for the domains in which the rules apply. Another type of interaction is found in the set of rules having to do with phenomena of relative prominence and rhythm, which require a treatment in terms of grids as far as the content of the rules is concerned and a treatment in terms of prosodic theory as far as their domains are concerned. Thus, rules such as those discussed by Hayes (to appear) that account for the metrical patterns in English verse modify the grid representation of prominence within domains specified by prosodic theory (see also Chapter 10).

A model of the prosodic subsystem of phonology differs crucially from the traditional generative model of phonology in two fundamental areas: the structure of the representations and the nature of the rules. In this section, we briefly present the basic notions we will make use of throughout this book, as well as the principles governing the representations and rules of the system.

Phonological representations

   In contrast with the linear representations of traditional generative phonology, prosodic phonological representations consist of a set of phonological units organized in a hierarchical fashion. The phonological units, defined on the basis of mapping rules incorporating information from the various components of the grammar, are grouped into hierarchical structures, or trees, in accordance with the following principles that establish the geometry of such trees.

>   *Principle 1.* A given nonterminal unit of the prosodic hierarchy, X^p, is composed of one or more units of the immediately lower category, X^{p-1}.
>   *Principle 2.* A unit of a given level of the hierarchy is exhaustively contained in the superordinate unit of which it is a part.[2]
>   *Principle 3.* The hierarchical structures of prosodic phonology are n-ary branching.
>   *Principle 4.* The relative prominence relation defined for sister nodes is such that one node is assigned the value strong (s) and all the other nodes are assigned the value weak (w).

Given that the internal structure of each prosodic constituent is characterized by the same geometrical configuration, the rules that construct the trees of the different prosodic categories will all have the same form, that of rule (1), which will thus have to be formulated only once in Universal Grammar.

(1)   *Prosodic Constituent Construction*
      Join into an n-ary branching X^p all X^{p-1} included in a string delimited by the definition of the domain of X^p.

For the convenience of the reader, however, we will give the specific rule for constructing the trees of each category in the respective chapters, where the variables are replaced by the appropriate values. It should be noted that the parallelism among the trees of all the prosodic categories is analogous to the parallelism expressed by the X-bar convention in syntactic theory, according to which it is also the case that the internal geometry of all phrasal nodes is essentially the same.

   The four principles given above, along with the rule in (1), allow us to construct phonological representations of the abstract form given in (2).

(2)

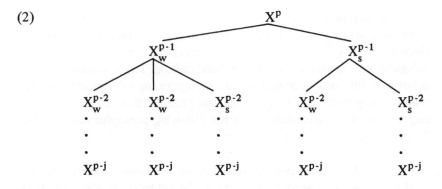

By the same token, each of the four structures in (3) is ruled out by Principles 1-4, respectively.

(3)   a. *   ...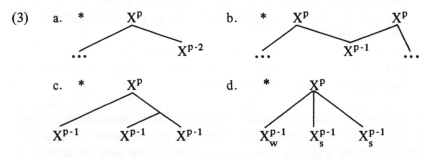

The first two principles and the type of restrictions they place on prosodic tree structure are relatively uncontroversial, since a theory in which one or both are lacking would allow a virtually unlimited number of possible structures. The last two principles, on the other hand, are more controversial, and in fact, the position we are taking here differs from that found in earlier work (including our own) on prosodic phonology. In Principle 3, it is proposed that prosodic structures are n-ary branching, in contrast with earlier claims that they are binary branching.[3] The question of binary *vs.* n-ary branching structures has received much attention in various areas of generative linguistic theory, and it is likely to remain a controversial issue for years to come, with respect to phonology as well as to the other components of the grammar. At this time, however, it seems most advantageous to posit n-ary branching structures for the prosodic hierarchy for a number of reasons.[4]

First of all, n-ary branching structures are simpler than binary branching structures in the sense that the former are essentially flat, while the latter allow, in principle, trees of unlimited depth, as illustrated below.

(4) a. 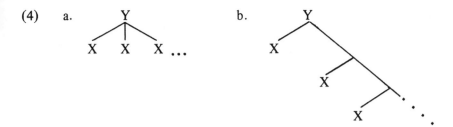 b.

Binary branching trees thus lead to the creation of a much richer internal structure than do n-ary branching trees. This additional structure is not, however, motivated phonologically. For example, in order to group three elements into a binary structure, an intermediate node must be created, as illustrated in (5b). No such intermediate structure exists in the n-ary branching structure in (5a).

(5) a. 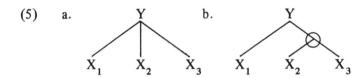 b.

The extra (circled) node in the binary branching tree represents a level of structure that does not correspond to any constituent in phonological theory. That is, there do not seem to be any rules or other phenomena that crucially need to refer to a constituent defined as a subpart of a constituent Y in this way. This fact, although recognized, was minimized in the past by claiming that only those nodes with category labels were constituents with respect to the formulation and application of phonological rules (see Selkirk, 1980b; Nespor, 1983).

Finally, it was suggested in Nespor and Vogel (1982) that the additional constituent structure found in binary branching trees might have a role, if not in specifying the domain of phonological rules, at least in accounting for restructuring of constituents under certain circumstances. It was claimed, for example, that a very long constituent Y could be broken into shorter constituents only in such a way that the Y that 'split off' from the original one was a constituent in the original structure, as seen in (6a). Similarly, particularly short Xs could be regrouped into longer ones only if the newly created X corresponded to a node in the original structure, as illustrated in (6b).

(6)   a.

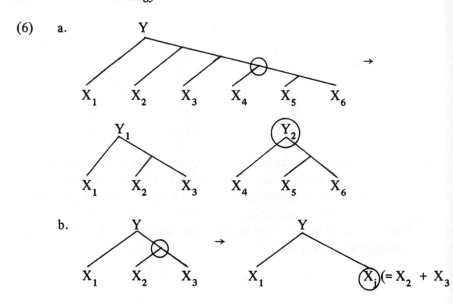

Contrary to our original proposal, it seems now that restructuring cannot be constrained in the way just seen. That is, while most cases seem to follow such a constraint, there are some cases in which the constituent structure of binary branching trees makes incorrect predictions about which units may be regrouped when a long Y is broken down into shorter ones, and when short Xs may be grouped into larger ones (see Chapter 7).

The branching structure of phonological trees was originally argued for also on the grounds of stress assignment. It is in relation to this point that the fourth principle, too, differs from earlier assumptions of prosodic and metrical phonology. It was originally claimed that the assignment of strong and weak values of relative prominence depended on the structure of the trees, and specifically on such factors as whether or not a given node branched and the direction of branching of the tree (see among others, Liberman and Prince, 1977; Wheeler, 1981). It is interesting to note that the binary structures and assignment of *s* and *w* to the sister nodes in such structures have recently been rejected by several of their original proponents in favor of another mechanism, the metrical grid (see Prince, 1983; Selkirk, 1984b). In any case, it is clear that the principles that assign stress to binary branching structures cannot be valid for the n-ary structures we are adopting here. Instead, we propose to replace the stress assignment rules with a simpler convention, Principle 4 above, which specifies, for a given type of constituent in the prosodic hierarchy, which sister is the strong one. For example, it might be stipulated that the rightmost constituent X, in the constituent Y that immediately dominates X, is strong. All other sisters of the strong node are weak. As will be seen in the following chapters, some of the principles that determine the values strong and weak are universal in nature, while others are language specific. As far as the details of the patterns of relative prominence and the rules that modify these patterns are concerned, however, a more complex system will undoubtedly be needed, for example, one that combines the properties of the grid with the domains of the prosodic hierarchy, as was suggested above.

Turning now from the abstract structures to the specific units of the phonology, we propose that the prosodic hierarchy consists of seven units, each of which will be motivated in subsequent chapters. These seven units, from large to small, are: the phonological utterance (U), the intonational phrase (I), the phonological phrase (ϕ), the clitic group (C), the phonological word (ω), the foot (Σ), and the syllable (σ). While there is no *a priori* reason that the phonology of a given language must include all seven units, we will make the assumption here that this is the case, an assumption that can be motivated on both general and theory-specific grounds. First of all, a theory that requires all languages to have a specific set of phonological units is stronger than one that allows some languages to have some units and other languages to have other units. Secondly, given that one of the central claims of the present proposal is that each level of the phonological hierarchy is defined in terms of mapping rules representing the interface between phonology and other components of the grammar, the absence of a phonological category X^i in some language would have as a consequence that in that language there is no interface of a specific type between the phonological component and the rest of the grammar, while in another language, in which category X^i is present, this interface does exist. Such a situation would be undesirable since it would allow grammars to vary in such fundamental ways as the number and nature of the interactions among the various components, leading, furthermore, to an increase in the number of possible grammars. Of course, the issue of the number of phonological categories in a given language is an empirical one. It should be noted, however, that it does not suffice to say, as Selkirk (1980a) suggests in her analysis of Sanskrit, that if we find no rules in a given language that make reference to a phonological unit X^i, we can conclude that X^i does not exist in that language. First of all, it is always possible that a rule that refers to X^i exists but has not yet been discovered. Secondly, and more importantly, the fact that there may be no phonological rule whose domain of application is X^i does not necessarily mean that X^i is not relevant for the overall phonological pattern of the language. That is, it may still be necessary in order to define relative prominence relations, or to account for other types of phenomena, such as the commonly observed constituent-final lengthening which may occur in positions determined in relation to X^i. If, on the other hand, it turned out to be the case that all of the languages that appeared not to have phonological rules that refer to X^i shared some other feature as well, this would be a more convincing type of evidence that X^i may be absent in a particular category of languages characterized by this feature. Thus far, however, we have not come across any such generalizations.

Finally, before we proceed to a discussion of the rules in prosodic phonology, let us briefly return to our claim that the terminal category of the prosodic hierarchy is the syllable, since a number of recent proposals have argued for the existence of internal structure within the syllable, and in particular, for the relevance of the rhyme unit. It should be noted, first of all, that saying that the syllable is the terminal category of the prosodic phonological system does not mean that the syllable is not further divisible or that it does not have internal structure. It is clear, for example, that a syllable is at least divisible into segments. Furthermore, we do not exclude the possibility that the segments may be grouped into other subsyllabic units, such as onsets and rhymes. We only wish to exclude segments, onsets, and rhymes from the prosodic hierarchy, an exclusion made on the grounds that these subsyllabic units are not organized in accordance with the principles governing all the other units above the syllable level, and do not serve as the domain of application of phonological rules.

In considering the organization of the units within the syllable, we immediately encounter conflicts with several of the principles proposed above. For example, the division into onset and rhyme, as proposed by Fudge (1969), and more recently by Halle and Vergnaud (1978), Kiparsky (1979), and Selkirk (1980b), among others, does not conform to Principle 1 on two accounts. First, a syllable cannot be composed of 'one or more' onsets, or 'one or more' rhymes; one of each is the maximum. Second, it must be assumed that the units of a given level, such as the X^{p-1} level referred to in Principle 1, are all of the same type. This is clearly not the case for onsets and rhymes, which are distinct types of units with distinct characteristics.[5] Furthermore, in the case of ambisyllabic segments, we may find an element that is at the same time a member of the rhyme of one syllable and the onset of another. In such cases, neither the rhyme nor the onset is exhaustively contained in the superordinate unit, the syllable, in violation of Principle 2 above. Principle 3 would also be violated by an analysis of the syllable into onset and rhyme constituents, since such a division is generally assumed to be binary in nature, as is the internal structure of the onset and rhyme constituents themselves. This is illustrated by the universal representation of syllable structure proposed by Kiparsky (1979: 432).

(7)

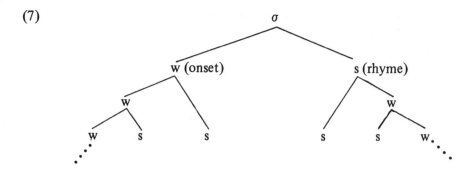

Not only would the inclusion of onset and rhyme units in the prosodic hierarchy introduce violations of the principles that govern without exception the other prosodic categories, it would also create constituents that are different from all the others in that they do not crucially serve as the domain of application of phonological rules. That is, while the onset and rhyme units may be relevant in accounting for stress patterns and certain phonotactic constraints, as shown for example by Harris (1983) for Spanish, they are not needed in accounting for the domain of application of (segmental) phonological rules. Any domain formulated in terms of an onset or rhyme can be (at least) equally effectively formulated in terms of a syllable (see Vogel, 1985). Thus, we are not claiming that onset and rhyme constituents have no role in phonology, but rather that they cannot, in any case, be considered constituents of the prosodic hierarchy.

One last question that must be examined here is the possibility that the segment be considered the lowest constituent in the prosodic hierarchy, instead of the syllable. In fact, if we consider the following n-ary branching representation of a syllable divided into segments, it would seem that the four principles given above are satisfied.

(8)

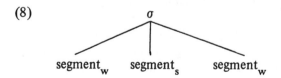

In the case of ambisyllabic segments, however, we encounter a violation of Principle 2, a problem seen in relation to onsets and rhymes as well. That is, we find a segment that is not exhaustively contained in the constituent that immediately dominates it.

It might be possible to claim that the creation of ambisyllabicity results from low-level phonetic processes, and therefore that such violations of the Strict Layer Hypothesis do not exist at the phonological level.

While this does not seem totally unreasonable, there is reason to believe, nevertheless, that such an account is unnecessary, and that there are, instead, better arguments for not considering the segment part of the prosodic hierarchy. Specifically, the existence of ambisyllabicity seems to be part of a more general freedom of segments to be involved in relations that do not conform to a notion of 'strict layers'. That is, not only may a single segment be associated with two syllables, as in the case of ambisyllabicity, but two (or more) segments may be associated with a single feature, as in the case of harmony phenomena, as seen in (9).

(9)   a. σ   σ   b. segment   segment

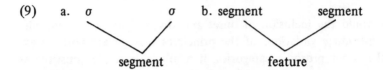

                segment   feature

The segment is, furthermore, fundamental to all of the subsystems of phonology. That is, the segmental tier, or more abstract segmental skeleton, forms the core in the subsystem represented by autosegmental theory, as illustrated by the typically autosegmental structures (9). The basic units of metrical grid theory, syllables, also have as their terminal elements units that generally coincide with segments (see Selkirk, 1984b), and in lexical phonology, it is clear that segments constitute a crucial part of the representation of the units of the system and of the phonological rules. Thus, rather than looking for a way to justify the claim that segments are constituents of the prosodic hierarchy, it seems more correct to assume that segments, or at least their positions, are the central core of phonological representations and that they are in fact the common unit of all the subsystems, the point at which they intersect.

Phonological rules

In considering the rules relating to prosodic phonology, it is necessary to distinguish between two basic types: the mapping rules that represent the interface between the phonological component and the other components of the grammar, and the phonological rules proper. The former are the rules that define the units of the prosodic hierarchy and will be discussed in the chapters on the various phonological units. In this section, we will be concerned only with the latter type, that is, the rules responsible for changes in the phonological pattern. We will limit ourselves furthermore, to the formal properties of rules that modify linear sequences of segments, as opposed to rules that modify prominence relations and autosegmental associations. Examples of the various types of segmental rules, as well as rules that affect prominence relations and autosegmental associations, can be found throughout the discussion of the different phonological constituents in relation to their domain of application.

In a prosodic framework, as in a traditional generative framework, phonological rules can carry out a specific set of operations that modify sequences of sounds. The crucial difference between the rules in the two frameworks is that in the traditional generative framework, phonological rules operate in domains defined in terms of morpho-syntactic constituents, while in the prosodic framework, they apply in domains defined in terms of the phonological hierarchy. Since in traditional generative phonology the domain of application of most phonological rules was assumed to be the word, the domain is often not explicitly expressed in rules. In prosodic phonology, on the other hand, no such assumption can be made, and the domain of application must be stated explicitly for all rules.

Selkirk (1980a) distinguishes three types of prosodic rules: domain span, domain juncture, and domain limit rules. The same division is maintained in the present work. Thus, all segmental phonological rules, in order to be considered well formed, must be formulated as one of these three types, characterized as follows, where A and B are segments, one of which may be null; X, Y, and Z are strings of segments, all of which may be null; and D_i and D_j stand for prosodic categories (see Selkirk, 1980a:111-12):

(10)   a.   *domain span:*

$$A \rightarrow B \ / \ [...X\_Y...]_{D_i}$$

     b.   *domain juncture:*

$$\text{i) } A \rightarrow B \ / \ [...[...X\_Y]_{D_j} [Z...]_{D_j} ...]_{D_i}$$

$$\text{ii) } A \rightarrow B \ / \ [...[...X]_{D_j} [Y\_Z...]_{D_j} ...]_{D_i}$$

     c.   *domain limit:*

$$\text{i) } A \rightarrow B \ / \ [...X\_Y]_{D_i}$$

$$\text{ii) } A \rightarrow B \ / \ [X\_Y...]_{D_i}$$

Selkirk (1980b) makes reference, in addition, to prosodic transformations which, at first glance, appear not to fall into any of the three categories just given. For example, Selkirk (p.585) gives the following formulation of Defooting in English:

(11) $[_\omega [_{\Sigma_w} [_\sigma C\breve{V}]_\sigma]_{\Sigma_w} ...]_\omega \rightarrow [_\omega [_{\sigma_w} CV]_{\sigma_w} ...]_\omega$

Closer examination of this rule reveals, however, that it can be reformulated as the third type of prosodic rule, that is, as a domain limit rule, in the following way:

(12) $[[C\check{V}]_\sigma]_{\Sigma_w} \rightarrow [CV]_{\sigma_w} / [\underline{\quad}...]_\omega$

Since all of the prosodic transformations used by Selkirk can be rewritten along the same lines, we see no need at this point to enlarge the set of phonological rule types to include more than the original three. A more general question can still be raised in relation to the types of phenomena treated by prosodic transformations. That is, since they do not modify strings of segments, but rather the phonological representation itself, it is not clear that they should be treated by phonological rules at all. We will not examine such phenomena further here, however, since we have limited our discussion to those phonological rules that modify strings of segments.

As we have mentioned, the prosodic subsystem of the phonology consists of seven units and three basic rule types. It is not the case, however, that all seven units may freely constitute the domains, D_i and D_j, referred to in the rules, as can be seen in Table 1, where '+' indicates that a given combination of prosodic unit and rule type is possible, and '−' indicates that it is not possible.

Table 1. Phonological constituents and phonological rule types

		SPAN	JUNCTURE (DOMAIN D_j) $\sigma\ \Sigma\ \omega\ C\ \phi\ I\ U$							LIMIT
DOMAIN (D_i)										
syllable	(σ)	+	−	−	−	−	−	−	−	+
foot	(Σ)	+	+	−	−	−	−	−	−	+
phonological word	(ω)	+	+	+	−	−	−	−	−	+
clitic group	(C)	+	+	+	+	−	−	−	−	+
phonological phrase	(ϕ)	+	+	+	+	+	−	−	−	+
intonational phrase	(I)	+	+	+	+	+	+	−	−	+
phonological utterance	(U)	+	+	+	+	+	+	+	−	+

What Table 1 shows is that all seven of the prosodic categories may, in principle, serve as the domain (D_i) in span rules, as indicated by the plus signs in the first column. The same is true for limit rules, as indicated by the plus signs in the last column. The situation with juncture rules, however, is somewhat more complex, since these rules make reference to two categories: the category of the adjacent units involved in the juncture (D_j), and the unit within such a juncture must occur in order for the rule to apply (D_i). Since the prosodic categories are organized hierarchically, it follows that the juncture of two units of a particular type can only occur within a larger unit that comprises the two units in question. We must thus exclude *a priori* any domain juncture rule in which D_j, the domain of juncture, is not smaller than D_j, the domain within which the juncture occurs. Such cases are indicated by the minus signs in the columns under the juncture rules. Thus, of the 63 ways of combining prosodic categories and rule types, only 35 are logically possible. It may turn out that not all of these 35 logical possibilities are in fact real possibilities for prosodic rules, but we will not enter into a discussion of this issue here.[6]

1.2.2. *The other components*

One of the central aspects of prosodic phonology, as we have said above, is the interaction between phonology and the other components of the grammar. Since we make use of a number of nonphonological notions throughout this book, we will briefly outline here those characteristics of the morphological, syntactic, and semantic components that are relevant to our discussion of phonology, as well as certain problems regarding the interaction between the phonological and the other components of the grammar.

Morphology

In recent years there has been much discussion about the nature of morphological representations and processes of word formation within generative grammar.[7] Whether the forms represented in the lexicon are primarily morphemes (as proposed, for example, by Halle 1973) or words (as proposed, for example, by Aronoff 1976) is of relatively little importance to the model of phonology we propose here. The same can be said about the nature of the word formation processes; that is, nothing in our model of phonology depends crucially on whether words are built by word formation rules of the type proposed by Aronoff (1976), by rewriting rules analogous to those in $\bar{X}$ syntax, as proposed by Selkirk (1982), or by some other type of mechanism. This is not to say, however, that the choices made in relation to these issues have no implications for the phonology. Instead, the point we wish to make here is that the consequences of such choices on the prosodic phonology are relatively minor, and the various possibilities would most likely require relatively small adaptations with respect to the model proposed here. We will therefore not take a position regarding the nature of morphological representations and word formation rules.

The only aspects of morphology that are relevant to our model of prosodic phonology are those notions that are referred to by the mapping rules that relate morphological structure to phonological structure. In particular, the mapping rules must have access to certain aspects of morphological structure and must be able to distinguish a number of different morphological units. First of all, they need to be able to make reference to what we will call the morphological word, that is, a unit that corresponds to the terminal node of a syntactic tree. In addition, it is necessary to distinguish simple (underived) words from complex (derived and compound) words. In this regard, furthermore, the rules that build phonological structure must have access to the stem of a word – that is, the underived, uninflected form of a word – and to any inflectional or derivational affixes (prefixes, suffixes, and infixes). As will be seen, in particular in the chapter on the phonological word (Chapter 4), different languages make use of the various morphological notions in different ways. What is central in all cases, however, is the fact that the construction of certain phonological constituents depends on specific aspects of morphological structure, though the resulting phonological structures are not necessarily isomorphic to the constituents of morphology.

It should be noted that once the mapping rules have used the morphological information needed to create the appropriate phonological constituents, this information is no longer available to phonological rules. In other words, any phonological rule that applies in a domain created on the basis of morphological structure may refer only to the phonological domain, not to the morphological elements in the corresponding morpho-syntactic tree.

There are, of course, also phonological processes that must make direct reference to morphological structure and/or specific morphological elements in the formulation of their environments. Such rules must clearly be ordered before the rules that apply in a strictly phonological domain, since, as we have mentioned, at this point the morphological structure is no longer available. Since such morpho-phonological rules are different from the purely phonological rules that are the subject of the present work, we will not discuss further how this type of interaction between morphology and phonology must be handled. We will assume here that morpho-phonological processes are accounted for by a different type of mechanism, such as the one proposed recently within the framework of lexical phonology (see, among others, Kiparsky, 1982; Mohanan, 1981; Rubach, 1984; Booij, to appear). It should be noted, though, that if we accept a model of lexical phonology which assumes that internal morphological structure is erased at the end of each cycle, certain problems arise with respect to the ordering of different types of phonological rules. While at first glance, it seems possible to order all the rules of lexical phonology before all the rules of prosodic phonology (assuming that the rules of postlexical phonology correspond to the prosodic rules of the present proposal), a closer examination reveals a complication with such a simple model. That is, it is not possible for the output of the rules of lexical phonology to constitute the input to the rules of prosodic phonology, because the output of lexical phonology no longer contains information about the internal morphological structure of the items in question. As will be seen below, in order to create certain prosodic constituents, in particular the phonological word, the mapping rules must indeed have access to certain aspects of morphological structure (see Chapter 4). One possible solution would be to allow the mapping rules to apply before, or at least independently from, the rules of lexical phonology. In this way, the lexical phonology rules could apply before the prosodic rules, although their output would not be the only input to the subsystem of prosodic phonology. In any case, it seems that the accomodations necessary in order to obtain the correct type of interaction between the lexical and prosodic subsystems of the phonology will not require major modifications in either theory. We will leave working out the details of these modifications for future research.

Syntax

The theory of syntax that we will assume in the present study is organized as in Figure 1.

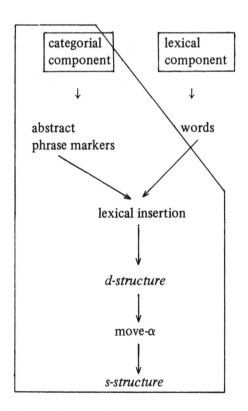

Figure 1. Schematic model of syntax

Within this theory, two subsystems must be distinguished: the first contains the principles and operations that hold universally, and the second contains a set of parameters according to which languages may differ from each other.

In the model of syntax represented in Figure 1, the categorial component is a context-free grammar that generates abstract phrase markers. The context-free rules of this component are assumed to be formulated according to the X-bar ($\bar{\text{X}}$) theory, in the version of Chomsky (1970). The $\bar{\text{X}}$ theory is not assumed to be universal; there are languages, the so-called free word order languages (see Hale, 1981), that appear not to fit the configurational structure determined by the $\bar{\text{X}}$ theory. Such languages are usually referred to as W* languages, as opposed to $\bar{\text{X}}$ languages (those that do fit the $\bar{\text{X}}$ theory), a distinction that turns out to be relevant for the prosodic subsystem of phonology (see Chapter 6).

A fundamental claim of $\bar{\text{X}}$ theory is that there is a parallelism in the internal structure of the phrases of a language. Thus, the lexical categories N, V, A (extended to include P by Jackendoff 1974, and van Riemsdijk, 1978) need not be mentioned in the phrase structure rules, since they represent the values that the variable X may assume.

The basic format of a phrase structure rule is: $X^n \rightarrow \ldots X^{n-1} \ldots$, where the maximal value that n may have is an empirical question. In principle, it is also possible that this value varies from language to language or from category to category within a language, along some parameter. For the purposes of this book, however, we will assume that the maximal value of n is 2. Each phrase will thus have three distinct levels: X, $\bar{\text{X}}$, and $\bar{\bar{\text{X}}}$. X is the head; the sister nodes of X in $\bar{\text{X}}$ are referred to as the complements of X, and the sister nodes of $\bar{\text{X}}$ in $\bar{\bar{\text{X}}}$ are referred to as the specifiers of X.

The maximal value of X, in our case $\bar{\bar{\text{X}}}$, is called the maximal projection of X. The linear ordering of specifiers and complements with respect to the head varies according to two parameters of universal grammar to allow for the different basic orders found in $\bar{\text{X}}$ languages. One parameter defines the recursive side with respect to the head in a given language, that is, the unmarked side for embedding, and the other parameter specifies whether a language also uses the nonrecursive side, that is, whether specifiers and complements are on the same side or on opposite sides with respect to the head (see Graffi, 1980). The majority of the languages investigated in this book are SVO languages, and thus the unmarked position of the complements within a phrase is to the right of the head. In an SOV language, on the other hand, the unmarked order will typically be one in which the complements precede the head. As far as the position of specifiers goes, SVO languages tend to use both sides of a phrase and thus have the specifiers to the left of the head. It is a tendency of SOV languages, on the other hand, to use only the recursive side of phrases and thus to have both specifiers and complements to the left of the head.

Another assumption we will make is that X is analyzable as a bundle of two syntactic category features: [±N] and [±V], as represented in the matrix below (from Chomsky, 1970).

	+N	−N
+V	A	V
−V	N	P

Figure 2. Syntactic category feature matrix

The sentences of a language are assumed to be divided into root sentences, those that are not dominated by a node other than S, or S̄ and nonroot sentences (see Emonds, 1976). Thus, for instance, coordinated sentences are typically root sentences, while subordinated sentences are not.

Lexical insertion rules insert the words that have been generated by the lexical component into the abstract phrase markers that have been generated by the categorial component. When no lexical item is inserted in an NP position, the phonologically empty category [e]$_{NP}$ is inserted instead. The output of these operations represents the deep structure level (d-structure).

The transformational rules, indicated by move-α in Figure 1, map d-structures onto s-structures. When the element moved by a transformation is an NP, a trace is left behind, coindexed with the moved NP. The presence of different types of empty elements at the s-structure level makes this level of representation a rather abstract object. While empty elements are relevant for both syntax and logical form, they will be shown not to play any role for prosodic phonology.

Semantics

The s-structure generated by the syntax represents the input to the semantic component, in particular to the logical form component, the interpretive part of the grammar that deals with meaning and has as its output logical form. The logical form component does not include an exhaustive semantic theory but is exclusively a theory of those aspects of meaning that may be determined *a*) within a sentence, and *b*) without making reference to the extralinguistic knowledge of speakers or their systems of beliefs.

Since the internal organization of the logical form component(LF), and of semantics in general, plays a somewhat peripheral role in the discussion to be developed in this book, we will briefly discuss here the more relevant issue of semantics with respect to the rest of the grammar, and in particular, the relation between specific semantic notions and phonological rules. LF is usually assumed to have a position parallel to that of the phonological component with respect to s-structure. That is, it is generally accepted that both components have s-structure as input and are autonomous subsystems with respect to each other. Within this view, the organization of the grammar is graphically represented in the T-model (see Chomsky and Lasnik, 1977). In this model, the phonological component is on the left side of the grammar and the logical form component is on the right side, as schematically represented below.

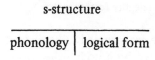

Figure 3. T-model of grammar

An alternative to the T-model has been proposed by van Riemsdijk and Williams (1981), who argue in favor of a linear organization of the different modules of the grammar where, in particular, the phonological component is ordered after the logical form component.

For the theory of prosodic domains developed in this book, it is not really relevant whether the linear model or the T-model is assumed, since both models are incapable of accounting for a set of phonological phenomena. Specifically, there is empirical evidence, discussed in Chapter 8, that indicates *a*) that there are phonological rules that apply across sentences, and *b*) that certain semantic relations that are not subsumed under the logical form component are interpreted phonologically. Since the T-model and the linear model both represent types of sentence grammars, it follows that phenomena of the first type fall beyond the field they cover. Furthermore, neither model provides a mechanism by which semantic information other than that included in logical form may be interpreted phonologically.

What is needed instead is a model of grammar in which the prosodic phonological component has access both to strings larger than a sentence and to specific structural relations that hold between these strings. Thus, a discourse component must be incorporated in the grammar alongisde a sentence component. (See, among others, Woitsetschlaeger, 1976; Williams, 1977; and Platzack, 1979, for proposals for different subsystems of a discourse component.)

1.3. Data

While this book is primarily a theoretical work it rests on a large corpus of empirical data collected over a number of years by the authors. The bulk of the data that form the empirical basis of the book comes from languages spoken by the authors. The largest corpus of data includes many hours of tape recordings of more than 40 middle-class native speakers of standard Italian gathered by the authors in Italy in the period between 1978 and 1982. The speakers were recorded reading and/or imitating, in as natural a way possible, a series of test sentences representative of an unmarked colloquial style of Italian. In addition, twenty speakers were consulted for grammaticality judgments of sentences containing the phenomena under investigation. Large amounts of data were also collected for American and British (RP) varieties of English and for Modern Greek (henceforth, simply Greek). For each of the phenomena studied in these languages, at least five native speakers were recorded reading a series of sentences and then asked to give grammaticality judgments on similar types of constructions. In addition, data found in the literature and, where possible, also judgments of native speakers, constitute the basis of our analyses and observations of phonological phenomena found in a number of other languages, including Spanish, Dutch, French, Quechua, Turkish, Yidiɲ, Japanese, Hungarian, Sanskrit, and Latin.

Beyond the data that constitute the basis of our proposal regarding the organization of the prosodic subsystem of phonology, we have also used other types of data to independently evaluate certain aspects of the theory. In particular, the results of a perception test we conducted with 48 speakers of standard northern Italian have been used to evaluate the role of prosodic constituents in the interpretation of ambiguous sentences (see Chapter 9). In addition, 4720 lines of Dante's *Divina Commedia* were scanned in order to test the role of prosodic domains in determining the distribution of metrical stress in Italian hendecasyllabic verse (see Chapter 10).

Type of speech

The phonological phenomena analyzed in this book are limited to those occurring at a normal rate of speech, that is, neither artificially slow nor artificially fast. In this way, we have eliminated from investigation forms that occur exclusively in slow speech, such as those used in dictation, where, for example, the intervocalic *t* of *water*, which is normally flapped in American English, is often aspirated instead. By the same token, we have excluded phenomena found only in fast speech, which often lead to sequences not otherwise permitted in the language, such as certain cases of Vowel Deletion in American English, as in the pronunciation [pʰtʰɛʲɾə] for the word *potato*, and the well known *mangiarsi le parole* 'word-eating' in Italian. We have, furthermore, limited our investigation to a colloquial style of speech and, unless explicitly mentioned, to unemphatic and noncontrastive pronunciations.

Phenomena

Within the type of speech we are considering, we have restricted our attention further to those phenomena that can be considered strictly phonological in nature in that they involve changes in sound patterns in contexts that can be specified wholly in terms of phonological notions. We have thus excluded from consideration many phenomena that were central to early generative phonological theory, that is, phenomena that must make reference to specific morphological or syntactic characteristics of the elements involved. On these grounds, we do not consider a rule such as the *z*-Devoicing rule in English (cf. *abu*[*z*]*e* vs. *abu*[*s*]*ive*) to be a strictly phonological phenomenon since it must specify a particular morpheme in its formulation: z → [−voice] / __+ive (see Chomsky and Halle, 1968: 232). Similarly, a rule such as the Main Stress Rule of English must be excluded from consideration since it crucially refers to syntactic labels in order to correctly assign primary stress to words such as the noun *pérvert* and the verb *pervért*. In contrast to such rules that make explicit reference to morphological and syntactic notions in their formulation, we will be concerned in this book only with prosodic rules, that is, rules whose domain of application may be defined exclusively on the basis of the units of the phonological hierarchy mentioned above.

While the phenomena treated in traditional generative phonology were usually those operating at and below the word level, the majority of the rules examined in the present study apply between words in larger domains. They thus fall into the category of rules often referred to as external sandhi rules. We prefer to use the more general term 'sandhi rules', for two reasons. First, most of the rules that apply across words also apply in analogous segmental contexts within words, as in the case of the Gorgia Toscana, the rule of Tuscan Italian that 'aspirates' voiceless stops intervocalically between words (e.g. *molti* /k/*ammelli* → *molti* [*h*]*ammelli* 'many camels') as well as within words (e.g. *fo*/k/*a* → *fo*[*h*]*a* 'seal'). Second, in the linguistic tradition external sandhi rules are opposed to internal sandhi rules — rules that apply across morphemes within a word — whereas in the view of prosodic phonology presented in this book, where there is an entire hierarchy of constituents, the word is not the reference point but just one of the prosodic categories.

While sandhi rules represent the major object of study here, some attention will also be given to phenomena such as pauses and intonation contours, given that these aspects of the sound pattern are also sensitive to the constituent structure defined by the units of the phonological hierarchy. Since the present study is phonological rather than phonetic in nature, however, we are not concerned with measurements of the pauses and intonation contours themselves. Furthermore, we are interested in 'perceived pauses' rather than 'actual pauses', since what is perceived as a pause can actually correspond phonetically to a variety of phenomena, including changes in pitch and duration, only sometimes corresponding to a complete cessation of phonation (see Downing, 1970:10). Finally, we do not analyze the actual intonation patterns themselves, but rather discuss only the domains throughout which intonation contours may extend.

NOTES

1. For a pregenerative discussion of this problem, see, for example, Pike (1947).
2. A restriction with the same effect as Principles 1 and 2 is formulated by Selkirk (1984b) under the name of the 'Strict Layer Hypothesis'. The same name will be used here.
3. Although 2 is, in fact, one of the possible values of n, we follow the general practice in phonology according to which n is always taken to have the maximum possible value.
4. See also Leben (1982), Rischel (1982), van der Hulst (1984), and Hayes (to appear), all of whom reject binary branching structures in favor of n-ary branching structures.
5. Van der Hulst (1984) proposes to solve this particular problem by having syllables dominate morae rather than onsets and rhymes. We do not include morae in our prosodic hierarchy, since we are not aware of evidence that they serve as the domain of application of phonological rules.
6. See Vogel (1984a) for a detailed discussion of this problem and a proposal for further restricting the set of well-formed prosodic rules.
7. Various theoretical positions within the generative framework are discussed in Scalise (1984).

Chapter 2

Motivation for Prosodic Constituents

2.0. Introduction

Among the processes that involve a modification of the sound pattern of a language, there is a qualitative difference between those processes that must be formulated with rules that make direct reference to specific morphological or syntactic properties of the elements involved and those that can be formulated without making direct reference to such information. It is the latter type of processes, those in which there is no systematic correspondence between the domains that must be referred to in the formulation of the process and the constituents of the morpho-syntactic hierarchy, that constitute the strictly phonological rules of a language, henceforth referred to as purely phonological or simply phonological rules, a subset of which consists of the prosodic rules that are the focus of this book.

In the first part of this chapter, we will briefly discuss the types of rules that are not subsumed under our definition of purely phonological rules. In the second and third sections, a number of arguments will be presented that demonstrate why morphological and syntactic constituents cannot constitute the domains of application of certain phonological rules. This failure of morpho-syntactic constituents is taken as evidence of the need for some other type of constituents, which we propose are the constituents of the prosodic hierarchy, discussed in Chapters 3 through 8. The specific types of criteria used in order to motivate the postulation of a prosodic constituent will be discussed in the last section of this chapter.

2.1. Phonological processes in nonphonological contexts

Since we are concerned here with purely phonological rules, that is, those rules that make reference only to phonological elements in their formulation, we must be able to distinguish these rules from other processes in which phonological information alone is not adequate. In order to make clearer the type of phenomena we will consider in this book, we will briefly examine below the properties of the types of rules we do not intend to discuss further. Strictly phonological rules, and in particular prosodic rules, will be discussed in subsequent chapters in relation to the prosodic constituents that serve as their domains of application.

2.1.1.   *Morphological contexts*

There are many phonological processes that apply only under specific morphological conditions. These may be divided into two general groups on the basis of the type of morphological information required. That is, there are some rules that only need to 'see' morphological structure, and others that also need to 'see' specific morphemes or types of morphemes.

The rules that need to have access to morphological structure are those that have typically been accounted for by different types of boundaries in their formulations within the SPE framework. For example, the fact that Nasal Assimilation in English applies to the prefix *in-* but not to the prefix *un-* was captured in the SPE framework by allowing the rule to apply across '+' boundaries but not across '#' boundaries. The rule, therefore, applies in the case of *illegal* and *irresponsible*, but not in the case of *unlawful* and *unreliable*, because of the different boundaries in their underlying representations:

(1)   a.   in + legal   → illegal
             in + responsible → irresponsible
       b.   un # lawful   → *ullawful
             un # reliable   → *urreliable

In more recent proposals, such as the Level Ordering Hypothesis (see Siegel, 1974, 1977; Allen, 1978) and Lexical Phonology (see Kiparsky, 1982; Mohanan, 1981), the boundaries have been replaced by other mechanisms that also take morphological structure into account, and thus allow assimilation to apply in cases like those in (1a), but not those in (1b).[1] Regardless of the mechanism chosen to represent the facts of Nasal Assimilation, it is clear that whether or not the rule applies is not a purely phonological issue. The words below in (2) show that assimilation does not apply in the absence of a morphological juncture, and, as the examples in (1b) above and the additional examples in (3) show, it does not apply at all morphological junctures either.

(2)   only   → *olly
       Stanley   → *Stalley
       Henry   → *Herry

(3)   sudden – ly   → *suddelly
       man   – like → *mallike
       sun   – less → *sulless

Thus, the formulation of the rule of Nasal Assimilation must take into account information about the morphological structure of the words in question. This type of rule is, therefore, different in nature from the strictly phonological rules we will consider in subsequent chapters of this book.

Another example of a rule that must take morphological structure into account is the Vowel Deletion rule of Italian that deletes an unstressed vowel before another vowel only when the vowels are separated by a morpheme juncture. Thus, the rule applies in the words in (4a), but not in those in (4b).[2]

(4) a. fama   − oso   → famoso   'famous'
         giallo − astro → giallastro 'yellowish'
         fiore   − aio   → fioraio   'florist'
         castoro − i   → castori   'beaver + pl.'
     b. paura   → *pura   'fear'
         caotico   → *cotico   'chaotic'
         meandri   → *mandri   'meanders'

In both the English and Italian examples, in order for the relevant phonological processes to apply, the formulation of the rule must contain not only phonological information, but also information about the morphological structure of the items involved. It is not necessary, however, to provide any morphological information other than that relating to the structure. Structural information is not adequate, however, for all morpho-phonological rules. For example, there are rules that apply only to specific lexical categories or in the presence of specific morphemes. The first type can be illustrated on the basis of the Main Stress Rule in English (see SPE). This rule applies differentially to different lexical categories, such that primary stress is assigned to the first syllable of the noun and to the last syllable of the verb in the following set of minimal pairs:

(5) a. [récord]$_N$ *vs.* [recórd]$_V$
     b. [pérvert]$_N$ *vs.* [pervért]$_V$
     c. [súbject]$_N$ *vs.* [subjéct]$_V$
     d. [éxtract]$_N$ *vs.* [extráct]$_V$

The second type of rule can be exemplified by the rule of z-Devoicing in English. As was mentioned in Chapter 1, this rule applies only in the presence of a particular morpheme, *-ive* (see SPE), as illustrated by its application in (6a), but its lack of application in (6b).

(6) a. abu[z]e + ive → abu[s]ive
     b. abu[z]e + ing → abu[z]ing (*abu[s]ing)

Another rule that applies only in the environment of a specific morpheme is the rule of Affrication in Italian (see Scalise, 1983). This rule changes [t(:)] to [t(:)s] before the suffix *-ione* (after the application of Vowel Deletion), as illustrated in (7).

(7)   corre[t:]o – ione → corre[t:s]ione   'correction'
       distin[t]o – ione → distin[ts]ione   'distinction'
       danna[t]o – ione → danna[ts]ione[3]   'damnation'

Affrication does not apply in the same segmental context (i.e. before [j]V...) present in other suffixes, as seen in (8a), nor does it apply in the same segmental context where no morpheme juncture intervenes, as seen in (8b).

(8)   a.   carre[t:]o – iere → *carre[t:s]iere   'wagoner'
             (cf. carre[t:]iere)
             den[t]e – iera → *den[ts]iera   'denture'
             (cf. den[t]iera)
             insala[t]a – iera → *insala[ts]iera   'salad bowl'
             (cf. insala[t]iera)
       b.   ottiene → *o[t:s]iene   '(he) obtains'
             (cf. o[t:]iene)
             sen[t]iero → *sen[ts]iero   'path'
             (cf. sen[t]iero)
             e[t]iopico → *e[ts]iopico   'Ethiopian'
             (cf. e[t]iopico)

What all the rules discussed in this section have in common is the fact that they carry out phonological modifications in a context that must contain morphological information as well as phonological information. They cannot, therefore, be considered purely phonological rules, and their domains of application cannot be expressed in terms of prosodic phonological constituents. This is not to say that all rules that apply at or below the word level are necessarily morpho-phonological rules. It will be seen in Chapters 3 and 4, in fact, that there are also purely phonological rules that apply at and below the word level, their domains of application being formulated in terms of prosodic phonological constituents. We will assume that the former type of rule is to be handled by a mechanism such as lexical phonology, while the latter will be handled by the prosodic subsystem of phonology. Consequently, only the latter type of rules will be discussed further in this book.

2.1.2. Syntactic contexts

Given that there are (at least) two types of rules that change the sound pattern of a language at or below the word level – those that belong to the prosodic subsystem of phonology and those that belong to another subsystem – an empirical question arises as to whether a parallelism exists between the phonology at and below the word level, on the one hand, and that above the word level, on the other hand. That is, one can ask whether above the word level, too, there are two types of phonological rules, those that make reference to syntax and those that belong to the prosodic subsystem of phonology. In the discussion of phonological rules operating above the word level, it will be shown in Chapters 5 through 8 that a number of rules that were thought to have a syntactic domain of application belong, instead, to prosodic phonology, in that direct reference to syntactic structures does not yield a proper definition of their domains while reference to prosodic constituents can handle such cases. The question we will now address is whether there is also a group of phonological rules above the word level that belongs to another, not purely phonological, subsystem of the grammar, as is the case for word-internal rules.

In early generative grammar, no attempt was made to specify the domains of application of sandhi rules applying across words. The pioneering work in the field is that of Selkirk (1972), who proposed that by translating the syntactic constituent analysis in such a way that information about the bracketings is made accessible to phonological rules, it is possible to account for the domain of application of phonological rules applying across words, for example Liaison in French. The specific way in which this translation is carried out is by inserting word boundaries into the phrase marker, following the conventions proposed in SPE and Selkirk (1972). While phonological rules could not look into the syntactic structure of a sentence, they could see such boundaries. For example, as was mentioned in Chapter 1, it was claimed that Liaison could apply across one boundary, but was blocked if more boundaries intervened between two words. That syntactic constituents could not be exactly identified with the domains of application of phonological rules, however, was already clear in Selkirk's work itself, where special conventions were needed both to delete a word boundary in certain syntactic structures, thus allowing Liaison in contexts in which it would otherwise be blocked, and to insert a word boundary when the opposite effect was needed (see also Rotenberg, 1975, 1978).

Once it became clear that syntactic constituents were not the answer to the problem of defining the domain of application of at least some phonological rules, several linguists attempted to define the domains of a number of rules in terms of other types of syntactic notions. A syntactic distance analysis was proposed by Rotenberg (1975, 1978) to account for the domain of application of French Liaison; the relevance of left branches in a syntactic tree was proposed by Napoli and Nespor (1979) in the form of the Left Branch Condition, to account for the domains in which the Italian rule of Raddoppiamento Sintattico applies. Similarly, Clements (1978) proposed that certain tonal rules of Ewe are sensitive to the distinction between left and right branching structures. Most of these rules have been subsequently reanalyzed in terms of phonological, or prosodic, constituents (see Selkirk, 1978b, for Liaison; Nespor and Vogel, 1982, for Raddoppiamento Sintattico and Liaison; Hayes, to appear, for the tonal rules of Ewe; and Chapters 5 through 8 below for a variety of other rules). Since the specification of the domain of application of a rule in terms of a constituent is theoretically simpler – that is, more restrictive – than a specification of such a domain that refers to subsets of specific types of constituents, such a solution is to be preferred to one that refers to syntactic structures.

There are, however, rules that apply across words that need to refer to information expressed by the (syntactic) labeled bracketings. That is, certain rules apply across two words only if they are contained within a specific syntactic constituent; other rules apply only if the word that undergoes the modification has a specific syntactic label.

The first type of rule is exemplified by two vowel deletion rules of Greek discussed in Kaisse (1977). The first rule, Unrounded First Vowel Deletion, deletes the final vowel of $word_1$ in a sequence $word_1$ $word_2$ if the vowel is unrounded and $word_2$ also begins with a vowel, but only under the condition that the two words are within an NP. The second rule, Less-Sonorant Vowel Deletion, deletes one of the two vowels in a sequence $word_1$ $word_2$, where $word_1$ ends with a vowel and $word_2$ starts with a vowel. The specification of which vowel is deleted is complicated and not relevant to the present discussion. The relevant point here is that the two words must belong to the same VP.

The second type of rule, that which must see the syntactic label of the word which undergoes the rule, can be exemplified by a vowel deletion rule of Italian (see van Hoorn, 1983; Vogel et al., 1983). Thus rule, Verb Final Vowel Deletion, optionally deletes the final vowel of a word if *a*) the vowel is immediately preceded by a $\begin{bmatrix} +\text{coronal} \\ +\text{sonorant} \end{bmatrix}$ consonant, preceded, in turn, by a vowel, *b*) another word follows within a specific domain, and *c*) the word where the deletion takes place is a verb. Thus, while in (9a) the final vowel of the verb may be deleted, deletion of the final vowel of a noun in a similar segmental context yields the ungrammatical sentence given in (9b).[4]

(9)   a.   So che vuol[∅] nuotare.   (< vuole)
             'I know he wants to swim.'

b. *Ho le suol[Ø] nuove. (< suole)
'I have new soles.'

It should be noted that the different syntactic relation between the words directly involved in the rule is not the crucial factor. Consider the items in (10), where in both cases the word that presents the segmental environment for deletion is the head of a phrase and the following word is its complement. Deletion, nevertheless, applies to the verbal but not to the nominal head (with the exception of a small group of nouns ending in *-re* (see van Hoorn, 1983; Vogel et al., 1983)).

(10) a. parlan[Ø] bene   (< parlano)
          'they speak well'
      b. *un gabbian[Ø] bianchissimo   (< gabbiano)
          'a very white seagull'

Similarly, syntactic categories play a crucial role in the Down Step rule of Igbo where, in the sequence ...V́ # V́CV́ (where ' ' indicates high tone), a rule applies to lower the initial tone of the second word in certain domains, if this word is a noun (see Welmers and Welmers, 1969; Welmers, 1973; Kenstowicz and Kisseberth, 1977). The application of this rule is illustrated below, where the initial tone of *ánú̩*, a noun, is lowered in example (11a), whereas the initial tone of *o̩cá*, an adjective, is not modified in example (11b).

(11) a. wètá á'nú̩   (V̕' = vowel with a down-stepped tone)
          'bring meat'
      b. ùwé ócá
          'a white garment'

From these and similar examples described in various works (Kenstowicz and Kisseberth, 1977; Kaisse, 1977; among others), the conclusion must be drawn that a separate subsystem of rules exists in which reference is made to the information borne by labeled bracketings. Thus, the answer to the question raised at the beginning of this section is that a parallelism does exist between the types of rules operating at and below the word level and the types of rules operating above the word level. That is, in both areas, a distinction must be drawn between those phonological processes that are to be handled by purely phonological rules and those that are to be handled by rules that also take other than phonological information into account.

2.2.   *Failure of morphologically specified contexts of prosodic phenomena*

As has been seen in the preceding sections, there are certain phonological
rules that apply in contexts that are specified directly in terms of morpho-
syntactic constituents. This is not the case, however, for all phonological
rules. It will be shown in this section that there are rules whose domain of
application cannot be formulated in terms of morpho-syntactic constituents. The first language we will consider here as an illustration of this
point is Yidiɲ, a language spoken in Northern Queensland Both the data and
analyses reported here are based on Dixon (1977a, b). In Yidiɲ, there is
a phonological rule that lengthens the penultimate vowel of any underived
word with an odd number of syllables, as can be seen below, where the
examples in (12a) are words with an odd number of syllables, and thus
show Penultimate Lengthening (PL), while the examples in (12b) are
words with an even number of syllables, and therefore do not undergo the
rule.

(12)   a.   gudá:ga   'dog'
            mad̪í:ndaŋ   'walk up'
       b.   múd̪am   'mother'
            gumbiraŋa   'pick up'

In derived words, whether or not the sequence root + suffix forms a
domain of application of Penultimate Lengthening depends on the number of syllables contained in the suffix. If the suffix is monosyllabic
and is affixed to a root with an even number of syllables, thus yielding
the desired environment for Penultimate Lengthening – that is, a derived
word with an odd number of syllables – then the rule applies, as shown in
(13).

(13)   a.   galí:-na
            go   (purp.)
       b.   ŋunaŋgara:-nda
            whale   (dat.)

If, however, a bisyllabic suffix is affixed to a root with an odd number of
syllables, thus forming a derived word with an odd number of syllables,
PL does not apply, as seen in (14), although the word contains the desired
environment consisting of an odd number of syllables. Instead, the penultimate syllable of the stem is lengthened.

(14)   mad̪i:nda-ŋaliŋ
       walk up   (pres.)

It should be noted that the two types of suffixes, monosyllabic and bi-syllabic, cannot be assigned to different morphological categories. That is, there are no morphological regularities, such as linear ordering with respect to each other, that might suggest the existence of two morpholog-ical classes of suffixes. They behave in different ways phonologically because of different phonological characteristics (i.e. number of syllables) that cannot be captured, in a non *ad hoc* way, in morphological structure.

Further evidence that morphological constituency cannot define the context of application of Penultimate Lengthening is offered by derived words that contain the sequence root + bisyllabic suffix + monosyllabic suffix. The sequence formed by the two suffixes behaves like an underived word as far as PL is concerned, as shown in (15).

(15) gumari–daga–ɲu → gumá:ridagá:ɲu   'to have become red'
      red   (inch.)(past)

While the lengthening in the root can easily be expressed in terms of morphological boundaries, there is no way to formulate the lengthen-ing in -*daga:-ɲu* in terms of morphological boundaries, since there is no constituent of morphological structure that exhaustively includes the two suffixes. Another rule deletes the final -*u* in the surface form.

Additional support for the claim that the domains of application of phonological rules are not necessarily isomorphic to morphological constituents can be found in another phonological rule of Yidiɲ, Stress Assignment, which assigns stress to alternating syllables. In the morpholog-ical word in (15), the stressed syllables are the second and the fifth ones. That is, there are two adjacent unstressed syllables, the third and the fourth ones. Since this is a forbidden sequence in Yidiɲ, we are led to the conclusion that the domain of Stress Assignment is not the morphological word, and that, more generally, the morphological word is not a constitu-ent as far as phonological rules are concerned.

Further evidence that constituents of the morpho-syntactic hierarchy cannot be considered the domains of application of at least some word-level phonological rules comes from two assimilation rules of Greek (see Householder, 1964: Nespor, 1986). One rule, Nasal Assimilation, as-similates a nasal consonant in point of articulation to a following non-continuant consonant; the other rule, Stop Voicing, voices a stop when it is preceded by a voiced consonant. The application of the two rules is exemplified in (16), where it is shown that the rules apply across mor-phemes within a word.

(16) συν+πλέκω '(I) knit'
      sin+pléko → si[mb]léko

Nasal Assimilation and Stop Voicing, however, are not strictly word internal but may apply in certain cases across word boundaries as well.
For example, they may apply across two words when word$_1$ is an article
and word$_2$ a noun, or when word$_1$ is the negative element δεν and word$_2$
a verb, as shown in (17). They may not apply, however, when word$_1$
is an auxiliary and word$_2$ a verb, as shown in (18).

(17) a. τον#πατέρα   'the father (acc.)'
          ton#patéra → [tombatéra]
      b. δεν#πειράζι   '(it) doesn't matter'
          ðen#pirázi → [ðembirázi]

(18) έχουν#πλέξει   '(they) have knitted'
      éxun#pléksi → *[éxumbléksi]

Since in each of these examples the two words in question are separated
by a single word boundary, but the phonological rules apply in the first
two cases but not in the third, a theory of phonology that makes use of
boundaries to define the domains of application of phonological rules is
inadequate. In order to account for the facts just illustrated within such
a theory, it would be necessary to posit a morpheme boundary rather
than a word boundary between articles and nouns and between negative
elements and verbs, so that the rules would be word internal. This solution, however, aside from being *ad hoc*, is untenable for syntactic
reasons. That is, since boundaries reflect morpho-syntactic structure,
positing a morpheme boundary between articles and nouns and between
negative elements and verbs would amount to claiming that these strings
are dominated by a single terminal node in syntactic structure. Such a
claim is false, however, since other words may intervene to separate the
two elements of the string.

To summarize, what the examples from Yidiɲ and Greek show is that
a phonological theory in which the domains of application of phonological rules must be expressed by making reference to morphological
boundaries and word boundaries is inadequate, given that the constituents
of morphological structure are not necessarily isomorphic to the domains
of application of a set of phonological rules. An account of these and
other phenomena in a variety of languages, whose domains of application
must be expressed in terms of another type of constituent, the phonological word, forms the foundation of Chapter 4.

2.3.   *Failure of syntactically specified contexts of prosodic phenomena*

In considering phonological rules operating across words, a problem arises that is analogous to the one seen in relation to rules that apply within the word. That is, it is necessary to define the domains of application of such rules. While in traditional generative theory it was supposed that these domains directly correspond to syntactic constituents (see Chomsky and Halle, 1968; Selkirk, 1972), it has been demonstrated in more recent work that such a claim cannot be maintained. In this light, several alternative proposals have been made in which different syntactic notions have been used to characterize the domains of phonological rules operating between words (Bierwisch, 1966; Rotenberg, 1978; Clements, 1978; Napoli and Nespor, 1979). While all of these proposals have contributed to our understanding of the phenomena in question, they nevertheless have certain shortcomings in that they fail to correctly predict all cases of application of a given rule, or are not sufficiently general to be applicable to a large number of other phenomena.

In the following sections, we will examine in some detail several of the problems associated with the claim that syntactic constituents are the domains of application of phonological rules. Specifically, we will show that syntactic structures fail in three respects. First of all, it will be demonstrated that direct reference to syntactic constituents either results in the loss of generalizations or leads to incorrect predictions about the application of a number of phonological rules, evidence that these constituents cannot be the appropriate domains for the rules in question (section 2.3.1). Secondly, while it follows from a strictly syntactic approach in which phonology directly refers to s-structures that empty elements are visible to phonological rules, we will demonstrate that such a position is untenable (section 2.3.2). Finally, we will examine in some depth the inadequacy of syntactic constituents as the domains of intonation contours, a point that has already been touched on in the traditional generative literature (section 2.3.3).

2.3.1. *Noncorrespondence between syntactic constituents and domains of phonological rules*

The inappropriateness of syntactic constituents as the domains of application of phonological rules will be demonstrated on the basis of three different types of problems. First of all, it will be shown that direct reference to syntactic constituents does not make the correct predictions about the domains of phonological rules. Secondly, whereas syntactic constituency is determined uniquely in terms of structural factors, it will be shown that a nonstructural factor, the length of a given string, is relevant to the phonology in that constituents of the same syntactic nature but different lengths exhibit different behaviors as far as the application of phonological rules is concerned. Finally, in contrast with the implicit prediction made by a syntactic constituent approach to phonology that the largest possible domain of application of a phonological rule is the sentence, it will be demonstrated that there exist phonological rules that apply in larger domains.

Bracketings

If we try to express the domains of certain phonological rules in terms of syntactic constituents, we find that the bracketings of these constituents do not delimit units that account for the application of the rules, as can be illustrated by Raddoppiamento Sintattico in Italian.

Raddoppiamento Sintattico (RS) is a rule of central and southern varieties of Italian that lengthens the initial consonant of word$_2$ in a sequence word$_1$ word$_2$. RS does not apply, however, in just any sequence of two words, but requires that two phonological conditions be met. These conditions vary a great deal according to the regional variety of Italian. We will consider here only the variety spoken in the Tuscan region, the one most commonly described in traditional works on Italian (Fiorelli, 1958; Camilli, 1965; Pratelli, 1970; Lepschy and Lepschy, 1977). The phonological condition on word$_1$ is that it must end in a stressed vowel. Thus, RS applies in (19a), but not in (19b).[5]

(19)   a.   La scimmia aveva appena mangiato metá [b:]anana.
            'The monkey had just eaten half a banana.'
       b.   Il gorilla aveva appena mangiato quáttro [b]anane.
            'The gorilla had just eaten four bananas.'

The phonological condition on word$_2$ requires that the onset of the first syllable be either a single consonant or a cluster other than *s* followed by another consonant. RS applies, therefore, in (20a) and (20b), but not in (20c).

(20)   a.   Il ragno aveva mangiato metá [f:]arfalla.
            'The spider had eaten half a butterfly.'
       b.   Il ragno aveva mangiato metá [g:]rillo.
            'The spider had eaten half a cricket.'
       c.   Il ragno aveva mangiato metá [s]corpione.
            'The spider had eaten half a scorpion.'

These conditions on the two individual words in a given sequence, however, are not sufficient to determine the occurrence of RS. Thus, although the phonological conditions on word$_1$ and word$_2$ are met in (21), RS does not apply.

(21)   a.   La volpe ne aveva mangiato metá [p]rima di addormentarsi.
            'The fox had eaten half of it before falling asleep.'

b. Il gatto aveva catturato un colibrí [m]olto pregiato.
    'The cat had caught a highly valued hummingbird.'

The examples in (21) illustrate that in order for RS to apply, word$_1$ and word$_2$, in addition to fulfilling the phonological requirements just mentioned, must be in a particular relation to each other. It is the specification of this relation that is problematic if it is to be expressed in terms of syntactic constituents. The cases that are most problematic are those in which the same types of syntactic constituents are treated differently by a given phonological rule, a situation that a purely syntactic analysis, by definition, cannot handle.

Consider first the following examples which illustrate that different sister nodes behave differently with respect to RS.

(22) a. $\overset{w_1}{}$ $\overset{w_2}{}$ $\overset{w_3}{}$
      Ha appena comprato un colibrí [b:]lú [k]on le ali sottilissime.
      'He just bought a blue hummingbird with very thin wings.'

      b. $\overset{w_1}{}$ $\overset{w_2}{}$ $\overset{w_3}{}$
      Caccerá [k:]aribú [k]ol fucile e cervi con l'arco e le frecce.
      'He will hunt caribous with a rifle and deer with a bow and arrow.'

      c. $\overset{w_1}{}$ $\overset{w_2}{}$ $\overset{w_3}{}$
      Un levriero costerá [s:]uppergiú [m]ezzo milione.
      'A greyhound will cost about half a million (lire).'

      d. $\overset{w_1}{}$ $\overset{w_2}{}$ $\overset{w_3}{}$ $\overset{w_4}{}$
      Disegnó [b:]alene blú [k]on inchiostro di lapislazzuli.
      'He draw blue whales with lapislazuli ink.'

Although the syntactic structures of (22a-c) differ somewhat, in each sentence the three words relevant to the present discussion are in the same abstract relation to each other, as represented schematically in (23a), where "H" stands for the head of the phrase and "C" for a complement. The abstract relation among the four crucial words in (22d), on the other hand, is represented in (23b).

(23) a. 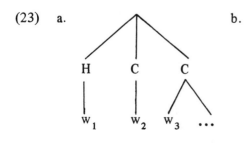   b.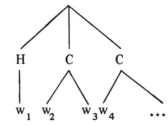

While in each of these four sentences the segmental environment for RS is met in two positions, that is, between w_1 and w_2 and between w_2 and w_3 in (22a-c), and between w_1 and w_2 and between w_3 and w_4 in (22d), the rule applies only in the first position. There is no way, however, in (22a-c) for the head of the phrase to be grouped into a syntactic constituent together with its first complement (w_2), but not with the second complement, whose initial word is w_3. Similarly, in (22d), syntactic constituency does not allow us to group the head of the phrase (w_1) with its first complement (w_2 and w_3) to the exclusion of its second complement, whose initial word is w_4. Since the head and complements are sister nodes, there is no way to form a unit that consists only of the head and its first complement. Thus, the domain of application of RS cannot be identified with any of the syntactic constituents available in this case.

That syntactic constituents cannot account for the domain of application of RS can be further illustrated with the following example, where a series of right branching elements does not uniformly exhibit RS even though the proper phonological conditions are present.

(24) a. Ho visto tré [k:]olibrí [b:]rutti.
          'I saw three ugly hummingbirds.'
      b. Ho visto tré [k:]olibrí [k]osí [b:]rutti.
          'I saw three such ugly hummingbirds.'

In (24a), RS applies in both of the environments in which the phonological conditions on the individual words are satisfied, that is, between *tré* 'three' and *colibri* 'hummingbirds' and between *colibri* and *brutti* 'ugly'. In (24b), however, there are three environments in which the phonological conditions for RS are met, that is, between *tré* and *colibri*, between *colibri* and *cosi* 'such' and between *cosi* and *brutti*, but the rule applies only in the first and third cases. Since all of the words in question are grouped in a parallel way in syntactic structure, as can be seen in (25), there is no reason to expect RS not to apply between w_2 and w_3 in (25b), since it applies in all the other positions.

(25) w_1 w_2 w_3
      a. ...[tré [colibrí [brutti]]]
           w_1 w_2 w_3 w_4
      b. ...[tré [colibrí [cosí [brutti]]]]

While in (25a) the repeated application of RS seems to indicate that the rule applies throughout an entire constituent, it can be seen that this is not the case in (25b), where the rule does not apply throughout a similar type of constituent. That is, if it is claimed that the domain of application of RS is a syntactic constituent, it would be necessary to claim, further-more, that in the example in (25b), w_1 and w_2 form an exhaustive consti-tuent. There is, however, no syntactic constituent that groups these two words together to the exclusion of w_3 and w_4.

Another rule that shows the inappropriateness of syntactic constituents as the domains of phonological rules in still another respect is the much discussed phenomenon of Liaison, as illustrated in (26). While Liaison applies in all styles of French, we are concerned here only with its applica-tion in informal speech.

(26)   a.   Les giraffes et les éléphants sont ses meilleurs⌣amis.
           'Giraffes and elephants are his best friends.'
      b.   Claude a des perrochets / intolérables.
           'Claude has some intolerable parrots.'

In syntactic terms, *meilleurs* 'best' is the complement of *amis* 'friends', just as *intolérables* 'intolerable' is the complement of *perrochets* 'parrots'. That is, *meilleurs* and *amis* in (26a), just as *perrochets* and *intolérables* in (26b), are sister nodes directly dominated by the same type of node. It is, therefore, impossible to predict in terms of syntactic constituents that Liaison applies in the first case but not in the second.

The three problems just discussed show that we cannot identify the domains of application of phonological rules with syntactic constit-uents, since it was shown that neither of the two rules under consideration applies uniformly throughout a constituent of a given type. That is, there is no way to capture in terms of syntactic constituent structure the fact that similar constituents behave differently with respect to the same phonological rule.

Length of constituents

Another problem that arises if syntactic constituents are posited as the domains of application of phonological rules is related to the length of the constituents involved. Since constituents in syntax are defined in terms of certain structural relations among the words of a given string, the number of words involved is irrelevant. That is, as far as the syntax is concerned, a constituent of a certain type composed of one word is structurally equivalent to another constituent of the same type composed of five, ten, or any number of words. If syntactic constituents are taken as the domains of application of phonological rules operating above the word level, this means that, under the appropriate segmental conditions, a given phonological rule should operate uniformly within all syntactic constit-uents of a certain type. That is, a constituent composed of two words, the minimum necessary for the application of a phonological rule operating above the word level, should exhibit the same phonological behavior as the same type of constituent of any other length. It will be demonstrated here that certain phonological rules, in fact, do not apply throughout all consituents of a given type, but rather are sensitive to the length of the constituents.

Let us consider the rule of Gorgia Toscana (GT) in Italian. This rule is traditionally described as a phonological phenomenon of Tuscan Italian that results in varying degrees of so-called aspiration of the voiceless stops [p], [t], [k] in intervocalic position, or more precisely, between two [−consonantal] segments (see, among others, Lepschy and Lepschy, 1977; Giannelli and Savoia, 1979). Since GT varies somewhat in different areas of Tuscany, we will limit our discussion to the variety spoken in the province of Florence. The most common form of GT changes [p], [t], and [k] into [ϕ], [θ], and [h], respectively, both within and across words, as the examples in (27) and (28) illustrate.

(27) a. lu[ϕ]o   (< lu[p]o)   'wolf'
      b. crice[θ]o (< crice[t]o)   'hamster'
      c. fo[h]a   (< fo[k]a)   'seal'

(28) a. Lo zoo ha appena comprato una nuova [ϕ]antera.
          $\overset{w_1}{}$ $\overset{w_2}{}$
          (< [p]antera)
          'The zoo has just bought a new panther.'

      b. Ci sono tantissimi [θ]arli nella mia scrivania.
          $\overset{w_1}{}$ $\overset{w_2}{}$
          (< [t]arli)
          'There are lots of wood-worms in my desk.'

      c. Sta arrivando uno stormo di [h]orvi neri.
          $\overset{w_1}{}$ $\overset{w_2}{}$
          (< [k]orvi)
          'A flock of black crows is arriving.'

Gorgia Toscana, however, does not apply across just any two words. In the examples in (29), cases are seen in which the rule operates within a VP, while in the examples in (30), cases are seen in which the rule does not normally apply between an NP and a VP, even though the appropriate phonological conditions are present (i.e., the consonant in question is in intervocalic position).

(29) a. aveva [h]onosciuto Arcibaldo   (<[k]onosciuto)
          '(he) had met Arcibaldo'
      b. viaggia [h]ol cammello   (<[k]ol)
          '(he) travels by camel'

    c.   si lamenta [h]ostantemente   (< [k]ostantemente)
        '(he) complains constantly'

(30) a.   Le zanne dell'elefante bianco dell'Africa orientale [k]ostano
        sempre di piú in Europa.
        (?*[h]ostano)
        'The tusks of the white elephant of eastern Africa cost more and
        more in Europe.'
    b.   Quella banda segreta di ragazzi temuta da tutti [k]accia orsi
        ferocissimi solo per divertirsi.
        (?*[h]accia)
        'That secret band of boys feared by all hunts very ferocious
        bears just for fun.'
    c.   Certi tipi di uccelli trovati solo in Australia [k]ostruiscono nidi
        complicatissimi a due piani.
        (?*[h]ostruiscono)
        'Certain types of birds found only in Australia construct very
        complicated two-story nests.'

If the domain of application of GT is to be expressed in terms of syntactic constituents, for example the verb phrase, the prediction is made that the rule will not only apply in the VPs listed in (29), but in all VPs, including those in (31) below. By the same token, just as GT does not apply between the NPs and VPs in (30), it is expected that the rule will not apply between the NPs and VPs of the sentences in (32). As it turns out, however, contrary to the predictions, GT does not always apply in all the positions in which its segmental context is present within a VP, as indicated in (31). It normally does apply, however, across the NPs and VPs in (32). "_" and "⫞" in (31) indicate those segments to which GT normally does and does not apply across words, respectively.

(31) a.   Osservano il rarissimo colibrí peruviano con le penne azzure

        con un cannocchiale particolarmente adatto alla situazione.

        '(They) observe the very rare Peruvian hummingbird with blue
        feathers with binoculars that are particularly suitable for the
        situation.'
    b.   Hanno comprato un sacco di caramelle liquerizia e lattine di

        coca cola con i soldi che hanno guadagnato vendendo giornalini.

        '(They) bought a lot of candies, licorice, and cans of coca cola
        with the money they earned selling comic books.'

(32)   a.   Gli struzzi [h]orrono velocemente.   (< [k]orrono)
            'Ostriches run quickly.'
       b.   Un levriero [h]osta moltissimo.   (< [k]osta)
            'A greyhound is very expensive.'

It is obvious from these examples that the length of a given string is crucial in determining whether or not a phonological rule, in this case GT, applies. Thus, while it seemed from the examples in (29) that the domain of application might be, at least in part, identified with a phrasal node, specifically VP, the items in (31) show that when a VP is particularly long, GT tends not to apply in all positions. Similarly, while the sentences in (30) might lead one to the conclusion that GT is blocked across the boundary of two phrasal nodes, specifically NP and VP, those in (32) demonstrate that when the NP and VP in question are relatively short, GT in fact normally does apply.

This type of situation is by no means limited to the application of GT, or to Italian, for that matter. An analogous problem arises, for example, in specifying the domain of application of Nasal Assimilation (NA) in Spanish.

It has frequently been observed that in Spanish nasals are homorganic to a following consonant both within a word and across words (see among others, Navarro Tomás, 1957; Harris, 1969; Hooper, 1976). Examples of homorganic nasal and following consonant within and across words are given below:

(33)   a.   ga[m]ba   'shrimp'
       b.   co[m] piedad   'with pity'
       c.   elefa[n]te   'elephant'
       d.   si[n] tardar   'without delaying'
       e.   la[ŋ]gosta   'lobster'
       f.   come[ŋ] carne   '(they) eat meat'

NA does not, however, apply between just any two words. As was seen above in relation to GT, an examination of the domains in which NA does and does not apply reveals that they do not necessarily coincide with any syntactic constituent. While NA applies in the VPs in (34), it tends not to apply in those in (35).

(34)   a.   tiene[ŋ] cuatro gatos   (< tiene[n])
            '(they) have four cats'
       b.   canta[m] bien   (< canta[n])
            '(they) sing well'
       c.   no se vea aquella especia de escorpió[n] (< escorpió[n])
            tan frecuentemente en Brasil

'(one) doesn't see that species of scorpion very frequently in
Brazil.'

(35) a. Colecciona en todo el mundo plumas de tucá[n] para su sombrero preferido.
(?*tucá[m])
'(She) collects all over the world toucan feathers for her
favorite hat.'
b. Estudia el sistema comunicativo de algunos tipos de delfí[n]
con aparatos muy sofisticados.
(?*delfi[ŋ])
'(She) studies the communicative system of several types of
dolphin with very sophisticated apparatus.'

Furthermore, while NA appears to be blocked between NPs and VPs
on the basis of sentences such as those in (36), the sentences in (37)
show that it is not blocked between all instances of NP and VP.

(36) a. El nuevo canario de mi amiga Carme[n] canta solo cuando está
solo.
(?*Carme[ŋ])
'My friend Carmen's new canary sings only when it is alone.'
b. Su nuevo sombrero con tres plumas de tucá[n] cuesta sin duda
mas del sombrero de su hermano.
(?*tucá[ŋ])
'Her new hat with three toucan feathers undoubtedly costs
more than her brother's hat.'

(37) a. Mi faisá[ŋ] corre siempre.   (< faisá[n])
'My pheasant always runs.'
b. Eso tucá[m] parece enfermo.   (< tucá[n])
'That toucan seems sick.'

There are still other phonological rules, for example, Intervocalic Spirantization in Italian and s-Assimilation in Greek, that exhibit the same
general pattern just illustrated with GT and NA, in that they apply in a
given type of constituent if it is short, but not if it is long, or are blocked
across a particular type of boundary if the constituents on either side are
relatively long, but not if they are short. We will not illustrate these rules
here, but refer the reader to a more detailed discussion of this problem
in Chapter 7. The relevant point here is that such rules provide further
evidence that the domains of application of phonological rules operating
across words cannot be coextensive with the constituents provided by
syntax. That is, while it has just been demonstrated that the application

of certain phonological rules is sensitive to the length of the strings involved, the principles that define syntactic constituents do not take into account nonstructural factors such as length. There is, thus, a fundamental difference between the nature of the domains relevant for phonological rules and the constituents of syntax.

Beyond the sentence

We have just seen cases in which the domains of application of various phonological rules could not be expressed in terms of syntactic constituency either because the syntax provides inappropriate bracketings of the elements of a given string or because the phonology may be sensitive to length, a factor the syntax does not take into account. In both cases, the problem was essentially that the phonological rules in question did not apply uniformly throughout the constituents provided by the syntax. The last problem we will consider in this section is somewhat different from the first two in that it does not so much represent a mismatch between syntactic constituents and domains of application of phonological rules, but rather demonstrates that syntactic constituents, by definition, cannot delimit domains large enough to account for the application of certain phonological rules.

Let us first consider the well-known rule of Flapping in American English. The examples in (38) show that this rule applies both within words and across two words in a sentence.

(38)   a.   water   →   wa[ɾ]er
       b.   capital →   capi[ɾ]al
       c.   Wait a minute.   →   Wai[ɾ]a . . .
       d.   The white rabbit escaped from its cage.   →   . . .rabbi[ɾ]escaped..

Flapping, however, is not restricted to applying within a sentence; it may also apply across two words in different sentences, as the examples in (39) illustrate.

(39)   a.   Please wait. I'll be right back.   →   . . .wai[ɾ]I'll...
       b.   It's hot. Open the window.   →   . . .ho[ɾ]Open...
       c.   Don't shout. It's rude.   →   . . .shou[ɾ]It's...

It is not the case, however, that Flapping can apply across just any pair of sentences. The examples in (40) show that in some cases (i.e. where the two sentences are unrelated) the rule is blocked in exactly the same segmental contexts in which it was seen to apply in (39).

(40)   a.   They didn't wait. I'll be right back.   →   *. . .wai[ɾ]I'll...

    b.   Where's Scott? Open the window. → *...Sco[ɾ]Open...

    c.   Don't shout. Is Ed here? → *...shou[ɾ]Is...

Since the largest constituent in syntax is the sentence, there is no way in which the domain of application of Flapping can be identified with a syntactic constituent. That is, beyond the sentence there is no unit that allows us to group together, for example, the pairs of sentences in (39), and thus characterize the domain of Flapping in terms of this unit. The fact that Flapping does not apply across just any two sentences complicates the problem even further, since it automatically rules out the possibility of defining the rule's environment as being any place within the largest syntactic constituent, or across two such constituents.

    A similar problem arises with two other phenomena in another variety of English as well, Linking-*r* and Intrusive-*r* in Received Pronunciation. Both rules account for the pronunciation, in certain contexts, of an *r* that is not pronounced when the word in question is uttered in isolation. In the first case, the *r* is present orthographically, and in the second case, it is not present (see among others, Gimson, 1970). These rules apply, as does Flapping, within words, across words within a sentence, and across words in different sentences, as illustrated in (41), where "*r̸*" indicates an orthographic *r* that is not pronounced when the word is uttered in isolation.

(41)   a.   clea*r̸* + est → clea[r]est
        b.   gnaw + ing → gnaw[r]ing
        c.   That type of spide*r̸* is dangerous. → ...spide[r]is...
        d.   The giant panda eats pounds of bamboo a day. →
           ...panda[r]eats...
        e.   There's my brothe*r̸*. I have to go. → ...brothe[r]I...
        f.   Try that sofa. It's softer. → ...sofa[r]It's...

As was the case with Flapping, not all combinations of sentences permit the application of Linking-*r* and Intrusive-*r*. For example, the two rules in question would most probably be blocked in the pairs of sentences in (42), even though it was just seen that they apply in identical segmental contexts in (41e,f).

(42)   a.   There's my brothe*r̸*. I have a cold. → *...brothe[r]I...
        b.   Try that sofa. It's after midnight. → *...sofa[r]It's...

Once again, we are faced with the problem of how to represent the domain of application of phonological rules that can apply across two sentences, since the largest constituent provided by the syntax is the sentence. Furthermore, the fact that the rules apply across some sentences but not others provides additional evidence that we are dealing with rules that operate in specific contexts larger than the sentence, not simply in any sequence of sentences.

Finally, the Voicing Assimilation rule of Mexican Spanish discussed by Harris (1969) appears to be another example of a phonological rule that operates beyond the sentence. This rule, that voices *s* before a voiced consonant, may, under certain circumstances, apply across two sentences, as illustrated by the pair of sentences below (from Harris, p.60).

(43)   Los dos. Dámelos. → ...do[s^z]Dámelos.
       'Both of them. Give them to me.'

Harris points out further that the rule does not always apply across sentences; rather, it is blocked by an interruption in 'phonational activity'. Thus, although Harris does not provide any other examples, it seems quite likely that Voicing Assimilation represents, in fact, the same type of phenomenon we have just examined in American and RP varieties of English.

What all of these rules demonstrate is that syntactic constituency cannot provide the appropriate domains for the application of a specific type of phonological rule, that is, any rule that can apply across certain sentences but not others. Since the largest syntactic constituent is the sentence, there is by definition no way in which the domain of application of such rules can be identified with a constituent of syntactic structure. It seems, instead, that a more appropriate way to account for the application of the phonological rules in question would be in terms of a different type of unit, one that is not limited by the constituent structure of the syntactic component.

The combination of the problems examined above in which it was seen that a number of phonological rules do not apply uniformly throughout the strings delimited by syntactic constituents, and the problem of phonological rules operating beyond the sentence that has just been addressed here, quite clearly reveals the inadequacy of syntactic constituents as the domains of application of (at least some) phonological rules. That is, there is no simple one-to-one relation between the constituents of syntax and the strings within which phonological rules operate. Instead, it seems that units other than those provided by the syntactic component are necessary in order to account for the application of phonological rules operating above the word level.

2.3.2. Phonetically null syntactic constituents and phonological rules
       It has been proposed by a number of linguists that phonological rules

that apply between two words are sensitive to the presence of syntactic elements that do not have a phonetic matrix, such as traces and PRO (see, among others, Selkirk, 1972; Chomsky and Lasnik, 1977; Rizzi, 1979; Vanelli, 1979; Jaeggli, 1980). This position follows directly from the theoretical claim that the labeled bracketings of s-structure are carried directly into the phonological representation in the form of boundaries. That is, since s-structure consists of bracketed constituents that may contain phonetically null elements, it is claimed that such elements will affect the application of phonological rules applying across words. It is argued, specifically, that the effect of an empty element will show up where adjacency is a necessary condition for the application of a phonological rule. If a syntactic constituent is present between two words, these words obviously can not be considered adjacent and thus are not subject to the application of the phonological rule in question. There is no unanimous agreement, however, on which phonetically empty syntactic constituents are relevant for the definition of adjacency in phonology. Research in this area has taken essentially two directions, which we will examine below as the strong hypothesis and the weak hypothesis. According to the strong hypothesis, all empty elements have the same status that lexical items have in determining adjacency. That is, the occurrence of any such element between two words will prevent the application of a phonological rule whose environment is otherwise present (see, among others, Rizzi, 1979; Vanelli, 1979). According to the weak hypothesis, only certain types of empty elements, that is, those marked for case, are capable of blocking the application of phonological rules that apply across words (see Jaeggli, 1980; Chomsky, 1981). We will demonstrate below that syntactic constituents not represented phonetically are not capable, under any circumstances, of blocking the application of phonological rules and thus that both of the hypotheses are untenable.

The empty elements to which recent proposals attributed the power of blocking phonological rules are: traces of clitics, PROs, and traces of *wh*. Of these, the last type is clearly marked for case, the second type is clearly not marked for case, and the first type is somewhat controversial, in that it is considered by some linguists to be marked for case (Longobardi, 1980) and by others not to be so marked (Jaeggli, 1980; Chomsky, 1981). We will consider each of these categories separately.

Traces of clitics

If traces of clitics have an influence on the application of phonological rules, as has been proposed, for example, by Rizzi (1979), we would expect both *a*) that in a given language these traces would block the application of all phonological rules whose environment is defined on adjacent words, and *b*) that either all or none of the traces of the same type would block the application of a particular rule. Consider, however, the sentences in (44) and (45), which include the segmental environment for the phonological rule of Italian, Raddoppiamento Sintattico (see section 2.3.1 above). In the examples in (44) the rule is blocked, while in the examples in (45) the rule applies, despite the presence of traces of clitics in both sentences.

(44) a. Ne voglio comprare metá t_{CL} [s]ubito.   (no change)
          'I want to buy half of it immediately.'
      b. Ne incontreró tré t_{CL} [v]enerdí.   (no change)
          'I will meet three of them Friday.'

(45) a. Ne compreró t_{CL} [s:]ubito.   ($<$ [s]ubito)
          'I'll buy some immediately.'
      b. Lo incontreró t_{CL} [v:]enerdí.   ($<$ [v]enerdi)
          'I'll meet him Friday.'

The inconsistent behavior of RS[6] with respect to traces of clitics in these examples indicates that the traces cannot be the factor that determines in which contexts the rule is blocked, at least if a unified analysis of the phenomenon is to be given.

A possible solution in which traces of clitics are present at the moment of application of some phonological rules, for example the vowel deletion rule mentioned by Rizzi, and absent at the moment of application of others, for example RS, must be excluded since this would require the introduction of a new type of rule within the phonological component which would substantially deviate from the nature of the other rules of the component. That is, it would be necessary to introduce a type of rule that has as its only effect the deletion of syntactic material in order to create adjacency between two words that were at some other point considered structurally nonadjacent. It should be noted that the ungrammatical sentences given by Rizzi to show that Specifier Vowel Deletion (SVD) is blocked by phonetically null syntactic constituents can be excluded for independent reasons, as shown in Nespor and Scorretti (1985).

Pro

We will now consider the blocking effect of PRO, which was proposed by Rizzi (1979) and Vanelli (1979) to account for the context of application of the same rule used by Rizzi to argue in favor of the blocking effect of traces of clitics: Specifier Vowel Deletion. An argument similar to the one just given for traces of clitics can also be made for PRO on the basis of two other phonological rules of Italian: Gorgia Toscana (GT) and Intervocalic Spirantization (IS).

GT, as shown in section 2.3.1 above, applies both within words and at the juncture between two adjacent words. The rule applies, however, in the sentences in (46), in which, according to the analysis proposed by Rizzi (1979) and Vanelli (1979), w_1 and w_2 are not structurally adjacent since the empty element PRO intervenes between them.

(46) a. Tu dai da mangiare al puma australiano e io a quello PRO $\overset{w_1}{}$
$\overset{w_2}{}$[ϕ]eruviano.
($<$[p]eruviano)
'You feed the Australian puma and I the Peruvian one.'
  b. Ci sono due leoni obesi e quattro PRO [θ]utti magri. $\overset{w_1}{}$ $\overset{w_2}{}$
($<$[t]utti)
'There are two obese lions and four very thin ones.'
  c. Ho visto un passero pennuto e uno PRO [h]alvo. $\overset{w_1}{}$ $\overset{w_2}{}$
($<$[k]alvo)
'I saw a feathered sparrow and a bald one.'

Similarly, in the sentences in (47), GT applies between w_1 and w_2 in additional types of constructions in which it is commonly accepted that PRO separates the two words in question, although Rizzi and Vanelli do not explicitly mention these cases.

(47) a. Il mio cavallo é stato tutto un mese senza PRO [ϕ]ascolare. $\overset{w_1}{}$ $\overset{w_2}{}$
($<$[p]ascolare)
'My horse has gone a whole month without grazing.'
  b. Il pappagallo ha trovato come PRO [θ]orturarci con le nostre $\overset{w_1}{}$ $\overset{w_2}{}$
parole.
($<$[t]orturarci)
'The parrot has learned how to torture us with our own words.'
  c. Il mio barbagianni crede di PRO [h]antare meglio di un $\overset{w_1}{}$ $\overset{w_2}{}$
usignolo.
($<$[k]antare)
'My barn owl thinks he sings better than a nightingale.'

Another segmental rule of Tuscan Italian is Intervocalic Spirantization, the rule that changes the affricates [tʃ] and [dʒ] into the corresponding fricatives [ʃ] and [ʒ] between two vowels (see Lepschy and Lepschy, 1977). As is the case with GT, IS applies both within words and across words:

(48)   a.   cri[ʃ]eto   (< cri[tʃ]eto)   'hamster'
       b.   fa[ʒ]ano   (< fa[dʒ]ano)   'pheasant'

(49)   a.   Questo dev'essere un uovo di [ʃ]efalo.
             (< [tʃ]efalo)
             'This must be a mullet egg.'
       b.   Le [ʒ]iraffe si abbeverano al tramonto.
             (< [dʒ]iraffe)
             'Giraffes drink at sunset.'

The sentences in (50) illustrate that IS applies in the same environments as GT across intervening PROs in the type of analysis proposed by Rizzi and Vanelli.

(50)   a.   Hanno trascurato l'armadillo zoppo per concentrarsi tutti su
             w_1 w_2
             quello PRO [ʃ]eco.
             (< [tʃ]eco)
             '(They) neglected the limping armadillo so all could concentrate on the blind one.'
                                           w_1 w_2
       b.   Parlava di un pinguino nano e di uno PRO [ʒ]igante.
             (< [dʒ]igante)
             '(He) was talking about a dwarf penguin and a giant one.'

IS, like GT, applies across other instances of PRO as well, as seen in (51).
                                     w_1 w_2
(51)   a.   Non hanno ancora capito come PRO [ʃ]ercare l'upupa.
             (< [tʃ]ercare)
             'They haven't yet figured out how to locate the hoopoe.'
                                                       w_1
       b.   La mia foca non puó resistere un solo giorno senza PRO
             w_2
             [ʒ]ocare a palla con Pierino.
             (< [dʒ]ocare)
             'My seal can't go even one day without playing ball with Pierino.'

These sentences lend further support to the point made above in relation to traces of clitics, that is, that a phonetically empty element does not have any effect on the application of phonological processes. That is, GT and IS apply between two words that contain the relevant phonological characteristics, the adjacency of the two words being totally unaffected by the presence or absence of PRO. We must conclude, then, that

PRO does not have the same status as phonologically non-null constituents, in that it does not count in determining whether two words are adjacent for the purposes of phonology.

At this point we must reject the strong hypothesis according to which all phonetically empty elements, including those not marked for case, may intervene between two words in the way a lexical item may, to interrupt the adjacency of the words.

Traces of wh

We will now examine data relevant to the weak hypothesis, that is, sentences in which it is case-marked empty elements, specifically traces of *wh*, that intervene between two words that otherwise satisfy the requirements for the application of phonological rules. Raddoppiamento Sintattico and Gorgia Toscana are both examples of rules that apply freely across case-marked traces, as shown in (52) and (53), respectively.

(52) *Raddoppiamento Sintattico*
  a. Cosa filmerá t_{wh} [d:]omani?
      (< [d]omani)
      'What will he film tomorrow?'
  b. Filippo é il cavallo che monteró t_{wh} [d:]omani.
      (< [d]omani)
      'Filippo is the horse that I will ride tomorrow.'

(53) *Gorgia Toscana*
  a. Chi hai fotografato t_{wh} [h]ol pappagallo sulla spalla?
      (< [k]ol)
      'Who did you take a picture of with the parrot on his shoulder?'
  b. Questi sono i picchi che abbiamo comprato t_{wh} [h]ol sussidio
      statale.
      (< [k]ol)
      'These are the woodpeckers that we bought with the national grant.'

Phonological rules that apply across intervening case-marked traces are found not only in Italian, but in all the languages we have investigated. Consider, for instance, Nasal Assimilation in Spanish. While the sentences in (54) show that NA applies between two words that are structurally adjacent, the sentences in (55) show that the rule also applies freely across traces of *wh*.

(54) a. El faisa[m] peruano tiene la cola mas larga.
          (< pavó[n])
          'The Peruvian pheasant has the largest tail.'

b. Quisiera ver un airó[n] tambien.
(< airó[n])
'I would like to see a heron too.'

c. Ha escrito un articulo sobre el sistema comunicativo del delfí[ŋ] canadiense.
(< delfí[n])
'He has written an article about the communicative system of Canadian dolphins.'

(55)   a. Qué come[m] t_{wh} para navidad las tortugas?
(< come[n])
'What do turtles eat for Christmas?'

b. Este es el coyote que fotografia[m] t_{wh} para la rivista.
(< fotografia[n])
'This is the coyote that they are taking a picture of for the magazine.'

The last phonological rule we will discuss to illustrate the irrelevance of the feature "case" for phonological rules is Linking-*r* in Received Pronunciation. While a word-final *r* is usually deleted, it is retained in connected speech if the following word begins with a vowel, as illustrated in (56). (See Chapter 8 for a detailed analysis of this rule.)

(56)   a. I'd prefer a monkey.
b. A caterpillar is a wormlike larva of a butterfly or moth.

Linking-*r* applies, as do the other rules seen in this section, also when there is an intervening case-marked trace, as is shown in (57).

(57)   a. What would you order t_{wh} instead?
b. I can't think of what I could wear t_{wh} otherwise.

These facts, along with those of Italian and Spanish, lead us to the conclusion that phonological rules are not affected by the presence of phonetically empty syntactic constituents marked for case.

Let us now consider a stress rule in Italian and one in English. The Italian rule exhibits a mixed type of behavior in that it is never blocked when the trace of *wh* intervening between the two words involved in the rule is left either by relative clause formation or by indirect questions, while it may be blocked when the trace is left by the movement involved in the formation of direct questions. The English stress rule, however, shows a more consistent pattern, in that it typically applies across all traces of *wh*, regardless of their origin.

Consider first the rule of Stress Retraction (SR) found in standard northern Italian. In a sequence of word$_1$ word$_2$, where w_1 has primary stress on the last syllable and w_2 is stressed on the first syllable, SR retracts the primary stress of w_1 (see Nespor and Vogel, 1979). This rule applies freely across t_{wh} in (58a) and (58b), examples of relative clauses and indirect questions, respectively, but it does not apply in (58c), a direct question.

(58)   a.   Ho giá capito quello che fáro t_{wh} dópo.
         ($<$ faró)[7]
         'I've already understood what I will do afterwards.'
     b.   Ci si domanda cosa fára t_{wh} dópo.
         ($<$ fará)
         'One wonders what he'll do afterwards.'
     c.   Cosa dirá t_{wh} dópo?
         (?*díra)
         'What will he say afterwards?'

Iambic Reversal (IR), a stress retraction rule of American English (see Liberman and Prince, 1977), however, does not usually exhibit the mixed behavior just seen in Italian with respect to traces of *wh*. That is, IR applies in (59a), (59b), and (59c), examples of relative clauses, indirect questions, and direct questions, respectively.

(59)   a.   The picture that I'm going to réproduce t_{wh} láter is the one
         Emily took.
         ($<$ reprodúce)
     b.   They asked me which company Martha répresents t_{wh} nów.
         ($<$ represénts)
     c.   What are they going to éxport t_{wh} néxt?
         ($<$ expórt)

As Nespor and Scorretti (1985) observe, attributing the blocking of SR in Italian in (58c) to the presence of a trace would pose serious problems to the commonly accepted unified derivation of the three phenomena under consideration: relative clause formation, indirect questions, and direct questions. It also seems to be in conflict with the uniform behavior of IR in the same three types of constructions in English. Following Nespor and Scorretti (1985), we believe that the low acceptability of the direct questions in Italian in which SR has applied cannot be attributed to the presence of a trace but rather must be attributed to the intonation pattern of these questions. Specifically, the unacceptability of SR in (58c) is due to the fact that the word in question, *dirá*, contains the peak of an intonation contour, and in general material in this position is resistant to any type of reduction. This analysis is further confirmed by the facts of English. In direct questions, such as the one in (59c), the peak of the intonation contour is not typically on the word which is subject to IR, and thus the primary stress may be retracted. Under certain circumstances, however, it is possible for the word in question to be the peak of the contour, and in such cases IR is in fact blocked, as SR is in Italian. This happens, for example, when there is contrastive stress or emphasis on the word that would otherwise undergo Iambic Reversal, as illustrated by the following sentences:

(60)   a.   Who are they going to íntroduce t_{wh} néxt?
            (< introdúce)
       b.   I said, who are they going to introdúce t_{wh} néxt, not who
            are they going to invite next.
            (*íntroduce)

We can thus conclude that it is not the syntactic properties of the constructions under consideration, but rather their phonological properties that are responsible for the application or nonapplication of Stress Retraction and Iambic Reversal.

Given that traces of *wh* are invisible to phonological rules that depend on the adjacency of two words, as are the other types of phonetically empty elements seen above, we can conclude that the weak hypothesis about the influence of empty nodes on phonology must be rejected also, at least if it is formulated in the general fashion found in Chomsky (1981). While the hypotheses discussed above clearly have no general validity, it could still be claimed that they are valid for a subset of the rules of the phonological component. That is, it might be possible that a subcomponent of the phonology is sensitive to the presence of empty elements, while another subcomponent, presumably ordered after the first, is blind to nonphonetic material. To show that this is not the case, it would be necessary to demonstrate that all the rules that have been claimed to be sensitive to empty elements are in fact only sensitive to phonological material. These rules include *to*-Contraction and Auxiliary Reduction in American English (see King, 1970; Lakoff, 1970; Zwicky, 1970; Selkirk, 1972; Kaisse, 1983, among others) and Specifier Vowel Deletion in Italian (see Rizzi, 1979; Vanelli, 1979). We will not provide a reanalysis of these rules here, since it would involve a syntactic discussion that would lead us too far from the topic of the present chapter. An analysis of these rules that does not rely on the presence of traces, however, can be found in Nespor and Scorretti (1985), where it is shown that these rules, like all phonological rules, are not sensitive to nonphonological material. We may thus conclude that the hypotheses made about the influence of empty categories on phonological rules must be rejected.

2.3.3. Noncorrespondence between syntactic constituents and domains of intonation contours

The noncorrespondence between the limits of intonation contours and major syntactic breaks is a phenomenon often mentioned in the linguistic literature. The type of sentence most often cited as an illustration of this phenomenon is one containing a restrictive relative clause. It has been noted that complex sentences containing restrictive relative clauses present a problem for intonation in that 'the intonation breaks are ordinarily inserted in the wrong place' (Chomsky, 1965:13). Underlying Chomsky's statement is the assumption that if intonation breaks were in the 'correct' place, they would directly reflect the surface syntactic structure of the sentence, in particular, the direction of embedding. Compare the bracketings of the sentences in (61) and (62), where those in (61) illustrate the syntactic constituent analysis and those in (62) reflect the intonational structure.

(61)   This is [the cat that caught [the rat that stole [the cheese]]]

(62)   [This is the cat] [that caught the rat] [that stole the cheese]

According to Chomsky and Halle (1968:372), this discrepancy between how things are and how things should be is 'obviously a matter of performance rather than of grammatical structure'. In this regard the notion of 'phonological phrase' is introduced, and rules that insert the boundaries of such phrases 'will have to take account of syntactic structure, but they will also involve certain parameters that relate to performance, e.g. speed of utterance'.

While it seems clear that the presence and position of intonation breaks are to some extent connected to such factors as the rate of speech and the length of an utterance, this does not necessarily mean that the occurrence of intonation breaks is not rule governed like other performance phenomena such as hesitations. Instead, the specification of the positions in which intonation breaks may occur follows from the constituent structure of prosodic trees, and is thus a matter of competence, as will be shown in Chapter 7.[8]

The flexibility of the domains over which intonation contours are spread is another area in which it can be seen that intonation domains cannot be directly determined by syntactic constituent structure. In section 2.3.1, we have illustrated the flexible nature of the domains of application of sandhi rules and have argued, on the basis of the inflexibility of syntactic structure, that syntactic constituents cannot form the domains of application of phonological rules applying across words. The same flexibility can also be seen in relation to the domains over which intonation contours extend, and thus provides further evidence that syntactic constituents are not the appropriate structures for defining the domains of intonation contours. For example, while it is possible to read the sentence below with three separate intonation contours, as indicated by the bracketings in (63a), a pronunciation with the intonation contours indicated by the bracketings in (63b) is also possible. Even a pronunciation without internal intonation breaks, that is, with one single intonation contour as in (63c), is possible.

(63)   a.   [The frog] [ate a fly] [for lunch]
      b.   [The frog] [ate a fly for lunch]
      c.   [The frog ate a fly for lunch]

While it would be possible to describe the data in (63) in terms of syntactic constituents by saying that an intonation break may optionally occur after each syntactic phrase, i.e. at the end of the maximal projection of any category X, this is not the correct generalization. For example, it can be seen that such a principle would yield the unacceptable division into intonation domains in (64), where each break indicated corresponds to the end of a syntactic phrase.

(64) *[Bruce] [never] [understood], [I believe], [why Paul]
      [can't see the Southern Cross] [from his home in Brittany]

In conclusion, we have provided some evidence that the analysis into constituents offered by the syntax does not correspond to the division into possible domains of intonation contours. This issue will be taken up again in Chapter 7.

2.4.   *On motivating a phonological constituent*

Up to this point, we have shown that morpho-syntactic constituents cannot account for the domain of application of all types of phonological rules. We will now motivate the postulation of phonological constituents that do account for such domains. The specific criteria that will be used to motivate phonological constituents throughout this book derive, in part, directly from the notion of constituent in general; they are the same criteria that are used to motivate a constituent analysis in syntax. There are other criteria, however, that are specific to phonology. The first two criteria mentioned below are the more general ones related to the notion of constituent. The last two, however, are specific to phonology since they are related to the fact that phonological constituents represent an analysis of strings of sounds.

In generative grammar, the formal configuration adopted to represent the internal structure of a sentence is the constituent structure tree. In both phonology and syntax this tree is a representation of the hierarchical grouping of the elements of a string into constituents and the left-to-right order of these constituents. A string is considered a constituent in phonology, as in syntax, if *a*) there are rules of the grammar that need to refer to it in their formulation, or *b*) there are rules that have precisely that string as their domain of application. In phonological theory, however, these are not the only motivations for positing a constituent (see also Nespor, 1983). It is also possible for a string to be a constituent even if the first two criteria are not met, if the string is the domain of phonotactic restrictions. Thus, a constituent X would be motivated, for example, in a language in which a sequence of a nasal consonant immediately followed by a liquid is ill formed within a given domain X, but is allowed when the two segments are in different Xs.

Finally, even in the absence of phonological phenomena that need to refer to the domain X for one of the reasons mentioned above, X may be posited as a constituent of the phonological hierarchy for still another reason. That is, a phonological constituent, unlike a syntactic constituent, can also be motivated on the basis of a fourth criterion, the relative prominence relations among the elements of a string. Consider the case in which, for example, a constituent X^n cannot be motivated in a given language on the basis of any of the first three criteria. It might nevertheless be the case that in this language, stress peaks within the constituent X^{n+1} are neither distributed in a regularly alternating pattern nor located in positions that are specifiable in terms of syntactic constituents. The lack of periodicity in the recurrence of these stress peaks, together with the lack of connection between the location of the peaks and a given position within syntactic constituents, indicates that there must be some principle responsible for the distribution of stress other than an abstract alternation rule or a rule that makes direct reference to syntactic structure. In such a case, another type of constituent that accounts for the stress pattern would be motivated. We propose that it is precisely in such situations that a phonological constituent X^n can be posited on the basis of the fourth criterion mentioned above: relative prominence relations within a given string. It should be noted that such a constituent has the function of delimiting the domains of stress patterns, independently of the mechanism chosen to represent the actual prominence relations and the rules that modify them.

While prosodic and morpho-syntactic constituents are in principle nonisomorphic, it should be noted that an occasional case of isomorphism between the two does not constitute grounds for rejecting a specific prosodic constituent in a given language. Replacement of a prosodic constituent by a syntactic constituent in the case of isomorphism would, in fact, have undesirable results. First of all, since prosodic rules may refer to more than one constituent, in the case that one of these constituents is morpho-syntactic, two different hierarchies would be referred to by a single phonological rule. Secondly, even in the case of prosodic rules that need to mention only one category, allowing the rules of a given level to refer to a morpho-syntactic constituent would create a heterogeneous situation. That is, the majority of the prosodic rules would refer to one hierarchy while the rules of a single level would refer to the other hierarchy.

To summarize, we have claimed that there are four possible types of motivation for positing a constituent in the phonological hierarchy. It is on the basis of such motivations that each of the constituents of the prosodic hierarchy will be established in Chapters 3 through 8.

NOTES

1. It should be noted that Siegel actually proposes that *in-* and *un-* are both Class I affixes. She thus fails to account for the difference in assimilation patterns, a difficulty that is resolved within the same theoretical framework by Allen, however, who assigns *in-* to Level I and *un-* to Level II.
2. See Scalise (1983) for a more detailed discussion of this rule.
3. A subsequent rule that lengthens /ts/ in intervocalic position will give the pronunciation *danna[t:s]ione*.
4. It should be noted that we are concerned here only with a colloquial style of speech, not with poetic language, in which deletion phenomena are more widespread.
5. Here and elsewhere in the book, primary stress is indicated with an acute accent, even when this is in conflict with the orthographic conventions of Italian.
6. The same argument can be made on the basis of other phonological rules of Italian, such as Gorgia Toscana, Stress Retraction, and Intervocalic Spirantization.
7. The acute accent mark on a nonfinal syllable of a word that undergoes Stress Retraction should not be interpreted as being equivalent to a primary stress. Thus, for example, *fáro* (< *faró*) in (58a) is not necessarily phonetically identical to the word *fáro* 'lighthouse'. Stress Retraction changes the prominence relations within a word by destressing the last syllable and stressing a previously unstressed syllable. The fact that it does not necessarily create a stress as strong as word primary stress on the newly stressed syllable is not relevant here.
8. It has also been suggested by Langendoen (1975), though for different reasons, that the position of intonation breaks is dependent on competence rather than performance.

Chapter 3

The Syllable and the Foot

3.0. Introduction

As was mentioned in Chapter 1, we take the syllable to be the smallest constituent of the prosodic hierarchy. The foot is the next constituent in the hierarchy, and consists of one or more syllables. The fact that the syllable and the foot have been grouped here into a single chapter is not an indication that there is less to say about these two constituents than about the others, each of which has been afforded an entire chapter. To the contrary, an exhaustive treatment of both the syllable and the foot would require more than a chapter each, given the explosion of research dealing with these units that the field of phonology has witnessed in recent years. We have therefore had to make a selection of the issues to discuss here, and have decided to restrict our attention to only those aspects of the syllable and foot that are most relevant to the rest of this book. Thus, this chapter does not contain an overview of the various positions taken in relation to the two units in question in the recent phonological literature, nor does it attempt to analyze the various controversies surrounding these units. Rather, it is an investigation of the roles the syllable and foot play in a theory of prosodic phonology. Specifically, it concentrates on the syllable and the foot as domains of phonological rules, as well as certain other related issues. The reader will be referred to representative works dealing with important issues related to the syllable and foot that are not treated here.

3.1. The syllable

While the syllable is not a new notion in phonology, it has only recently been incorporated into generative theory. In the early and mid 1970s, the main discussion surrounding the syllable was whether or not it belonged in a theory of generative phonology. Major advances were made in the direction of accepting the syllable by Hooper (1976) within the framework of natural generative phonology (see also Hooper, 1972; Vennemann, 1971,1974) and by Kahn (1976) within the autosegmental framework.[1] Once the syllable was accepted, there was a rapid increase in the amount of research dealing with various aspects of its nature and role in phonology, and our understanding of the syllable has deepened greatly in a number of areas due to work on issues such as the internal structure of the syllable and syllable templates,[2] relations among the segments within a syllable,[3] syllabification and resyllabification,[4] the autosegmental representation of syllables,[5] and studies of the syllable in specific languages.[6]

The existence of such a large body of research on the syllable allows us to dispense with a discussion of a number of issues here, such as how to determine the division of a string of segments into syllables and what constitutes a well-formed syllable. This is not to say that all the problems in these areas have been resolved, but rather that it is possible to assume a certain familiarity with these problems by now (see notes 2-6 for bibliographical indications). We will therefore take the syllable as the starting point in our investigation of the various syllable- related phenomena treated in this chapter. That is, we will assume that the universal and language-specific principles that determine the organization of segments into syllables are known, and in the case of syllable-level phonological rules, that the division of a string into syllables has already been established at the point at which our analysis of the rules begins.

3.1.1.   The domain of the syllable

Although we will not be concerned here with the principles of syllabification *per se*, it is nevertheless necessary to consider the question of the domain within which syllabification applies, since it is in the definition of this domain that we find the interaction between the phonological and morpho-syntactic components of the grammar. That is, the principles of syllabification group segments into well-formed syllables throughout a string whose boundaries must be defined on the basis of nonphonological elements, as will be seen here in relation to English and Dutch.

Let us consider, for example, the following sequence of consonants and vowels:

(1) C_0 V   C   V C_0

In English, and probably universally, the basic principles of syllabification would divide a string such as the one in (1) as in (2).[7]

(2) $[C_0$ $V]_\sigma$ $[C$ V $C_0]_\sigma$

Of course, this type of division does not only apply to the bisyllabic string given here, but represents the general principle that places an intervocalic consonant at the beginning of the syllable to its right, rather than at the end of the syllable to its left, part of the Maximal Onset Principle. This, in fact, is the correct division for the example in (3a), but not for those in (3b-d), where the brackets indicate syllable constituents;[8] the symbols within the brackets are orthographic.

(3)   a.   pecan   → $[pe]_\sigma\ [can]_\sigma$
        b.   brookite   → $*[broo]_\sigma\ [kite]_\sigma$
        c.   pack ice (N) → $*[pa]_\sigma\ [ckice]_\sigma$
        d.   pack ice (VP) → $*[pa]_\sigma\ [ckice]_\sigma$

An indication that the syllabification in (3a) is correct and that those in (3b-d) are not is the fact that the velar stop [k] at the beginning of the second syllable is aspirated in *pecan* but not in the other examples. That is, if the correct syllabification of all of the items in (3) were as predicted by (2), with [k] at the beginning of the second syllable, we would expect [k] to be aspirated in all four cases, since the second syllable in each case begins a new foot.[9] Instead, the correct divisions of (3b-d) are such that [k] belongs to the first syllable, as in (4), and is thus in a position in which it is not aspirated.

(4)   a.   brookite   → $[brook]_\sigma\ [ite]_\sigma$
        b.   pack ice (N) → $[pack]_\sigma\ [ice]_\sigma$
        c.   pack ice (VP) → $[pack]_\sigma\ [ice]_\sigma$

The difference between *pecan* and the other items is that *pecan* is monomorphemic while the others are cases of a derived word with a neutral or Class II affix (in the terminology of SPE and Siegel (1974), respectively), a compound word, and a syntactic phrase.[10] In addition to accounting for syllabification of monomorphemic words, (2) also accounts for the division of segments into syllables in words derived with nonneutral or Class I affixes, as seen in (5).

(5)   a.   ethnicity   → $[eth]_\sigma\ [ni]_\sigma\ [ci]_\sigma\ [ty]_\sigma$
        b.   racketeer → $[ra]_\sigma\ [cke]_\sigma\ [teer]_\sigma$

It should be noted that the [t] in (5b) is aspirated, since it is not only syllable initial but also foot initial (see section 3.2.2).

What the examples in (3) and (5) show is that syllabification does not apply in the same way to all strings of segments, but rather is sensitive to certain aspects of the morphological structure of the items in question.

In particular, the domain throughout which syllabification occurs in English is a stem plus any adjacent nonneutral affixes, as was seen in (3a) and (5). Syllabification does not apply across the boundaries between a stem and a neutral affix, as was seen in (3b), or between one neutral affix and another, as can be seen in (6).

(6)   sleeplessness → [sleep]$_\sigma$ [less]$_\sigma$ [ness]$_\sigma$
       (*[slee]$_\sigma$ [ple]$_\sigma$ [ssness]$_\sigma$)

While (6) does not contain ...VCV... sequences like the other examples, it nevertheless illustrates the more general point about the domain of syllabification. That is, syllabification does not create the clusters [pl] and [sn] in the morphological contexts illustrated above, though these clusters are perfectly acceptable at the beginning of a syllable in English (cf. *plea, snooze*).

Finally, syllabification does not apply across the members of a compound, nor does it apply across words in a phrase, as was seen in (3c) and (3d), respectively. It should be recalled that we are interested in 'normal' colloquial speech in this book. Thus, while we do not wish to exclude the possibility that resyllabification may be found across words in English in other types of speech, in particular in fast or sloppy speech, we believe that such phenomena are fundamentally different from the ones under investigation here and, consequently, we do not consider them further. We also do not wish to exclude the possibility of low-level phonetic rules of (partial) resyllabification similar to Kahn's (1976) ambisyllabicity rules, which account for the difficulty speakers of English have in dividing certain strings of segments into syllables. Rules of the latter type, however, appear to reflect the fact that an utterance consists of a continuous flow of speech sounds, without sharp boundaries between one sound and another, and thus is quite different from the type of syllabification under examination here (see also note 17).

Contrary to our observation that resyllabification does not apply across words in English is Kiparsky's (1979) claim to the effect that it does. Kiparsky's position is based on his analysis of Flapping across words, which he accounts for by first laxing a consonant, *t* in this case, when it follows a [−consonantal] segment within a foot. Cyclic resyllabification subsequently places the lax *t* at the beginning of a following vowel-initial word, where it is voiced by a post-cyclic rule, yielding a segment that is phonetically interpreted as a flap. While this set of operations does generate flaps where they are observed, it rests on an assumption we do not share: that resyllabification normally applies across words.

In favor of his position, Kiparsky mentions that *an aim* may have the same pronunciation as *a name*. This does not seem to be a representative case, however, but seems instead to depend on the special (weak) phonological status of the article *an*. An *n* does not appear to be resyllabified in other types of constructions, so for example, *Anne ate* does not have the same junctural properties as *innate*. This point becomes even clearer if we consider a segment that has a noticeable difference in its pronunciation in syllable-final *vs.* syllable-initial position. In English, *l* is such a segment, since it is 'dark' finally and 'clear' initially (cf. *pa*[ɫ] vs. [*l*]*ap*). If resyllabification takes place across words, we would expect a clear *l* in *call Andy*, the *l* having been moved into syllable-initial position. This is not what we find, however. Instead, the *l* of *call Andy* is dark, and thus is quite distinct from the unquestionably syllable-initial *l* in *Yolanda*. While it might be possible to resolve the problem by saying that the final dark *l* of *call* is moved as is to the onset of the following syllable, there is no evidence for such a claim. Furthermore, there appears to be a general constraint in English against dark *l*s in syllable-initial position. In fact, when resyllabification of a syllable-final *l* to syllable-initial position does take place, this results in a change from a dark to a clear articulation (cf. vigi[ɫ] vs. vigi[l]ant, vigi[l]ante). Note that where resyllabification is blocked before a Class II suffix, the dark *l* remains (cf. vigi[ɫ]ish).

Returning now to the problem of Flapping, the fact remains that this rule does apply across words, as in *caught Andy*. There is no more motivation for saying that the *t* in *caught Andy* is syllable initial than there is for saying that the *l* in *call Andy* is syllable initial. Flapping must therefore be explained in some other way. (See Chapter 8 for an alternative proposal in which Flapping is analyzed as a *U* domain rule, and see sections 3.1.2 and 3.2.2 for a discussion of the related phenomena of Glottalization and Aspiration.)

Another language in which an interaction between phonology and morphology at the syllable level can be seen is Dutch, where the facts are quite similar to those of English seen above (see, among others, Booij, 1977; van der Hulst, 1984). By way of illustration, let us consider a medial sequence of nasal + obstruent which would normally be divided in Dutch, and perhaps universally, such that the nasal closes the preceding syllable and the obstruent begins the following syllable, giving the structure in (7), where *N* and *O* stand for 'nasal' and 'obstruent', respectively.

(7) $[C_0 \ V \ N]_\sigma \ [O \ V \ C_0]_\sigma \ldots$

This type of syllable division is illustrated in (8).

(8)   a.   kompas   → $[\text{kom}]_\sigma [\text{pas}]_\sigma$ 'compass'
       b.   pompoen   → $[\text{pom}]_\sigma [\text{poen}]_\sigma$ 'pumpkin'

The same syllable structure is also found when the nasal and obstruent cluster is at the end of a stem when the stem is followed by an inflectional suffix or by a derivational suffix belonging to a particular class (which might be likened to the Class I or nonneutral affixes in English in some, though not all, respects (see Booij, 1977)). Examples of an inflected word and of a word derived with the relevant type of affix, which we will call type X, are given in (9a) and (9b), respectively, where "_" indicates the position of the juncture between the stem and its affix.

(9)   a.   *stem + inflectional affix*
       lamp-en   → $[lam]_\sigma [pen]_\sigma$ 'lamps'
       stamp-en   → $[stam]_\sigma [pen]_\sigma$ 'stamp (inf.)'
       b.   *stem + type X affix*
       damp-ig   → $[dam]_\sigma [pig]_\sigma$ 'vaporous'
       stamp-er   → $[stam]_\sigma [per]_\sigma$ 'stamper'

When a suffix belonging to the other class, which we will call type Y, is present, however, syllabification cannot divide the N + O cluster into two syllables, as seen in (10a). The same pattern is observed with a prefix and a stem, and with adjacent members of a compound, as seen in (10b) and (10c), respectively.

(10)
a.   *stem + type Y affix*
       lamp-achtig → $[lamp]_\sigma [ach]_\sigma [tig]_\sigma$ $(*[lam]_\sigma [pach]_\sigma [tig]_\sigma)$
       'lamplike'
       klomp-achtig → $[klomp]_\sigma [ach]_\sigma [tig]_\sigma$ $(*[klom]_\sigma [pach]_\sigma [tig]_\sigma)$
       'wooden shoe-like'

b.   *prefix + stem*
       ont-erven   → $[ont]_\sigma [er]_\sigma [ven]_\sigma$ $(*[on]_\sigma [ter]_\sigma [ven]_\sigma)$
       'disinherit'
       ont-eigenen   → $[ont]_\sigma [ei]_\sigma [ge]_\sigma [nen]_\sigma$ $(*[on]_\sigma [tei]_\sigma...)$
       'dispossess'
c.   *compound*
       lamp arm   → $[lamp]_\sigma [arm]_\sigma$ $(*[lam]_\sigma [parm]_\sigma)$ 'part of a lamp'
       lamp olie   → $[lamp]_\sigma [olie]_\sigma$ $(*[lam]_\sigma [polie]_\sigma)$ 'kerosene'

As the examples in (11) show, it is also impossible for syllables to group together segments that belong to separate words in a phrase.

(11) *separate words*

    (doe de) lamp aan   → ...[lamp]$_\sigma$ [aan]$_\sigma$ (*...[lam]$_\sigma$ [paan]$_\sigma$)
    '(put the) lamp on'
    (een) ramp aanbrengen → ...[ramp]$_\sigma$ [aan]$_\sigma$ [breng]$_\sigma$ [en]$_\sigma$
                                (*...[ram]$_\sigma$ [paan]$_\sigma$...)

    'cause (a) disaster'

What both the English and the Dutch examples show is that the definition of the domain of the syllable depends crucially on certain types of nonphonological information. It will be seen, in fact, in Chapter 4 that the domain for syllabification, or the domain within which syllables must be well formed, is the phonological word, and that syllabification may be used as a test for determining the definition of the phonological word (see also Booij, 1983; van der Hulst, 1984).

    Thus far, we have only mentioned the possibility of syllabification within words and have shown that English and Dutch do not permit syllabification across words in a phrase. It is well known, however, that certain languages such as Italian and Spanish typically do permit syllabification across words. Let us consider again the case of an intervocalic consonant and its syllabification seen above in (1) and (2), respectively, repeated below as (12).

(12) C_o V   C   V C_o → [C_o V]$_\sigma$ [C V C_o]$_\sigma$

As was said above, this rule, and syllabification in general, are limited to applying within the phonological word. Thus, syllabification of the same string of consonants and vowels gives different results depending on whether the segments are all part of the same word or not, as illustrated by the English examples in (13) and the Dutch examples in (14), where the symbols within the brackets this time are phonetic.

(13)   a.   pecan   → [pi]$_\sigma$ [kæn]$_\sigma$
      b.   pique Anne → [pik]$_\sigma$ [æn]$_\sigma$ (*[pi]$_\sigma$ [kæn]$_\sigma$)

(14)   a.   alarm   → [a]$_\sigma$ [larm]$_\sigma$
           'alarm'
      b.   al arm   → [a]$_\phi$ [arm]$_\phi$ (*[a]$_\phi$ [larm]$_\phi$)
           'already poor'

Unlike these examples, the Italian and Spanish examples in (15) and (16), respectively, show that a particular string of segments is syllabified in the same way within a word and across words.[11]

(15)   a.   adocchio   → [a]$_\sigma$[[dɔk]$_\sigma$ [kjo]$_\sigma$
            '(I) sight'

       b.   ad occhio (nudo) → [a]$_\sigma$ [dɔk]$_\sigma$ [kjo]$_\sigma$...   (*[ad]$_\sigma$ [ɔk]$_\sigma$...)
            'with (the bare) eye'

(16)   a.   alelado   → [a]$_\sigma$ [le]$_\sigma$ [la]$_\sigma$ [ðo]$_\sigma$
            'stupified'

       b.   al helado   → [a]$_\sigma$ [le]$_\sigma$ [la]$_\sigma$ [ðo]$_\sigma$ (*[al]$_\sigma$ [e]$_\sigma$...)
            'to the ice cream'

In fact, the application of syllabification across words gives a result that is indistinguishable from the syllabification of the same sequence of segments which is already divided with the consonant in question at the beginning of a syllable. Compare the results of syllabification of the pairs of expressions in Italian and Spanish given in (17) and (18), respectively.

(17)   a.   non ho   → [no]$_\sigma$ [nɔ]$_\sigma$ (*[non]$_\sigma$ [ɔ]$_\sigma$)
            '(I) don't have'

       b.   no no   → [nɔ]$_\sigma$ [nɔ]$_\sigma$
            'no no'

(18)   a.   las aves   → [la]$_\sigma$ [sa]$_\sigma$ [βes]$_\sigma$ (*[las]$_\sigma$ [a]$_\sigma$ [βes]$_\sigma$)
            'the birds'

       b.   la sabes   → [la]$_\sigma$ [sa]$_\sigma$ [βes]$_\sigma$
            '(you) know it'

The Italian and Spanish examples seem to lead to the conclusion that the domain of syllabification in these languages, and other languages that allow syllabification across words, is a unit larger than the phonological word, the domain of syllabification seen in English and Dutch. Such a conclusion, however, would be partially incorrect. Instead, it is necessary to distinguish between two types of syllabification, one applying within the domain of the phonological word and the other applying within larger domains. The first type, which we will refer to here as 'syllabification' *tout court*, is universal in that all languages must have rules that ensure the existence of well-formed syllables at some level, which we take to be the phonological word (see also Selkirk, 1978b), though clearly the definition of a well-formed syllable varies from language to language. The second type, which we will refer to as 'resyllabification', is language specific in the sense that it is found in some languages but not in others, and applies in a domain that must be further specified.[12] In addition, the details of the resyllabification rule, that is, which segments are resyllabified and under what conditions, varies from language to language.

It can be demonstrated, furthermore, that in languages that allow syllabification across words, both syllabification at the word level and resyllabification at a higher level are needed. That is, it is not sufficient to have only one rule in such languages that applies post-lexically, once and for all throughout an utterance, or some smaller domain within the utterance, after the individual words have been inserted into their syntactic structures. Specifically, it can be shown that there are certain phonological rules that must apply in relation to the (phonological) word-level syllable structure, before resyllabification takes place. The application of these rules to the syllable structure provided by a single post-lexical syllabification would yield the wrong results. This can be seen in both Spanish and French.

In Spanish, the combination nasal + glide (N + G) constitutes a well-formed syllable-initial sequence, as seen in the examples in (19a,b), which begin with [nw], and those in (19c,d), which begin with [nj].

(19) a. nuevo   'new'
      b. nuez   'walnut'
      c. nieve   'snow'
      d. nieto   'grandson'

Thus, in accordance with the Maximal Onset Principle, a word-internal sequence of N + G is syllabified with the vowel that follows it rather than with the vowel that precedes it, as seen in (20). The first two examples contain the phonetic sequence [nw] and the last two contain the sequence [nj].

(20) a. manual   → $[ma]_\sigma$ $[nual]_\sigma$ 'manual'
      b. anual   → $[a]_\sigma$ $[nual]_\sigma$ 'annual'
      c. poniendo   → $[po]_\sigma$ $[nien]_\sigma$ $[do]_\sigma$ 'placing'
      d. quinientos → $[qui]_\sigma$ $[nien]_\sigma$ $[tos]_\sigma$ 'five hundred'

On the basis of such examples, one might expect N + G sequences in adjacent words to be syllabified in the same way, too, given that Spanish is a language that permits syllabification across words. In fact, this is what would happen if there were only one rule of syllabification that applies post-lexically to a string of words. It does not happen, however, as is shown in (21), where the first example contains the phonetic sequence [nw] and the second one contains [nj].

(21) a. un huevo   → $[un]_\sigma$ $[hue]_\sigma$ $[vo]_\sigma$ $(*[u]_\sigma$ $[nhue]_\sigma$ $[vo]_\sigma)$
          'an egg'

b.   un hielo   → [un]$_\sigma$ [hie]$_\sigma$ [lo]$_\sigma$ (*[u]$_\sigma$ [nhie]$_\sigma$ [lo]$_\sigma$)
'an ice'

An indication that the correct syllabification of these examples is with the nasal and the glide in separate syllables is the fact that, as part of a more general phenomenon of nasal assimilation, a nasal assimilates in point of articulation to a following glide, but only if the two segments are not tautosyllabic (see Hooper, 1972,1976). We thus find a velar nasal in (21a) and an alveopalatal nasal in (21b), as indicated in the transcriptions in (22a) and (22b), respectively, where [ñ] indicates the alveopalatal nasal (see Harris, 1969).

(22)   a.   un huevo   → [uŋweβo]
       b.   un hielo   → [uñjelo]

No such assimilation takes place, however, when the nasal and glide are in the same syllable:

(23)   a.   nuevo   → [nweβo]   (*[ŋweβo])
       b.   nieto   → [njeto]   (*[ñjeto])

If the only syllable structure assignment is by post-lexical rules applying to an entire sentence, there is no way to account for the difference in nasal assimilation patterns before glides within a single word and before glides in a separate word. In both cases, the nasal and glide would be syllabified at the beginning of the syllable with the following vowel, the position in which it was seen that assimilation does not occur. It is necessary, therefore, to allow syllabification rules to apply to individual (phonological) words, and thus to assign, at this point, the nasal and glide in cases such as (21) to separate syllables. The fact that Spanish allows syllabification across words, as seen earlier in (16b) and (18b), is accounted for by the subsequent application of resyllabification rules.[13]

Liaison in French is another rule that applies across words. Together with Enchaînement, it accounts for the pronunciation of a word-final consonant and its resyllabification to the beginning of the following word, at least in informal styles of speech:[14]

(24)   a.   tout ouvert   → [tou]$_\sigma$ [tou]$_\sigma$ [vert]$_\sigma$ 'completely open'
       b.   les îles   → [le]$_\sigma$ [sîles]$_\sigma$ 'the islands'
       c.   mes oncles   → [me]$_\sigma$ [soncles]$_\sigma$ 'my uncles'

These divisions of segments into syllables follow the same patterns found word internally:

(25) a. coutumière → [cou]$_\sigma$ [tu]$_\sigma$ [mière]$_\sigma$ 'customary (fem.)'
     b. asile   → [a]$_\sigma$ [sile]$_\sigma$ 'asylum'
     c. maison → [mai]$_\sigma$ [son]$_\sigma$ 'house'

It might at first seem possible to have a single set of syllabification rules and assign syllable structure only after the individual words have been combined into a sentence. This is not possible, however, since there is another rule that must make reference to the syllable structure of the word, and making reference to the structure that arises from syllabification across words throughout a larger domain would yield the wrong results. In French, neither [e] nor [ə] may occur in a closed stressed syllable. In this environment, both vowels become [ɛ] (see, among others, Schane, 1968; Basbøll, 1978; Lowenstamm, 1979,1981). Thus, we find *sèche* [sɛʃ] 'dry (fem.)' but *sécher* [seʃe] 'to dry' and *première* [prəmjɛr][15] 'first (fem.)' but *premier* [prəmje] 'first (masc.)'. In a system in which syllabification rules apply only after words have been inserted into syntactic structures, these rules will assign syllable structure to the phrases in (26) as indicated; the transcription within the brackets is roughly a phonemic one.

(26) a. la première année → *...[prə]$_\sigma$ [mje]$_\sigma$ [ra]$_\sigma$ [né]$_\sigma$
       'the first year'
     b. sa première idée → *...[prə]$_\sigma$ [mje]$_\sigma$ [ri]$_\sigma$ [de]$_\sigma$
       'his first idea'

In these examples, the /e/ in *première* is in an open syllable. Since the rule that changes an underlying /e/ to [ɛ] applies only in closed syllables, it does not apply to the items in (26). This is not the correct result, however, since *première* is pronounced with [ɛ], even in phrases such as those above. It is necessary, therefore, that syllable structure be assigned first at the (phonological) word level. This places the vowels in question in closed syllables, as shown in (27).

(27) a. la première année → ...[prə]$_\sigma$ [mjer]$_\sigma$ [a]$_\sigma$ [ne]$_\sigma$
     b. sa première idée → ...[prə]$_\sigma$ [mjer]$_\sigma$ [i]$_\sigma$ [de]$_\sigma$

The rule that changes /e/ to [ɛ] can now apply. Only subsequently does a rule of resyllabification move the syllable-final consonant to the beginning of the following syllable. This gives the correct results, as seen in (28).[16]

(28) a. ...[prə]$_\sigma$ [mjɛ]$_\sigma$ [ra]$_\sigma$ [ne]$_\sigma$
     b. ...[prə]$_\sigma$ [mjɛ]$_\sigma$ [ri]$_\sigma$ [de]$_\sigma$

The Spanish and French examples show that even in languages that allow syllabification across words, the syllabification procedure that accounts for this phenomenon cannot be the only one in the language. It is necessary to distinguish between the syllabification across words that applies throughout larger domains relatively late in the derivation of a sentence, what we have been calling 'resyllabification', and the more basic syllabification that applies earlier in the derivation and has as its domain the phonological word. While, as we have said, all languages have word-domain syllabification, which has the effect of ensuring the well-formedness of syllables within strings delimited by the boundaries of phonological words, not all languages have resyllabification. Whether or not resyllabification is allowed is a parameter of the phonology that must be fixed for each language. It may turn out, further, that this parameter is related to other aspects of a language: it is probably not a coincidence that resyllabification tends to be present in Romance languages but absent in Germanic languages.[17]

What still remains to be determined is the larger domain within which resyllabification takes place in those languages in which the phenomenon occurs. Above the word level, there are four prosodic constituents, each of which is potentially a domain for resyllabification. In French, it seems that the domain of obligatory Liaison is the phonological phrase (see Chapter 5 below, and Selkirk, 1978b), while in Spanish the domain appears to be larger – the intonational phrase, or perhaps even the phonological utterance. In Italian, on the other hand, it is more difficult to determine the domain of resyllabification, since there are so few consonant-final words, and most of these are not members of any of the major lexical categories (e.g. *non* 'not', *con* 'with', *il* 'the (masc. sg.)', *per* 'for'). Combinations of such words and a following vowel-initial word, needed for resyllabification, always form a phonological phrase (see Chapter 5), making it appear that this is the domain for resyllabification, as it is in French. Additional data and other types of phenomena are necessary in order to evaluate more accurately the domain of resyllabification in Italian. One such phenomenon, Raddoppiamento Sintattico, will be discussed in Chapter 6, where it will be shown that the domain of resyllabification in Italian is, in fact, the phonological phrase. The question of the domain of resyllabification in general, however, as well as its relation to other aspects of the phonology of a given language, is one that deserves more attention in the future.

3.1.2. The syllable as a phonological domain

While the rules of syllabification and resyllabification must refer to larger domains such as the phonological word and the phonological phrase, the syllable itself also serves as the domain of application for other rules.

In fact, as we will show, it is the smallest unit in phonology that serves as the domain of (segmental) phonological rules.

Much work in recent years has been devoted to motivating and characterizing the internal organization of the syllable. Such studies (among others, Kiparsky, 1979; Harris, 1983) argue for syllables structured as in (29), along the lines proposed earlier by linguists such as Pike and Pike (1947) and Fudge (1969).

(29)

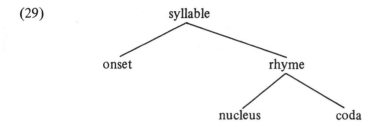

Much of the motivation for this structure comes from the relationship observed between syllable structure, in particular the rhyme, on the one hand, and stress placement and tone, on the other (see also Newman, 1972; Hyman, 1977; Hayes, 1981). Another type of motivation comes from the fact that languages tend to have strong restrictions on how segments may be combined within syllables. While these two types of motivation seem quite convincing as far as the role of subsyllabic units in such areas as stress and tone assignment and phonotactic restrictions is concerned,[18] they do not provide motivation for the use of these units as domains of segmental phonological rules. There have also been attempts to extend the role of subsyllabic units into this area as well, and Harris (1983), for example, argues that the rhyme, in particular, is the domain of application of a number of segmental rules in Spanish. The problem with this, however, is that the same rules can also be viewed as motivation for the syllable as a domain in phonology, as will be seen below.

According to Harris, the best way to describe a Velarization rule found in certain dialects of Spanish is to say that n becomes [ŋ] when it is in the rhyme of a syllable (p.46):

(30)   n → ŋ
          |
          R

This accounts for the velarization observed in the following examples (from Guitart, 1979, 1980, cited in Harris):

(31)   a.   cantan   → ca[ŋ]ta[ŋ]   '(they) sing'

b.   instituto   → i[ŋ]stituto   'institute'
c.   constante   → co[ŋ]sta[ŋ]te 'constant'

The formulation of Velarization in (30) has the advantage, according to Harris, of applying to any nasal segment in a rhyme, whether it is syllable final (as in the case of the two *n*s in (31a)) or not (as in the case of the *n*s in the first syllables of (31b,c), which are followed by *s* in the same syllable). Any rule that has the form of (30), or in more general terms, the form of (32) (from Harris, p.40), however, can also be formulated in a straightforward and simple way by referring to the syllable with no loss of generalization, as seen in (33).

(32)   x   → y / ___
                      |
                      R

(33)   x   → y / ___ C_0]$_\sigma$

Thus, the velarization rule in (30) can be reformulated as in (34).

(34)   *Velarization*

n   → ŋ /___ C_0]$_\sigma$

The same argument can be made for the six other rules Harris formulates as rhyme-domain rules, as seen in Table 1 (taken from Vogel, 1985).
    The question now is whether rules such as those just seen should be taken as evidence for the rhyme or for the syllable as a domain of phonological rules. Clearly a phonological system that allows a given phenomenon to be formulated in two ways is weaker than one that allows only one formulation. It is necessary, therefore, to find some way of choosing one of the two types of formulations. There is nothing in the rules seen thus far that seems to particularly favor either a rhyme formulation or a syllable formulation. Let us consider, however, the rule of Glide Strengthening that accounts for the presence of the fricative [ž] in the words in (35c,d), but of the glide [i̯] in those in (35a,b).

(35)   a.   ley   →   le[i̯]   'law'
       b.   comiendo   →   co-m[i̯]endo   'eating'
       c.   leyes   →   le-[ž]es   'laws'
       d.   creiendo   →   cre-[ž]endo   'believing'

Harris formulates the following syllable-domain rule for Glide Strengthening (p.58):

(36)   i̯   → ž / [$_\sigma$ ___

Table 1. Comparison of rules formulated with rhymes and syllables (only relevant syllable divisions are indicated with "__")

Rule	Harris's number	Page	Harris's formulation	Alternative formulation	Examples
Velarization	3.3a	46	n → ŋ / __ R	n → ŋ / __ C_o]$_\sigma$	constante → co[ŋ]s-ta[ŋ]-te 'constant' cantan → ca[ŋ]-ta[ŋ] '(they) sing'
Aspiration	3.3b	46	s → h / [+son]__ R	s → h / [+son]__]$_\sigma$	tienes → tiene[h] '(you) have' después → de[h]-pué[h] 'after'
Liquid Gliding	3.7	48	L → i̯ / __ R	L → i̯ / __ C_o]$_\sigma$	perspectiva → pe[j]s-pectiva 'perspective' revolver → revo[i̯]-ve[i] 'revolver'
Lateral De-palatalization	3.15	51	L → l / __ R	L → l / __]$_\sigma$	donce/L/ → donce[l] 'lad' be/L/dad → be[l]-dad 'beauty'
Nasal De-palatalization	3.21	53	ñ → n / __ R	ñ → n / __]$_\sigma$	re/ñ/cilla → re[n]-cilla 'quarrel' desde/ñ/ → desde[n] 'disdain'
r-Strengthening (i)	3.45	63	r → r̄ / [+cons]__ R	r → r̄ / [+cons][$_\sigma$__	honra → hon-[r̄]a 'honor' alrededor → al-[r̄]edador 'around'
r-Strengthening (iii) (emphatic speech)	3.49	65	r → r̄ / __ R	r → r̄ / __C_o]$_\sigma$	mártir → má[r̄]-ti[r̄] 'martyr' superstición → supe[r̄]s-tición 'superstition'

This rule cannot be reformulated as a rhyme-domain rule of the form in (32), though Harris considers the glide in question to be part of the rhyme, since it does not apply to just any glide in a rhyme, but only to one that is not preceded by another segment in the same syllable. Thus, there are certain syllable-domain rules that cannot be reformulated in terms of the rhyme domain, though all rhyme-domain rules can be reformulated as syllable-domain rules. We propose to resolve the problem mentioned above of how to determine whether a given phenomenon should be expressed as a rhyme- or as a syllable-domain rule by excluding completely the possibility of rhyme-domain rules; the smallest domain for segmental phonological rules is the syllable. That is, while the rhyme may play a role in stress and tone assignment and in the formulation of phonotactic constraints, it does not serve as a domain for segmental phonological rules. The result is a more constrained, and thus more highly valued, system since it contains one less domain for the application of segmental rules and since it eliminates the situation in which there is no way to choose between two formulations of a rule, and perhaps also prevents a duplication of functions, which arises when both the rhyme and the syllable are potentially the domain of a single phenomenon.

As we have just seen, there are (at least) eight rules in different varieties of Spanish that make reference to the syllable in their formulation.[19] While all of these rules have been formulated as domain limit rules, that is, rules that apply in relation to either the right side or the left side of a syllable, it should be noted that one of the rules, Aspiration, can also be formulated as a span rule. That is, it is not necessary to explicitly represent the fact that the *s* that is aspirated is at the right end of a syllable. That the *s* in question will always be in this position is accounted for by general constraints on syllable structure in Spanish. In other words, the *s* in question cannot be in any other position if it is preceded by a [+sonorant] segment, as specified in the context of the rule. Thus, instead of the formulation of the rule given in Table 1, we could formulate Aspiration as a syllable span rule:

(37)   s   →   h / [...[+son] _____ ...]$_\sigma$

Since nothing may, in fact, appear in the position indicated by the rightmost '...', the domain span formulation yields the same results as the domain limit formulation. We will not choose between the two possibilities at this point, since it is not clear whether one type of rule is more highly valued than the other, and both rules are formulated in a very simple way. It should be pointed out in relation to the span interpretation, however, that it makes use of information about Spanish syllable structure that must in any case be expressed in the grammar and may, for this reason, be considered a more desirable formulation.

The phenomena we will examine in the rest of this section show that the syllable is the domain of application of segmental rules in languages other than Spanish and that syllable-level rules, in addition to applying as limit or span rules, may also apply at the juncture between two syllables as domain juncture rules.

Let us first consider a rule of English, Glottalization. As is well known, Glottalization is one of the three rules that account for the major allophonic variation of *t*, as well as of the other voiceless stops in American English. (For a discussion of the other rules, Aspiration and Flapping, see section 3.2 below and Chapter 8, respectively.) In segmental terms, it can be said that a *t* is glottalized following a [−consonantal] segment when the *t* is *a*) in absolute final position, *b*) followed within a (phonological) word by a consonant other than *r*, and *c*) followed by a consonant or a glide in an adjacent word. As the examples in (38) show, these environments are precisely those that place *t* in syllable-final position (see, among others, Kahn, 1976, 1980).

(38) a. wait   → $[\text{wai}[t^{ʔ}]]_\sigma$
     b. report   → $[\text{re}]_\sigma \; [\text{por}[t^{ʔ}]]_\sigma$ [20]
     c. giant   → $[\text{gi}]_\sigma [\text{an}[t^{ʔ}]]_\sigma$ [21]
     d. atlas   → $[\text{a}[\; t^{ʔ}]]_\sigma \; [\text{las}]_\sigma$
     e. witness   → $[\text{wi}[t^{ʔ}]]_\sigma \; [\text{ness}]_\sigma$
     f. wait patiently → $[\text{wai}[t^{ʔ}]]_\sigma \; [\text{pa}]_\sigma \ldots$
     g. wait reluctantly → $[\text{wai}[t^{ʔ}]]_\sigma \; [\text{re}]_\sigma \ldots$
     h. wait wearily   → $[\text{wai}[t^{ʔ}]]_\sigma \; [\text{wea}]_\sigma \ldots$

It should be noted that when a word-final *t* is followed by a vowel in an adjacent phonological word, either in a compound or in a phrase, Glottalization does not occur, as illustrated below.

(39) a. night owl   → *$\text{nigh}[t^{ʔ}]$ owl
     b. heart ache   → *$\text{hear}[t^{ʔ}]$ ache
     c. wait a minute   → *$\text{wai}[t^{ʔ}]$ a minute
     d. wait eagerly   → *$\text{wai}[t^{ʔ}]$ eagerly

In these examples, we find a flap instead of a glottalized *t*. One way to exempt such cases from Glottalization is to claim that the word-final *t* is resyllabified to the onset of the following syllable, the solution adopted by Kiparsky (1979). As we have argued above, however, this is not a viable solution. The solution we adopt here, instead, is to allow the Flapping rule to apply before the Glottalization rule. The *t*s in environments like those in (39) will be flapped, and will therefore not be subject to the later application of Glottalization, since Glottalization applies to voiceless stops, not to flaps (see also Vogel, 1981).

On the basis of the above observations, we can formulate Glottalization as a syllable-domain rule, and in particular, a domain limit rule, as seen in (40).

(40)   *Glottalization*

$$t \;\rightarrow\; t^{?} \;/\; [\;\ldots[-\text{cons}] \;\underline{\quad\quad}\;]_{\sigma}$$

Another rule that has the syllable as its domain of application is Schwa Insertion in certain varieties of Dutch (see, among others, Booij, 1981; Trommelen, 1983; van der Hulst, 1984). According to this rule, a schwa may be inserted between a liquid and a following noncoronal obstruent, but only when the liquid and the obstruent are in the same syllable.[22] Compare the examples in (41), in which Schwa Insertion applies, and those in (42), in which it does not apply.

(41)

a.	park:	$[\text{park}]_{\sigma}$	→ par[ə]k	'park'
b.	helpster:	$[\text{help}]_{\sigma}\,[\text{ster}]_{\sigma}$	→ hel[ə]pster	'helper (fem.)'
c.	helft:	$[\text{helft}]_{\sigma}$	→ hel[ə]ft	'half'
d.	melk:	$[\text{melk}]_{\sigma}$	→ mel[ə]k	'milk'
e.	melkachtig:	$[\text{melk}]_{\sigma}\,[\text{ach}]_{\sigma}\,[\text{tig}]_{\sigma}$ →	mel[ə]kachtig	'milklike'
f.	melkauto:	$[\text{melk}]_{\sigma}\,[\text{au}]_{\sigma}\,[\text{to}]_{\sigma}$ →	mel[ə]kauto	'milk van'

(42)

a.	parkiet:	$[\text{par}]_{\sigma}\,[\text{kiet}]_{\sigma}$	→ *par[ə]kiet	'parakeet'
b.	pulpig:	$[\text{pul}]_{\sigma}\,[\text{pig}]_{\sigma}$	→ *pul[ə]pig	'pulpy'
c.	Margreet:	$[\text{Mar}]_{\sigma}\,[\text{greet}]_{\sigma}$	→ *Mar[ə]greet	proper name
d.	wolkig:	$[\text{wol}]_{\sigma}\,[\text{kig}]_{\sigma}$	→ *wol[ə]kig	'cloudy'
e.	melkerij:	$[\text{mel}]_{\sigma}\,[\text{ke}]_{\sigma}\,[\text{rij}]_{\sigma}$ → *mel[ə]kerij	'milk farm'	

It should be noted that Schwa Insertion applies in (41e,f), even though the liquid and obstruent sequence *lk* is followed by a vowel, an environment in which we might not expect the two segments to be tautosyllabic. Compare these cases to those in (42d,e), where in a similar segmental environment the rule does not apply. The difference is that the *l* and the *k* are, in fact, tautosyllabic in (41e,f), but not in (42d,e). It will be recalled that the domain for syllabification in Dutch is the phonological word, which often does not include affixes with the stem. Since *-achtig* is one of the suffixes that form a phonological word on their own, the *k* of *melk* cannot be syllabified with the vowel-initial syllable of the following suffix. It remains at the end of *melk*, where it is tautosyllabic with *l*, thus creating the appropriate environment for Schwa Insertion. A similar situation is found in the compound *melkauto*, since the two members of the compound form separate phonological words in Dutch. Thus, the *k* must remain at the end of the first syllable, rather than being syllabified with the following vowel-initial syllable, which belongs to a separate phonological word. By contrast, the suffixes *-en* and *-erij* in (41d) and (41e), respectively, do not form separate phonological words (see Booij, 1977). The *k* thus forms the onset of the following syllable in these cases and the context for Schwa Insertion is not created.

The facts of Schwa Insertion are captured by the following syllable-domain rule, where 'L' represents a liquid:

(43)   *Schwa Insertion*

$$\emptyset \rightarrow \partial \ / \ [\ \dots \ L \ \_\_\_\_ \ [-\text{cor}] \ C_0 \ ]_\sigma$$

Formulated as such, Schwa Insertion is a syllable limit rule that applies in relation to the right end of a syllable, with one or more consonants optionally appearing after the [−coronal] segment, as indicated by the presence of C_0 in the rule. This case was seen in (41c).

It should be noted that Schwa Insertion, like Aspiration in Spanish, has an alternative formulation as a span rule. That is, since general restrictions on Dutch syllable structure require that the relevant position for the application of the rule, between a liquid and a following noncoronal obstruent, be on the right end of a syllable, it is not necessary to express this information explicitly in the rule.[23] As a span rule, Schwa Insertion can be expressed as in (44).

(44) $\emptyset \rightarrow \partial \ / \ [\dots L\_\_\_\_ \ [-\text{cor}]\dots]_\sigma$

Another syllable domain rule is Strengthening in Tamazight Berber (see Saib, 1978). This rule changes the nonstrident fricatives [θ] and [ð] to the corresponding stops [t] and [d] when they are preceded by their strident counterparts [s] and [z], but only if the segments in question are tautosyllabic. Consider the examples in (45), given by Saib (p.98). The final transcription, between unlabeled brackets, is phonetic; the dots under certain segments indicate phonetic emphasis.

(45)   a.   /θafusθ/:   [θa]$_\sigma$ [fusθ]$_\sigma$ → [θafust]   'little hand'
       b.   /θazðusθ/:   [θaz]$_\sigma$ [ðuzθ]$_\sigma$ → [θazðust]   'little mortar'
       c.   /θəkkəsð/:   [θək]$_\sigma$ [kəzð]$_\sigma$ → [θəkkəzd]   'you took off'
       d.   /θəmmizð/:[θəm]$_\sigma$ [mizð]$_\sigma$ → [θəmmizd]   'you stretched'

When the two fricatives are not in the same syllable, Strengthening does not apply, as can be seen above in the first sequence of /zð/ in (45b) and in the examples below.

(46)   a. /usθu/:   [us]$_\sigma$ [θu]$_\sigma$ → [usθu]   (*[ustu]) 'yarn'
       b. /i+zðəy/: [iz]$_\sigma$ [ðəy]$_\sigma$ → [izðəy]   (*[izdəy]) 'he linked'

As these examples show, Strengthening applies in relation to the right end of a syllable. We can thus formulate the rule as follows:[24]

(47)   *Strengthening*

$$
\begin{bmatrix} +\text{cont} \\ +\text{ant} \\ +\text{cor} \\ -\text{strid} \end{bmatrix} \rightarrow [-\text{cont}] \ / \ [\dots \begin{bmatrix} +\text{cont} \\ +\text{ant} \\ +\text{cor} \\ +\text{strid} \end{bmatrix} \underline{\quad\quad}]_\sigma
$$

All of the syllable-domain rules seen thus far except one are domain limit rules or domain span rules, and of these, all limit rules except one apply in relation to the right end of the syllable. The only syllable limit rule seen above that applies in relation to the left end of the syllable is Glide Strengthening in Spanish, formulated in (36). Another syllable limit rule that applies in relation to the left end of the syllable is what can be called Alveopalatalization, a rule of English that changes the point of articulation of *t* from alveolar to alveopalatal before *r*. The alveopalatal *t* is, furthermore, either unaspirated, [c], or aspirated, [c^h], [25] depending on whether or not it is in the appropriate context for the usual Aspiration rule (see Kahn, 1976). Alveopalatalization is thus found in the examples in (48) but not in those in (49).

(48)   a. treat: [treat]$_\sigma$ → [c^h]reat
      b. street: [street]$_\sigma$ → s[c]reet
      c. retrieve: [re]$_\sigma$ [trieve]$_\sigma$ → re[c^h]rieve
      d. citrus: [ci]$_\sigma$ [trus]$_\sigma$ → ci[c]rus
      e. destroy: [de]$_\sigma$ [stroy]$_\sigma$ → des[c]roy
      f. nitrate: [ni]$_\sigma$ [trate]$_\sigma$ → ni[c^h]rate

(49)   a. night rate: [night]$_\sigma$ [rate]$_\sigma$ → *nigh[c] rate
      b. rat race: [rat]$_\sigma$ [race]$_\sigma$ → *ra[c] race
      c. cut rate: [cut]$_\sigma$ [rate]$_\sigma$ → *cu[c] rate
      d. tight rope: [tight]$_\sigma$ [rope]$_\sigma$ → *tigh[c] rope

The application of Alveopalatalization can be accounted for by the rule in (50), a left-end syllable limit rule. It should be noted that there may be another consonant to the left of the *t* that undergoes the rule. Given the general phonotactic restrictions on English syllable structure, this consonant may only be *s* (cf. (48b,e)).

(50)   *Alveopalatalization*

　　　t   →   c / [(C)_____ r...]$_\sigma$

Finally, it should be noted that Alveopalatalization is another rule that can be formulated as a syllable span rule rather than a syllable limit rule on the basis of more general constraints on syllable structure. That is, since in English the only place within a syllable in which we find *(s)t* followed by *r* is at the left end, the Alveopalatalization rule could alternatively be formulated as the span rule in (51) and still yield the correct results.

(51)   t   →   c / [..._____r...]$_\sigma$

The only syllable-domain rule mentioned above that is not a limit or a span rule is the rule of *r*-Strengthening (i) in Spanish. This rule, originally formulated as a rhyme-domain rule by Harris (1983), can be reformulated, in accordance with our proposal to eliminate the rhyme as a phonological domain, as a syllable-domain rule (see Table 1, above). As can be seen in (52), *r*-Strengthening (i) is a domain juncture rule. That is, it applies at the juncture of two syllables, on some larger domain, D_j, possibly the phonological word.

(52)   *r-Strengthening (i)*

　　　r   →   r̄ / [... [... [+cons]]$_\sigma$ [_____ ...]$_\sigma$ ...]$_{D_j}$

An *r* is thus strengthened when it is preceded by a [+consonantal] segment in a separate syllable (as in (53)), but not by a [+consonantal] segment in the same syllable (as in (54)).

(53)   a.   honra: [hon]$_\sigma$ [ra]$_\sigma$ → hon[r̄]a   'honor'
　　　 b.   alredador: [al]$_\sigma$ [re]$_\sigma$...   → al[r̄]edador   'around'

(54)   a.   otro: [o]$_\sigma$ [tro]$_\sigma$ →*ot[r̄]o   'other'
　　　 b.   agricultor: [a]$_\sigma$ [gri]$_\sigma$...   →*ag[r̄]icultor   'farmer'

Another phenomenon that occurs at the juncture between syllables is Consonant Gradation (CG) in Finnish. CG comprises a fairly complex set of changes that have the effect of 'weakening' oral stops: geminates simplify, in homorganic sonorant + stop clusters the stop assimilates totally to the sonorant, *t* becomes *d*, *p* becomes *v*, and *k* is deleted (see Prince, 1984). Examples (from Keyser and Kiparsky, 1984) of several of these changes are given below.

(55) a. halute + ten → halut̲ten → halut̲en [26]
      b. pure + ten   → purt̲en   → purr̲en
      c. tule + ten   → tult̲en   → tullen
      d. saa + ten   → saat̲en   → saad̲en

As both Prince (1984) and Keyser and Kiparsky (1984) point out, Consonant Gradation applies to a consonant that is not in the first syllable of a word, and more specifically, to one that is preceded by a [+sonorant] segment in the adjacent syllable. The syllable in which CG occurs must, furthermore, be heavy. Since there are no long vowels or diphthongs outside the first syllable (at least of stems), and since CG applies to syllables other than the first one, the only type of syllable to which the rule applies is one with a short vowel and a final consonant (see Prince, p.241). On the basis of these observations, it can be seen that CG fits the definition of a syllable-domain juncture rule. Such a rule can be formulated as in (56), where 'weak' is a cover term representing the various changes the consonants in question may undergo, and D_j represents the larger domain within which the rule applies, most likely the phonological word as in the case of *r*-Strengthening (i).[27]

(56) *Consonant Gradation*

$$
\begin{bmatrix} +\text{cont} \\ -\text{son} \end{bmatrix} \rightarrow \text{`weak'} \quad / \quad [...[... [+\text{son}]]_\sigma [\underline{\quad} V\ C]_\sigma ...]_{D_j}
$$

The last rule we will consider here is Emphasis in Arabic. The velarization or pharyngealization that characterizes Emphasis is conditioned in most dialects by the presence in a syllable of an emphatic consonant. All segments in a syllable with such a consonant receive emphasis (see van der Hulst and Smith, 1982). Consider the examples in (57), given by van der Hulst and Smith, where emphasis is indicated in the traditional way with a dot under an emphatic segment.

(57) a. ṛab: [ṛab]$_\sigma$ → [ṛab]   'lord'
      b. ṭiin: [ṭiin]$_\sigma$ → [ṭiin]   'mad'
      c. ṛaagil: [ṛaa]$_\sigma$ [gil]$_\sigma$ → [ṛaagil]   'man'
      d. bukṛa: [buk]$_\sigma$ [ṛa]$_\sigma$ → [bukṛa]   'tomorrow'
      e. ṛaaʕid: [ṛaa]$_\sigma$ [ʕid]$_\sigma$ → [ṛaaʕid]   'military rank'

Van der Hulst and Smith analyze Emphasis as an autosegmental spreading rule which operates on the syllable domain, and as such it is somewhat different from the segmental rules seen thus far. In other words, Emphasis is a rule of autosegmental association that is bound to a specific phonological domain, which shows, as van der Hulst and Smith point out, that there are at least some rules that require both a theory of autosegmental associations and a theory of phonological domains.[28]

On the basis of the various rules examined above, there does not seem to be any doubt as to the validity of the syllable as a domain of phonological rules. In fact, examples were seen of the syllable as the domain of all three types of prosodic rules: domain limit, domain juncture and domain span rules. In several cases, it was shown that two formulations are possible for a given rule, a syllable limit formulation and a syllable span formulation. However, since both formulations are simple and straightforward, and since we do not at this point have any reason for favoring one type of rule over another, we have not made a choice between the two alternative formulations.

We will now examine the next level in the prosodic hierarchy, the foot, one which is more controversial than the syllable.

3.2. The foot

In the model of prosodic phonology we are proposing in this book, syllables are not grouped directly into words, but rather are first grouped into intermediate-sized constituents, feet. Most of the arguments in favor of the foot in generative phonology, and in particular in metrical theory, have been based on stress assignment. That is, the foot was seen as fundamental in determining the positions of stressed *vs.* stressless syllables within words and larger strings (see, among others, Liberman and Prince, 1977; Halle and Vergnaud, 1978; Kiparsky, 1979; Selkirk, 1980b; Hayes, 1981). More recently, however, it has been argued by several of the original proponents of the foot (see in particular Prince, 1983; Selkirk, 1984b) that the correct way to account for stress patterns in a language is not in terms of the foot, but rather in terms of the metrical grid. This position is taken even further, and it is claimed that the foot does not exist as a constituent in phonology at all since '[m]ost alleged foot-sensitive rules can be recast as rules sensitive to the stressed-stressless distinction' (Selkirk, 1984b:31). While metrical grid theory offers interesting advantages over an arboreal theory with feet as far as stress is concerned, it is not clear that it can obviate the role of the foot as a domain of other types of phonological rules. Even if it were the case that all foot-sensitive rules can, in fact, be formulated in relation to grid configurations, this does not necessarily mean that the foot should be eliminated from phonological theory. In fact, such an approach to the role of the foot is reminiscent of some of the early arguments against the syllable as a unit of phonology (see, among others, Kohler, 1966; Leben, 1973). Furthermore, on analogy to what was found in relation to the syllable, one might suspect that one of the risks in eliminating the foot as the domain of certain phonological rules is that the alternative accounts will nevertheless require that the definition of the foot be built into the formulation of the rule itself. The result would thus be a loss of generalization. In section 3.2.2, we will examine several phonological rules that apply in relation to the foot, and on the basis of these rules argue that the foot is indeed a valid constituent of phonology. First, however, in section 3.2.1, we will consider several questions related to the structure of the foot.

3.2.1.   The structure of the foot

In general terms, the structure of a foot can be characterized as consisting of a string of one relatively strong and any number of relatively weak syllables dominated by a single node (see, among others, Liberman and Prince, 1977; Kiparsky, 1979). As Hayes (1981) has shown on the basis of an analysis of a large number of languages, however, there are fairly strong restrictions on the grouping of syllables into feet in a given language. That is, a language may either have binary feet, consisting of two syllables each, or unbounded feet, consisting of any number of syllables. In exceptional cases, languages with binary feet may also have ternary feet, though this option is marked and the positions in which ternary feet may occur tend to be quite limited. One last type of foot that may also be found as a marked structure is the 'degenerate' one-syllable foot.

Hayes (1981) has shown, furthermore, that languages may differ not only in the number of syllables they allow in a foot, but also in whether or not syllable structure is relevant in determining foot structure. That is, in certain languages the weight of a syllable must be taken into account in constructing feet, yielding so-called quantity sensitive feet; in other languages, feet are constructed without regard to syllable weight, yielding so-called quantity insensitive feet. This parameter combines with the parameter of binary *vs.* unbounded feet to give the four possible foot types in (58).[29]

(58)   a.   binary, quantity sensitive
       b.   binary, quantity insensitive
       c.   unbounded, quantity sensitive
       d.   unbounded, quantity insensitive

We will assume here that Hayes's characterization of the various foot types is basically correct. We differ with Hayes (1981), however, as far as the nature of foot trees is concerned. While Hayes maintains that feet are binary branching, in accordance with the principles of an arboreal metrical theory (see also Liberman and Prince, 1977; Kiparsky, 1979; Selkirk, 1980b, among others), in the model we are proposing here, all prosodic constituents are n-ary branching (see Chapter 1). This difference in foot structure shows up only in ternary and unbounded feet; binary feet and degenerate one-syllable feet are obviously represented in the same way in both systems. One problem with binary branching feet is that they contain more structure than is necessary, as was discussed in Chapter 1; furthermore, this structure makes predictions that are not, in fact, borne out. Let us consider a binary branching foot tree such as the one in (59), which represents an unbounded foot with its strongest syllable on the left.

(59)

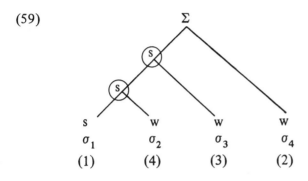

This type of tree creates internal nodes that define constituents consisting of subparts of the entire foot tree, as indicated by the circles in (59). That is, the upper circled node establishes a constituent consisting of syllables σ_1 - σ_3 and the lower circled node establishes a constituent of syllables σ_1 - σ_2. This additional constituent structure is superfluous, however, since there are no rules that make crucial reference to them, although we would expect such rules to exist given that one motivation of a particular constituent structure is the existence of rules that make reference to that structure. In a theory that makes use of binary branching trees, it is necessary to make a distinction between nodes with a category label and those without a category label (see Nespor, 1983). In a theory that makes use of n-ary branching trees, however, no such distinction is needed since all nodes have a category label.

Another problem with binary branching trees is related to the stress patterns they give rise to. According to the usual interpretation of the stress pattern represented by a tree like the one in (59), based on Liberman and Prince's (1977) algorithm, the strongest syllable is the leftmost one, σ_1, as indicated by the stress value (1) under the syllable; secondary stress falls on σ_4, as indicated by the value (2). Syllables σ_3 and σ_2 are increasingly weaker. As Leben (1982:182) points out, 'we do not need foot-internal structure in order to signal relationships between primary and secondary stress, since on current assumptions the foot is defined as containing one and only one stressed syllable.' Thus, the complex stress relations within the foot predicted by a binary branching structure are also superfluous. Both this problem and the one seen above are avoided by n-ary branching trees. The flatter structure of such trees does not contain any intervening nodes between the foot and the syllable, as illustrated in (60). In this type of structure, therefore, there are no constituents present other than the foot and the syllables it dominates. As far as stress is concerned, there is only one strong syllable per foot, in this case the leftmost one. All other syllables are weak, and there are no further predictions about relative prominence relations among them.

(60)

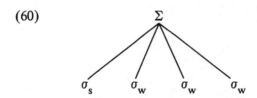

Leben (1982) shows, furthermore, that the same types of information used by Hayes to build binary branching trees can also be used to build n-ary branching trees that capture all of the same necessary structure but none of the unnecessary structure. Compare the binary and n-ary representations in (62) that correspond to the statement in (61), a statement typical of those used by Hayes in his construction of feet. Note that the *s* and *w* labels on the feet indicate their relative prominence within the word tree; primary stress is thus on the syllable marked [+A].

(61)   Assign maximal unbounded right-dominant feet right to left such that no recessive [i.e. weak] node contains [+A].
        (Leben's (10), p.182)

(62)   a.   binary branching tree

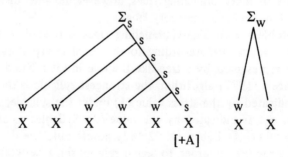

b.   n-ary branching tree

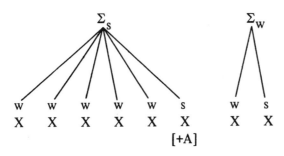

(slightly modified form of Leben's (11), p.182)

The stress pattern expressed by the above statement and tree structure is quite similar, in fact, to one mentioned by Hayes, that of West Greenlandic Eskimo. It should be noted, however, that Hayes (1981:58) uses a statement that refers to the dominant node rather than the recessive node. That is, Hayes states that syllables with branching rhymes are stressed, as is the final syllable. West Greenlandic Eskimo does not make use of word trees, however, according to Hayes, so the foot nodes might not be labeled as in (62).

The type of structure in (62a) is fairly similar, furthermore, to another type of structure found in Hayes's system, one which leads to another point of difference between Hayes's proposal and ours. In Khalkha Mongoljan, stress is placed on the first long vowel, or on the first vowel in words without any long vowels (see Hayes, pp.63-64). This type of stress pattern can be accounted for by a rule such as the one in (63).

(63)   On a projection of [+syllabic] segments within the rhyme, assign at the left edge of a word a maximally unbounded right-dominant foot such that the dominant node branches; if there are no long (i.e. branching) vowels, stress the first syllable.

If we indicate a branching node with the feature [+A], we would assign the foot structure in (64a) to the same sequences of Xs seen above in (62). According to Hayes, the Xs that are not assigned to the foot created by (63) are joined directly into the left-dominant word (ω) tree by Stray Syllable Adjunction, as shown in (64b).

(64) a. foot tree

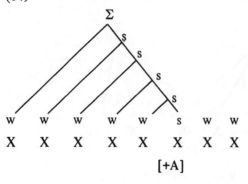

[+A]

b. word tree

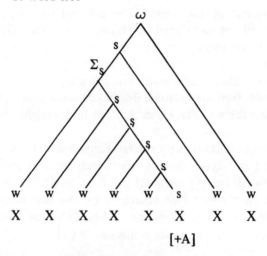

[+A]

Examples of this type of structure and of the structure built when a word contains no long (i.e. branching) vowels are given in (65a) and (65b), respectively (from Hayes, p.64).

(65) a.

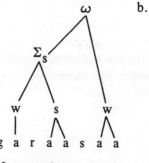

'from one's own hand'

b.

'leadership'

Both of these structures are unacceptable in the system we propose, aside from the binary branching trees, because they violate the Strict Layer Hypothesis.[30] In (65a), the final syllable is dominated, along with the foot, by the phonological word node. In (65b), the phonological word dominates a string composed only of syllables. According to the Strict Layer Hypothesis, however, all syllables must be grouped into feet before feet are grouped into phonological words. Within the framework proposed by Hayes (1981), not only is it possible for a given phonological constituent of the size of the phonological word or smaller to be present in some languages and absent in others, it is also possible for a given constituent to be present in some words and absent in other words of the same language.

The way we propose to analyze the examples in (65) is as in (66).

(66)   a.   b.

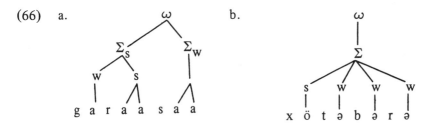

These structures can be built with the same statement used for building the structures in (64). The only difference is that before the word tree is constructed, any syllables that are not part of a foot must be joined into a (separate) foot. In a phonological system that includes the Strict Layer Hypothesis, this operation does not have to be stated explicitly since it follows directly from the hypothesis. Thus, while n-ary branching trees and the additional foot structure no longer allow us to make a statement to the effect that all of the dominant nodes of a foot must branch in a given language (see Vergnaud and Halle, 1978; Hayes, 1981), what we have instead is more uniform tree structure throughout the language, and across languages, at no additional cost to the grammar.

It should be noted, finally, that the two-foot analysis we are proposing for a string of Xs such as that in (64) predicts that there are two strong syllables in the word, while the one-foot-plus-two-additional-syllables analysis in (64b) predicts that there is only one strong syllable. If languages with words such as the one to which we would assign two feet, in fact, have one stress per word and no secondary stresses, we could account for this with a language-specific phonetic interpretation convention to the effect that the only strong node that is actually perceived as such is the one that corresponds to the primary word stress, in this case, the leftmost stress. Given more recent work on stress patterns (in particular Prince, 1983;

Selkirk, 1984b), however, it seems fairly unlikely that a language will in effect have only one strong syllable in a long polysyllabic word. Clearly, more detailed studies of languages like Khalkha Mongolian are needed.

To summarize briefly, in the model we are proposing, the foot is a constituent of the prosodic hierarchy. Like all other prosodic constituents, it is n-ary branching. A general principle of the system will guarantee that only one syllable per foot is strong, and language-specific rules will determine which one it is. In the case of long unbounded feet, it is possible that additional rhythmic alternations may be introduced by general rhythmic principles of the type discussed in the framework of grid theory. We will not be concerned further here with the rule for assigning foot structure. Instead, as in our discussion of the syllable, we will assume that the necessary rules have operated at the point at which our discussion of foot-domain phonological rules, in the next section, begins. Finally, while some languages may allow a process of 'refooting' to apply across words in a way analogous to resyllabification, we take the basic domain for the construction of feet to be the phonological word, as it is for syllables (see also Selkirk, 1978b; Chapter 4 below).

3.2.2.   *The foot as a phonological domain*

While the definition of the foot is intimately related to stress, as was seen in the preceding section, stress is not the only phonological phenomenon that is related to the foot. In fact, as we will show in this section, there are several different types of phenomena that must make reference to the foot. In particular, we will examine a number of phonological rules, a phonotactic constraint, and a definition of poetic rhyme, all of which depend on the foot for their formulation. It will be shown, furthermore, that despite the close relation between the foot and stress, the foot cannot be replaced as a phonological domain by stress patterns. That is, there are certain rules that cannot be formulated in terms of stress and others whose formulation in terms of stress requires more complicated rules and results in the formalization of a relationship between stress and other phenomena that otherwise seems improbable.

Let us first consider Aspiration in English. While this rule applies to all three voiceless stops, *p*, *t*, and *k*, we will limit our attention here to *t*, since the Aspiration of *t* interacts with two other rules that affect *t* in American English: Glottalization, which was seen above, and Flapping, which will be discussed in Chapter 8. Examples of the contexts in which Aspiration applies are given in (67) and examples of contexts in which it does not apply are given in (68). The foot structure is also given.[31]

(67)   a.   time   → [t^h]ime   [time]$_\Sigma$

        b.   tuna   → [t^h]una   [tuna]$_\Sigma$

c.	toucan	→ [tʰ]oucan	[tou]$_\Sigma$ [can]$_\Sigma$
d.	typhoon	→ [tʰ]yphoon	[ty]$_\Sigma$ [phoon]$_\Sigma$
e.	terrain	→ [tʰ]errain	[te]$_\Sigma$ [rrain]$_\Sigma$
f.	detain	→ de[tʰ]ain	[de]$_\Sigma$ [tain]$_\Sigma$
g.	detention	→ de[tʰ]ention	[de]$_\Sigma$ [tention]$_\Sigma$
h.	entire	→ en[tʰ]ire	[en]$_\Sigma$ [tire]$_\Sigma$
i.	curtail	→ cur[tʰ]ail	[cur]$_\Sigma$ [tail]$_\Sigma$
j.	satire	→ sa[tʰ]ire	[sa]$_\Sigma$ [tire]$_\Sigma$
k.	reptile	→ rep[tʰ]ile	[rep]$_\Sigma$ [tile]$_\Sigma$
l.	infantile	→ infan[tʰ]ile	[inf an]$_\Sigma$ [tile]$_\Sigma$
m.	longitude	→ longi[tʰ]ude	[longi]$_\Sigma$ [tude]$_\Sigma$
n.	tree toad	→ [tʰ]ree [tʰ]oad³²	[tree]$_\Sigma$ [toad]$_\Sigma$
o.	sweet tooth	→ sweet [tʰ]ooth	[sweet]$_\Sigma$ [tooth]$_\Sigma$

(68)	a.	sting	→ *s[tʰ]ing	[sting]$_\Sigma$
	b.	abstain	→ *abs[tʰ]ain	[ab]$_\Sigma$ [stain]$_\Sigma$
	c.	austere	→ *aus[tʰ]ere	[au]$_\Sigma$ [stere]$_\Sigma$
	d.	after	→ *af[tʰ]er	[after]$_\Sigma$
	e.	alter	→ *al[tʰ]er	[alter]$_\Sigma$
	f.	satyr	→ *sa[tʰ]yr	[satyr]$_\Sigma$
	g.	shatter	→ *sha[tʰ]er	[shatter]$_\Sigma$
	h.	hospital	→ *hospi[tʰ]al	[hospital]$_\Sigma$
	i.	night owl	→ *nigh[tʰ] owl	[night]$_\Sigma$ [owl]$_\Sigma$
	j.	flat iron	→ *fla[tʰ] iron	[flat]$_\Sigma$ [iron]$_\Sigma$

What (67) and (68) show is that a *t* is aspirated if and only if it is the first segment of a foot. When it is preceded by another segment, *s*, or by one or more syllables, it is not aspirated ((68a-c) and (68d-h), respectively). Since resyllabification does not apply across phonological words in English, as was seen above, a *t* at the end of the first member of a compound cannot be transferred to the onset of the second member. It remains foot final and is therefore not aspirated (as in (68i,j)). We can thus formulate the following foot limit rule which expresses the fact that Aspiration only applies at the left end of a foot (see also Vogel, 1981):

(69) *Aspiration*

$$t \rightarrow [+asp] \ / \ [\underline{\quad\quad} ...]_\Sigma{}^{33}$$

It should be noted that the Strict Layer Hypothesis requires that all syllables be grouped into feet, before the feet may be grouped into phonological words. This means that even a stressless syllable may form a foot if it is the only syllable preceding another foot in a word. Thus the first

syllable of *terrain*, (67e), forms a foot by itself, a sister of the foot constituted by the second syllable. The same is true of the first, stressless
syllables of *detain, detention, entire* and *curtail* in (67f-i).[34] This analysis
of foot structure yields the correct results since the initial *t* of *terrain* is
aspirated, despite the fact that the first syllable is stressless. If *te* were not
a foot, the Aspiration rule in (69) could not apply to it. As far as (67f-i)
are concerned, we see further that a stressless syllable is not joined rightward into a single foot with what follows, since doing so would mean
that the *t*s at the beginning of the second syllable of each of these examples would not be foot initial and (69) could not apply to them.

Our analysis of Aspiration shows that by referring to the foot, we
can formulate the rule that accounts for this phenomenon in a simple
way. The same cannot be done by making reference only to stress. While
it is clear that stress does have something to do with Aspiration, it is not
the only factor involved. The connection between stress and Aspiration
has to do with the fact that a foot usually begins with a stressed syllable;
thus, a *t* at the beginning of a stressed syllable is aspirated. We have seen,
however, that there are also cases in which a *t* is aspirated in another
position, at the beginning of a word, even when it is in an unstressed syllable, the case of *terrain*. Thus, a stress account of Aspiration would require two separate statements of the environment – one that does, in fact,
make reference to stress, and one that makes reference to some other
property of the remaining cases, i.e. to the fact that they are word initial.
The combination of these two statements is in effect the definition of the
foot in English, so we do not really gain anything with such a formulation.

It should be noted that in the analysis of English word stress proposed by Selkirk (1984b), the first syllable of words such as *terrain*
actually receives stress at one point in the process of grid construction.
This is accomplished by the Initial Beat Rule (IBR). Such syllables are
also destressed, however, by a subsequent rule. In order to claim that
Aspiration applies only in relation to stress, it would be necessary to allow
it to apply after IBR but before Destressing. Such a solution is excluded,
however, by a fundamental principle of Selkirk's proposal, namely that
phonological rules (such as Aspiration) apply to the output of the syntax-
phonology mapping, that is, after the grid structure has been established,
not in the middle of the grid construction procedure. Thus, a stress-only
account of Aspiration is not a viable alternative. We conclude, therefore,
that the best account of Aspiration is the foot-domain rule in (69), since
it is simpler than the other possibility that requires two distinct statements
of the environment of the rule. Reference to the foot furthermore allows
us to capture a generalization with respect to the environment of Aspiration that is lost if the environment is characterized in two different ways.
Finally, it was seen that the two statements needed for the stress account
are actually only a restatement of the foot domain in English.

Let us now consider four more rules of English, *l*-Devoicing, Diphthong Shortening, Obligatory *n*-Velarization, and Mutual *k-r* Assimilation. As Kiparsky (1979) shows, the domain of all of these rules is the foot. We will first examine *l*-Devoicing (LD). This rule applies to an *l* that is preceded by a voiceless consonant, only if the two segments are in the same foot. It thus applies to (70a) and (70b), but not to (70c) (see Kiparsky, 1979:440).

(70) a. Islip   → Is[l̥]ip   [Islip]$_\Sigma$
      b. eye-slip → eye s[l̥]ip   [eye]$_\Sigma$ [slip]$_\Sigma$
      c. ice-lip   → *ice [l̥]ip   [ice]$_\Sigma$ [lip]$_\Sigma$

These same examples serve to illustrate the domain of Diphthong Shortening (DS), which accounts for the short variant of [aw] and [aj] before a voiceless consonant. We thus find a short diphthong in (70a) and (70c), where the relevant phonetic sequence [ajs] is found within a single foot. In (70b), however, the rule does not apply, since the diphthong [aj] and the following voiceless consonant [s] are in separate feet. It is clear that the domain of both LD and DS must be larger than the syllable since, as Kiparsky (p.440) points out, there is no way in which *Islip* can be syllabified ('short of the absurd *Isl-ip*') such that both rules can be accounted for in relation to syllable structure. That the two rules do not apply in larger domains than the foot has already been seen. We can thus formulate *l*-Devoicing and Diphthong Shortening as in (71) and (72), respectively.

(71) *l-Devoicing*
      l   →   [−vce] / [... [−vce] _____ ...]$_\Sigma$

(72) *Diphthong Shortening*

$$\left\{ \begin{array}{c} aw \\ aj \end{array} \right\} \rightarrow [-\text{long}] \; / \; [\ldots \underline{\quad} [-\text{vce}] \ldots]_\Sigma {}^{35}$$

As these formulations show, LD and DS are both foot span rules, that is, they apply any time their segmental context appears within the foot domain.[36]

Let us now consider the possibility of accounting for the same phenomena in terms of stress rather than the foot. On the basis of the examples in (70), the only correlation that appears to exist is between the absence of application of the rules and the fact that the relevant segments are in separate syllables both of which bear a fairly high degree of stress, corresponding at least to the third grid level in the sense of Prince (1983) and Selkirk (1984b). We could therefore state that LD and DS apply to the relevant

segments except when they are part of a rhythmic pattern consisting
of two stresses of level three or more. Thus, the rules do apply if *a*) the
segments are part of the same syllable (cf. LD in *eye-slip*) or *b*) the segments are part of a different rhythmic pattern (cf. LD in *Islip*, with a
stressless second syllable). It should be noted, however, that the characterization of 'different rhythmic pattern' in (*b*) is not adequate. It is
necessary to specify further that the pattern must be one of sharply
decreasing stress, since the opposite situation, sharply increasing stress,
also blocks LD, as in *mislead*, which does not have a devoiced *l*. We must
thus complicate our stress-only specification of the context in which the
rules in question do not apply, or better yet, specify the contexts in
which the rules do apply. We can say that the rules apply when there is no
stress change (for tautosyllabic segments) or when there is a sharply
decreasing pattern. Such a statement, however, is not much more than a description of the possible contexts within a single foot in which the rules
may apply. Furthermore, even if it is possible to specify the contexts for
LD and DS in terms of stress, it is not clear that there really exists any
relationship that we would want to capture between the voicing of *l* and
stress or between the vowel length phenomenon in question and stress
(though there are other vowel length phenomena that are related to stress).

The problems we have just seen also arise with the other two rules,
Obligatory *n*-Velarization (OV) and Mutual *k-r* Assimilation (MA). As
Kiparsky (1979:439-40) points out, an *n* is obligatorily velarized before
a velar stop in words like *ink* (*i*[ŋ]*k*) and *increment* (*i*[ŋ]*crement*), but is
only optionally velarized in words like the verb *incréase* and the noun
incrèase. Furthermore, *k* and *r* undergo mutual assimilation to what can
be indicated as [KR] in words like *crew* ([*KR*]*ew*), *increase* (V, N) (*in-
*[*KR*]*ease*), and *increment* (*in*[*KR*]*ement*), but not in words like *back-rub*
and *cock-roach*. Since words like *increment* undergo both OV and MA,
it is not possible to account for the rules in terms of the syllable. That is,
it is not possible for *n* to be obligatorily velarized before a tautosyllabic
velar and for MA to apply to tautosyllabic *k* and *r*, because such an analysis would require that the entire sequence *nkr* be tautosyllabic, and this
would violate the principles governing English syllable structure. If, however, we make reference to the foot, both phenomena can be handled very
simply as foot span rules. To see that the foot is indeed the domain of OV
and MA, consider the foot structure of the words in question:

(73) a. ink: [ink]$_\Sigma$ → i[ŋ]k   *OV*
      b. crew: [crew]$_\Sigma$ → [KR]ew   *MA*
      c. incréase (V): [in]$_\Sigma$ [crease]$_\Sigma$ → in[KR]ease   *MA*[37]
      d. incrèase (N): [in]$_\Sigma$ [crease]$_\Sigma$ → in[KR]ease   *MA*
      e. increment: [increment]$_\Sigma$ → i[ŋKR]ement   *OV, MA*

If we try to account for the application of OV and MA in terms of stress rather than the foot, we encounter the same difficulties seen above in relation to *l*-Devoicing and Diphthong Shortening. That is, we must state that the rules apply either *a*) when there is no change in the stress pattern to cover the cases of application within a syllable (e.g. *ink, crew*) or *b*) when there is a sharply decreasing stress pattern (as in *increment*). The rules do not apply when the segments in question are in a sequence of stressed syllables (cf. the absence of OV in *increase*) or when there is a sharply increasing stress pattern, such as the transition from the stressless second syllable to the stressed third syllable in compound words like *garden club* and *cotton candy*, where Obligatory *n*-Velarization does not apply. Once again, our conclusion is that the foot analysis is to be preferred because it is simpler and because it expresses a generalization about the contexts in which OV and MA apply. Moreover, it is not clear that there is any reason to expect a relationship between stress and the occurrence of either Obligatory *n*-Velarization or Mutual *k-r* Assimilation, although by formulating the rules in terms of stress we are in effect encoding precisely such relationships.

The foot also plays an important role in Chinese (see Yip, 1980). In fact, there seems to be an interaction among tone, stress, the foot, and several segmental phonological rules. According to Yip, the foot is built on the basis of the tonal structure of syllables. There is a constraint in Mandarin, as well as in several other dialects examined by Yip, that allows only one fully toned syllable per foot. In a foot with more than one syllable, only the first bears tone; the others are toneless (e.g. *xǐhuan* 'like', *hǎode* 'good ones'). Under certain circumstances, a foot may consist of two originally toned syllables, but in these cases a tone-deletion rule applies to make the second syllable toneless in conformity with the general constraint on foot structure, as seen in (74), a slightly modified form of Yips's example (p.97).

$$(74) \quad \text{lǎohǔ} \xrightarrow[\text{sandhi}]{\text{tone}} \text{láohǔ} \xrightarrow[\text{formation}]{\text{foot}} [\text{láohǔ}]_{\Sigma} \xrightarrow[\text{deletion}]{\text{tone}} [\text{láohu}]_{\Sigma}$$

'tiger'

Stress is assigned to the foot (and to the word) and thus also interacts with tone since it is on the basis of tone that feet are constructed in the first place. Typically, stress is on the first syllable of a foot, that is, on the fully toned syllable (e.g. *páshanglaile* 'jumped up', where only the first

$$\begin{array}{cccc} 1 & 0 & 0 & 0 \end{array}$$

syllable bears tone and stress (Yip, p.92). It is therefore likely that if it were only for stress, we might not need the foot constituent. An abstract rhythmic pattern represented by a metrical grid might be sufficient to handle stress assignment as well as certain tone sandhi rules that apply to 'terminal *s* nodes' in Yip's analysis (p.22). However, there are also segmental rules, in particular Gemination and Stop Voicing in the Chinese language Amoy, that according to Yip have the foot as the domain. Fairly similar rules are also found in Mandarin. The question is whether these rules, too, can be accounted for in terms of stress rather than the foot.

In Amoy, the stress patterns are very similar to those in Mandarin, with the exception of an additional marked pattern before one particular suffix.[38] When the suffix a^{53}, which often has a diminutive meaning, is added to another morpheme, the two form a single foot, with the marked *w-s* prominence pattern; the unmarked pattern is with the strong syllable on the left, as in Mandarin. Other tone-bearing morphemes form separate feet on their own. Compare the structure that results from the addition of a^{53} with the structure that results from the usual word formation process, for example with the addition of the morpheme a^{21}, illustrated in (75a) and (75b), respectively (from Yip, p.100).

(75)   a. $tshin^{21} + a^{53}$: $[[tshin^{21}]_{\sigma_w} [a^{53}]_{\sigma_s}]_\Sigma$ 'small scale'

  b. $tshin^{21} + a^{21}$: $[[tshin^{21}]_\sigma]_\Sigma [[a^{21}]_\sigma]_\Sigma$ 'scale box'

The segmental rule of Gemination applies to the final consonant of a syllable when it is followed by a vowel-initial syllable, but only if the two are within the same foot. This can be seen in relation to the items in (75). That is, Gemination applies in the first case but not in the second, as illustrated in (76a) and (76b), respectively.

(76)   a. $tshin^{21} a^{53}$ → $tshin^{55} na^{53}$ 'small box'
  b. $tshin^{21} a^{21}$ → $tshin^{53} a^{21}$ (*$tshin^{53} na^{21}$)
                                                 'scale box'

The rule of Stop Voicing also applies to a syllable-final consonant when it is followed within the same foot by a vowel-initial syllable. Thus, both Gemination and Stop Voicing apply in (77a), where $khap^{21}$ and a^{53} form a single foot, but they do not apply in (77b), where $khap^{21}$ and a^{21} are in separate feet.

(77)   a. $hang^{55} khap^{21} a^{53}$ → $hang^{33} khab^5 ba^{53}$ 'clam'
  b. $hang^{55} khap^{21} a^{21} a^{53}$ → $hang^{33} khap^5 a^{33} a^{53}$
      (*$hang^{33} khab^5 ba^{33} a^{53}$)   'clam box'

Gemination and Stop Voicing also apply within the more usual type of foot, in which the strong syllable is on the left. This is illustrated in (78a) and (78b) with the suffix *e* 'of' and the classifier e^{13}, respectively.[39] Note that *l* represents a type of flap.

(78)   a. tek^{21} e   → teg^{21} ge
        b. be^{53} $tsit^{54}$ e^{13} → be^{53} tsil-le

On the basis of the above observations, we can formulate the rules of Stop Voicing and Gemination as syllable juncture rules operating on the foot domain, as seen in (79) and (80), respectively, where gemination is represented by the feature [+long].

(79)   *Stop Voicing*

        C   →   [+vce]   / $[...[... \underline{\quad\quad}]_\sigma [V...]_\sigma ...]_\Sigma$

(80)   *Gemination*

        C   →   [+long] / $[...[... \underline{\quad\quad}]_\sigma [V...]_\sigma ...]_\Sigma$

As Yip (p.103) points out, while the foot allows a straightforward account of the rules in question, the same is not true if we appeal instead to surface stress patterns, since the rules apply in words with quite different patterns, 1-0 and 3-1, but not in words with the pattern 2-1. Even if stress were represented in terms of a grid configuration rather than integer values, the problem of accounting for the domains of Gemination and Stop Voicing remains. In fact, we encounter the same difficulties encountered earlier in English. While we might be able to formulate the stress patterns that allow the rules to apply in terms of grid levels corresponding to the syllables involved, the result is nevertheless a set of unrelated possibilities, in this case, a syllable with a high stress level followed by a stressless syllable (1-0) and a syllable with a low stress level followed by one with a high level (3-1). Gemination and Stop Voicing are blocked instead by the configuration of a fairly high stress level followed by a still higher one (2-1). Rather than capturing any generalizations about the application of the rules in question, such a formulation would make their domain seem quite *ad hoc*. The foot, on the other hand, permits a unified account of the application (*vs.* nonapplication) of the rules, as well as of two other phenomena we will not discuss here: the fact that melody deletion occurs with stress patterns 3-1 and 1-0 but not 2-1, and the fact that the suffix a^{53} exhibits a special rhythmic pattern in verse (see Yip, p.103).

Not only does the foot serve as the domain of application of certain segmental phonological rules as seen thus far, it has been proposed that the foot is also the domain of a number of autosegmental association rules. The rule of Nasalization in Applecross Gaelic, for example, is analyzed by

van der Hulst and Smith (1982) as a process of nasal spreading that applies
throughout the domain defined by the foot (unless blocked by certain
segments). The foot in Applecross Gaelic consists of a stressed syllable
followed by all the remaining syllables in a (phonological) word. The
stressed syllable is usually the first syllable of a stem. Prefixes and proclitic elements never receive stress and according to van der Hulst and
Smith, these weak syllables, when they are present, are joined directly
into the word tree with the following foot. The same occurs with the occasional weak syllable to the left of the stressed syllable in monomorphemic words. Thus, /kʰatʰríanə/ 'Catherine' would have the structure
in (81a). As was mentioned above, however, such a structure violates the
Strict Layer Hypothesis, according to which a phonological word may
only dominate feet, not syllables. We therefore propose that the first
syllable also constitutes a (degenerate) foot on its own, as in (81b), a point
we will return to below.

(81)   a.   b.

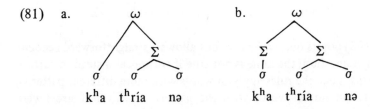

According to the characterization of the foot structure in (81b), each of
the items in (82) is analyzed as consisting of one foot, while each of the
items in (83) is analyzed as consisting of two feet (from van der Hulst
and Smith, p.318).

(82)   a. /kʰə́nʸil/:   [kʰə́nʸil]_Σ   'meeting'
        b. /ãjəɫ/:   [ãjəɫ]_Σ   'angel'
        c. /mã.r + içən/:   [mã.riçən]_Σ   'mothers'

(83)   a. /ɣa + ɛ́çkʸənʸ/:   [ɣa]_Σ [ɛ́çkʸənʸ]_Σ 'seeing him'
        b. /kʰɔ + vĩa.t/:   [kʰɔ]_Σ [vĩa.t]_Σ   'how much'
        c. /kʰatʰríanə/:   [kʰa]_Σ [tʰríanə]_Σ 'Catherine'

The application of the Nasalization rule extends in a word from a stressed
nasal vowel forward until the end of the word is reached and backward
to and including the consonantal onset of the stressed syllable (see Ternes,
1973, cited in van der Hulst and Smith). The only elements that can block
Nasalization within this domain, which has been defined by van der Hulst
and Smith as the foot in Applecross Gaelic, are: *a*) a stop within the
domain, or *b*) one of the vowels /e/, /o/, or /ə/. The examples below il-

lustrate the application of Nasalization and the environments in which it is blocked. Specifically, (84a) shows an entire foot nasalized, while (84b) and (84c) show nasalization blocked by the presence of a stop to the left and to the right, respectively. (84d) shows that the rule is also blocked by the presence of one of the nonnasalizing vowels (from van der Hulst and Smith, p.319).

(84) a. /ʃɛ́nɛ.var/   → [ʃɛ̃nɛ̃.ṽar̃]$_\Sigma$ 'grandmother'
      b. /strãi.ɣ/   → [strã́i.ɣ̃]$_\Sigma$ 'string'
      c. /kʰɔ̃ispaxk/ → [kʰɔ̃ispaxk]$_\Sigma$ 'wasp'
      d. /mã.riçən/   → [mã.r̃ĩçən]$_\Sigma$ 'mothers'

The fact that Nasalization does not extend beyond the foot boundary is seen in (85).

(85) /kʰɔ + vĩa.t/   → [kʰɔ]$_\Sigma$ [ṽĩã.t]$_\Sigma$ 'how much'

It should be noted that the same predictions regarding the lack of application of Nasalization beyond the foot are made by both of the structures seen above in (81). Nasalization does not spread into the first syllable of (81a), because it is not dominated by the foot that dominates the syllables to its right, or by any foot, for that matter. Nasalization does not spread into the first syllable in (81b), because it is in a separate foot from the one with the nasalized vowel that gives rise to the nasal spreading. Even though the domain of Nasalization is the foot, it should be noted that no incorrect predictions arise from assigning stressless syllables to the left of the main stress to a separate foot. We will never find Nasalization in such a foot, since the phenomenon originates only with a stressed nasalized vowel. The unstressed syllables to the left of the main stress cannot, therefore, give rise to Nasalization.

While van der Hulst and Smith account for Nasalization as an auto-segmental spreading rule that applies throughout the foot domain, as we have seen, it might nevertheless be possible to account for the domain of this rule in terms of stress.[40] That is, we could say that the rule applies within the domain defined by a syllable stress at a particular level of the grid, for example level 3, plus all the syllables to its right within a word. The question remains, however, as to whether such a formulation is desirable, even though it is much simpler than the stress formulations of the other rules we have examined thus far. It should be noted that the stress formulation of the domain of Nasalization corresponds exactly to the definition of the (non-degenerate) foot in Applecross Gaelic. We are thus confronted once again with a problem similar to the one seen in relation to the syllable earlier in the history of generative phonology. It is possible to formulate the domain of a phonological rule without making reference to a particular phonological constituent, in this case the foot not the syllable, but in order to do so we must incorporate the definition of the constituent into the rule itself. In the case of the syllable, the constituent has clearly won over the formulation that includes the definition of the syllable. We think that in the case of the foot, too, the constituent should be preferred over the formulation that contains the definition of the foot. While in the case of Applecross Gaelic Nasalization both the foot solution and the stress solution are quite simple and straightforward, the foot solution allows us to make generalizations that the stress solution does not. That is, since the nature of the foot may vary from language to language, if we refer only to the (stress) definition of the foot in our rules, we will be unable to relate rules across languages that define the foot differently. We would thus lose the ability to make generalizations about those rules that apply in domains that are larger than the syllable but smaller than the word. Instead, it would seem that there is no connection, for example, between a rule that applies in a domain beginning with a stressed syllable and continuing to the end of a word, such as Applecross Gaelic Nasalization, and another rule that applies between, but not across, stresses of a given height in the metrical grid, or a rule that has an even more complicated formulation in terms of stress such as the rules of English and Chinese seen above. By making reference to the foot, on the other hand, the differences among languages are only relevant at the stage of foot construction. That is, different languages may have different rules for building feet, but once the feet are created we can make reference to this level of analysis in general, without regard for the rules that create it.

The same line of reasoning makes a foot treatment preferable even when dealing with a single language. That is, if there is more than one rule in a language that applies within the same domain, say between stresses of a given height on the metrical grid, it would be advantageous to be able to make reference to this particular configuration only once, rather than specifying it each time it is needed in the formulation of a rule. This can be done by using the stress information, or whatever other type of information is necessary, to define a foot constituent. Once the foot is defined, it can be referred to directly in any rule that applies in relation to the domain it delimits.

This is, in fact, essentially the type of argument that led Hayes (1982) to propose a foot analysis of a number of rules in Yidiɲ, although in this case the alternative being considered was a segmental one. As Hayes points out in relation to the rules in question, since 'rules which delete or modify segments based on an odd-even syllable count are not especially common – it would be a colossal coincidence to find eight of them in a single language if all applied on an independent basis, particularly when the language in question has an alternating stress pattern' (p.101). Thus, rather than stating for each rule the segmental, or rhythmic, configuration that essentially characterizes an alternating stress pattern, it is simpler and more insightful to formulate only once the rules for foot construction and there- after allow the phonological rules to refer directly to this constituent. It should be noted, furthermore, that while some of the rules of Yidiɲ are of the type that often do depend on stress (e.g. length adjustments), there are other segmental rules that are not so clearly related to stress (e.g. Rhotic Dropping). While all of the rules can be expressed in relation to the foot, it is not clear that they all can, or should, be expressed as stress-dependent rules. To separate the rules into two groups, those that are accounted for in terms of stress and those that are not, would cause us to miss the generalization that they all share the property of being foot-dependent in one way or another.

Before we conclude our discussion of the foot, there are two more phenomena that are worth mentioning. The first one has to do with pho- notactic restrictions in Žuǀʼhõasi, a Namibian language.[41] In this lan- guage, one of four tones is possible on a word consisting of a single CV syllable: high (´), high mid ('), low mid (` ), and low (¯) (see Smith, in preparation, who bases his analysis on Snyman, 1975). The same four tones are possible on words consisting of CVV or CVN, as are the addi- tional two combinations of a low mid tone followed by a high mid tone ( ` ') and a low tone followed by a low mid tone (¯ `). It turns out, furthermore, that the same six tone patterns, and only these, are also found in words consisting of a sequence of two syllables: CVCV or CVVCV. That is, although any single syllable may bear one of four basic tones, in bisyllabic words we actually find fewer than half of the possible combina- tions that would result from freely combining the different syllable types (i.e. 6 out of 16). Smith takes this as evidence that such bisyllabic sequen- ces constitute a unit, specifically a foot, in Žuǀʼhõasi. What is particularly interesting is that the foot, as just defined, is not only the domain of constraints on possible tone sequences, but is also the domain of another phonotactic restriction. That is, the intervocalic consonant within the foot may only be one of the following four (with very few exceptions): *b, m, r, n.* This is indeed a very strong restriction since, according to Snyman's (1975:125) inventory, there are over 50 consonant phonemes in the language. Examples of words containing the four consonants are given below.

(86) a. pàbú   'pumpkin'
      b. tȧmȧ   'kindly'
      c. ǀõarà   'complete'
      d. nǂòanà   'tell'

That the restriction on intervocalic consonants only applies to those consonants that are in intervocalic position within a foot can be seen in (87), where reduplication creates longer words, with the result that consonants other than the four mentioned above can be found between vowels. In all of these cases, however, the consonant in question is at a juncture of two feet; it is not foot internal. The relevant consonants are underlined in the examples.

(87) a. [gùmá]$_\Sigma$ [gūmà]$_\Sigma$ 'whisper'
      b. [ǀxàná]$_\Sigma$ [ǀxanà]$_\Sigma$ 'drill'
      c. [kx'ū]$_\Sigma$ [kx'ùnì]$_\Sigma$ 'move'
      d. [ǂ'àa]$_\Sigma$ [ǂ'àmà]$_\Sigma$ 'gather'

Without referring to the foot, it is not possible to account for the observations about the distribution of tonal and consonantal patterns in Žulʼhõasi. That is, if we consider any two adjacent syllables, it seems as if any consonant may appear intervocalically, as seen in (87), and that any sequence of tones is possible (e.g. the sequence '– in (87a,b)). Since, however, there are quite strong restrictions on the consonants and tones that may appear in specific environments, if we are not able to refer to the constituent defined as the foot, we miss two important generalizations about the language.

The last phenomenon we will consider is poetic rhyme in Dutch. Dutch verse makes use of the following three types of rhyme (from van der Hulst, 1984:58):

(88) a. *Masculine rhyme*
          hoog –   droog   'high   – dry'
          kaal –   schraal   'bald   – scanty'
      b. *Feminine rhyme*
          hoge –   droge   'high   – dry'
          kale –   schrale   'bald   – scanty'
      c. *Extended rhyme*
          hogere – drogere   'higher – drier'
          handelen – wandelen   'to trade – to walk'

Without reference to the foot, each of these types of rhyme patterns must be described separately in terms of the number of syllables involved and either the rhyme or onset portion of the first syllable. We are thus unable to express the fact that all three types of rhyme can actually be defined in the same way. That is, as van der Hulst (1984:58) points out, they all consist of the final foot of a word minus the onset of the first syllable. If any of the elements within the unit thus defined are different, the rhymes are not well formed, as illustrated by the unacceptable feminine and extended rhymes given in (89a) and (89b), respectively.

(89) a. *harten – parken 'hearts – parks'
      b. *kinderen – tintelen 'children– to twinkle'

We could also account for the poetic rhyme unit in terms of stress, without referring to the foot. That is, we could define the unit as consisting of everything between the last syllable corresponding to a certain height in the metrical grid and the end of the word, minus the onset of the first syllable. This characterization of the rhyme unit, however, is little more than the definition of the (word-final) foot in Dutch. As we mentioned in relation to Applecross Gaelic Nasalization, however, there are definite drawbacks to an account of a phenomenon that requires the definition of a particular constituent to be present in the formulation of the phenomenon. We therefore take the definition of the poetic rhyme unit in Dutch as further evidence of the foot as a domain in phonology.

3.3. Conclusions

In this chapter, we have examined the two smallest constituents of the prosodic hierarchy, the syllable and the foot. Given the amount of research that has been dedicated to these two units in recent years, a chapter clearly does not provide enough space to even touch on all of the major issues surrounding them. We have therefore focused our attention on the domain of the syllable and certain aspects of the structure of the foot, and even more importantly, on the role of both units as domains of phonological rules, given that the model of prosodic phonology we are advocating is a theory of domains.

As far as the domain of the syllable is concerned, we have shown that syllabification rules must be divided into two categories: *a*) a set of rules that apply within the domain of the phonological word, and *b*) a set of resyllabification rules that apply across phonological words. While all languages have rules of the first type, which account for the fact that the definition of a well-formed syllable in a given language must be satisfied within the larger domain of the phonological word, not all languages have the second type of rules. Instead, we have proposed that the possibility of resyllabifying across phonological words depends on a parameter of phonology that must be set by individual languages. This parameter, in fact, allows us to distinguish between the Romance languages, which typically allow resyllabification across (phonological) words, and the Germanic languages, which do not.

The syllable is also the domain of phonological rules. In fact, we have argued that it is the smallest domain of segmental phonological rules. Although it has been proposed that the rhyme subcomponent of the syllable is also the domain of certain phonological rules, we have demonstrated that any rule that can be expressed as a rhyme-domain rule can also be expressed as a syllable-domain rule. The rhyme as a domain of phonological rules is thus superfluous. Of the rules that apply in relation to the syllable examined in this chapter, most were seen to be domain limit rules. Examples were also given, however, of domain juncture rules and of a domain span rule.

Although the domain of the foot was not discussed in detail as was the domain of the syllable, we have proposed that there are certain parallels between the two smallest phonological constituents in this regard. That is, we take the domain of basic foot formation to be the phonological word for all languages, while only certain languages may have the possibility of refooting across phonological words. We examined in more detail the structure of the foot, drawing primarily on the insights found in the work of Hayes (1981). We accept Hayes's basic distinctions between binary and unbounded feet and between quantity sensitive and quantity insensitive feet. Beyond this, however, our analysis of foot structure diverges from that of Hayes. That is, we have argued that feet group syllables into n-ary branching trees rather than the binary branching trees found in the metrical tree framework. Not only is the n-ary analysis in keeping with the rest of our model, in which all the other prosodic levels are organized into n-ary branching trees, it also offers several more specific advantages. The structure it creates is simpler than a binary branching structure, in the sense that it does not contain superfluous foot-internal constituents that do not have any further role in phonological theory. In addition, n-ary branching trees do not predict any particular prominence relations among the weak syllables of the foot. Such prominence relations are, however, predicted by binary branching trees, although they are not in fact motivated. Finally, our proposal differs from that of Hayes in that in ours the Strict Layer Hypothesis requires that all syllables be grouped into feet before the feet are grouped into phonological words. Hayes (1981) does not have a Strict Layer Hypothesis, and thus allows syllables to be sisters of feet in phonological words; in some cases, too, a phonological word directly dominates a string of syllables without any intervening foot nodes.

Since the definition of the foot is very closely tied to the notion of stress, the question arises as to whether the foot is actually needed as a phonological constituent. That is, if all the rules that apply in relation to the foot can be handled equally well by making reference directly to abstract rhythmic patterns, it might be possible to avoid the introduction of the foot as a unit of phonological analysis. We have shown, however, that the domain defined by the foot allows us to account for the application of a number of phonological rules in a simpler and more straightforward way than would be possible if direct reference were made only to stress patterns. We have argued, furthermore, that even if it is possible to account for some segmental rules fairly simply in terms of stress, it is not clear that this is desirable, for several reasons. First of all, the stress account typically requires that the definition of the foot be incorporated in the formulation of the rules. As was seen in the past in relation to the syllable, this is a typical indication that we are dealing with a constituent and not a chance sequence of segments, or in this case, stressed and unstressed syllables. In addition, since the definition of the foot may vary somewhat from language to language, if phonological rules are formulated in terms of the definition of the foot, we lose the ability to generalize about foot-level rules across languages. Finally, in the case that a language has more than one rule operating in relation to the domain we are calling the foot, it is more economical to define the foot once and then let the various rules make direct reference to this constituent, rather than defining it each time it functions as the domain of a phonological rule. In such cases, a foot approach also allows us to express a generalization about the domain of application of a set of rules that is otherwise missed if each rule formulates the domain separately.

In addition to phonological rules operating in the foot domain, two other foot-dependent phenomena were examined: phonotactic constraints and poetic rhyme. In these cases, too, it was shown that direct reference to the foot allows us to capture generalizations that would otherwise be missed. Our conclusion is that the foot is indeed a necessary constituent of phonological analysis, one which plays a role distinct from the role played by the abstract rhythmic patterns of the language despite the close relation between the two.

NOTES

1. See Vogel (1982) or an earlier version in English (Vogel, 1977) for a discussion of the controversy surrounding the syllable and for additional references on the topic. See Bell and Hooper (1978) for an early collection of articles on the syllable and its structure.
2. See, among others, Vergnaud and Halle (1978), Kiparsky (1979), Selkirk (1980b), Harris (1983), van der Hulst (1984). See also Pike and Pike (1947) and Fudge (1969) for earlier work in this area.
3. See, among others, Hooper (1976), Lowenstamm and Kaye (1981), Steriade (1982), Selkirk (1984a).
4. See, among others, Kahn (1976), Vogel (1977), Vergnaud and Halle (1978), McCarthy (1979), Lowenstamm (1981), Lapointe and Feinstein (1982), Noske (1982). See also Kurylowicz (1948) for an earlier discussion of this issue.

5.   See, among others, Kahn (1976), Clements and Keyser (1983).
6.   See, among others, Kahn (1976), Vogel (1977), Harris (1983), Trommelen (1983), van der Hulst (1984).
7.   According to Dixon (1970), the Australian language Olgolo may be a counter-example, with a preference to divide the sequence as $[C_0 VC]_\sigma [VC]_\sigma$.
8.   We use brackets as a space-saving representation of phonological tree structure. Where the content of syllables is concerned, the brackets should not be interpreted as claiming that syllabification necessarily divides strings into discrete, non-overlapping units. In many cases, brackets provide an adequate representation of the syllabic structure under examination. In the case of ambisyllabic segments, however, brackets cannot be used and it is necessary instead to use the tree representation.
9.   See section 3.2.2 for a discussion of Aspiration in English.
10.   There is not complete consensus in the literature about which are the non-neutral and neutral affixes, or the corresponding Class I and Class II affixes in Siegel (1974, 1977), and Allen (1978), or the Root-level and Word-level affixes in the terminology of Selkirk (1982). We have therefore chosen examples with affixes that are uncontroversial whenever possible.
11.   We are referring to the situation in normal connected speech. Clearly there is a difference if a pause is introduced between the two words in (15b) and (16b), but this is not relevant to the point we are making here.
12.   The term resyllabification is also used sometimes to refer to cyclic readjustments of syllable structure that apply within a word in relation to the addition of affixes to a stem (see, among others Selkirk, 1984b). We will not use the term in this way here.
13.   The fact that nasals assimilate to glides in separate syllables but not in the same syllable is probably due to the phonetic properties of a syllable-initial glide as opposed to a glide that is not syllable initial. In fact, syllable-initial /w/ and /j/ are often strengthened to the corresponding obstruents $[g^w]$ and $[\hat{y}]$ (see Hooper, 1976; Harris, 1983). When this happens, the cases in question can be subsumed under the more general phenomenon of nasal assimilation before an obstruent. It should be noted that in this case, too, it is necessary to assign syllable structure first to individual words and only later allow resyllabification to take place. A single, late syllabification procedure would once again place a nasal at the beginning of a syllable before a glide in an adjacent word. The glide would thus not be syllable initial and would not undergo strengthening to an obstruent. The context for nasal assimilation before an obstruent would consequently not be present.
14.   A distinction must be made between Liaison and Enchaînement in formal styles of speech, where it is possible to find Liaison without Enchaînement (see Encrevé, 1983). That is, in certain formal styles a word-final consonant may be pronounced without being resyllabified to the beginning of the following word. Since we are interested in colloquial speech, however, this distinction is not relevant to the present work. When we discuss the application of Liaison from now on, it should be understood that this includes the concomitant application of Enchaînement.
15.   [ɛ], and other vowels, are long before a final *r* and in certain other environments. Since length is not crucial to our discussion, however, it will not be indicated.
16.   Several linguists (e.g. Selkirk, 1978; Booij, 1983) have proposed that Closed Syllable Adjustment is more correctly analyzed as a foot-domain rule rather than a syllable-domain rule. While this is not an uncontroversial position (see Noske, 1982, for example,) it should be noted that even if the domain of the rule is the foot, it is necessary to have two distinct syllabification processes in French. That is, the /r/ in *première année* must be part of the final syllable — and foot — of the first word at

the point at which the rule changing /e/ to [ɛ] applies; it may be resyllabified to the onset of the second word only after the vowel change has taken place. If this were not the case, and the only process of syllabification — and foot construction — placed the /r/ at the onset of *année*, then the /e/ of *première* would never be followed in the same syllable — or foot — by a consonant (/r/ in this case), as required by both the syllable and foot accounts of the vowel-changing rule in question.

17. It should be noted that there may be low-level phonetic rules of resyllabification in all languages, including Germanic languages (see also Trommelen, 1983). This is a different type of phenomenon, however, and is most likely controlled by different mechanisms than those that are relevant to the present discussion.

18. This position is not accepted by all linguists. See, for example, Clements and Keyser (1983), who argue that the rhyme is not needed in order to account for these types of phenomena.

19. See also Hooper (1972, 1976) and García-Bellido (1979) for a discussion of syllable-dependent rules in Spanish.

20. See Kahn (1976) for a discussion of the [—consonantal] properties of *r* in English.

21. See Malécot (1960) and Kahn (1976) for a discussion of the [—consonantal] properties of certain nasals in English.

22. It should be noted that Trommelen (1983) actually proposes that the domain of Schwa Insertion is the rhyme. Since this rule, like all other rhyme-domain rules, can be reformulated as a syllable-domain rule, Trommelen's analysis is not in conflict with the analysis discussed here. It should be noted, in addition, that according to Booij (1981), Schwa Insertion also applies, at least in certain varieties of Dutch, between a liquid and a tautosyllabic coronal obstruent if it is a nasal (i.e. [n]). The final formulation of the rule of Schwa Insertion in (43) below could easily be modified to take this possibility into account if necessary, though we will not do so here. Finally, it should be noted that in some varieties of Dutch, Schwa Insertion may also apply across two syllables if they are in the same foot (cf. *balken* → *bál*[ə]*kĕn* 'beams' vs. *balkon* → **bǎl*[ə]*kón* 'balcony'). In these varieties, the domain of Schwa Insertion is not the syllable, but the foot.

23. We are grateful to Harry van der Hulst for having pointed this out to us.

24. Saib does not actually formulate the rule.

25. Although the symbol [c] is used for a palatal stop in the alphabet of the International Phonetic Association, it is used here to represent an alveopalatal stop, since there is no other IPA symbol for this type of articulation.

26. The *e* of the stem is deleted by a rule of *e*-Deletion that precedes Consonant Gradation (see Keyser and Kiparsky, 1984).

27. It should be noted that Prince (1984) and Keyser and Kiparsky (1984) argue in favor of an autosegmental treatment of Consonant Gradation. Our view of CG is not necessarily incompatible with certain aspects of an autosegmental treatment and it might be that we are dealing here with a phenomenon that depends on the interaction between the autosegmental and prosodic subsystems of the phonology. See, however, Anderson (1982) on the use of the autosegmental formalism for segmental phonological rules, which would include most aspects of CG. In any case, it should be recalled in relation to our formulation of CG, that our use of labeled brackets to represent syllable structure is only a shorthand notation for hierarchical structure. It is not meant to exclude the possibility of ambisyllabic segments, which in fact seem to be needed in the analysis of Finnish.

28. Actually, Anderson (1982) argues that such phenomena, too, can and should be formulated as segmental rules, ones that apply iteratively to the appropriate string

of segments. A thorough evaluation of this claim is beyond the scope of this book since it would require an evaluation of autosegmental theory in general. It should be noted, however, that on the analysis proposed by Anderson, while we would no longer need the theory of autosegmental associations, the theory of domains remains essential in order to specify precisely which segments are to be affected by the rule.

29. A further division of quantity sensitive feet can be made into quantity sensitive and what van der Hulst calls quantity determined feet (see also Halle and Vergnaud, 1978; Hayes, 1981). In this case, the combinations with the parameter of binary *vs.* unbounded gives six possibilities.

30. Note that even though foot formation needs to see rhyme structure, what is actually joined into larger constituents are syllables, not just parts of syllables.

31. Our foot divisions are consistent with Selkirk's (1980b) characterization of the foot in English.

32. Note that the aspirated *t* of *tree* will become [c^h] by the rule of Alveopalatalization discussed in section 3.1.2.

33. This rule applies before Flapping (see Chapter 8).

34. See also Kiparsky (1979:436), according to whom *nitrate, agree,* and *Montana* each consist of two feet.

35. This rule is most likely part of a more general rule that accounts for the presence of a long vowel before a voiced consonant or finally and a short one before a voiceless consonant (cf. *bead/bee* vs. *beat*). We will therefore not provide a more formal statement of Diphthong Shortening than is given in (72).

36. An alternative account would be to allow *s* in *Islip* to be ambisyllabic, and thus tautosyllabic both with *s* in the first syllable and with *l* in the second syllable. LD and DS could then be formulated as syllable domain rules. We do not adopt this alternative here, however, precisely because it depends on the notion of ambisyllabicity. That is, since it is possible to account for all the rules under consideration here with reference to independently motivated phonological constituents, it is superfluous to introduce the additional notion of ambisyllabicity at this point. The same argument holds for Obligatory *n*-Velarization and Mutual *k-r* Assimilation discussed below. It should be noted, though, that we do not exclude the possibility of ambisyllabicity in English in general (cf. Section 3.1.1 above); we exclude it only as part of the account of the phonological rules under consideration here.

37. The cases of optional *n*-velarization will be handled by a more general rule of optional nasal assimilation that also accounts for the possible assimilation of nasals across words (e.g. *brown cow* $\xrightarrow{opt}$ *brow*[ŋ] *cow*).

38. The numbers on the morphemes in the following discussion of Amoy indicate tone. The tone changes seen in the examples below do not concern us here.

39. It seems that the rules are only optional before *e*[13].

40. Note that according to Anderson (1982) a rule such as Nasalization should not be treated as an autosegmental rule at all, but rather as an iterative segmental rule. See also notes 27 and 28.

41. The symbol [ǀ'] in the name of the language stands for a type of dental implosive. Other uncommon symbols encountered in the examples below are: [ǀ], another type of dental implosive; [ǀx], a dental infricate (fricative produced with inwardly sucked air); [kx'], a velar affricate; [ǂ] and [ǂ'], two types of alveopalatal implosive (see Snyman, p.125).

Chapter 4

The Phonological Word

4.0. *Introduction*

The phonological word is the lowest constituent of the prosodic hierarchy which is constructed on the basis of mapping rules that make substantial use of nonphonological notions. In particular, the phonological word (ω) represents the interaction between the phonological and the morphological components of the grammar.

The phonological word is the category that immediately dominates the foot. More specifically, as required by the Strict Layer Hypothesis (see section 1.2.1 above), all the feet of a given string must be grouped into phonological words, and no other category may be so grouped. Each foot is thus exhaustively included in a ω; that is, it is never the case that the syllables of a single foot belong to different phonological words.

Whether the syllable and the foot are already present in the lexicon, as proposed for example by van der Hulst (1984), and are thus available at the point at which the domain of ω is defined, or whether they are constructed within this domain once it has been defined, is not a question that can be easily resolved. In the first case, σ and Σ structure must be adjusted following the application of word formation processes in order to establish more optimal syllables and feet. In the second case, σ and Σ structure is created at the ω level, a procedure that automatically yields optimal syllables and feet; readjustment is therefore not necessary. The interaction between the phonological and morphological components of the grammar will in either case take the form of a definition of ω that maps morphological structure onto phonological structure. Within the ω domain we can then proceed either to readjust the syllables and feet when necessary or to construct them in accordance with universal principles and possible language-specific constraints.

As we have said above, the mapping rules which define ω represent the interaction between morphology and phonology. That is, they regroup the terminal elements of morphological structure in such a way that the resulting units do not necessarily correspond to any morphological constituent.

Although the nonisomorphism between the constituents of the pro-

sodic and the morpho-syntactic hierarchies is the most compelling argument in favor of the existence of two separate hierarchies in the grammar,
as was shown in Chapter 2, occasional isomorphism is not excluded *a
priori*, and it will be shown that isomorphism between ω and a morphological unit is, in fact, the norm in some languages such as Greek and Latin
(see section 4.1 below). The superiority of a theory of prosodic phonology
that does not directly refer to morpho-syntactic boundaries, however, is
not undermined by sporadic cases of isomorphism (see section 2.4).

While it has been claimed by a number of linguists (among others,
Booij, 1983) that there are three basic possibilities for the domain of the
phonological word, that is, that it is larger, smaller, or equal to the terminal
element of a syntactic tree, it is our contention that only the second and
the third options exist, a point that will be demonstrated in this chapter.

4.1. ω *domain equal to the terminal element of the syntactic tree*

In this section, we will consider the case of languages in which the phonological word has the same domain as the terminal element of a syntactic
tree. That is, it includes the stem, all affixes, and both members of compound words. In such languages there is in principle a left–right symmetry.
That is, if both prefixes and suffixes occur in a given language, these two
categories are treated in the same way by the phonology. This does not
imply that these languages have no morpho-phonological processes that
apply to subparts of words; our claim is that no purely phonological rules
affect strings larger than the foot and smaller than the phonological word
as just defined.

4.1.1.   Greek

The first language we will consider in which the phonological word has
the same extension as the terminal element of a syntactic tree is Demotic
Greek. There are two assimilation rules of Greek that have ω as their
domain of application. Though both apply in a larger domain as well (see
Nespor, 1986, and Chapter 5 below), their application is obligatory
only within the phonological word. These two rules are Nasal Assimilation
(NA) and Stop Voicing (SV) (see Householder, 1964). As was mentioned
in Chapter 2, the first rule assimilates a nasal in point of articulation to
a following noncontinuant consonant. This rule is exemplified in (1),
where it is shown that NA applies in underived words (1a,b) and in derived
words, both between the prefix and the stem (1c,d,e), and between two
prefixes (1f,g). These examples, together with those in (2), also illustrate

the application of the second rule, SV, which obligatorily voices a stop
when it is preceded by a nasal.

(1) a. τεμπέλης [tembélis]
         'lazy'
     b. τσαμπουνίζω [tsambunízo]
         '(I) shout'
     c. συμπονώ [simbonó] < [sin+ponó]
         '(I) have compassion'
     d. συμπίνω [simbíno] < [sin+píno]
         '(I) drink in company'
     e. εμπειρία [embiría] < [en+piría]
         'experience'
     f. συγκαταλέγω [singataléγo] < [sin+kataléγo]
         '(I) include among'
     g. συγκαταβαίνω [singatavéno] < [sin+katavéno]
         '(I) condescend'

(2) a. καντίλα [kandíla]
         'small lamp'
     b. συνταξιδεύω [sindaksiðévo] < [sin+taksiðévo]
         '(I) travel in company'
     c. έντιμος [éndimos] < [en+tímos]
         'honored'

In order to show that the domain of the phonological word is indeed the
terminal element of a syntactic tree, we must still demonstrate that the
two members of a compound belong to the same ω. This cannot be shown
on the basis of NA and SV, since there are no compounds in which the
first member ends with a nasal consonant. It can be shown, however, on the
basis of stress placement – which also has as its domain the phonological
word – that the two members of a compound do, in fact, belong to the
same ω constituent.

It should be observed first of all that there is a well-formedness condition in Greek that requires primary word stress to fall on one of the last
three syllables of a word. This is exemplified in (3)-(5).

(3) a. άλογος   [áloγos]   'horse'
     b. κόκκινος   [kókinos]   'red'
     c. ντρέπομαι   [drépome]   '(I) am ashamed'

(4) a. πατέρας   [patéras]   'father'
     b. γεμάτος   [yemátos]   'full'
     c. πηγαίνω   [piyéno]   '(I) go'

(5) a. αχινός   [axinós]   'sea urchin'
     b. πιθανός   [piθanós]   'probable'
     c. αγαπώ   [ayapó]   '(I) love'

In certain cases, the location of stress is predictable on the basis of morphological information. For example, in diminutives derived with the suffix *-άκι* ([–áki]), primary stress always falls on the penultimate syllable. In other cases, however, there is no way to predict on which syllable stress falls, as is clear from the existence of minimal pairs such as those in (6)-(9).

(6) a. οπός   [opós]   'juice'
     b. όπως   [ópos]   'like'

(7) a. ορός   [orós]   'serum'
     b. όρος   [óros]   'condition'

(8) a. πεινώ   [pinó]   '(I) am hungry'
     b. πίνω   [píno]   '(I) drink'

(9) a. δευτέρι   [ðeftéri] 'account book'
     b. δεύτεροι [ðéfteri] 'second pl. masc.'

A first indication that the two members of a compound word form a single phonological unit is the fact that in compounds, as in other types of words, there is only one primary stress. The stress of the compound does not necessarily fall on any of the syllables that bear primary stress before compound formation; in fact, most of the time it does not. Another indication that the two members of a compound in fact constitute a phonological word is the fact that they respect the same well-formedness condition that applies to stress in simple words. That is, stress must fall on one of the last three syllables of the compound, as shown in (10)-(12).

(10) a. κουκλόσπιτο   <   κύκλα   σπίτι
          [kuklóspito]   <   [kúkla]   [spíti]
          'doll's house'   'doll'   'house'
      b. ασπρόμαυρος   <   άσπρος   μαύρο
          [asprómavros] <   [áspros]   [mávros]
          'black and white'   'white'   'black'

c. ξυλόκολλα   <   ξύλος   κόλλα
    [ksilókola]   <   [ksílos]   [kóla]
    'wood glue'   'wood'   'glue'

(11) a. νυχτοπούλι   <   νύχτα   πουλί
         [nixtopúli]   <   [níxta]   [pulí]
         'night bird'   'night'   'bird'

  b. σπιρτοκούτι   <   σπίρτον   κουτί
      [spirtokúti]   <   [spírton] [kutí]
      'matchbox'   'match'   'box'

  c. ψυχοπαίδι   <   ψυχή   παιδί
      [psixopéði]   <   [psixí]   [peðí]
      'adopted child'   'spirit'   'child'

(12) a. νυχτοφυλακή   <   νύχτα   φυλακή
         [nixtofilakí] <   [níxta]   [filakí]
         'night guard'   'night'   'guard'

  b. φιλοφρονώ   <   φίλος   φρονώ
      [filofronó]   <   [fílos]   [fronó]
      '(I) entertain'   'friend'   'think'

  c. ξυλοθημονιά   <   ξύλος   θυμονιά
      [ksiloθimonyá] <   [ksílos]   [θimonyá]
      'wood stack'   'wood'   'stack'

In compounds, unlike in simple words, the location of primary stress is largely predictable on the basis of the quality of the last vowel of the compound. That is, if the last vowel is a back vowel, the word is most often stressed on the antepenultimate syllable; if it is a front vowel, the word tends to be stressed on the penultimate syllable. Final stress in compounds is fairly uncommon, but when it occurs it is often predictable on the basis of morphological information. Regardless of the specific rules for assigning stress to compounds, what is relevant here is that compound words form one phonological word since *a*) they have only one primary stress, just as noncompound words do, and *b*) they must fulfill the same well-formedness condition on the position of stress that noncompound words must fulfill.

Having established the domain of the phonological word in Greek, we may now formulate the two rules seen above, Nasal Assimilation and Stop Voicing, in the following way:

(13)   *Nasal Assimilation* (obligatory)

$$[\text{+nas}] \rightarrow \begin{bmatrix} \alpha \text{ cor} \\ \beta \text{ ant} \end{bmatrix} \;/\; [\ldots \underline{\hspace{1cm}} \begin{bmatrix} -\text{cont} \\ \alpha \text{ cor} \\ \beta \text{ ant} \end{bmatrix} \ldots]_\omega$$

(14)   *Stop Voicing* (obligatory)

$$[-\text{cont}] \rightarrow [\text{+vce}] \;/\; [\ldots \; [\text{+nas}] \; \underline{\hspace{1cm}} \ldots]_\omega$$

As the formulations of NA and SV show, these are ω span rules. That is, they apply any time their segmental context is present within the ω domain.

An additional rule of Demotic Greek that has ω as its domain of application is a rule that in certain varieties of the language optionally deletes a nasal before a continuant consonant. Sequences of nasal + continuant consonant are almost totally absent from Demotic Greek, although they are very common in Katharevousa, which was the official language until 1974 but is now hardly spoken at all. When they do occur in Demotic Greek, however, the nasal consonant is optionally deleted, as exemplified in (15).

(15)   a.   ἄνθρωπος [ánθropos] and [áθropos]
             'human being'
       b.   συμβιβασμός [simvivazmós] and [sivivazmós]
             'compromise'

The rule of Nasal Deletion (ND) may now be formulated in the following way:

(16)   *Nasal Deletion* (optional)

$$[\text{+nas}] \rightarrow \emptyset \;/\; [\ldots \underline{\hspace{1cm}} \begin{bmatrix} +\text{cont} \\ +\text{cons} \end{bmatrix} \ldots]_\omega$$

It should be noted that ND is a ω span rule, as are NA and SV, seen above. To sum up briefly, we have demonstrated on the basis of stress placement, two assimilation rules, and one deletion rule that the domain of the phonological word in Greek is equal to the terminal element of a syntactic tree. That is, it was shown that the rules in question apply within a domain that consists of one, or in the case of compounds two, stems plus all adjacent affixes. While the rules of stress assignment are limited to the ω domain, the assimilation and deletion rules are not. It will be shown in Chapter 5 that the clitic group, the constituent of the prosodic hierarchy that immediately dominates the phonological word, must also be taken into consideration in order to give an exhaustive account of these phenomena. That is, it will be shown that these rules exhibit different degrees of application in the two categories. As we have shown above, Nasal Assimilation and Stop Voicing apply obligatorily in ω, and Nasal Deletion applies optionally in the same domain. In the clitic group, the obligatoriness of the rules is reversed.

4.1.2. Latin

The next language that will be discussed here to exemplify the domain of ω equal to the terminal element of a syntactic tree is Classical Latin. That the phonological word in Latin has this extension can be seen from the fact that the Main Stress Rule applies in the same way to simple, derived, and compound words. In polysyllabic words, this rule assigns primary stress to the penultimate syllable if it is heavy. Otherwise it assigns stress to the antepenultimate syllable. This is illustrated in (17), (18) and (19), with simple, derived, and compound words, respectively.[1]

(17) a. stratḗgus   'chief'
      b. pópŭlum   'people'

(18) a. stomachṓsus   'irritated'
      b. homúncŭlus   'little man'

(19) a. vivirā́dix   'offshoot'
      b. vivípărus   'viviparous'

While Latin clitics have been claimed to form one phonological word with their host on the basis of the observation that they influence the stress of the word to which they cliticize, (see for instance Booij, 1983), we believe this not to be the case. Notice, in fact, that stress assignment in the group word + clitic does not follow the stress rule mentioned above. In the sequence word + clitic, the main stress falls instead on the syllable that immediately precedes the clitic, regardless of its weight (see Niedermann, 1953; Cupaiolo, 1959; Traina and Bernardi Perini, 1977). This rule, Clitic Group Stress, is exemplified in (20), where the clitic -*que* is cliticized to words whose final syllables have different internal structure and weight and nevertheless all bear primary stress.

(20)	a.	rosăque	'and the rose (nom.)'
	b.	rosámque	'and the rose (acc.)'
	c.	rosăque	'and the rose (abl.)'

Only in cases in which the sequence word + clitic no longer has the original meaning, and can thus be considered a single word rather than a sequence analyzable as word + clitic, does the Main Stress Rule apply (see Niedermann, 1953; Cupaiolo, 1959), as exemplified in (21).

(21)	a.	úndĭque	'everywhere'
	b.	dénĭque	'finally'
	c.	plérăque	'most things (fem. nom.)'

If this analysis is correct, there should be minimal pairs that differ phonologically only with respect to the location of their primary stress, depending on whether the sequence word + clitic is still analyzed as such or represents, instead, a new (single) word. This type of minimal pair does indeed exist, as exemplified in (22).

(22)	a.	ităque	'and so'
	b.	ităque	'therefore'

This issue will be treated in more detail in Chapter 5, where it will be shown that the stress (readjustment) rule exemplified in (20) has as its domain of application the clitic group, that is, the constituent of the prosodic hierarchy that immediately dominates the phonological word.

What the examples above have shown is that the Main Stress Rule applies to sequences consisting of a single stem, or two stems in the case of compounds, plus any adjacent string of affixes. We take this as evidence that such strings, which correspond to the terminal element of a syntactic tree, constitute a phonological unit and in particular the phonological word.

4.1.3. ω *domain (i)*

On the basis of the domain of the phonological word in languages like Greek and Classical Latin, we may now proceed to give the definition of ω for languages in which ω is coextensive with the constituent dominated by the terminal node of the syntactic stree, which we will call Q.

(23) ω *domain (i)*
     The domain of ω is Q.

As we mentioned above, this is not the only possibility for the phonological word. We will now turn to an analysis of the domain of ω in languages where this domain is smaller than the one just defined.

4.2. ω domain smaller than the terminal element of the syntactic tree

In this section, we will present an analysis of the phonological word in languages in which its domain is smaller than the constituent dominated by the terminal node of a syntactic tree. There is more than one possibility for the construction of ω in this case; each possibility will be discussed and exemplified in a separate subsection. Despite their differences, all of these cases of ω construction share the characteristic of regrouping the morphological units of a word in such a way that the end result is not isomorphic to any constituent of the morpho-syntactic hierarchy.

4.2.1. ω domain equal to stem plus affixes

The first case of a phonological word whose domain is smaller than the terminal element of a syntactic tree is found in languages in which both underived and derived words form a ω. That is, for all noncompound words, there is isomorphism between the morpho-syntactic and the prosodic hierarchies. In the case of compound words, however, the extension of the word-level constituent in the two hierarchies is different. That is, in compounds, each stem forms a phonological word together with its adjacent affixes. In languages that have both prefixes and suffixes, one ω thus includes the prefixes together with the first member of the compound, and a separate ω includes the second member of the compound and its adjacent suffixes. It is clear that in cases in which the affixes represent derivations of the compound as a whole, the phonological and the morphological divisions of the constituents do not coincide. In the case of suffixes the mismatch would be of the kind illustrated in (24).

(24)   a.   morphological constituency   b. phonological constituency

In the following two sections, we will exemplify this particular type of ω domain on the basis of Sanskrit and Turkish.

4.2.1.1. Sanskrit

A definition of the type of phonological word just described has been proposed by Selkirk (1980a) for Sanskrit. The mapping rules proposed by Selkirk on the basis of observations found in Whitney (1889) specify that each word of a syntactic marker constitutes a ω domain, unless it is composed of a compound stem, in which case the first member constitutes one ω and the second member plus its affixes a separate ω. Selkirk shows that the phonological word so defined is the domain of application of several phonological rules. Among these are Final Voicing, a rule that assimilates a [−sonorant] segment in voicing to the following segment only at a ω juncture, as exemplified in (25) with two compound words.

(25)   a.   sat − aha   →   sad − aha   'good day'
        b.   tat − namas →   tad − namas   'that homage'

A ω internal combination of morphemes does not trigger Final Voicing, as shown in (26).

(26)   a.   vāc+ya   →   vācya   'speak (ger.)'
        b.   marut+i   →   maruti   'wind (loc.)'

A second ω juncture rule of Sanskrit, Stop to Nasal, optionally assimilates a stop in nasality to a following nasal segment, as exemplified in (27).

(27)   a.   tat namas   → tad namas   → tan namas
        b.   tristup nūnam → tristub nūnam → tristum nūnam

Two additional rules are given by Selkirk to show that ω plays an essential role in determining where a phonological phenomenon may take place. These rules are Final Cluster Reduction and Final Deaspiration and Devoicing. The first rule deletes all but the leftmost postvocalic consonant in a ω final cluster, as shown in (28). The second deaspirates and devoices aspirated nonsonorant consonants if ω final, as shown in (29), as well as in (28b,c).

(28)   a.   bhavant+s   → bhavan   'being (nom. masc. sg.)'
        b.   tristubh+s → tristup   'type of meter (nom. masc. sg.)'
        c.   pad+s   → pat   'foot (nom. masc. sg.)'

(29)   a.   agnimath   → agnimat   'producing fire by friction'
        b.   labh − sye → lap − sye   'I shall sieze'
        c.   virudh   → virut   'plant'

The fact that the four rules we have just considered all have the same domain of application, one which, furthermore, is not isomorphic to any constituent of the morpho-syntactic hierarchy, is evidence that a constituent with precisely this extension must be posited in the prosodic hierarchy of Sanskrit. It should be noted that the first two rules are formally ω juncture rules on the U domain. That is, they apply when the segmental context is present at the boundary of two phonological words throughout a phonological utterance. The last two rules, on the other hand, are ω limit rules and apply at the end of any ω, given the correct segmental conditions.

Before proceeding to give the definition of the type of phonological word just seen in Sanskrit, that is, one that includes a stem and all adjacent affixes, we will examine another language in which the ω constituent has exactly the same domain.

4.2.1.2. Turkish

The second language we will use to exemplify the lack of one-to-one correspondence between the domain of the phonological word and the lowest constituent of the syntactic hierarchy is Turkish. In particular, we will show that the extension of the ω domain is equal to a stem plus its adjacent affixes in Turkish, as it is in Sanskrit.

With the exception of a limited group of words (see Lewis, 1967: 21), all monomorphemic words in Turkish have primary stress on the last syllable. Thus, the Main Stress Rule assigns stress to the vast majority of monomorphemic words as illustrated in (30).

(30) a. yaλníz 'alone'
b. somún 'loaf'
c. doğú 'fast'
d. çocúk 'child'
e. odá 'room'

The Main Stress Rule also applies to derived words; that is, the last syllable of a derived word bears primary stress, no matter how many suffixes the word contains, as the derivations of *çocúk* 'child' and *odá* 'room' show.

(31) a. çocúk 'child'
b. çocuklár 'children'
c. çocuklarimíz 'our children'
d. çocuklarimizín 'of our children'

(32) a. odá 'room'
b. odadá 'in the room'
c. odadakí 'that which is in the room'
d. odadakilér 'those who are in the room'
e. odadakilerdén 'from those who are in the room'

While these examples show that the domain of the Main Stress Rule in Turkish includes an entire derived word, we have not yet shown that this is the largest domain of stress assignment. That is, if we assume that the phonological word is equivalent to the domain within which stress is assigned, we have thus far only shown that ω must include at least derived words. To show that the domain of ω is, in fact, smaller than the terminal element of the syntactic tree, we must provide evidence that the two members of compounds do not behave as a single ω. As Lees (1961) observes, of the two primary stresses that the members of a compound word have in isolation, only the first remains after compounding; the main stress of the second member is reduced to secondary stress. The stress pattern of compounds is exemplified in (33).

(33)   a.   düğünçiçeği   'butter cup'
            of yesterdayflower
       b.   çáy evì   'tea house'
            tea house

This pattern, however, besides being different from that found word internally, is precisely the one found in independent words which are joined together in a phonological phrase (see Chapter 6). This stress pattern is thus a first indication that each of the members of a compound forms part of a separate ω in Turkish.

Additional evidence that the two members of a compound do not form a single phonological word is provided by Vowel Harmony. In Turkish, there is a rule whose effect is that of harmonizing within a certain domain all vowels for the feature [back] and high vowels for the feature [round].[2] In Chapter 5, it will be shown that this domain is the clitic group and that the rule works from left to right. That is, the first vowel of a word determines the quality of all the following vowels of the sequence word + clitics. The application of the rule in affixed words is exemplified in (34) and (35) below, where the vowels of the suffixes harmonize with the vowels of the stem. Specifically, the forms of the genitive and plural morphemes are *-in* and *-ler*, respectively, after the front unrounded vowel in *ev*, while these same morphemes have the forms *-un* and *-lar* after words such as *vapur* and *burun*.

(34)   a.   ev – in   'of the house'
            house (gen.)
       b.   vapur – un   'of the steamer'
            steamer (gen.)

(35)   a.   ev – ler   'houses'
            house (pl.)
       b.   burun – lar   'noses'
            nose   (pl.)

The two members of compounds, however, do not form a single domain
for the harmony rule, as may be seen in (36).

(36)   bugün   'today'
            this day

What this shows is that there are, in fact, two separate harmony domains
in compound words. Since, as was mentioned above, the clitic group is
the domain of Vowel Harmony in Turkish, we must conclude that there
are two clitic groups in compound words. Furthermore, given the Strict
Layer Hypothesis, it follows that compounds in Turkish must also contain
two separate phonological words. On the basis of the two rules just exemplified, the Main Stress Rule and Vowel Harmony, we may now draw
the conclusion that in Turkish, as in Sanskrit, the domain of the phonological word is not necessarily isomorphic to any constituent of the morpho-
syntactic hierarchy. In both cases the mismatch is of the type illustrated
in (24) above in which ω does not include the entire element that corresponds to the lowest constituent in the syntactic hierarchy, but only a part
of it.

4.2.1.3. ω domain (iia)

   In section 4.1.3 above, we have given the definition of the first type
of ω, that found in languages in which the domain of ω is equal to the
terminal element of the syntactic tree. On the basis of the preceding
analysis of Sanskrit and Turkish, we may now give the definition of a
second type of phonological word.

(37)   ω domain (iia)
       a.   The domain of ω consists of a stem and any linearly adjacent
            string of affixes.
       b.   Any unattached element forms a ω on its own.

The first part of this definition has the effect of forming one phonological word from each noncompound word, whether it is underived or derived. It forms two ωs in the case of compound words, one with the first
member of the compound plus (in languages in which they exist) any prefixes, and the other with the second member of the compound plus any
suffixes. The second part of the definition, on the other hand, ensures

that other elements that do not qualify as stems, for example conjunctions and clitics, also form a ω as required by the Strict Layer Hypothesis.

4.2.2. ω domain and additonal morphological and phonological factors

The phonological word discussed in section 4.2.1 has a domain that, though not necessarily isomorphic to any morpho-syntactic constituent, is symmetrical in the sense that it does not crucially distinguish prefixes from suffixes, that is, left from right side with respect to the stem. In addition, it does not need to refer to any phonological information other than that inherent in the Strict Layer Hypothesis, that is, that a ω is formed by grouping together constituents of the level immediately below it, feet.

The phonological word we will discuss now has a domain that not only is nonisomorphic to any morpho-syntactic constituent, but is also asymmetric. That is, the definition of such a ω must distinguish prefixes from suffixes (i.e. left from right side). Furthermore it may take into account specific phonological criteria in addition to those inherent in the Strict Layer Hypothesis. The first type of phonological word, the one that must take into account specific morphological factors, will be exemplified on the basis of Hungarian. The second type of ω, the one for which specific phonological information is needed in its definition, will be exemplified on the basis of Italian and Yidiɲ.

4.2.2.1. Hungarian

In this section, we will show that the domain of the phonological word in Hungarian includes a stem plus any linearly adjacent string of suffixes. The two members of a compound thus form two different ωs: the first includes only the first stem, the second includes the second stem plus any suffixes of the compound. In addition, the category of elements often referred to as preverbs, which we will refer to here simply as prefixes, also form independent ωs.

We will begin with an analysis of Vowel Harmony (see among others, Vago, 1976), and show that its domain of application is the phonological word as just described. The claim that ω is the domain of Vowel Harmony is not new; it is also found in Booij (1984b), where the domain of ω, however is not defined in an exhaustive way.

In Hungarian, all vowels other than *i, í,* and *é* (where *i* and *é* are the alphabetic symbols for the phonetic [iː] and [eː]) participate in Vowel Harmony. The harmonizing feature is [back], as exemplified in (38) and (39), where it can be seen that a stem plus its suffixes form a domain for harmony, and thus a ω (see Booij, 1984b).

(38)   a.   [ölelés]$_\omega$ 'embracement'
       b.   [ölelés-nek]$_\omega$ 'embracement + (dat. sg.)'

(39) a. [hajó]$_\omega$ 'ship'
      b. [hajó-nak]$_\omega$ 'ship + (dat. sg.)'

The examples in (40), on the other hand, indicate that the first and second members of a compound constitute separate harmony domains and thus separate ωs.

(40) a. [Buda]$_\omega$ [Pest]$_\omega$ 'Budapest'
      b. [könyv]$_\omega$ [tár]$_\omega$ 'library'
          book   collection

In (41), it may be seen that while the first and second stems of a compound are separate harmony domains, the suffix of the compound is included in the harmony domain of the second stem (see Vago, 1980). We thus have evidence for the claim that a stem plus any linearly adjacent string of suffixes form one ω.

(41) [lát]$_\omega$ [képünk]$_\omega$ 'our view'   (látkép = view; ünk = our)

The final point that remains to be demonstrated in order to establish the domain of ω defined above is that prefixes do not harmonize with the stem to which they are affixed. In (42) this point is demonstrated on the basis of the fact that the vowels of verbal prefixes do not have the same value for the feature [back] as the vowels of the stem.

(42) a. be – utazni   'to commute in'
          in   commute
      b. fel – ugrani   'to jump up'
          up   jump
      c. oda – menni   'to go there'
          there go

Within a theory of phonology that includes the Strict Layer Hypothesis, the fact that prefixes do not harmonize with the following stem is evidence that they must be considered as forming separate ωs in Hungarian. It should be noted that other types of similarities between prefixes and words have been observed in Hungarian as well as in other languages (see, among others, Tompa, 1972; Strauss, 1982; Scalise, 1983; Booij and Rubach, 1984). It is therefore not surprising that these two types of elements have the same phonological status in some languages.

The phonological word in Hungarian is not only the domain of harmony, but also of other phenomena. For example, Palatalization, a rule that assimilates *d, t, l, n* to a following *j*, yielding the corresponding palatal

124   *Prosodic Phonology*

sounds (see Hall, 1944), applies within ω as defined above, as shown in (43). It does not apply between two phonological words, however, as exemplified in (44), (45), and (46), where the rule is blocked between the two members of a compound, between a prefix and the following stem, and between two words, respectively.

(43)   [men+jen]$_\omega$ → me[ɲ]en   'let him go'
       go (Pe 3 sg. imp.)

(44)   [alúl]$_\omega$ – [járó]$_\omega$ → *alú[j]járó³   'tunnel'
       under   path

(45)   [fel]$_\omega$ [jönni]$_\omega$ → *fe[j]önni   'to come up'
       up   come

(46)   [én]$_\omega$ [jövök]$_\omega$ → *é[ɲ]övök   'I come'
       I   come

To conclude this section on Hungarian, let us summarize the main characteristics of the type of phonological word found in this language. First of all, it is not isomorphic to any morpho-syntactic constituent, as can be seen from the fact that while the two members of a compound form two different ωs, the suffixes of a compound form one ω with its second stem. In this respect, it is the same as the ω constituent discussed in the previous section and exemplified with data from Sanskrit and Turkish. Secondly, the definition of the ω domain in Hungarian must refer to morphological constituents in an asymmetric way, in that any string of suffixes is included in one ω with the linearly preceding, adjacent stem, while prefixes form a ω on their own. In this respect, it is different from the ω domain seen in the previous section.

4.2.2.2. *Italian*

In this section, an analysis of Italian will be given in which it is shown that the phonological word is a necessary constituent of phonological analysis, since there is no one-to-one relation between ω and any constituent of the morpho-syntactic hierarchy, and, furthermore, that the construction of ω must make reference to specific phonological information other than that expressed by the Strict Layer Hypothesis. On the basis of this analysis, we will propose that additional phonological notions may be used in the construction of ω only under specific circumstances.

Let us begin by examining the domain of application of a rule that voices an intervocalic *s*. We will demonstrate that this domain is not isomorphic to any constituent of the morpho-syntactic hierarchy, and claim that it is equivalent instead to the phonological word. We will then show that the ω constituent thus defined is needed in the formulation of several other phonological rules of Italian (see Nespor, 1984).

Intervocalic s-Voicing (ISV) is a rule of standard northern Italian which applies within words,[4] but not across words, as seen in (47) and (48), respectively.

(47) a. a[z]ola   'button hole'
      b. a[z]ilo   'nursery school'

(48) a. la [s]irena *la [z]irena   'the siren'
      b. hanno [s]eminato *hanno [z]eminato '(they) have seeded'

ISV does not apply, furthermore, between a word and an enclitic element (see (49)) or between a proclitic element and a word (see (50)).

(49) telefonati[s]i *telefonati[z]i
      'having called each other'

(50) lo [s]apevo *lo [z]apevo
      '(I) knew it'

The environment that triggers ISV cannot be identified with the morphological word, however, since even word internally, ISV applies in some cases but not in others. The items in (51) and (52) exemplify the morphological contexts in which ISV does and does not apply, respectively.

(51) a. *within a morpheme*
          a[z]ola   'button hole'
      b. *between a lexical morpheme and its inflection:*
          ca[z]e   (house (pl.))   'houses'
      c. *between a lexical morpheme and its derivational suffix:*
          ca[z]ina   (house (dim.))   'little house'
      d. *between a derivational prefix and a lexical morpheme:*
          re[z]istenza   'resistance'
      e. *between the second member of a compound and the inflection:*
          ficcana[z]i   'busy bodies'

(52) a. *between a derivational prefix and a lexical morpheme:*
          a[s]ociale   'asocial'
      b. *between the two members of a compound:*
          tocca[s]ana   'cure all'

The domain of application of ISV is thus a constituent that in non-compound words includes a stem, its derivational and inflectional suffixes, and, in certain cases, also its derivational prefixes. In compound words, on the other hand, the second member of the compound forms a constituent with the suffixes, and the first member forms a separate constituent.

We will now show that the necessary constituents cannot be found in the morphological hierarchy; the context of application of ISV thus can not be identified with any morphological category. Take, for instance, the word *ri[s]uddivi[z]ione* 'resubdivision'. This word contains the prefix *ri-*, which can be attached to verbs but not to nouns, and the suffix *-ione*, which is used to make nouns from verbs.[5] Given the bases required by these affixes, the only possible morphological structure for *risuddivisione* is the one given in (53).

(53) $[[\text{PRE}[\quad]_V]_V\text{SUF}]_N$

Instead, the structure that we would need for a morphological constituent to be the domain of application of ISV is the one in (54), where the stem forms a constituent with the suffix to the exclusion of the prefix.

(54) $[\text{PRE}[[\quad]_V\text{SUF}]_N]_N$

The structure in (53) is not possible for *risuddivisione*, however, since, as we have just said, *ri-* may only be prefixed to verbs, not to nouns.

That the domain of application of ISV cannot be identified with a morphological constituent can also be seen in compound words with the morphological structure shown in (55).

(55) $[[[\text{ficca}]_V\,[\text{naso}]_N]_N+\text{i}]_N$ ficcana[z]i   'busy bodies'

We have already shown in (51e) and (52b) that ISV applies between the second member of a compound and its inflection, but not between the two members of a compound. There is no morphological constituent, however, that exhaustively includes the second member of a compound and the inflection, as may be seen in (55), where the plural inflection refers to the compound *ficcanaso* and not to its nominal subpart *naso* 'nose'. That is, *ficcanasi* refers to more than one person sticking a nose into other people's business, not to one person who sticks more than one nose (*nasi*) into other people's business.

The fact that the domain of application of ISV is not isomorphic to any constituent of the morpho-syntactic hierarchy can be taken as evidence that the domain must be a phonological one. Given that the domain is larger than the foot, since ISV applies both within and across feet (see (56a,b)) but smaller than a string of two words (see (56c,d)), we can conclude that the domain of ISV is the phonological word.

(56) a. Σ Σ
        | /\
        a[z]ilo   'nursery school'

     b.   Σ
         /\
         ca[z]o   'case'
     c. la [s]alamandra   *[z]   'the salamander'
     d. gatto [s]iamese   *[z]   'Siamese cat'

It is clear from the contexts in which ISV applies, however, that the definitions of ω given above for other languages are not adequate for Italian. We will therefore examine now the specific criteria on which ω is based in Italian. It has already been shown that *a*) in noncompound words, the stem plus all suffixes, whether derivational or inflectional, form a single ω, and *b*) in compound words, the first stem forms a ω domain[6] and the second stem plus the suffixes of the compound form another ω domain. The only point that remains unclear from (51) and (52) concerns the prefixes, since some appear to form a ω with the following stem and others do not. The question now is what determines whether or not a prefix is joined into the same ω with the following stem.

One characteristic that distinguishes (51d) from (52a) repeated as (57) and (58) for convenience, is the fact that the prefix *re-* in (57) is affixed to a stem that is not an independent word in contemporary Italian, that is, one that cannot undergo lexical insertion, while the prefix *a-* in (58) is affixed to a word.

(57) re[z]istenza   'resistance'

(58) a[s]ociale   'asocial'

It should be noted, furthermore, that words such as (57) are not analyzed as derived words by native speakers; that is, while the prefix *re-* means 'again' (cf. reintegrare 'reintegrate'), the meaning of the word *resistenza* does not include the notion of 'again'. The example in (58), on the other hand, is for any native speaker a word derived with the negative prefix *a-*. The meaning of *asociale* is, in fact, 'not social'. We may thus draw the conclusion so far that in historically prefixed words that are not analyzed as such synchronically, the prefix forms a phonological word with the following stem. That this is the appropriate conclusion may be seen on the basis of the additional examples in (59) and (60), where synchronically analyzable and non-analyzable words, respectively, are given.

(59) a.   bi[s]essuale   'bisexual'
      b.   ri[s]uonare   'to ring again'
      c.   ultra[s]ensibile   'supersensitive'

(60) a.   bi[z]estile   'leap year'
      b.   ri[z]acca   'undertow'
      c.   pre[z]unzione   'arrogance'

The minimal pair in (61) illustrates further the difference between those prefixes that are synchronically analyzable and those that are not. Specifically, (61a) has the predicted meaning of 'hear in advance', and thus includes two distinct ωs, across which ISV does not apply. (61b), however, has an idiosyncratic meaning. That is, it is not analyzed as a prefixed word by native speakers, and thus forms only one ω, within which ISV predictably applies.

(61) a.   pre[s]entire   'to hear in advance'
      b.   pre[z]entire   'to have a presentiment'

Consider, however, the examples in (62).

(62) a.   di[z]armo   'disarmament'
      b.   di[z]onesto   'dishonest'
      c.   di[z]intossicare   'disintoxicate'
      d.   di[z]uguale   'unequal'
      e.   di[z]innescare   'defuse'

All of the words in (62) are derived with the negative prefix *dis-* in a very regular way, as can be seen from the fact that every word has the predicted negative meaning. ISV applies in all of these examples, indicating that the behavior of *dis-* differs from that of the other prefixes examined above. It should be noted that the behavior of *dis-* cannot be explained along the lines proposed for English according to which prefixes are divided into two classes on the basis of their position in morphological structure (see among others, SPE; Siegel, 1974; Selkirk, 1982), since *dis-* can both precede and follow other prefixes such as *pre-* which do not trigger ISV, as seen in (63).[7]

(63) a.   predisintossicazione   (pre-dis-)
           'predisintoxication'
      b.   dispremunirsi   (dis-pre-)
           'dis-pre-arm oneself'

Since the peculiar behavior of *dis-* cannot be due to its position in morphological structure, and given certain distributional characteristics of Italian phonology in general, we propose, instead, that the behavior of *dis-* is due to the fact that it ends in a consonant. With the exception of a small group of function words such as *il* 'the (masc. sg.)', *in* 'in', *con* 'with', *per* 'for' and *non* 'not', consonant-final words are extremely uncommon in standard Italian, and totally absent in most regional varieties of Italian, where different phonological rules apply in order to avoid them.[8] Thus, there seems to be a general well-formedness condition that forbids consonant-final phonological words, or at least represents a strong tendency to avoid them whenever possible. It is on these grounds that we propose to include *dis-* and consonant-final prefixes in general (i.e. *bis-*, *mis-*, *in-*, *con-*, *per-*, etc.) within a ω with the adjacent element.[9] That is, while vowel-final prefixes have the form of independent words, consonant-final prefixes do not. Thus, while the former can constitute independent phonological words, the latter cannot. It should be noted, in addition, that in the case in which a consonant-final prefix has a ω to its left that consists of a vowel-final prefix, and one to its right including a stem or another prefix, the direction of attachment is rightward, i.e. in the direction of the stem, as the application of ISV in the example in (63a) above shows.

To sum up briefly, the domain of the phonological word in Italian is such that a stem forms a ω with all suffixes and with those prefixes that end in a consonant. Prefixes that end in a vowel form independent ωs, as required by the Strict Layer Hypothesis, according to which the sisters of a ω must be other ωs. Finally, prefixes which do not form independent ωs always attach in the direction of the stem. We can formulate ISV as a ω span rule in a maximally simple way as seen in (64), whereas the expression of the domain of application of this rule in terms of morphological constituents would not amount to more than a list of disparate environments.

(64)   *Intervocalic s-Voicing*

$$\begin{bmatrix} +\text{cont} \\ -\text{vce} \\ +\text{cor} \\ +\text{ant} \end{bmatrix} \rightarrow [+\text{vce}] \quad / \quad [\ldots[-\text{cons}]\underline{\quad}[-\text{cons}]\ldots]_{\omega}$$

To show that ω, as defined above, is not an *ad hoc* solution valid only for ISV, we will now examine several other phonological rules of Italian and show that their domains, too, correspond to the ω defined for ISV.

The first rule we will consider is Vowel Raising (VR). Of the seven vowels of Italian, two low vowels, [ɛ] and [ɔ], may occur only in syllables that bear primary stress, or in other words, are the DTE of a word.[10] If morphological derivation or inflection has the effect of moving the primary stress of a word from [ɛ] or [ɔ] to another position, an ill-formed word is created. A rule therefore applies to change [ɛ] and [ɔ] into [e] and [o], respectively, thus reestablishing a well-formed word, as exemplified in (65).

(65)   a.   t[ɔ́]lgo   vs. t[o]gliévo   '(I) take out / (I) was taking out'
       b.   l[ɛ́]ggo   vs. l[e]ggévo   '(I) read / (I) was reading'
       c.   p[ɔ́]co   vs. p[o]chíno   'little / little (dim.)'
       d.   t[ɛ́]rra   vs. t[e]rríccio   'earth / loam'

That suffixes form a single ω with the preceding element(s), and that ω is the domain of Vowel Raising, is further illustrated by the minimal pair in (66b) and (66c), where the derived word is distinguished from the phrase by the application *vs.* nonapplication of the rule.

(66)   a.   s[ɔ́]lito   'usual'
       b.   s[ò]litaménte   'usually'
       c.   s[ɔ́]lita ménte   'usual mind'

The examples in (67) show that the rule fails to apply in the case of compounds, indicating that the primary stress of the first member is not reduced as it is in derivation.

(67)   a.   t[ɔ́]sta páne   →   t[ɔ́]stapáne
            toast   bread   'bread toaster'
       vs. t[ɔ́]sta+tóre   →   t[ò]statóre
            'toaster'
       b.   p[ɛ́]lle róssa   →   p[ɛ́]llleróssa
            skin   red   'redskin'
       vs. p[ɛ́]lli+cína   →   p[è]llicína
            'small piece of skin'

Since a phonological word may contain at most one primary stress, the data in (65) show that suffixes form one ω with the stem, while the data in (67) show that in compound words there must be two ωs.

By making use of the ω domain, we can thus formulate a ω span rule of Vowel Raising in the following way, where the specification of [−DTE] accounts for the fact that the rule applies when the vowel in question does not bear primary stress in the domain indicated, the phonological word.

(68)   *Vowel Raising*

$$
\begin{bmatrix} +\text{syll} \\ +\text{mid} \\ -\text{hi} \end{bmatrix} \rightarrow [+\text{hi}] \;/\; [\cdots \underset{[-\text{DTE}]}{\underline{}} \cdots]_\omega
$$

Additional evidence in favor of the ω domain as defined above comes from Vowel Lengthening (VL). This rule lengthens the vowel of the strong syllable which is the DTE of a word (i.e. the vowel with primary word stress) if and only if it is in an open syllable which is not word final. The application of the rule is exemplified in (69), and its nonapplication in word-final position is exemplified in (70).

(69)   a.   p[á:]pero   'duck'
      b.   tap[í:]ro   'tapir'
      c.   pap[á:]vero   'poppy'
      d.   tartar[ú:]ga   'turtle'

(70)   a.   carib[ú]   'caribou'
      b.   colibr[í]   'hummingbird'

That the domain of application of VL is best described by making use of the phonological word can be seen from the facts that *a*) the rule applies with any type of suffix (see (71)), *b*) the rule applies in bisyllabic prefixes but not in underived words that begin with similar syllables (see (72) and (73)), and *c*) the rule applies twice when the appropriate local phonological environment occurs in both members of a compound (contrast (74a), (75a), and (76a) with (74b), (75b), and (76b), where noncompound words with a similar syllabic structure undergo the rule only once).

(71)   a.   gatt[í:]no   'little cat'   (< gatto + ino)
      b.   abbai[á:]va   '(it) was barking'   (< abbaia + va)
      c.   utilit[á:]rio   'utilitarian'   (< utile + itá + rio)

(72)   a.   p[á:]ramilit[á:]re 'paramilitary'
      b.   p[a]rametr[í:]co 'parametric'

(73)   a.   s[ú:]pervel[ó:]ce   'superfast'
      b.   s[u]perstizi[ó:]so 'superstitious'

(74)   a.   c[á:]pop[ó:]polo   'chief'
      b.   c[a]teg[ó:]rico   'categoric'

(75)   a.   d[ó:]polav[ó:]ro   'afterwork'
       b.   d[i]vinat[ó:]re   'seer'

(76)   a.   div[á:]no létto   'sofa bed'
       b.   tav[o]linetto   'very small table'

The rule of VL can now be formulated in the following way:

(77)   *Vowel Lengthening*

$$V \rightarrow [+\text{long}] \, / \, [...[... \underline{\quad}]_\sigma \, X]_\omega$$
$$[+\text{DTE}]$$

where $X \neq \emptyset$

The phonological word as defined above is also the domain of a rule of Total Nasal Assimilation (TNA). Sequences of a nasal consonant immediately followed by a sonorant consonant are ill formed when word-internal in Italian,[11] but are allowed across words, as exemplified in (78) and (79), respectively.

(78)   a.   *inregolare   'irregular'   (cf. irregolare)
       b.   *inmaturo   'immature'   (cf. immaturo)
       c.   *conlaterale   'collateral'   (cf. collaterale)

(79)   a.   in rime   'in rhyme'
       b.   con molti   'with many'
       c.   con loro   'with them'

To avoid the unacceptable nasal + sonorant sequences, TNA applies to the items in (78), but not to those in (79). It can be shown that the restriction and the consequent application of TNA, which totally assimilates the nasal to the following sonorant consonant, have as their domain the phonological word. In particular, the rule applies when the ill-formed sequences are created through prefixation, that is, when a prefix ending in a nasal consonant is adjacent to a word beginning with a sonorant consonant, as can be seen in (80).

(80)   a.   in+raggiungibile   →   irraggiungibile   'unreachable'
       b.   in+legale   →   illegale   'illegal'
       c.   in+morale   →   immorale   'immoral'
       d.   con+rispondere   →   corrispondere   'to correspond'
       e.   con+legare   →   collegare   'to put together'

The rule applies, in addition, within a phonological word consisting of a consonant-final prefix followed by a vowel-final prefix, as shown in (81a), and does not apply across the two members of a compound, since they form two different ωs, as shown in (81b).

(81)   a. $[\text{in+ri}]_{\omega} + [\text{producibile}]_{\omega} \rightarrow \text{i[r:]iproducibile}$
            'irreproducible'
       b. $[\text{man}]_{\omega} [\text{rovescio}]_{\omega} \rightarrow *\text{ma[r:]ovescio}$
            'slap'

The appropriate formulation of Total Nasal Assimilation as a ω span rule is given in (82).

(82)   *Total Nasal Assimilation*

$$[\text{+nas}] \rightarrow \begin{bmatrix} \alpha\text{nas} \\ \beta\text{ant} \\ \gamma\text{cor} \\ \delta\text{lat} \end{bmatrix} \Big/ [\ldots \underline{\hspace{1cm}} \begin{bmatrix} \text{+son} \\ \alpha\text{nas} \\ \beta\text{ant} \\ \gamma\text{cor} \\ \delta\text{lat} \end{bmatrix} \ldots]_{\omega}$$

A final confirmation of the definition of ω given above, and in particular, of the claim that vowel-final and consonant-final prefixes behave differently with respect to ω formation, is the fact that the former, unlike the latter, may be factored out. If we assume, following a proposal by Booij (1984a), that the condition necessary in order for an element to be factored out (see Siegel, 1974) is that this element must be a ω (see section 4.2.3.1 below), the following data are easily accounted for.

(83)   a.   i pro e gli antifascisti < i profascisti e gli antifascisti
            'the pro- and the antifascists'
       b.   *in ⎱ e amorale < immorale e amorale
            *im ⎰
            'immoral and amoral'
       c.   *dis e superintegrato < disintegrato e superintegrato
            'unintegrated and superintegrated'

In (83a), it can be seen that the vowel-final prefix *pro-* may be factored out, while in (83b) and (83c), it can be seen that it is not possible to factor out a consonant-final prefix. The example in (83b) shows, furthermore, that factoring out is equally impossible before and after the application of the assimilation rule in (82) (see also Scalise, 1983).

On the basis of the various phenomena of Italian analyzed in this section, all of which operate in the domain defined as ω, we can conclude that the ω proposed above is indeed a necessary constituent of the prosodic hierarchy of Italian.

As has been demonstrated above, the ω construction rules needed for Italian regroup the terminal elements of the morphological tree in such a way that the end result is a constituent that is not necessarily isomorphic to any morpho-syntactic constituent. Furthermore, these rules make a crucial distinction between prefixes and suffixes. It has been shown, moreover, that in the case of prefixes, specific phonological factors must be taken into account. In particular, a prefix is joined into a ω with the following item only if it is of a form (in this case, consonant-final) that in principle may not stand alone as a separate word. We would like to propose this as a more general condition on the use of phonological factors in the ω construction rules. That is, it is our proposal that the phonological word is constructed, in general, with rules that use morpho-syntactic notions, but in those cases in which such rules produce constituents that from a phonological point of view are not well formed in a given language, specific phonological notions may be taken into consideration as well.

In the next section, we will discuss Yidiɲ, another language in which phonological notions must be taken into account in the definition of the ω domain. It will be seen that the general condition we have just proposed in relation to Italian holds for Yidiɲ as well.

4.2.2.3. Yidiɲ

A very interesting description of Yidiɲ, an Australian language spoken in Northern Queensland, is found in Dixon (1977b). Yidiɲ has contrastive vowel length, and the central feature of its phonology is the interaction of vowel length and syllable count (see Dixon, 1977a). There is a rule, for example, which lengthens the penultimate vowel of a word if and only if the word has an odd number of syllables, as was seen in Chapter 2. Consider the following examples:

(84)   a.   gudá:ga   'dog (abs.)'
       b.   múḍam   'mother (abs.)'
       c.   maḍi:ndaŋ   'walk up (pres.)'
       d.   gáliŋ   'go (pres.)'

The nouns in (84a) and (84b) are coextensive with the nominal stem, since the absolutive inflection is ∅; the forms in (84c) and (84d) contain a verbal stem plus the present inflection ŋ (see Dixon, 1977b). In both cases, the number of syllables of the surface form is equal to the number of syllables of the stem, and it may be seen that the rule of Penultimate Lengthening applies in (84a) and (84c), which contain an odd number of syllables, but not in (84b) and (84d), which contain an even number of syllables.

The rule appears to apply also after morphological operations that have altered the number of syllables, as may be seen in (85).

(85) a. gudaga – gu → gudagagu 'dog (purp.)'
      b. muḍam – gu → muḍa:mgu 'mother (purp.)'

The first example shows a stem with an odd number of syllables and a surface form with an even number of syllables. The second example, to the contrary, shows a stem with an even number of syllables and a surface form with an odd number of syllables. Penultimate Lengthening (PL) applies to the second form but not to the first, showing that the phonological word must include the suffixes in order for the syllable count to be correct. It does not, however, include all suffixes (see Dixon, 1977b), as shown in (86).

(86) gumari – daga – ɲu → gumá:ri dagá:ɲu
      red   (inch.) (past)
      'to have become red'

Assuming that ω is the domain of application of Penultimate Lengthening, (86) shows that in the morphological word *gumá:ridagá:ɲu* there are two ωs, one containing the simple stem and one containing the two suffixes. A broader investigation of the data reveals *a*) that a suffix forms a ω with the stem if it is monosyllabic, but forms a separate ω if it is bisyllabic (Dixon, 1977b), and *b*) that it is not possible to divide the suffixes into morphological classes according to their relative order of occurrence in derived words, since bisyllabic suffixes can both precede and follow monosyllabic suffixes. The distinction is exclusively phonological and must therefore be accounted for in the phonological component. In particular, we propose that it is incorporated in the definition of the ω domain. This definition must thus specify that a ω consists of either a stem or a bisyllabic suffix together with any adjacent string of monosyllabic suffixes to their right; there are no prefixes in Yidiɲ.

Since a word in Yidiɲ must contain at least two syllables (see Dixon, 1977a, 1977b), the definition of ω may be reformulated by saying that a ω is formed by either a stem or a suffix that can be a well-formed independent word, together with any adjacent string of monosyllabic suffixes to the right.

The situation is strikingly similar to that of Italian prefixes: they also form separate ωs when they can stand as independent words. Our contention – that a definition of the ω domain may mention phonological notions only if more general rules defining ω exclusively on the basis of morpho-syntactic notions yield ill-formed elements – is thus valid for Yidiɲ as well.[12]

4.2.2.4.   ω domain (iib)

In sections 4.1.3 and 4.2.1.3 above, definitions have been given for ω in languages in which its domain is equal to Q and for languages in which its domain is equal to the stem plus all adjacent affixes, respectively. The ω domain in languages such as those just analyzed in sections 4.2.2.1-4.2.2.3 is defined in (87) below, where Q is the terminal element of a syntactic tree.

(87)   ω *domain (iib)*
    I. The domain of ω consists of
        a. a stem;
        b. any element identified by specific phonological and/or morphological criteria.
    II. Any unattached elements within Q form part of the adjacent ω closest to the stem; if no such ω exists, they form a ω on their own.

This rule defines ω for all three languages analyzed in the preceding sections. As was the case for the ω definition in (37), this definition too must provide a way for nonstems (such as clitics, conjunctions, and complementizers) to be dominated by a ω, as required by the Strict Layer Hypothesis. Such a provision is expressed by the last part of (87II) above. The only variable point of (87) is that (87Ib) allows for two possibilities: *i*) that only morphological criteria are present, and *ii*) that both morphological and phonological criteria are present. Hungarian is an example of the first type of language, in that the only additional information that must be taken into account is whether an affix is a prefix or a suffix, which is a morphological notion. Italian and Yidiɲ, on the other hand, are examples of the second type of language. In Italian, as in Hungarian, the morphological notion needed is the distinction between prefix and suffix; the additional phonological notion that is needed in Italian is the well-formedness condition on the structure of a possible word. Similarly, in Yidiɲ the additional phonological notion needed is that of the well-formedness of the word, while the only additional morphological notion that must be referred to is that of affix.

4.2.3.   ω domain and diacritic features

This section will be devoted to the phonological word whose construction rules must take into account specific diacritic features. That is, the general types of morphological and phonological notions required for the construction of ω in the previous sections are not sufficient in certain languages to distinguish the elements that form independent ωs from those that are grouped into a ω with specific adjacent elements. The language we will analyze to exemplify this type of phonological word is Dutch.

4.2.3.1. Dutch

On the basis of the observation that the phonological word in Dutch is the domain of syllabification (see Booij, 1983), it has been proposed that each member of a compound word forms a separate ω domain (see also Chapter 3 for a discussion of syllabification in Dutch). The minimal pair in (88), suggested to us by Geert Booij, illustrates this point since the sequence of consonants *dsp* is syllabified in different ways in the two examples. That is, we find the division $d - sp$ in the first example, but the division $ds - p$ in the second example. The latter division shows that resyllabification does not occur across the two members of a compound, since if it did we would expect the division $d - sp$ in this case too, in accordance with the Maximal Onset Principle (see, among others, Pulgram, 1970; Vennemann, 1972; Kahn, 1976; Vogel, 1977).

(88) a. $[[\text{lood}]_\sigma]_\omega$ $[[\text{spet}]_\sigma]_\omega$ 'drop of lead'
      b. $[[\text{loods}]_\sigma]_\omega$ $[[\text{pet}]_\sigma]_\omega$ 'sea captain's cap'

The fact that no resyllabification takes place in (88b) shows that the two stems of a compound are separate domains of syllabification, thus two separate ωs.

Another ω-dependent phenomenon that Booij (1985) analyzes is Coordination Reduction in Dutch, a rule that deletes the second part of a complex word under identity with the second part of the following complex word in a coordinate structure, as exemplified in (89) and (90).

(89) a. landbouw en tuinbouw
      b. land en tuinbouw
          'agri(culture) and horticulture'

(90) a. een elfjarige, twaalfjarige jongen
      b. een elf, twaalfjarige jongen
          'an eleven-, twelve-year-old boy'

Phonetic identity is not, however, a sufficient condition for deletion. This may be seen from the ungrammaticality of the examples below, where (91) illustrates the impossibility of deleting part of an underived word, and (92) and (93) the impossibility of deleting certain derivational morphemes.

(91)   a.   vogels and vlegels
      b.   *vo and vlegels
         'birds and impertinent persons'

(92)   a.   blauwig en rodig
      b.   *blauw en rodig
         'bluish and reddish'

(93)   a.   absurditeit en banaliteit
      b.   *absurd en banaliteit
         'absurdity and banality'

As Booij points out, an additional condition on the application of the rule is required, namely that the deletable element must be a constituent of prosodic structure: a phonological word. That is, *-gels, -ig*, and *-iteit* are not independent ωs and cannot be deleted; *-bouw* and *-jarige*, on the other hand, do constitute independent ωs and thus can be deleted.

It should be observed, furthermore, that the elements that may be deleted by Coordination Reduction in Dutch cannot be expressed as a constituent of the morpho-syntactic hierarchy, since there is no one-to-one relation between ω as defined above and any morpho-syntactic constituent. This is exemplified in (94).

(94)   a.   Ik heb twee en drietenigen in de dierentuin gezien.
         (< tweetenigen en drietenigen)
         'I have seen both two- and three-toed (ones) in the zoo.'
      b. $[[[\text{drie}]_A [\text{teen}]_N \text{ig}]_A \text{e}]_N \text{n}]_{Npl}$
         'three-toed (ones)'

While phonologically *tenigen* is a constituent, specifically a ω, morphologically it is not a constituent, since [ten+ig] does not exist as an adjective in Dutch, and since neither [tenig+e] nor its hypothetical plural [tenige+n] exists as a noun. Thus, while Coordination Reduction can be formulated in a simple way by making reference to the prosodic hierarchy, a definition of its domain in terms of morphological constituents would require an *ad hoc* and complicated specification of morphemes and boundaries.

Further evidence for the phonological word as a constituent in Dutch is the phenomenon of *r*-Coloring (RC) (see van der Hulst, in preparation). RC accounts for the modification in quality of the long vowels *ee* ([e:]), *oo* ([o:]), and *eu* ([ø:]) when they are followed by *r* – only, however, if the vowel and *r* are in the same ω, as seen in the examples in (95), given by Sassen (1979). The vowels that undergo RC are underlined.

(95) a. sm<u>e</u>ris   'copper'
      b. v<u>o</u>re   'furrow'
      c. ple<u>u</u>ris   'pleurisy'

As van der Hulst points out, the fact that words like those in (95) consist of a single foot is not relevant for the application of RC since the rule also applies across feet, as seen in the examples (96), where the syllables *ro, ra, ri* are foot initial.

(96) a. <u>e</u>rósie   'erosion'
      b. d<u>o</u>ráde   'dorado'
      c. ple<u>u</u>rítis   'pleurisy'

RC also provides further evidence for treating the two members of a compound as separate ωs since it does not operate when the vowel is at the end of the first member of the compound and the *r* is at the beginning of the second member, as illustrated below.

(97) a. meereis   (*m<u>ee</u>reis)   'travel together'
      b. poring   (*p<u>o</u>ring)   'ring of a "po" '
      c. keuring   (*ke<u>u</u>ring)   'ring of a "keu" '

Thus far, we have seen that each stem in a compound belongs to a separate ω, but a question remains as to the status of affixes. Here too, syllabification can be used to show that prefixes form independent phonological words (see van der Hulst, 1984). Consider the items in (98).

(98) a. [ont]$_\sigma$ [erven]   *[on]$_\sigma$ [terven]   'to disinherit'
      b. [ver]$_\sigma$ [edelen]   *[ve]$_\sigma$ [redelen]   'to ennoble'
          [her]$_\sigma$ [eiken]   *[he]$_\sigma$ [reiken]   'to adjust'

The first column contains the appropriate syllabification of the three derived words, while the second column contains the incorrect syllable division we would obtain if the words in question were a single ω. The example in (99) shows, in addition, that each prefix forms an independent ω by itself.

(99) [ver]$_\sigma$ [ont]$_\sigma$ [schuldigen]   *[ve]$_\sigma$ [ront]$_\sigma$ [schuldigen] 'to excuse'

That is, the syllable structure of the two prefixes is not what we would expect if they formed a single ω. Instead, the division between the two morphemes is maintained, despite the fact that it violates the Maximal Onset Principle.

As far as suffixes are concerned, the situation is more complicated, in that some suffixes behave as if they were independent phonological words, while others do not. This, too, can be seen on the basis of syllabification, as illustrated below (see Booij, 1983).

(100) a.   [rood]$_\sigma$ [ach]$_\sigma$ [tig]$_\sigma$ (< rood+achtig)   'red-like'
      b.   [roo]$_\sigma$ [dig]$_\sigma$ (< rood+ig)   'reddish'

That the syllabifications in (100) are correct may be seen from the fact that the final *d* of *rood* in the first example is devoiced, as are all syllable-final oral obstruents in Dutch. The final *d* of *rood* in the second example remains voiced, however, since it is the onset rather than the coda of a syllable. These examples indicate that while the suffix *-achtig* is a separate ω, the suffix *-ig* is not. Since there is no morphological or phonological criterion on the basis of which the *-achtig* type of suffix can be distinguished from the *-ig* type of suffix,[13] it has been proposed by van der Hulst (1984:66ff) that the phonologically independent suffixes be marked with a diacritic feature which he calls [+W]. This feature indicates that the elements bearing it form the kernel of a phonological word in the same way that prefixes or stems do. The suffixes that are not so marked, on the other hand, form part of the preceding phonological word.

A reasonable question to ask at this point is why in some languages the status of certain elements as independent ωs is derivable from specific characteristics of the language, while in others it must be marked diacritically. One possibility is that the cases in which diacritic features must be used reflect changes that have taken place in the historical development of the language. That is, diacritics must be used since the synchronic situation in fact contains certain forms that reflect patterns found in earlier stages of the language.

4.2.3.2. ω domain (iic)

On the basis of the domain of ω in Dutch just discussed, we may now proceed to define the last type of phonological word (see van der Hulst, 1984, for a similar proposal).

(101) ω domain (iic)
   I.   The domain of ω consists of
        a. a stem;
        b. any element identified by specific phonological and/or morphological criteria;
        c. any element marked with the diacritic [+W].
   II.   Any unattached elements within Q form part of the adjacent ω closest to the stem; if no such ω exists, they form a ω on their own.

It should be noted that the only difference between this ω domain and that in (87) is the addition of Ic; everything else is unchanged. Although we have not found examples of a language in which the definition of ω requires both phonological criteria of the type mentioned in Ib and diacritic features, we have not excluded this option from (101) since there is no *a priori* reason that such languages should not exist. This is, of course, an empirical question, one which hopefully will be resolved in future research.

4.3. General ω construction and conclusions

In this chapter, we have discussed the domain of the phonological word in various languages, and have proposed that several options are available for the definition of ω. As we mentioned above, the phonological word is the level of the prosodic hierarchy that represents the mapping between the morphological and the phonological components of the grammar. The morphological notions that are used to define ω, however, are not the same in all languages. There are languages, such as Greek and Classical Latin, that refer to the maximal projection of the morphological tree, that is, the terminal element of the syntactic tree (which we call Q). Other languages, such as Sanskrit and Hungarian, must refer to the stem and to either prefixes or suffixes or both. Still other languages, such as Dutch, must also make reference to diacritic features. In addition, we have shown that in some languages, such as Italian and Yidiɲ, certain phonological notions based on well-formedness conditions of the specific languages must also be taken into account.

All of the possibilities we have seen are expressed in the general definition of the ω domain given in (102).

(102) ω *domain*
- A. The domain of ω is Q.
- or
- B. I The domain of ω consists of
  - a. a stem;
  - b. any element identified by specific phonological and/or morphological criteria;
  - c. any element marked with the diacritic [+W].
  - II. Any unattached elements within Q form part of the adjacent ω closest to the stem; if no such ω exists, they form a ω on their own.

Despite the number of options allowed by (102), it should be noted that there are certain types of potential ω domains that are excluded. That is,

(102) predicts that no language exists in which ω is larger than the terminal element of a syntactic tree. We are thus left with two possibilities, that is, that ω is either equal to or smaller than the terminal element of a syntactic tree. The definition in (102) predicts, furthermore, that there will never be more than one ω in a single stem. In addition the prediction is made that in a language in which ω includes both members of a compound, there will be no affixes or sequences of affixes that form independent ωs. The first part of (102BII) predicts that any unattached element between two already formed ωs, only one of which contains a stem, will always be grouped with the ω that includes the stem.

We have also demonstrated that the definition of ω regroups morphological elements in such a way that the end result is not necessarily coextensive with any morpho-syntactic constituent, thus confirming the non-isomorphic character of the prosodic and the morpho-syntactic hierarchies.

Once we have the basic definition of the phonological word that maps morphological structure onto phonological structure, it is possible to proceed to the actual construction of the phonological word constituent. Given the general principles that govern the prosodic hierarchy, ω must be n-ary branching and it must exhaustively dominate one or more constituents of the level immediately below it, the foot, and no other type of constituent. While ω is the constituent that varies most from language to language, the language-specific differences are encoded in the mapping rules that define ω, not in the ω construction rule itself, which may be formulated in a maximally simple and general way, as in (103).

(103) ω *construction*
Join into an n-ary branching ω all Σ included within a string delimited by the definition of the domain of ω.

Which foot within a phonological word is labeled strong depends on a parameter that must be set for each language. Given recent work on stress systems, however (among others, Hyman, 1977; Vergnaud and Halle 1978; Hayes, 1981), this parameter will allow only a very restricted number of possibilities. That is, in the unmarked case the strong foot will consistently be either the leftmost one or the rightmost one in the phonological word tree of a given language.

Finally, it should be recalled that the syllable and the foot have the same domain as the phonological word. Since our rule of ω construction groups together Σ, it is clear that the phonological structure below the ω level must be present at the point at which ωs are created, whether the σ and Σ are already present in the lexicon or are constructed for the first time within the strings delimited by the definition of ω. That is, the syllables of a phonological word must, in any case, have been joined into n-ary branching feet by the general rule of Prosodic Constituent Construction.

NOTES

1. There are some morphologically predictable counterexamples to this generalization. For example, compound verbs whose second member is *făcio* maintain the stress on the penultimate syllable even in cases in which this is in conflict with the stress rule (see Cupaiuolo, 1959).
2. Vowel Harmony in Turkish is not without exceptions (see, among others, Lees, 1961; Lewis, 1967; Clements and Sezer, 1982).
3. Phonetically, the sequence [l] + [j] is realized as [j] (see, among others, Vago, 1980).
4. It should be noted that in other varieties of Italian, there are some underived words in which [s] contrasts with [z] and thus two separate underlying segments are required. In the varieties of northern Italian under examination here, however, such a contrast does not exist and the occurrence of [z] is predictable. There are several apparent exceptions, such as *preside* 'chairman' and *presidente* 'president'. These words are pronounced, at least in some varieties of northern Italian, with an intervocalic [s], although they are no longer analyzable as *pre+side* and *pre+sidente*. The fact that many similar words, such as *residente* 'resident', are pronounced with intervocalic [z] in the same position, however, shows that the small group of words mentioned above is more a historical than a regular phenomenon to be handled by a synchronic rule.
5. The fact that the stem *suddivis-* (from *suddivid-*) is itself derived is not relevant to the present discussion and thus not discussed in the text.
6. Although the first stem of a compound in Italian is usually not suffixed, in those cases in which there is a suffix, it forms a ω with the preceding stem (e.g. $[nav+i]_\omega$ $[traghett+o]_\omega$ 'ferry boats').
7. Although such complex words are not usually found in Italian dictionaries, it is not difficult to imagine situations in which they might be used.
8. Most consonant-final words used in the Italian language today are of foreign origin. The type of readjustment that these words undergo to avoid the word-final consonant varies depending on the region, on the type of consonant and on the structure of the last syllable (see Lepschy and Lepschy, 1977). For instance, in Tuscan varieties, a final *l* is usually deleted, as in (i).

(i) a.   alcool   →   [alko]
    b.   würstel   →   [vuste]

If a word ends in *m*, however, an *e* is added to avoid a closed final syllable as in (ii).

(ii)   reclam   →   [rekláme]

Sometimes the final consonant before the *e* is lengthened, as in (iii).

(iii)   tram   →   [tram:e]

We will not go into the details of these phenomena, since they would bring us too far from the topic of the present section.

9. There are a few consonant-final monosyllabic prefixes that behave differently, such as *sub* and *ex*, when they are found in relatively new words. They do not typically conform to the phonological rules of Italian and will have to be marked with a special feature.

10. The term DTF (Designated Terminal Element) is used in this book, following Liberman and Prince (1977), to refer to the terminal element of a prosodic tree that is dominated uniquely by strong nodes.

11. The sequences *nr* and *nl* are found in several proper names, for example, *Enrico* and *Manlio*. We do not believe these examples to be sufficient counterevidence to our well-formedness condition. Instead, these names will have to be indicated as being idiosyncratically not subject to TNA.

12. A formal account of Penultimate Lengthening and other rules of Yidiɲ phonology has been proposed by Hayes (1982) within the framework of metrical theory. We will not discuss Hayes's very interesting analysis, since we are concerned here with the domain within which Penultimate Lengthening applies, a question that is not addressed by Hayes. Instead, Hayes only reports that the 'word', which is not better specified, is the domain of foot construction. It is interesting to observe here, however, that the substitution for Hayes's 'word' of the ω constituent just defined yields the correct results.

13. A list of the two types of Dutch suffixes may be found in Booij (1977:72-73).

Chapter 5

The Clitic Group

5.0. Introduction

It has long been recognized that the problematic behavior of clitics is due to their hybrid nature: 'Enclisis is neither true suffixation nor juxtaposition of independent elements. It has the external characteristics of the former, . . . the inner feeling of the latter' (Sapir, 1930:71). Said in other words, a clitic is 'a form which resembles a word, but which cannot stand on its own as a normal utterance . . . ' (Crystal, 1980:64). The latter definition corresponds to the original meaning of the term 'clitic', from the Greek κλίνω 'to lean'. Though there are both syntactic and phonological ways in which clitics 'lean', we will concentrate here on their phonological dependence.

The most common approach in phonology is to consider clitics either as belonging to the phonological word, in which case they are considered similar to affixes, or as belonging to the phonological phrase, in which case they are considered similar to independent words (see, among others, Booij, 1983; Zwicky, 1984). In section 5.1 it will be shown that clitics cannot always be forced into either one of these categories, because their phonological behavior is often different from that of both affixes and independent words. That is, there are phonological phenomena that are characteristic only of the group consisting of a word plus clitic(s). On the basis of these observations, we conclude that there must be a constituent of prosodic structure that has exactly this extension. Section 5.2 contains a proposal as to the domain of this constituent, the clitic group (C), first proposed as a constituent of the prosodic hierarchy by Hayes (to appear). In addition, a specific case is examined which demonstrates the nonisomorphism between this particular level of prosodic structure and any constituent of the morpho-syntactic hierarchy. In section 5.3 we will offer further evidence for the clitic group as the domain of application of a number of phonological rules in different languages.

5.1. The mixed behavior of sequences of word plus clitics

It has been observed by Zwicky (1977) that some combinations of a word plus a clitic show '#' behavior, that is, they behave as if they were two independent words; others show '+' behavior, that is, they behave as if they were just one word. Still others show the first type of behavior with regard to some phonological rules and the second type of behavior with regard to other phonological rules. In other words, some clitics behave like independent words, some like affixes, and some either like words or affixes depending on the specific rule.

As an example of the first type of clitic, Zwicky mentions clitic pronouns in Spanish. Evidence of their word external status is the fact that they do not affect in any way the location of stress on their host. Thus *dándo* 'giving' maintains its initial stress also when it is followed by two clitics, as in *dándonoslos* 'giving them to us', despite the fact that the new string has main stress on the fourth-to-last syllable, a result that does not represent a possible word stress pattern in Spanish.

A second example of a language in which clitics are word external is Turkish. As Zwicky points out, Turkish words have primary stress on the last syllable. When a clitic is present at the end of the word, however, the position of stress on the host word remains unchanged (e.g. *aliyorlársa* 'if they had caught it', where *sa* is a clitic personal ending). In both Spanish and Turkish, the fact that clitics do not have any influence on the word stress of their host is, according to Zwicky, sufficient reason to consider clitics as word-external elements.

Classical Latin, on the other hand, is adduced as an example of a language in which clitics are considered to be word internal. Evidence for this claim, according to Zwicky, is a stress rule triggered by cliticization (Clitic Group Stress). That is, when an enclitic is attached to a word, the primary stress is shifted from its original position in the word to the syllable that immediately precedes the clitic. Consider the following examples:

(1)   a.   vírum   'the man (acc.)'
      b.   virúmque   'and the man (acc.)'

(2)   a.   vídēs   'you see'
      b.   vidḗsne?   'do you see?'

(3)   a.   cum vóbis   'with you (pl.)'
      b.   vobíscum   'with you (pl.)'

A similar type of reasoning has been used by other linguists to evaluate the status of clitics in a variety of languages (see, among others, Booij, 1983; Nespor, 1984, 1986). For example, another language in which clitics show word-internal behavior in the sense defined by Zwicky is Demotic Greek, where a new stress pattern is produced by Stress Readjustment when an enclitic is attached to a word with primary stress on the antepenultimate syllable (see Warburton, 1970; Nespor, 1986). This pattern is exemplified in (4).[1]

(4)   a.   *ο άνθρωπος*   [o ánθropos]
          'the person'
     b.   *ο άνθρωπός μας*   [o ánθropòs mas]
          'our person'

More recently, Zwicky (1984) has argued that the term clitic be used in a more precise and restricted way, and to this end, he proposed a series of tests, both syntactic and phonological, in order to distinguish clitics from independent words. As far as the phonological tests are concerned, the assumption is made that the difference between combinations of a clitic and a word and combinations of two words essentially represents the difference between a phonological word and a phcnological phrase. Thus, an element is a clitic if, together with a word, it is affected by internal sandhi rules; it is an independent word if, together with a word, it is affected by external sandhi rules. By the same token, if an element is counted as part of a phonological word for the purposes of stress assignment, it must be considered a clitic and not a word.

Zwicky (1984) thus attempts to restrict the use of the term clitic, something not done in Zwicky (1977). Nevertheless, the spirit of Zwicky's two articles is essentially the same as far as the phonological component is concerned. That is, either an element is word internal, i.e. a clitic, or word external, i.e. an independent word. It is precisely this approach that will be questioned throughout the present chapter.

Let us first consider Italian 'clitic' pronouns, true clitics as far as any syntactic test is concerned. According to any phonological test proposed by Zwicky, however, these elements would be qualified as independent words. They not only behave differently from the way clitics usually behave phonologically, but they also show, at least in one case, behavior typical of independent words.

First, the segmental rule of Intervocalic *s*-Voicing, which has the phonological word as its domain of application (see Chapter 4), does not apply across the juncture between a clitic and a word, as exemplified in (5) below.

(5)   a.   lo [s]aluto   (*[z])
          '(I) greet him'
     b.   essendo[s]i salutati   (*[z])
          'having greeted each other'

The rule does not apply between two clitics either, as shown in (6), where the clitics are underlined.

(6) a. ci [s]i va insieme   (*[z])

'we'll go there together'

b. andandoci[s]i insieme   (*[z])

'(our) going there together'

These facts show, according to Zwicky's test, that each clitic is an independent word.

A second rule, Raddoppiamento Sintattico, whose domain of application is larger than the word (see Chapter 6), also applies to a clitic. This rule, described above in section 2.3, is exemplified in (7), where the initial consonant of the enclitic pronoun is lengthened in both examples.

(7) a. da[m:]i   (< da mi)
         'give me'
     b. amó[l:]o   (< amó lo)
         '(he/she) loved him'   (archaic)

These facts are a positive indication, according to the clitichood test under examination, that Italian clitic pronouns are independent phonological words. The same conclusion may be reached on the basis of the behavior of the clitics with respect to stress. That is, they do not exhibit word internal behavior, as can be seen from the fact that sequences of word + clitic(s) violate the well-formedness condition of Italian that requires primary stress to fall on one of the last three syllables of a word.[2] This may be seen in (8), where the stress falls on the fifth- and even on the sixth-to-last syllable (see also Lepschy and Lepschy, 1977).

(8)
                σ́ σ σ σσ
     a. ind i caglielo   'indicate it to him'

                σ σ́ σ σσ
     b. d isegn amelo   'draw it for me'

                σ σ́ σ σ σ
     c. port at ecelo   'bring it to us'

                σ́ σ σ σ σ σ
     d. car icamecelo   'put it on it for me'

It should be noted, however, that considering these clitics independent elements, the same as any other words in the language, is not without problems, since clitics exhibit a well-known type of phonological dependency that other elements do not share. Specifically, they may never occur alone; that is, they may not be the only element of an utterance. Furthermore, they may not receive contrastive stress.

Thus, the hybrid nature of clitics is observed in Italian, too. While the elements in question are clearly clitics from a syntactic point of view, phonologically they behave neither as part of a word, nor as totally independent words. What we propose in relation to this problem is: *a*) whether or not an element is a clitic should be decided on the basis of nonphonological criteria, and *b*) a specific place must be created in phonological theory for clitics.

As far as the first part of the proposal is concerned, it is in agreement with the general conception of phonology as an interpretative component of the grammar, and in particular, with the theory of prosodic phonology proposed in the present study, since prosodic constituents are constructed by rules that map a nonphonological structure onto a phonological one. Despite the fact that it has often been observed that clitics share a number of nonphonological characteristics that are not typical of any other element, there is as yet no unambiguous way of defining clitics. For the time being, we will therefore just assume that a language may have some elements that are marked [+CL] in the lexicon (see Klavans, 1982).

As far as the second part of the proposal is concerned, that is, that phonological theory should have a specific place for clitics, it is our contention that this place is the prosodic constituent clitic group, which we will define and motivate in the next section.

5.2. The construction of the clitic group

The fact that specific combinations of a word and clitic(s) form the domain of application of certain phonological rules that do not apply in any other context in a given language provides motivation for a constituent of the prosodic hierarchy that groups exactly these elements. Hayes (to appear) proposes such a constituent, the clitic group (*C*), and motivates it on the basis of two segmental rules of English and certain constraints on the metrical patterns of several poems. According to Hayes (to appear), the clitic group directly dominates one or more phonological words and is dominated by the next category in the prosodic hierarchy, the phonological phrase (see Chapter 6). The hybrid nature of clitics, that is, their intermediate position between affixes and words, is thus reflected in the phonological component of the grammar, where a distinct constituent is posited between the phonological word – which groups affixes with stems – and the phonological phrase – which groups words with other words.

According to Hayes, the clitic group is the domain of application of *v*-Deletion and *s, z*-Palatalization in English. The first rule is a rule that has the effect of deleting a word-final [v] before a [−syllabic] segment in certain lexical items. The rule applies, however, only if the two words involved belong to the same clitic group. The application and nonapplication of the rule are exemplified in (9) and (10), respectively (from Hayes, to appear).

(9)   [Please]$_C$ [leave me]$_C$ [alone]$_C$
                         ↓
                         ∅

(10)   [Please]$_C$ [leave]$_C$ [Maureen]$_C$ [alone]$_C$
                         ↓
                         *∅

It should be noted, however, that *v*-Deletion is not the same type of rule as the others we are examining in this book, since it only applies in fast speech, according to Hayes. The second rule, which has the effect of palatalizing [s,z] before [š,ž], on the other hand, does conform to the nature of the other rules examined here. Hayes argues that the domain of *s, z*-Palatalization is the clitic group on the grounds that it applies in normal colloquial speech only between a clitic and its host, as can be seen by its application in (11) but not in (12a). Hayes points out further that the rule may also apply in 'fast or sloppy speech' in other contexts, as seen in (12b). We are not concerned, however, with the latter phenomenon.

(11)   [is Sheila]$_C$ [coming?]$_C$
                ↓
               [ž]

(12)   a.   [Laura's]$_C$ [shadow]$_C$ (normal rate of speech)
                       ↓
                      *[ž]

          b.   [Laura's]$_C$ [shadow]$_C$ (fast or sloppy speech)
                       ↓
                      [ž]

On the basis of the domain of application of these phenomena, Hayes gives rules to construct the *C* constituent. Basically, these rules say that a clitic group joins a clitic together with the lexical category which is its host. Whether a clitic chooses as host the word on its left or the word on its right is determined by syntactic structure. That is, a clitic is grouped with the constituent in which it shares more category memberships with the host. In the remainder of this section, we will take a somewhat different position with regard to the choice of the host. We will argue that in clitic group formation, as in the formation of other prosodic constituents, the division into constituents provided by the syntax is not always adequate. Specifically, with relation to the clitic group, syntactic constituency cannot always predict the direction in which the clitic finds its phonological host. This is thus an additional argument in favor of the nonisomorphism of the syntactic and prosodic hierarchies.

Let us consider again Stress Readjustment in Greek. As was mentioned in section 5.1 above, this rule applies to sequences of word + clitic, that is, within a clitic group in Hayes's terminology. Only enclitics are relevant to this discussion, since stress in Greek is not sensitive to the number of syllables to its left. Enclitics in Greek include personal pronouns (both direct and indirect objects) and possessives. These three types of enclitics are exemplified in (13) below.

(13) a. γράψε το   [γrápse to]
          'write it'
      b. γράψε μου   [γrápse mu]
          'write to me'
      c. το σπίτι μου   [to spíti mu]
          'my house'

The sequence word + enclitic must respect a well-formedness condition (WFC) on the location of stress. That is, there may not be more than two unstressed syllables to the right of the primary stress of a word. When the WFC is violated, as in (14) and (15) below, a rule applies to add a stress on the second syllable to the right of the originally stressed one (see note 1).

(14) a. διάβασε   [ðyávase]
          'read'
      b. διάβασè το   [ðyávasèto]
          'read it'
      c. διάβασè μου το   [ðyávasèmuto]
          'read it to me'

(15) a. γράψε   [γrápse]
          'write'
      b. γράψε το   [γrápseto]
          'write it'
      c. γράψε μού το   [γrápsemùto]
          'write it to me'

Furthermore, as was said in Chapter 4, Greek words must also respect a WFC that requires primary stress to fall on one of the last three syllables. The fact that this condition is the same as the one just seen for word + clitic sequences has been used to argue that clitics are word internal in Greek (see, among others, Nespor, 1986). It should be noted, contrary to this position, that the stress readjustment rules that apply word internally are different from those just illustrated in (14) and (15). To see this, let us consider again the stress pattern of compound words.

It was argued in Chapter 4 that a compound word forms just one phonological word in Greek. As in any other phonological word, the primary stress in compounds is on one of the last three syllables. We have seen, moreover, that the stress in a compound does not necessarily fall on any of the syllables that bear primary stress before compounding. Two examples are repated for convenience in (16) and (17).

(16)   [kuklóspito]   < [kúkla] [spíti]
         'doll's house' < doll   house

(17)   [nixtopúli]   < [níxta] [pulí]
         'night owl'   < night   bird

There are substantial differences between the stress readjustment that takes place in a clitic group and that which takes place in compounds. First of all, in the clitic group the original word stress never shifts to any other syllable, as it does in the case of compounds. Secondly, in the clitic group a new stress is added in a regular way only in those cases where there is a violation of the WFC. This is not the case with compounds. In (16), for example, the creation of a new stress pattern is not caused by a violation of the WFC. On the basis of these facts we can conclude that the sequence word + clitic is the domain of application of Stress Readjustment, a rule typical only of this sequence. Thus, the constituent clitic group is also motivated on the basis of Greek.

We can now proceed to examine the exact constituency of C in Greek. Of the enclitic elements exemplified in (13) above, the third type, the possessive, is the only one that is internal to a noun phrase. In particular, it follows the head noun if there are no nominal complements, but it may also precede the noun if there is an adjectival complement. Since adjectives precede the head noun in Greek, when an adjective is present, the possessive may be located between the adjective and the noun, as shown in (18).

(18)   a.   το ωραίο μου σπίτι   [to oréo mu spíti]
              'my nice house'

b. *ο δειλός σου φίλος*   [o ðilós su fílos]
   'your shy friend'

According to Hayes's clitic group formation rule, the clitics in (18) should be incorporated rightward into a clitic group together with the head noun, since it is with this noun that the possessives share the larger number of category memberships. The clitics, however, are incorporated leftward, as may be seen from the fact that they cause Stress Readjustment when more than two unstressed syllables, including the clitics, occur to the right of the main stress of the adjective. Examples of this context for readjustment are given in (19).

(19)   a.   [*το πρόσφατὸ μου*]$_C$ [*ἁρθρο*]$_C$
        [to prósfatò mu]$_C$ [árθro]$_C$
        'my recent article'
   b.   [*τα υποσυνείδητὰ μου*]$_C$ [*αισθήματα*]$_C$
        [ta iposiníðità mu]$_C$ [esθímata]$_C$
        'my unconscious feelings'
   c.   [*ο πιό*]$_C$ [*φιλόδοξὸς μου*]$_C$ [*φίλος*]$_C$
        [o pio]$_C$ [filóðoksòs mu]$_C$ [fílos]$_C$
        'my most ambitious friend'

If the possessives formed a clitic group with the following noun, Stress Readjustment would not take place (see also Malikouti–Drachman and Drachman, 1981). This is illustrated on the basis of the following minimal pair:

(20)   a.   [*ο δάσκαλὸς μου*]$_C$ [*το είπε*]$_C$
        [o ðáskalòs mu]$_C$ [to ípe]$_C$
        'My teacher said it.'
   b.   [*ο δάσκαλος*]$_C$ [*μου το είπε*]$_C$
        [o ðáskalos]$_C$ [mu to ípe]$_C$
        'The teacher said it to me.'

In (20a), the application of Stress Readjustment signals that *μου* is an enclitic with *δάσκαλος* as a host. The absence of readjustment in (20b), on the other hand, shows that *μου* is a proclitic with *είπε* as a host. Together these facts show that the constituency of the clitic group cannot be decided on purely syntactic grounds. There are some clitic elements that may only be enclitic, such as the Greek possessive. Others may only be proclitic, such as the articles in both Classical and Modern Greek. For these clitics the direction of phonological attachment is a property of the clitic itself. It is exactly in these cases that the clitic group formation rule does not necessarily respect syntactic constituency, but builds a new, nonisomorphic structure. This analysis is in agreement with the observation made by Klavans (1982, 1985) that a clitic can attach syntactically in one direction and phonologically in the opposite direction. The *C* construction rules proposed by Hayes are then appropriate only in the case of elements that can be both proclitic and enclitic, such as the personal pronouns in Greek exemplified in (21) below, or the similar personal pronouns in Romance languages.

(21) a. ο Αλέξανδρος μου το έδωσε
          [o aléksanðros mu to éðose]
          'Alexandros gave it to me.'
      b. Δώσε μού το αμέσως
          [ðóse mù to amésos]
          'Give it to me immediately.'

The first example in (21) shows that the two clitics μου and το are proclitics attached to the verb έδωσε. If they were enclitics, they would trigger Stress Readjustment on the preceding noun, but this does not occur. The application of Stress Readjustment in (21b), on the other hand, provides evidence that μου and το in this case are enclitics. Since the two personal pronoun clitics form a syntactic constituent with the verb, the clitic group formation rule proposed by Hayes correctly accounts for phonological cliticization in this case.

To sum up, we have demonstrated that phonological dependency on an element to the left or right must be an inherent property of certain clitics. We will call such clitics directional clitics (DCL), as opposed to clitics *tout court* (CL), which may, in principle, find their host either to the right or to the left. The definition of the domain that we propose is thus the one given in (22I); the second part of (22) contains the rule that establishes the internal structure of the *C* tree. This rule entails a maximally simple operation in accordance with the general principles that govern the prosodic hierarchy.

(22) *Clitic Group Formation*
      I. *C domain*
          The domain of *C* consists of a ω containing an independent (i.e. nonclitic) word plus any adjacent ωs containing
          a. a DCL, or
          b. a CL such that there is no possible host with which it shares more category memberships.

II. *C construction*

Join into an n-ary branching *C* all ωs included in a string
delimited by the definition of the domain of *C*.

It should be noted that the *b* part of the *C* domain definition, essentially
Hayes's proposal to join a CL leftward or rightward with the adjacent
element with which it shares more category memberships, produces
constituents whose domain does not have a counterpart in syntactic structure. The first part of the rule, however, regroups the terminal elements
of the syntactic tree in such a way that the resulting constituent need not
be isomorphic to any constituent of syntactic structure, as has been shown
to be the case for Greek possessives.

As far as the relative prominence of the clitic group is concerned, there
are two options. The first option is, as far as we know, the one chosen
by most languages of the world, that is, that the strong node is the phonological word that contains the nonclitic element. Whether a daughter of *C*
is strong or weak thus depends on its intrinsic nature rather than on its
position within *C*. This type of relative prominence within *C* is exemplified
on the basis of Italian and Greek in (23) and (24) below, respectively.

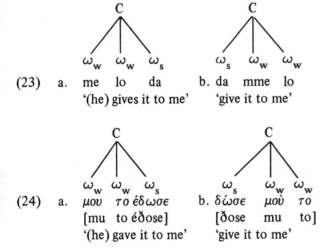

(23) a. me lo da   b. da mme lo
         '(he) gives it to me'   'give it to me'

(24) a. μου το έδωσε   b. δώσε μου το
         [mu to éðose]   [ðose mu to]
         '(he) gave it to me'   'give it to me'

It should be noted in the example in (24b) that the Stress Readjustment
rule of Greek described above does not alter the location of the primary
stress, which remains on the nonclitic element of *C*.

The first option for the assignment of relative prominence to the clitic
group is also exemplified by Latin, where, despite the application of
Clitic Group Stress described in section 5.1 above, the strong member of
C is the nonclitic element. It should be noted that although this rule may
have the effect of changing the position of word-internal stress, it is in-

dependent of the Main Stress Rule. That is, as was shown in section 4.1.2, Clitic Group Stress, unlike the Main Stress Rule, is not sensitive to syllable weight.

The second option is that the strong element of *C* is determined positionally, that is, that the ω which is labeled *strong* is defined on the basis of its position within *C*. This is the case in French, for example, where it is the rightmost ω of *C* which is labeled *s*, regardless of the particular item contained in this ω, as exemplified in (25).

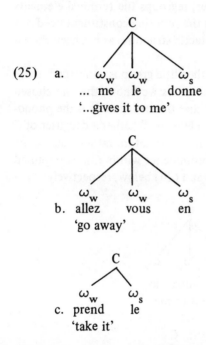

(25)　a.　ω_w　ω_w　ω_s
　　　　... me　le　donne
　　　　'...gives it to me'

　　　b.　ω_w　ω_w　ω_s
　　　　allez　vous　en
　　　　'go away'

　　　c.　ω_w　ω_s
　　　　prend　le
　　　　'take it'

In (25a), the *s* node is the nonclitic element of *C* since it occupies the rightmost ω. In (25b) and (25c), however, the strong node is a clitic since in both cases the rightmost ω node dominates a clitic element.

Other examples of clitic groups in which the strong element is determined positionally can be found in several Italian dialects. We will give examples from only two such dialects here. First, in the dialect of Viozene, in the northern region of Piedmont, the strong element of *C* is assigned to the rightmost phonological word by Clitic Group Stress, as it is in French. The relative prominence of this *C* is illustrated in (26) (see Rohlfs, 1949), where the underlined portion of the form is a clitic.

(26)　a.　vindirú　　　'sell it'
　　　b.　servirsí　　　'to help oneself'
　　　c.　portamarú　　'let's take it'

In several dialects spoken in the southern region of Calabria, on the other hand, the strong element of a clitic group is always the penultimate syllable, independently of whether this syllable is a clitic or is the last syllable of the nonclitic member of *C*. That is, there is a Stress Readjustment rule that places primary stress on the penultimate syllable of C and consequently has the effect of removing the primary stress from its original position in the host word. Examples are given in (27), where the clitic element(s) are again underlined (from Rohlfs, 1949).

(27) a. accidətíllə   '(you, pl.) kill him'
      b. mangiálu   '(you, sg.) eat it'
      c. mangiarisíndi   '(to) eat some of it for oneself'
          'eat + for oneself of it'

In (27a) and (27b), the strong element of the clitic group is the phonological word that contains the verb, while in (27c), it is the first clitic element after the verb. What all of these examples have in common is that the penultimate syllable of *C* is strong.

Having established the domain and the prominence relation of the clitic group on the basis of a number of phonological phenomena in different languages, we will proceed in the next section to offer further evidence in confirmation of this level of the prosodic hierarchy.

5.3. Additional evidence for the clitic group

In this section, we will show that the clitic group is the domain of application of several rules other than the rules of English for which it was originally proposed and the Stress Readjustment rule of Greek discussed in the previous section. It will be shown now that *C* is also the domain of application of four other rules of Greek. As was the case for Palatalization in English, the Greek rules not only apply within *C*, but also within another prosodic domain, the phonological word. In the two domains, however, the rules exhibit different degrees of application.

The first rule is Nasal Deletion (ND), a rule that optionally applies within the phonological word (see (16), Chapter 4). ND is not limited to the ω domain, but also applies across two ωs that belong to the same clitic group. In the latter domain, however, its application is obligatory.[3] Examples of the application of ND across ωs in *C* are given in (28a-c), while the examples in (28d-e) show that the nasal is indeed present when the segmental conditions on the second word are not met.

(28) a. το θέλω   [to θélo]$_C$ ($<$ [ton])
          '(I) want him'

b. τη θέα   [ti θéa]$_C$ (< [tin])
   'the view (acc.)'

c. τη βλέπω   [ti vlépo]$_C$ (< [tin])
   '(I) see her'

d. τον αγαπώ   [ton aγapó]$_C$ (* [to])
   '(I) love him'

e. την αλήθεια   [tin alíθia]$_C$ (* [ti])
   'the truth (acc.)'

That this rule has the clitic group as its domain of application, and not a larger domain, can be seen from the fact that it never applies between two ωs that belong to two different clitic groups, as illustrated in (29) below.

(29)   a. πριν φάω   [prin]$_C$ [fáo]$_C$ (* [pri fáo])
          'before (I) eat'

       b. έχουν δεί   [éxun]$_C$ [ði]$_C$ (* [éxu ði])
          '(they) have seen'

       c. όταν φύγω   [ótan]$_C$ [fíγo]$_C$ (* [óta fíγo])
          'when (I) leave'

Given these facts, we may now formalize the obligatory Nasal Deletion rules as a ω juncture rule on the *C* domain as in (30).

(30)   *Nasal Deletion* (obligatory)

$$[+\text{nas}] \rightarrow \emptyset \ / \ [\ldots[\ldots \underline{\hspace{1cm}}]_\omega \ [\ \begin{bmatrix} +\text{cont} \\ +\text{cons} \end{bmatrix} \ \ldots]_\omega \ldots]_C$$

Two other rules of Greek phonology that have *C* as their domain of application are the two assimilation rules already discussed in Chapter 4: Nasal Assimilation (NA) and Stop Voicing (SV). Their degree of application in the two categories is the reverse of what we have seen in the case of ND; that is, NA and SV are obligatory word internally and optional across words within a clitic group. Their application within *C* is exemplified in (31), while the examples in (32) show that the two rules do not apply across ωs that belong to different clitic groups. Since NA and SV apply in the same context, each form exemplifies both phenomena.

(31)   a. δεν πειράξει   [ðembirázi]   (< [ðen][pirázi])
          '(it) doesn't matter'

       b. τον πλέκω   [tombléko]   (< [ton][pléko])
          '(I) knit it'

(32) a. ὅταν πᾷς   [ótan pas]   (* [ótam bas])
          'when (you) go'
      b. ἔχουν πάει   [éxun pái]   (* [éxum bai])
          '(they) have gone'
      c. πρίν πλύνω   [prin plíno]   (* [prim blíno])
          'before (I) wash'

On the basis of these facts, we may now formalize optional NA and optional SV in the following way as ω juncture rules on the C domain.

(33) *Nasal Assimilation* (optional)

$$[+\text{nas}] \rightarrow \begin{bmatrix} \alpha\text{cor} \\ \beta\text{ant} \end{bmatrix} / [...[... \underline{\quad}]_\omega [\begin{bmatrix} -\text{cont} \\ \alpha\text{cor} \\ \beta\text{ant} \end{bmatrix} ...]_\omega ...]_C$$

(34) *Stop Voicing* (optional)

$$[-\text{cont}] \rightarrow [+\text{vce}] / [...[...[+\text{nas}]]_\omega [\underline{\quad}...]_\omega ...]_C$$

The fourth rule of Greek that applies within C is a rule that deletes non-high vowels, described by Kaisse (1977) under the name of Mirror Image Deletion. This is a ω juncture rule in C that applies whenever there are two adjacent phonological words within a clitic group, the first of which ends in a vowel and the second of which begins with a vowel. One of the two adjacent vowels is deleted. Specifically, the weaker of the two vowels is deleted according to a sonority scale where, of the nonhigh vowels, i.e. those that may be deleted, *e* is the weakest, *a* is intermediate, and *o* is the strongest. The rule is exemplified in (35).

(35) a. τα ἔχω   [ta éxo]   →   [tá xo]
          '(I) have them'
      b. με ὀδιγεί   [me oðiyí] →   [m óðiyí]
          '(he) leads me'

These examples show that it is not the position of the vowel that is relevant for the deletion rule, but its quality, which makes this particular *C*-internal rule different from the other vowel deletion rules of Greek (see Kaisse, 1977).

In addition, it can be seen in (35a) that although the vowel that is deleted was originally stressed, the stress itself is not deleted. Rather, it is moved to the vowel of the clitic, which was originally unstressed. Mirror Image Deletion is thus most likely another example of an interaction between the prosodic and the grid subsystems of the phonology, since it must refer to prosodic theory for the specification of its domain of application, while the specification of the stress readjustment itself seems to be most appropriately handled within grid theory.

Another language in which it can be shown that the clitic group is the domain of application of a phonological rule is Classical Latin. Enclitic elements in Classical Latin include -*que* 'and', -*ne* (interrogative marker), -*cum* 'with'. When one of these enclitics is added to the end of a word, Stress Readjustment takes place. As was shown in section 4.1.2 above, the stress rule operating in the clitic group is different from the stress rule operating in the word (see also Wanner, 1980). That is, within polysyllabic words, the Main Stress Rule assigns primary stress either to the penultimate or to the antepenultimate syllable. The penultimate syllable is stressed either if the word is bisyllabic (as in (36)) or, in the case of words with more than two syllables, if the penultimate syllable is heavy, that is, if it contains either a long vowel or a final consonant (as in (37)). Primary stress falls on the antepenultimate syllable otherwise (as in (38)).

(36)   a.   rósa   'rose'
       b.   úrbe   'city'

(37)   a.   amícus   'friend'
       b.   moléstus   'molest'

(38)   a.   fácĭlis   'easy'
       b.   pópŭlus   'people'

In contrast with the Main Stress Rule, Clitic Group Stress is not sensitive to syllable quantity. Instead, it blindly assigns primary stress to the syllable that immediately precedes the clitic, as exemplified in (39) and (40).

(39)   a.   rósă   'the rose (nom.)'
       b.   rosắque   'and the rose (nom.)'
       c.   *rósaque

(40)   a.   fémina   'the woman (nom.)'
       b.   feminắque   'and the woman (nom.)'
       c.   *féminaque

That we are dealing with two different stress rules may be illustrated even more clearly on the basis of the existence of minimal pairs, as seen in section 4.1.2 above. Consider the forms in (41) and (42). The first example

in each pair consists of a word + clitic combination, and is thus stressed
on the penultimate syllable. The second example, on the other hand,
contains the same sequences that have become lexicalized as a single word,
with a different, nonanalyzable meaning and thus follows the Main Word
Stress rule. In these cases, in fact, stress falls on the antepenultimate syllable, since the penultimate is light (see, among others, Niedermann, 1953;
Cupaiuolo, 1959).

(41)   a.   itáque   'and so'
       b.   itắque   'therefore'

(42)   a.   undíque   'and from there'
       b.   úndĭque   'everywhere'

The conclusion that must be drawn from these examples is that the combination word + clitic is a constituent which is the domain of application
of a stress rule typical of this constituent only. We may thus describe
this rule by saying that in a clitic group which branches, that is, one that
contains at least two phonological words, the main stress falls on the last
syllable of the first constituent.

It should be observed that the clitic group in Latin, too, is not necessarily isomorphic with any syntactic constituent. The interrogative enclitic
-*ne*, for example, may be used to question a single word, as in (43), as well
as a phrase containing more than one word, as in (44) (see Zanoni, 1948).

(43)   Solusne venisti? Non solus.
       'Did you come alone? Not alone.'

(44)   Abiitne solus pater? Solus.
       'Did father leave alone? Alone.'

While in (43) the question is focused on *solus* 'alone', in (44) the answer
to the question, *solus*, indicates that it is the whole phrase *abiit solus*
that is questioned and not the verb *abiit* alone. In this last case, there is
no syntactic constituent including only the verb and the enclitic -*ne*, while
this is exactly the domain of the prosodic constituent C.

Another language we will consider in which the clitic group is the
domain of application of a phonological rule is Turkish, where Vowel
Harmony spreads over a word plus its clitics (see, among others, Lewis,
1967). As was mentioned in Chapter 4, the harmonizing features in
Turkish are [back] for all vowels and [round] for high vowels, and the
rule works from left to right. That is, the first vowel of a word determines
the value for [back] and [round] of all the following vowels. The examples

in (45) and (46) which contain the interrogative clitic *mu* show that *C* is the domain of harmony.

(45)   a.   doğrú   'true'
       b.   doğrú mu   'true?'

(46)   a.   bügün   'today'
       b.   bügün mü   'today?'

An additional rule that is best formulated in terms of the clitic group is *t*-Deletion in Catalan, a rule which deletes the [t] of the cluster [nt] in word-final position, but is blocked if a clitic follows. This phenomenon is exemplified in (45) (from Zwicky, 1977), where the first example shows that the [t] is deleted *C*-finally and the second example shows that [t] must be retained when followed by another ω within *C*.

(47)   a.   [fèn]$_C$ [əsɔ́]$_C$ (< [fènt])   'doing this'
       b.   [[purtánt]$_\omega$ [u]$_\omega$]$_C$ (* [purtán u])   'bringing it'

These facts are easily accounted for by describing the domain of application of [t] deletion as ___]$_C$, that it, as a clitic group limit rule.

5.4. Conclusions

It has been shown in this chapter that what has often been observed to be a peculiar phonological behavior of a group of host-plus-clitic(s) is best accounted for within prosodic theory by establishing a constituent with exactly this extension. In this way we avoid the problems that arise in attempting to force clitics either into a single phonological word with their host or into a separate independent entity. That is, the mixed phonological behavior of clitics, a fact which distinguishes them from both affixes and words, is accounted for in terms of rules that have the clitic group as their domain of application.

Within the general view of prosodic theory developed in this book, each prosodic category incorporates specific information from the different components of the grammar. The clitic group is the first level of the prosodic hierarchy that represents the mapping between the syntactic and the phonological components, in that certain clitics, which may in principle either encliticize or procliticize, choose their direction of attachment according to the syntactic constituent structure.

This is not to say that *C* is always isomorphic to a constituent of syntactic structure. On the basis of data from Demotic Greek, in fact, it was shown that the phonological constituent clitic group is not necessarily isomorphic to any of the constituents of the morpho-syntactic hierarchy. The noncorrespondence between the domain of the clitic group and a constituent of the syntax is not peculiar to Greek. For example, *C*s that are not isomorphic to syntactic constituents also arise in any language that has sentential or phrasal clitics, that is, elements that may cliticize to a nonterminal node of the syntactic tree. Such a case was seen in relation to the interrogative enclitic *-ne* in Latin, which is joined into a prosodic constituent with one single word as its host, not the entire sentence or phrase with which it is associated. The result is thus a prosodic constituent that consists of one word plus the enclitic *-ne*, which in many cases does not have a corresponding constituent in syntactic structure.

NOTES

1. In marking the stress of these groups, we follow Setatos (1974:55), who says that in the unmarked pronunciation the primary stress remains in the original position; the new stress is a secondary stress. He also observes that in emphatic pronunciations the reverse pattern may be found. We do not consider such cases here, however, since emphatic speech is beyond the scope of the present study.
2. There is a restricted group of verbs with antepenultimate stress in the first person singular form of the present indicative. The third person plural of the present indicative and subjunctive forms of these verbs are exceptions to the generalization that primary stress must be on one of the last three syllables of a word, since they are stressed on the fourth-to-last syllable (cf. *teléfono* '(I) call'; *teléfonano* '(they) call'; *teléfonino* '(that they) call'). The existence of these verbal forms does not invalidate the well-formedness condition on stress, since they represent a small and predictable set of cases.
3. Although we will not go into a discussion here of the recently proposed grid treatment of sandhi rules, according to which the 'degree of connectedness' between adjacent elements determines the relative probability of a rule's application (see Selkirk, 1984b), it should be noted that Nasal Deletion poses a problem for such an analysis. Since the 'degree of connectedness' between a host and an adjacent clitic is lower than that between the segments within a single word, we would expect a rule that applies in both of these environments to apply more frequently within a word than between a word and a clitic. What we find in the case of ND, however, is the opposite: the rule applies obligatorily in the larger domain (*C*) and only optionally in the smaller domain (ω).

Chapter 6

The Phonological Phrase

6.0. Introduction

The constituent in the phonological hierarchy above the clitic group is the phonological phrase. That is, the phonological phrase (ϕ) is the constituent that groups together one or more clitic groups. As was mentioned in section 2.4, a phonological unit is motivated on the grounds that it is necessary in the formulation of phonological rules. In this chapter, we will motivate the constituent ϕ on the basis of the role it plays in defining the domain of application of Raddoppiamento Sintattico (RS), a phonological rule found in central and southern varieties of Italian.

While the original hypothesis about the domain of ϕ is made on the basis of one phonological rule of Italian (discussed in sections 6.1 and 6.2), the validity of the phonological phrase will be demonstrated on the basis of other phonological phenomena of Italian which apply in the same domain as RS (section 6.3). The syntactic notions that we propose to be relevant for the construction of ϕ are general enough that they can account for ϕ construction in all languages whose base rules are of the type defined by $\overline{X}$ theory. It will be shown in section 6.4 that the phonological phrase correctly defines the domain of application of phonological rules in a number of other languages. Section 6.5 contains some concluding remarks.

6.1. The domain of application of Raddoppiamento Sintattico and the phonological phrase

Since the domain of application of RS is not constant throughout all varieties of Italian, we have restricted our analysis here to the type of Italian spoken by educated speakers from Florence for two reasons. First of all, this is the variety that is most commonly described in grammars of Italian. The second, and more important, reason is that we have collected a large corpus of data for this particular variety.[1]

In Chapter 2, it was shown that RS is a rule that applies across words and that its domain of application cannot be identified with any syntactic constituent since syntactic constituents of the same type may behave differently with respect to the rule.

RS applies in a sequence of two ωs (ω_1 and ω_2) to lengthen the initial consonant of ω_2 if a) the consonant to be lengthened is followed by a sonorant, specifically a vowel or other nonnasal sonorant, and b) if ω_1 ends in a vowel which is the DTE (i.e. main stressed syllable) of ω. It should be noted that such vowels are short. This contrasts with the situation in nonfinal syllables, where a short stressed vowel in an open syllable would be ill formed in Italian. It was shown in Chapter 4, in fact, that a ω-internal rule applies to lengthen such vowels, thus yielding well-formed words. It can be seen that the same constraint on the occurrence of short vowels actually holds in some cases in sequences longer than a word as well. That is, a short stressed vowel in a ω-final open syllable is not considered well formed in certain positions within a sentence. It is in these cases that RS applies, and the rule may thus be seen as a resyllabification rule that has the effect of producing a well-formed structure by lengthening the initial consonant of the following word. The geminate consonant formed by RS cannot occupy only the initial position of ω_2, but must be divided over two syllables. It thus serves both as the coda of the final syllable of ω_1, creating in this way a closed syllable, and the onset of the initial syllable of ω_2. A closed syllable at the end of ω_1 yields a well-formed structure, since the stressed vowel is now in a position in which it is supposed to be short (see Vogel, 1977, for an analysis along these lines).

What remains to be specified for a complete analysis of RS is the larger domain in which it applies. That is, while RS only applies in the local segmental environment just described, it does not apply between just any two words that meet the required specifications. This may be seen in (1) and (2), where in both sentences there is a sequence of identical words, i.e. *perché Carlo*, and yet RS applies in the first but not in the second example.

(1) *Perché Carlo* non é venuto? → Perché [k:]arlo ...
    'Why didn't Carlo come?'

(2) Che c'é un *perché Carlo* lo sa. → ... perché [k]arlo ...
    'Carlo knows that there is a reason.'

While RS is a much studied phenomenon in Italian phonology (see, among others, Camilli, 1941,1965; Fiorelli, 1958; Leone, 1962; Pratelli, 1970), none of the traditional analyses has been able to predict exactly where RS applies. Napoli and Nespor (1979) have proposed to account for the domain of application of RS in syntactic terms within the generative framework. In this account, a proposal was made only for the definition of the contexts in which RS is allowed; no explicit predictions were made about when RS would actually apply. In the present chapter, we will address the latter issue, that is, the contexts in which RS actually applies (see also Nespor and Vogel, 1982). Examples of the contexts in which RS applies (marked with '‿') and of the contexts in which RS does not apply (marked with '//') are given in (3) and (4), respectively.

(3)   a.   Avrá‿trovato il pescecane.
           'He must have found the shark.'
     b.   La gabbia é‿giá‿caduta.
           'The cage has already fallen.'
     c.   È appena passato con tre‿cani.
           'He has just passed by with three dogs.'
     d.   Era venuto con tre‿piccoli cobra.
           'He came with three small cobras.'
     e.   Il tuo pappagallo é‿piú‿loquace del mio.
           'Your parrot is more talkative than mine.'

(4)   a.   Devi comprare delle mappe di cittá//molto vecchie.
           'You must buy some very old city maps.'
     b.   La gabbia era dipinta di giá//completamente.
           'The cage was already completely painted.'
     c.   Ne aveva soltanto tre//di bassotti.
           'He had only three dachshunds.'
     d.   L'entrata allo zoo costa di piú//per i turisti che per i locali.
           'The entrance to the zoo is more expensive for tourists than for locals.'
     e.   Guardó//piú attentamente e vide che era un pitone.
           'He looked more carefully and saw it was a python.'

It can be seen in (3a) that RS applies between an auxiliary and a verb, and in (3b) that it applies between an auxiliary and a preverbal adverb, and between a preverbal adverb and a verb. In (3c) and (3d), examples of RS are given between a quantifier and a noun, and between a quantifier and a prenominal adjective, respectively. Finally, (3e) shows that RS applies both between a copula and the comparative particle *piú*, and between *piú* and an adjective. The examples in (4), on the other hand, show contexts in which RS is blocked, that is, between an NP and an AP (in (4a)), between two adverbs (in (4b)), between a quantifier and a PP (in (4c)), between an adverb and a PP (in (4d)), and between a verb and a comparative adverb (in (4e)).

From such data it can be seen that RS applies to the left of the head of a phrase, within its maximal projection, but not to its right. This context is similar to that proposed by Selkirk (1978b) for English, on the basis of which she proposes a phonological phrase that joins all the specifiers of a head together with the head. The data in (3), however, show that the notion which is relevant for the context of application of RS is not that of specifier. It appears, instead, that RS applies to the left of a phrasal head, no matter what is found there. Often it is a specifier, but it can also be a phrasal complement, as in (3a), where RS takes place between an adjectival complement and its nominal head. The mapping rules that define the domain of ϕ (see (5) below) are based, as we mentioned above, on the assumption that the domain of ϕ is equal to the domain of RS. We propose, furthermore, that the fact that the environment for RS is the left rather than the right side of the head is not a language specific property of Italian, but instead is due to the fact that the left side of the head is the nonrecursive side of a phrase in Italian. We can generalize this observation and predict that in languages whose recursive side is to the left of the head, the phonological phrase will extend to its right. That is, if there are phonological rules at this prosodic level, they will apply between the head of a phrase and what follows.

The principles we propose for the definition of ϕ are given in (5), where the actual construction of the tree (5II) follows from the general principles of prosodic theory.

(5)   *Phonological Phrase Formation*
   I.   *ϕ domain*
      The domain of ϕ consists of a C which contains a lexical head (X) and all Cs on its nonrecursive side up to the C that contains another head outside of the maximal projection of X.[2]
   II.   *ϕ construction*
      Join into an n-ary branching ϕ all Cs included in a string delimited by the definition of the domain of ϕ.
   III. *ϕ relative prominence*
      In languages whose syntactic trees are right branching, the rightmost node of ϕ is labeled s; in languages whose syntactic trees are left branching, the leftmost node of ϕ is labeled s. All sister nodes of s are labeled w.

The intended interpretation of (5I) is that in which only V, N, and A are considered lexical heads, although several linguists have given syntactic reasons for considering P a lexical head as well, as was mentioned in Chapter 1. We do not take any position here as to whether or not P should be considered a major category in the syntactic component. Since P does not behave as a head for the purposes of phonology, however, if one considers P a lexical head for syntactic reasons, (5I) would have to be restated as in (5I'):

(5I')   The domain of ϕ consists of a C which contains a lexical head (X) with at least one positive specification according to the categorial feature system, and all Cs on its nonrecursive side up to the C that contains another head outside of the maximal projection of X.

Since P is specified as [−N,−V], the definition of ϕ will not treat it in the same way as N, V, and A, whose specifications are [+N,−V], [−N,+V], and [+N,+V], respectively.

Apart from such syntactic considerations, the point we want to stress here is that P differs from N, V, and A as far as the phonological component is concerned. It should be noted that this claim is not new. In SPE, for example, only N, V, and A are considered lexical categories for the purposes of stress assignment in English. A parallel situation is found in the morphological component: P normally does not serve as the head of a compound (see Scalise, 1984), nor does it normally undergo inflectional and derivational processes as N, V, and A do. Finally, there is evidence from an analysis of agrammatism in aphasics that N, V, and A form a distinct class. That is, they are the only categories which are typically retained in the speech of patients suffering from Broca's aphasia (see, among others, Kean, 1980).

A further point that should be mentioned in relation to (5I) is that it does not mention the elements that are joined into a ϕ with the head of a phrase. That is, as we mentioned above, it is the position and not the category of an element that is relevant. Thus, whatever is on the non-recursive side of X within its maximal projection, even another major category, is joined into the same ϕ. There are languages that have an unmarked position for complements – the recursive side with respect to the head of a phrase – but that also allow a complement to appear, in marked cases, on the nonrecursive side. In such languages the same category will be treated by the phonology as a major category in the first case and as a minor category in the second case. For example, in Romance languages, adjectives that are complements of nouns occur to the right of the noun in the unmarked case; they may also occur in certain cases, however, to its left. What (5I) claims is that in the second case, but not in the first case, adjectives will be joined into a phonological phrase together with the head N. In other words, major syntactic categories count as heads for the purposes of prosody only when they are in the unmarked position. Evidence that the same is true for the syntactic component as well is given by Emonds (1980). To explain the possibility of some extraction transformations in English and the impossibility of others, Emonds gives the 'Generalized Left Branch Condition', according to which 'no syntactic phrase C to the left of the lexical head N, A, V of a larger phrase is analyzable as C' (p. 34). He also states explicitly that this principle is not language specific and thus 'on the nonrecursive side' should replace 'to the left'.

Returning now to the phonological phrase in Italian, we must conclude that since Italian is syntactically right branching, that is, the recursive side with respect to the head is the right side, the strong node of ϕ is the rightmost C. In (6), examples are given of how a sentence is organized into ϕs.

(6)   a. $[[\text{Aveva}]_{C_w} \ [\text{giá}]_{C_w} \ [\text{visto}]_{C_s}]_\phi \ [[\text{molti}]_{C_w} \ [\text{canguri}]_{C_s}]_\phi$

'He had already seen many kangaroos.'

   b. $[[\text{Ho}]_{C_w} \ [\text{sognato}]_{C_s}]_\phi \ [[\text{che}]_{C_w} \ [\text{una}]_{C_w} \ [\text{civetta}]_{C_s}]_\phi$

$[[\text{era}]_{C_w} \ [\text{caduta}]_{C_s}]_\phi$

'I dreamed that an owl had fallen.'

   c. $[[\text{Gli avevo}]_{C_w} \ [\text{detto}]_{C_s}]_\phi \ [[\text{che}]_{C_w} \ [\text{Corinna}]_{C_s}]_\phi$

$[[\text{doveva}]_{C_w} \ [\text{riceverlo}]_{C_s}]_\phi$

'I had told him that Corinna was supposed to receive it.'

The fact that the category ϕ is the domain of application of Raddoppiamento Sintattico can be seen in (7) and (8). These are the sentences seen above in (3) and (4), respectively, but here they also contain indications of the ϕ structure.

(7)   a. $[\text{Avrá trovato}]_\phi \ [\text{il pescecane}]_\phi$
   b. $[\text{La gabbia}]_\phi \ [\text{é giá caduta}]_\phi$
   c. $[\text{É appena passato}]_\phi [\text{con tre cani}]_\phi$
   d. $[\text{Era venuto}]_\phi \ [\text{con tre piccoli cobra}]_\phi$
   e. $[\text{Il tuo pappagallo}]_\phi \ [\text{é piú loquace}]_\phi \ [\text{del mio}]_\phi$

(8)   a. $[\text{Devi comprare}]_\phi \ [\text{delle mappe}]_\phi \ [\text{di cittá}]_\phi \ // \ [\text{molto vecchie}]_\phi$
   b. $[\text{La gabbia}]_\phi \ [\text{erà dipinta}]_\phi [\text{di giá}]_\phi \ // \ [\text{completamente}]_\phi$
   c. $[\text{Ne aveva sóltanto tre}]_\phi \ // [\text{di bassotti}]_\phi$
   d. $[\text{L'entrata}]_\phi \ [\text{allo zoo}]_\phi \ [\text{costa di piú}]_\phi \ // \ [\text{per i turisti}]_\phi$
      $[\text{che per i lócali}]_\phi$
   e. $[\text{Guardó}]_\phi \ // \ [\text{piú attentamente}]_\phi \ [\text{e vide}]_\phi \ [\text{che era un pitone}]_\phi$

We can now proceed to formulate the rule of RS as in (9).

(9)   *Raddoppiamento Sintattico*

$$C \rightarrow [+\text{long}] \ / \ [...[... \ \underset{[+\text{DTE}]}{V} \ ]_\omega \ [\ \underline{\quad\quad} \ \begin{bmatrix} +\text{son} \\ -\text{nas} \end{bmatrix} \ ...]_\omega \ ...]_\phi$$

This formulation shows that RS is a ω juncture rule that applies on the ϕ domain.

It was argued in section 2.3 above that the domain of application of RS cannot be identified with any syntactic constituent, since within the same type of constituent we find examples of both application and non-application of RS. The rules that construct phonological phrases as proposed above divide a string into constituents that are crucially not isomorphic to the constituents of the syntactic hierarchy, as exemplified in (10).

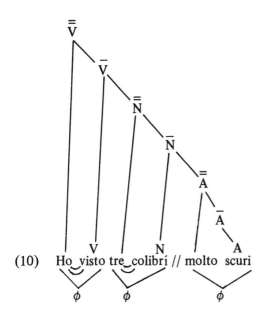

(10)   Ho visto tre colibrí // molto scuri

'I saw three very dark hummingbirds.'

While the sentence is divided into three phonological phrases, RS applies only in the first two, those which contain the proper segmental environment, that is, in *ho*[*v:*]*isto* and *tre*[*k:*]*olibri*. Syntactically, neither of these two strings forms a constituent. In fact, the only node that dominates both *ho* and *visto* is $\overline{\overline{V}}$, the node that also dominates the entire sentence; the first node that dominates both *tre* and *colibri* also dominates *molto scuri*. According to the syntactic division into constituents, there is no way of predicting that RS is blocked between *colibri* and *molto*, a sequence of words that fulfills the local phonological environment for RS. That is, while *colibri* and *molto* are, in fact, part of the same syntactic constituent, $\overline{\overline{N}}$, they are not part of the same phonological phrase. If RS depended on syntactic structure, we would expect the rule to apply between *colibri* and *molto*, as it does in the first part of the same $\overline{\overline{N}}$, that is, between *tre* and *colibrí*. There is a crucial difference between these two cases, however, and that is that *tre* and *colibrí* form a single ϕ, while *colibrí* and *molto* are in separate ϕs.[3] This generalization would be missed by a specification of the domain of application of RS that makes direct reference to syntactic notions, since such a specification would not amount to more than a list of environments. The superiority of prosodic constituents over syntactic constituents is thus demonstrated for RS. We will see below that this is the case for other rules as well.

As was mentioned above, RS can be seen in part as a rule of resyllabification, according to which the final syllable of word$_1$ is closed by part of the geminate consonant that is created at the beginning of word$_2$. The fact that RS applies within the ϕ domain can thus be taken as evidence that the domain of resyllabification in Italian is the phonological phrase, as it is in French (see section 3.1.1 above).

While the ϕ formation rule given in (5) defines constituents within which RS applies obligatorily, all other requirements being satisfied, RS may optionally apply in other domains as well. The next section is dedicated to the definition of these additional domains.

6.2. Restructuring of the phonological phrase

Given that the phonological phrase is the domain within which RS applies obligatorily, and given that RS applies optionally outside of ϕ as well, we propose in this section that the optionality is not in the application of RS but rather in the restructuring of the phonological constituent.

The application of RS between two words that do not belong to the same phonological phrase is illustrated in (11), where the contexts of optional application of RS are marked with '⌣'.

(11)   a.   [I caribú]$_\phi$⌣[nani]$_\phi$ [sono estinti]$_\phi$
              'Dwarf caribous are extinct.'
        b.   [Se prenderá]$_\phi$⌣[qualcosa]$_\phi$ [prenderá]$_\phi$⌣[tordi]$_\phi$
              'If he catches something, he will catch thrushes.'
        c.   [Ho visto]$_\phi$ [qualche fagiano]$_\phi$ [blu]$_\phi$⌣[chiaro]$_\phi$
              'I've seen a few light-blue pheasants.'

As may be seen in these examples, word$_2$ exhaustively forms a ϕ in all the additional contexts of application of RS. It should be noted, furthermore, that this nonbranching ϕ always contains the first complement of the adjacent head. The sentences in (12), on the other hand, show that RS does not apply if the first complement contains a branching ϕ (see Marotta, to appear, for duration measurements that show that the distinction between a branching and a nonbranching first complement of a head is crucial in determining the application of RS).

(12)   a.   [Porterá]$_\phi$ // [due tigri]$_\phi$ [fuori dalla gabbia]$_\phi$
           'He will take two tigers out of the cage.'
       b.   [Vaccineró]$_\phi$ // [tutte le scimmie]$_\phi$ [entro due giorni]$_\phi$
           'I will vaccinate all the monkeys within two days.'
       c.   [Venderá]$_\phi$ // [questo leopardo]$_\phi$ [in dicembre]$_\phi$
           'He will sell this leopard in December.'
       d.   [Hanno]$_\phi$ [dei caribú]$_\phi$ // [molto piccoli]$_\phi$
           'They have some very small caribous.'

We thus propose an optional rule for restructuring ϕ that has the effect of eliminating nonbranching ϕs. Specifically, this rule provides the possibility of restructuring a ϕ that is composed of a single C when certain syntactic conditions are met. These conditions are given in (13) below.

(13) ϕ *restructuring* (optional)
       A nonbranching ϕ which is the first complement of X on its recursive side is joined into the ϕ that contains X.

The effect of ϕ restructuring on the prosodic bracketing is illustrated in (14), where it can be seen that the w/s labels are also reassigned after restructuring.

(14) $[...C_w \ C_s]_\phi \ [C]_\phi \ \rightarrow \ [...C_w \ C_w \ C_s]_\phi$

If restructuring does take place, the examples given in (11) above will have the structures shown in (15) and RS will apply in the new contexts, as indicated by '‿'.

(15)   a.   [I caribú‿nani]$_\phi$ [sono estinti]$_\phi$
       b.   [Se prenderá‿qualcosa]$_\phi$ [prenderá‿tordi]$_\phi$
       c.   [Ho visto]$_\phi$ [qualche fagiano]$_\phi$ [blu‿chiaro]$_\phi$

Since ϕ is the domain of application of RS, when the rule applies between a head and its following nonbranching complement, this is an indication that restructuring has occurred (i.e. between *caribú* and *nani* in (15a), between *prenderá* and *qualcosa* and between *prenderá* and *tordi* in (15b) and between *blu* and *chiaro* in (15c)). If, on the other hand, RS does not occur in these environments, this is an indication that the nonbranching complement retains its status as a separate ϕ. Although we have said that ϕ restructuring is optional, it should be noted that its application is not merely a matter of chance. There are additional nonsyntactic factors that play a role in determining whether or not restructuring applies. For example, restructuring might turn out to be more frequent in fast speech than in slow speech. This would thus reflect the intuition of traditional grammarians, who claimed that in order for RS to apply between two words, they must belong to the same stress group (see Pratelli, 1970). Finally, it should be noted that since the rule of ϕ restructuring makes reference to the non-branching nature of the complement of a given head, and thereby implicitly to its length, this directly reflects the observation that length plays a crucial role in determining the application of RS, as well as other phonological rules (see Napoli and Nespor, 1979).

The nonisomorphism between syntactic and prosodic constituents is even clearer in the case of phonological phrases created by restructuring than it was for the phonological phrases constructed with the mapping rules in (5). That is, (13) crucially distinguishes between two groups of phrasal complements on the basis of their prosodic structure, a type of distinction that is impossible to make in the syntactic component since there are no rewriting rules that make reference to the branchingness versus nonbranchingness of a constituent.

6.3. Other ϕ-level phenomena in Italian

In this section we will demonstrate that the constituent ϕ allows us to account for two more phenomena of Italian: Stress Retraction and Final Lengthening.

Stress Retraction (SR) is a rule of standard northern Italian that has the effect of eliminating sequences of adjacent stressed syllables in certain environments (see Nespor and Vogel, 1979). Though the avoidance of clashes of primary stresses is a fairly general feature of Italian phonology, the particular phenomenon we will describe here is typical of northern varieties. SR applies in a sequence of two phonological words, ω_1 and ω_2, if ω_1 ends in a primary stressed vowel and ω_2 has its primary stress on the first syllable. In such cases the final stress of ω_1 is moved leftward to avoid the clash of primary stresses, as seen in (16).

(16)   a.   metá tórta   →   méta tórta
            'half a cake'
       b.   ònoró Búdda   →   ónoro Búdda
            'he honored Buddha'
       c.   si presèntèrá béne   →   si preséntera béne
            'it will be well presented'
       d.   dèlucìderó tútto   →   dèlucídero tútto
            '(I) will clarify everything'

It should be noted that there is a certain amount of overlap in the environment of SR and RS. In particular, when the final stressed vowel of ω_1

is followed by a stressed syllable at the beginning of ω_2, the conditions are met for both rules (though RS also applies in the absence of primary stress on the first syllable of ω_2). The two rules are not usually in conflict in the overlapping environment, however, since they typically apply in different varieties of Italian: SR in northern varieties and RS in central and southern varieties (see Nespor and Vogel, 1979).[4] Since we assume that stress is a matter of relative prominence and not absolute values, it is not the case that the 'new' primary stress is necessarily as strong as the original stress of ω_1 in isolation; it must only be stronger than the stress of the final (destressed) syllable of ω_1 in the sequence $\omega_1 \, \omega_2$ in connected speech. The syllable to which stress is 'retracted' is the first syllable in the case of bisyllabic words (e.g. (16a)), and the first syllable with secondary stress to the left of the primary stress in the case of words with more than two syllables (e.g. (16b-d)).[5]

SR, like RS, does not apply between just any two words that meet the local phonological conditions just mentioned. Instead, it applies only if ω_1 and ω_2 belong to the same phonological phrase. Examples of the application and nonapplication of RS are given in (17) and (18), respectively.

(17)   a. [Sára státa ammazzata]$_\phi$ la vipera (< sará státa)
          'The adder has probably been killed.'

       b. Ha giá contato [véntitre rágni]$_\phi$ (< ventitré rágni)
          'He has already counted twenty-three spiders.'

       c. [Le cítta nórdiche]$_\phi$ non mi piacciono (< cittá nórdiche)
          'I don't like Nordic cities.'

       d. [Péschera gránchi]$_\phi$almeno, se non aragoste. (< pescherá gránchi)
          'He will fish crabs at least, if not lobsters.'

(18)   a. [Le cittá]$_\phi$ [mólto nordiche]$_\phi$ non mi piacciono. (*cítta)
          'I don't like very Nordic cities.'

       b. [Pescherá]$_\phi$ [quálche granchio]$_\phi$ almeno, se non aragoste.
          (*péschera)
          'He will fish some crab at least, if not lobsters.'

       c. [La veritá]$_\phi$ [sálta fuori]$_\phi$ quasi sempre. (*vérita)
          'The truth almost always comes out.'

The examples in (17a,b) show that SR applies within a ϕ constructed on the basis of the mapping rules given in (5) above. Those in (17c,d) exemplify the application of SR within a restructured ϕ. The examples in (18), on the other hand, illustrate cases in which the words containing the adjacent primary stresses do not belong to the same ϕ; SR does not apply here, despite the presence of the two stresses. We may thus conclude that adjacent stresses do not always constitute a clash, but do so only within a certain domain. This behavior is not unique to Italian, and following our discussion of the second phenomenon of Italian, Final Lengthening (FL), we will show in section 6.4 that ϕ is the domain of rhythmic adjustments in other languages as well.

Although it is often claimed that lengthening takes place at the end of syntactic constituents, it is our contention that it is prosodic phrasing that makes the correct predictions as to where lengthening takes place, as we will demonstrate on the basis of Italian. Syntactic phrasing plays a role in lengthening only in the sense that the phonological phrase is built on the basis of syntactic notions. The reason such a distinction was not made earlier is most likely due to the fact that the two phrasings often do coincide. The example in (19) shows a sentence in which the prosodic and the syntactic phrasings coincide, while the example in (20) shows a sentence in which the ϕ phrasing and the syntactic phrasing differ in a crucial way.

(19) a. Ho mangiato [dei pasticcini ripieni]$_\phi$
      b. Ho mangiato $_{NP}$[dei pasticcini ripieni]$_{NP}$
          'I ate some filled donuts.'

(20) a. Ho mangiato [dei pasticcini]$_\phi$[ripieni]$_\phi$[di cioccolata]$_\phi$
      b. Ho mangiato $_{NP}$[dei pasticcini $_{AP}$[ripieni di cioccolata]$_{AP}$]$_{NP}$
          'I ate some donuts filled with chocolate.'

While the word *pasticcini* 'donuts' in (19) is neither ϕ final nor NP final, the same word in (20) is ϕ final, though it is not NP final, nor is it the end of any other syntactic phrase. It is thus in (20) that prosody and syntax make different predictions. If it is the prosodic constituents that are relevant for FL, then the word *pasticcini* should be longer in (20), where it is ϕ final, than in (19), where it is in the middle of a ϕ. If, on the other hand, the syntactic phrasing is relevant for FL, the word *pasticcini* should be of similar length in the two sentences. Since the word *pasticcini* is indeed longer in (20) than it is in (19), we have evidence that it is the prosodic division and not the syntactic division of a string into constituents that determines the position of FL. This is thus one more argument in favor of the phonological phrase as a distinct constituent level of the prosodic hierarchy. In Chapter 9 it will be shown, in addition, that Italian listeners can distinguish sentences that differ only in their ϕ phrasing, thus demonstrating the relevance of the notion of the phonological phrase for perception as well.

Finally, it should be noted that in cases in which two adjacent primary word stresses are found in separate ϕs and thus are not in the domain for SR, as seen in (18) above, the lengthening at the end of ϕ caused by the application of FL has the effect of introducing enough distance between the two primary word stresses to create well-formed rhythmical alternations of prominence. We will return to this point in Chapter 10 with reference to poetic meter.

6.4. *The phonological phrase in languages other than Italian*

The definition of the ϕ domain proposed in (5) above makes reference to very general syntactic notions, such as those of phrasal head and recursive side of a phrase with respect to the head. They thus make predictions about the ϕ domain not only for Italian but for all configurational languages, that is, languages whose syntactic structure can be represented within the $\overline{X}$ system. In this section, we will show that the phonological phrase proposed above is indeed the domain of application of a number of phonological rules in a variety of languages. As far as the ϕ restructuring rule is concerned, it will be shown that in addition to languages such as Italian where it is optional, there are languages in which restructuring is obligatory (see Hayes, to appear) and still other languages in which it is not an option at all (see also Nespor and Vogel, 1982).

6.4.1. *Other right recursive languages*
The first language we will consider is English. We will show that the phonological phrase is the domain of application of two phonological rules: Iambic Reversal (see Liberman and Prince, 1977) and the Monosyllable Rule (see Selkirk, 1972). This proposal is not new; in fact, ϕ was proposed as the domain of application of these rules by Selkirk (1978b). Since the domain of Selkirk's ϕ is somewhat different from ours, however, we will show that it is, in fact, our definition of ϕ that provides the appropriate description of the environments in which the two rules apply. In particular, we will demonstrate that the phonological phrase in English has the same domain as it has in Italian, as is to be expected given that both languages are right recursive. It will be shown, further, that restructuring of ϕ is optional in English, as in Italian, and that the rules given above are thus the correct rules for defining ϕ.

Iambic Reversal (IR) is a rule that has essentially the same effect as Stress Retraction in Italian, as is shown in (21). (See Liberman and Prince, 1977, for details of this phenomenon.)

(21) a. thirtéen mén   →   thírteen mén
      b. Tènnessé aír   →   Ténnessee aír

Like SR, this rule does not apply in just any sequence of two words that contains a stress clash. Liberman and Prince claim that the rule is optional and that 'the acceptability of a stress clash depends, in part, on the extent to which the interstress interval is prone to be lengthened, independently, by prepausal lengthening' (p.320). According to the analysis presented here, IR is not optional as to its environment, but rather is a ϕ internal rule, as is shown in (22)-(24).

(22) a. More than fífteen cárpenters are working in the house.
          (< fifteén)
      b. The kángaroo's life is full of surprises. (< kangaroó)

(23) a. John pérseveres gládly. (< persevéres)
      b. Given the chance, rabbits réproduce quíckly. (< reprodúce)

(24) a. John persevéres gládly and diligently. (* pérseveres)
      b. Given the chance, rabbits reprodúce véry quickly. (* réproduce)

The sentences in (22) exemplify the application of IR within ϕ as predicted by the definition of ϕ in (5); those in (23) show that IR applies within ϕ restructured according to the rule in (13); and those in (24) show that IR does not apply outside the ϕ domain. The examples in (23) and (24), moreover, offer additional evidence for the observation that the nonbranchingness of the first complement to the right of the head is the appropriate criterion for ϕ restructuring. This is also the crucial difference between the phonological phrase proposed by Selkirk (1978b) and that proposed here, since in Selkirk's proposal the phonological phrase may not extend to include any constituent to the right of the head of a phrase. Since there are, in fact, cases in which this is necessary, the present analysis must be preferred on empirical grounds.

It should be observed that in English, as in Italian, ϕ is also the domain of Final Lengthening. Liberman and Prince's observation that IR does not apply if the interval between the two stresses is lengthened is thus easily accounted for: since lengthening takes place at the end of ϕ, and since both words involved in IR must belong to the same ϕ, it is clear that the one phenomenon excludes the other.

Another rule of English that offers evidence for the ϕ level of prosodic structure is the rule that reduces monosyllabic words that do not belong to any of the lexical categories N, V, or A. As is demonstrated by Selkirk (1978b), this Monosyllable Rule applies only if the monosyllable is labeled weak with respect to another syllable in the same ϕ that is labeled strong. The fact that the rule applies in (25a) but not in (25b), which represent Selkirk's (1978b) examples with our division into constituents, is thus accounted for.

(25) a. [The sluggers]$_\phi$ [boxed]$_\phi$ [in the crowd]$_\phi$ (reduced *in*)
　　　b. [The cops]$_\phi$ [boxed in]$_\phi$ [the crowd]$_\phi$ (unreduced *in*)

In the first example, the preposition *in* is the leftmost node of a ϕ and is thus weak with respect to the strong node dominating *crowd*. Hence, *in* may undergo reduction. In the second example, on the other hand, *in* may not be reduced, since it is the rightmost node of the ϕ containing *boxed in*, and is thus labeled strong with respect to its sister, which is weak.

The second language we will discuss here in relation to the phonological phrase is French, a language in which the restructuring of ϕ is not an available option. That is, ϕ may only include a head X and whatever is on its nonrecursive side until another head outside of the maximal projection of X is reached. The rule we will consider is Liaison, a rule that applies in all styles of speech, but whose contexts of application become larger as the degree of formality increases (see Selkirk, 1972). We will restrict our attention to the colloquial style of speech, since it is only in this style that Liaison applies in a purely phonological environment. As has been shown in Morin and Kaye (1982), the contexts of application of Liaison in elevated styles of speech are partly morphologically determined. In colloquial French, however, the purely phonological Liaison rule applies within the domain of the phonological phrase, as exemplified in (26).

(26) a. Cette famille a [trois beaux‿enfants]$_\phi$
　　　　　'This family has three beautiful children.'
　　　b. Les enfants [sont‿allés]$_\phi$ à l'école.
　　　　　'The children went to school.'

The examples in (27) show that Liaison does not apply between words that belong to two different ϕs, and those in (28) show that it does not apply between the head of a phrase and the first nonbranching complement on the recursive side. The latter set of examples thus demonstrates that the restructuring of ϕ is not a property of French.

(27) a. Jean a [des livres]$_\phi$ // [assez nouveaux]$_\phi$
　　　　　'Jean has some rather new books.'
　　　b. Nos invités [sont arrivés]$_\phi$ // [en retard]$_\phi$
　　　　　'Our guests arrived late.'

(28) a. [Les maisons]$_\phi$ // [italiennes]$_\phi$ coûtent beaucoup.
　　　　　'Italian houses are expensive.'
　　　b. Le garçon [les aidait]$_\phi$ // [activement]$_\phi$
　　　　　'The boy helped them actively.'

It is interesting to observe that in most styles of speech, when Liaison applies, the final consonant of word$_1$ leaves the coda of this syllable and moves to the onset of the initial syllable of word$_2$. Liaison is thus a rule that triggers a process of resyllabification, as is Raddoppiamento Sintattico in Italian, although the details of the resyllabification differ in the two languages.

The ϕ constituency just proposed, without the possibility of restructuring, is not unique to French; it is also the domain of application, for example, of several rules that determine the occurrence of an extra-high tone in Ewe, a Bantu language spoken in Ghana (see Clements, 1978). We will not discuss these rules here, since they represent the same case exemplified by French. We will proceed instead to another type of situation, the case of a right recursive language where the inclusion of the first complement into the same ϕ with the head is obligatory. This situation is found in Chimwi:ni, a Bantu language spoken in the city of Brava in Somalia. This language has been analyzed by Kisseberth and Abasheikh (1974), the source of all the following examples, and its relevance for prosodic theory is discussed by Hayes (to appear). In Chimwi:ni, vowel length is generally contrastive, although there are specific environments in which it is predictable: *a*) word finally, where a vowel is predictably short if the end of the word coincides with the end of a phonological phrase, and long if it does not, *b*) before a heavy syllable within the same phonological phrase, where a vowel is short, and *c*) before a sequence of at least three syllables within the same ϕ, where a vowel is also predictably short. These facts can be accounted for by three shortening rules, Final Shortening, Pre-Length Shortening, and Pre-Antepenult Shortening, which may be formalized in the following way.

(29)　*Final Shortening*
　　　V: → V / [...＿＿＿]$_\phi$

(30)　*Pre-Length Shortening*
　　　V: → V / [...＿＿＿...[C$_o$ $\left\{ \begin{matrix} VC \\ V: \end{matrix} \right\}$]$_\sigma$...]$_\phi$

(31)　*Pre-Antepenult Shortening*
　　　V: → V / [...＿＿＿...$\sigma\sigma\sigma$]$_\phi$

Examples of the application of the three rules are given in (32), (33), and (34), respectively.

(32)　*Final Shortening*
　　a.　[xsoma: chuwo]$_\phi$　'to read a book'
　　b.　[xsoma]$_\phi$　'to read'

(33) *Pre-Length Shortening*
    a. [xkaɬa:ŋa]$_\phi$ 'to fry'
    b. [xkaɬaŋgo:wa]$_\phi$ 'to be fried'

(34) *Pre-Antepenult Shortening*
    a. [ku–reb–eɬ–an–a]$_\phi$ 'to stop for one another'
        ($<$ ku–re:–b–a   'to stop')
    b. [munt^{h}u uyu]$_\phi$ 'this person'
        ($<$ mu:nt^{h}u   'person')
    c. [xfuŋguɬa xalbi]$_\phi$ 'to open one's heart'
        ($<$ xfu:ŋguɬa   'to open')

It can be seen in (32a) that the final vowel of *xsoma* is long, since it is internal to ϕ. The same vowel is short in (32b), however, where it co-incides with the end of a ϕ. In (33), it is shown that while the verbal form *xkaɬa:ŋa* has a long vowel in the second syllable, this vowel becomes short if followed by a heavy syllable, as in (33b). The examples in (34) show the application of Pre-Antepenult Shortening, where it can be seen that the rule must count the syllables of a phonological phrase, independently of its division into lower-level constituents.

Thus far, it has been seen only that the phonological phrase is the domain of application of the first and third rules. As far as the second rule is concerned, it should be noted that on the basis of the examples in (33) this rule could be accounted for equally well in terms of the domain of the word. That the domain of Pre-Length Shortening is ϕ and not the word can be seen in (35), where the rules of Final Shortening and Pre-Length Shortening have both applied.

(35) [pauzize cho:mbo]$_\phi$ [mwa:mba]$_\phi$ 'he ran the vessel onto the rock'
     he ran   vessel   rock

Notice that both words that are in phrase-final position have a final short vowel, as predicted by rule (29). The first word, *pauzize*, on the other hand, should have a long final vowel, since it is phrase internal. This is not what we find, however, a fact which can be accounted for if the domain of rule (30) is ϕ. That is, the final vowel of *pauzize* will be shortened by (30) because it is followed by a heavy syllable within the same phonological phrase. As is pointed out by Hayes (to appear), these examples show that the phonological phrase in Chimwi:ni has undergone restructuring, with the result that the first complement of a head is included in a single ϕ with the head. The example in (35) also shows that the second complement of a head forms a separate ϕ, as can be seen from the presence of the long vowel in *cho:mbo*. If, instead, the three words were grouped into a single ϕ, this vowel would be shortened by the application of rule (31).

While we have seen above that restructuring is optional in Italian and English and forbidden in French, in Chimwi:ni, according to Hayes, it is obligatory. Hayes observes also that the restructuring of ϕ in Chimwi:ni is different from that of Italian and English for yet another reason; that is, the nonbranchingness of the first complement is not a requirement for restructuring in Chimwi:ni. An example of the fact that it is also possible for a branching complement to be joined into the same ϕ as the head is given in (36), where Pre-Antepenult Shortening applies before the branching complement *chuwo ichi* 'this book'.

(36) [somani chuwo ichi]$_\phi$ 'read this book' (< soma:ni)
      read   book   this

Hayes points out, furthermore, that the type of ϕ constituency we have just seen in Chimwi:ni is not peculiar to that language. Also in Kimatuumbi, another Bantu language (see Odden, 1980), the phonological phrase obligatorily includes the first complement on the recursive side, whether branching or not. The conclusion may thus be drawn that while ϕ obligatorily groups together a head and all material on the nonrecursive side, languages vary as to whether their ϕ may be restructured to include a complement on the recursive side as well, and as to whether this complement must be nonbranching (see Hayes, to appear).

6.4.2. Left recursive languages

All the rules we have discussed thus far in order to demonstrate the validity of the ϕ construction principles given in (5) above are found in languages in which the possibility of recursively embedding new material is to the right of the head. In order for (5) to be fully confirmed, however, evidence must be given from left recursive languages as well. The prediction made by (5) is that in such languages ϕ-level phonological rules apply to the right of the head in a domain that is the mirror image of the domain seen in the right recursive languages we have considered in the preceding sections.

Miyara (1981) analyzes a number of phonological rules that apply within the phonological phrase in Japanese, a left recursive language. The domain of the phonological phrase is defined by Miyara as follows:

(37) *Phonological Phrase: Japanese*
      X (Particle) (Quantifier) (Particle)
      where X is any string that does not contain a particle

On the basis of this definition and the examples found in Miyara, it appears that the domain of ϕ is equivalent to that predicted by our rule in (5).[6] That is, (37) may be translated into our terms in the following way: X is a head and forms a ϕ with whatever follows until another head outside of the maximal projection of X is reached.

The phonological phrase in Japanese is, as Miyara shows, the domain of Tone Assignment, several tone-shifting rules, and several segmental rules. Let us consider first the rule of Tone Assignment. In the Tokyo dialect, the surface tone melody of a ϕ constituent is predictable from whether the head is accented or not. That is, the particle has a low tone after an accented word and a high tone after an unaccented word. This is exemplified in (38), where a star above a vowel represents a lexical accent (from Miyara, 1981).

(38) a. $[\overset{*}{i} \lfloor \text{noti kara} \rfloor_\phi$ 'from the life'
          life from
      b. $[\text{sa} \lceil \text{kana kara} \rfloor_\phi$ 'from the fish'
          fish   from

Another ϕ-internal tonal rule, the Star Shift Rule, is found in the Matsue dialect of Japanese. This rule, formalized as in (39), has the effect of shifting the accent of a high vowel to ϕ-final position (from Miyara, 1981).

(39) $\begin{bmatrix} \overset{*}{V} \\ +hi \end{bmatrix} C_0 V \rightarrow \begin{bmatrix} V \\ +hi \end{bmatrix} C_0 \overset{*}{V} \; / \; [\ldots \underline{\quad}]_\phi$

Finally, the rather complex phenomenon of Reduction that occurs in casual speech also takes place exclusively within a phonological phrase, as illustrated in (40) (from Miyara, 1981).

(40) a. $[\text{kore-wa}]_\phi$ $\rightarrow$ koryaa   'this top'
      b. $[\text{ik-re ba}]_\phi$ $\rightarrow$ ik-e-ba $\rightarrow$ ikyaa   'go-if'
      c. $[\text{ker-re-ba}]_\phi$ $\rightarrow$ ker-e-ba $\rightarrow$ kryaa   'kick-if'

Since, according to our labeling convention, the strong node of ϕ in a left-branching language is the leftmost node, the reduction just seen can be taken as an indication of a more widespread pattern, the tendency for reduction phenomena to apply only to the weak nodes of a given tree.

The second left-branching language we will consider is Quechua. While Quechua uses almost exclusively the recursive side of a phrase with respect to the head, several elements (i.e. auxiliaries, copulas, existentials), can be found to the right of the head. It is these elements, and only these, that undergo Word Initial Voicing Assimilation when the last segment of the preceding word is voiced. Examples of the application of this rule, taken from Muysken (1977), are given below, where it can be seen that *ka*, a form of the verb 'to be', undergoes assimilation in (41a) where it is preceded by a voiced segment, but not in (41b) where it is preceded by a voiceless segment.

(41)   a.   [Pedro-mi *ga*-ni]$_\phi$ 'I am Pedro'
       b.   [gana-k *ka*-rka-ni]$_\phi$ 'I used to earn'

The rule does not apply, however, between a verb and a complement even when the segmental context is present, as illustrated in (42) and (43). This is an indication that Quechua does not allow ϕ to be restructured to include elements on the recursive side.

(42)   a.   [papa-da]$_\phi$ [*kara*-ni]$_\phi$ 'I serve potatoes'
       b.   *[papa-da]$_\phi$ [*gara*-ni]$_\phi$
            potatoes   serve

(43)   a.   [sumuk]$_\phi$ [*gushta*-ni]$_\phi$ 'I enjoy myself very well'
       b.   *[sumuk]$_\phi$ [*kushta*-ni]$_\phi$
            nice   enjoy

Another rule mentioned by Muysken that appears to be ϕ internal is the Reduction Rule exemplified in (44). It should be noted that this reduction, too, only affects weak elements since in Quecha, as in other left-branching languages, the strong node of ϕ is the leftmost one.

(44)   a.   [Xwana-mi a-ni]$_\phi$ → [Xwana-m-a-ni]
            'I am Juana'   'I'm Juana'
       b.   [Pedro-chu a-ngi]$_\phi$ → [Pedro-ch-a-ngi]
            'Are you Pedro?   'Are you Pedro?'

These examples provide further confirmation that the constituent ϕ, as defined in (5) above, expresses the domain of application of phonological rules in left recursive languages as it does in right recursive languages, though the construction of ϕ in the two types of languages results in structures that are essentially the mirror images of each other.

6.5.   Conclusions

In this chapter it has been demonstrated that the phonological phrase makes use of more general syntactic notions in its construction than does the clitic group, seen in Chapter 5. Specifically, while it was seen that only a very limited type of syntactic information is needed for C construction (i.e. whether a given clitic shares more category memberships in the syntactic tree with the element to its left or to its right), the rule for ϕ formation makes reference to such general notions as those of syntactic phrase and phrasal head, as well as to the parameter that establishes the direction in which sentences are embedded in a given $\bar{X}$ type language. In languages that embed sentences rightward, the domain of ϕ includes a phrasal head and whatever precedes it within the same phrase; in languages that embed sentences leftward, the domain of ϕ includes the phrasal head and whatever follows it within a phrase. That is, no reference is made to specific constituents that may precede or follow the head of a phrase, but only to general structural relations. The resulting phonological phrase thus provides another example of the nonisomorphism between the syntactic and prosodic hierarchies. That is, since ϕ construction treats phrasal complements differently according to their location with respect to the head, the constituent ϕ is often quite different from any syntactic constituent. Specifically, it was shown that complements are incorporated into a ϕ with the head if they are found on one side of the head, and that they form independent ϕs if they are found on the opposite side.

In addition to the ϕ formation rule just mentioned, a restructuring rule was also proposed for certain languages that has the effect of eliminating a nonbranching ϕ node if it contains the first phrasal complement on the recursive side of the phrase. If this condition is satisfied, restructuring may take place to incorporate a ϕ of the type just described into the same ϕ with the phrasal head. The restructured ϕ constituents are thus another case in favor of two separate hierarchies, in that a crucial distinction is made between the first complement and all other complements in phonology, while no such distinction can be made in syntax. Specifically, it was shown that elements that are sisters, and thus in some sense equal in a syntactic tree, are not treated in a uniform way by the mapping rules that form the prosodic constituent ϕ.

Finally, it should be noted that the restructured ϕ is the first constituent of prosodic structure that reflects the idea that length plays a role in the determination of prosodic categories. That is, since nonbranching complements are generally shorter than branching ones, the relative length of nonbranching *vs.* branching complements appears to be a crucial factor in determining the possibility of restructuring in certain languages. That is, there may be a general tendency to avoid forming particularly short (i.e. nonbranching) phonological phrases. As we will see in the following chapters, length plays an even greater role in larger prosodic categories.

While the phonological phrase was motivated in this chapter on the basis of the fact that it is the domain of application of a variety of rules in several languages, it will be shown in Chapters 9 and 10 that it is also a relevant constituent for other types of phenomena. Specifically, it will be demonstrated that ϕ is crucial for the first level of processing in speech perception and for the treatment of certain regularities in poetic meter.

NOTES

1. The data consist of tape recording and oscilloscopic measurements of over 100 sentences containing the various contexts for RS, spoken by six Florentine speakers of Italian.

2. There are languages in which a node expands to the left of the head of a phrase in some cases and to its right in other cases. Dutch is such a language, as may be seen from the following examples, where the expanded nodes are underlined.

i.   Het <u>nog te lezen</u> boek ligt op tafel.
     'The book that is still to be read is on the table.'
ii. Ik denk dat <u>ik een boek zal lezen</u>.
     'I think I will read a book.'

In (i) an expanded complement stands to the left of the phrasal head *boek* 'book', while in (ii) it stands to the right of the phrasal head *denk* 'think'. The rule in (5) does not make specific predictions for the domain of the phonological phrase in languages such as Dutch. In such cases, ϕ will have to be defined in a somewhat more complex way.

3. A syntactic proposal to account for the domain of application of RS that is not based on constituents, but rather on the more abstract notion of c-command, has been put forth by Kaisse (1985). The starting point of Kaisse's analysis is Napoli and Nespor's (1979) Left Branch Condition. According to Kaisse's proposal, RS applies between word$_1$ and word$_2$ when word$_1$ c-commands word$_2$ and word$_1$ is on a left branch. It should be noted, however, that while this principle correctly predicts the two applications of RS in (10), it fails to predict that RS is blocked between *colibrí* and *molto*. Unfortunately, we cannot go into a more detailed discussion of Kaisse's interesting proposal here, since Kaisse (1985) was not available to us at the time of the writing of the present book.

4. It has been suggested to us by Pier Marco Bertinetto (see also Savoia, 1974-75; Gianelli, 1976) that there may be some varieties of Italian in which both SR and RS occur (see, however, Marotta, to appear). In this case, since the presence of final stress is necessary for the application of RS, SR will have to be ordered after RS has applied.

5. For a discussion of the location of secondary stress in Italian, see Vogel and Scalise (1982).

6. We are assuming here that Japanese is a configurational language (see, among others, Hoji, 1982; Whitman, 1982; Saito and Hoji, 1983). If, on the other hand, Japanese is considered nonconfigurational, as proposed, among others, by Hale (1980) and Farmer (1980), its ϕ domain must be defined in some other way.

Chapter 7

The Intonational Phrase

7.0. Introduction

Now that the phonological phrase has been constructed, we can construct the next unit in the prosodic hierarchy, the intonational phrase (*I*). *I* groups together one or more ϕs on the basis of syntactic information, but as will be seen below, the nature of this information is more general than that needed for the definition of the ϕ domain. This shows clearly how the higher a constituent is in the prosodic hierarchy, the more general the nature of its definition becomes. In addition to the basic syntactic factors that play a role in the formation of intonational phrases, there are also semantic factors related to prominence and performance factors such as rate of speech and style that may affect the number of intonation contours contained in an utterance. Thus, any definition of the *I* domain must allow for this variability. While the relatively large degree of variability in the organization of a string into *I*s distinguishes *I* from the other prosodic constituents, it will be shown in this chapter that there are nevertheless syntactic and semantic constraints on what may constitute an intonational phrase. It will be shown, furthermore, that the strings delimited by the constituent *I* not only account for 'the domain over which an intonational contour is "spread" ' (Selkirk, 1978b:130), but they also represent the domain of application of a number of segmental phonological rules. Finally, it should be noted that while intonation contours are essential in the discussion of the *I* constituent of the phonological hierarchy, we will limit our discussion of these contours to their domains. We will not, therefore, discuss the actual phonetic patterns of the contours.[1]

7.1. Definition of the intonational phrase domain

In this section, we will discuss the basic rule for *I* formation. As will be seen, this rule uniquely partitions a sequence of ϕs into *I*s, and as it stands, does not allow for any variability in *I* structure. The variability that is characteristic of the intonational phrase level in the prosodic hierarchy will be treated in the next section, where it will be proposed that it is the result of a separate type of rule, that is, a restructuring rule.

The formulation of the basic *I* formation rule is based on the notions that the intonational phrase is the domain of an intonation contour and that the ends of intonational phrases coincide with the positions in which pauses may be introduced in a sentence.[2] It will be demonstrated below, however, that the domains established on the basis of intonation contours and the potential for pauses are the same as those needed to account for the application of a number of segmental rules in several languages.

One of the first things that is usually observed in relation to intonation contours is that there are certain types of constructions that seem to form intonation domains on their own. These constructions include parenthetical expressions, nonrestrictive relative clauses, tag questions, vocatives, expletives, and certain moved elements (see, among others, Bing, 1979; Downing, 1970; Ladd, 1980; Selkirk, 1978b, 1984b).[3] Examples of each of these structures are given in (1). Although the examples in (1) are all in English, it is our proposal that the same types of constructions will obligatorily form *I*s in all languages that make use of them.

(1) a. Lions [$_I$as you know]$_I$ are dangerous.
     b. My brother [$_I$who absolutely loves animals]$_I$ just bought himself an exotic tropical bird.
     c. That's Theodore's cat [$_I$isn't it?]$_I$
     d. [$_I$Clarence]$_I$ I'd like you to meet Mr. Smith.
     e. [$_I$Good heavens]$_I$ there's a bear in the back yard.
     f. They are so cute $_I$[those Australian koalas]$_I$.

While the different types of constructions that obligatorily form *I*s in some sense appear to constitute a rather disparate set of items, in another sense they all share a common property. That is, they all represent strings that are in some way external to the root sentence they are associated with. Following Safir's (1985) recent proposal in relation to nonrestrictive relative clauses, it seems that we might be able to account for the set of obligatory *I*-forming constructions on the grounds that they are all elements that, at the level of s-structure, are linearly represented but not structurally attached to the sentence tree.

It should be noted, in addition, that those types of constructions that obligatorily form an *I* do so regardless of where they occur in a sentence, as illustrated in (2).

(2) a. [$_I$As you know]$_I$ Isabelle is an artist.
     b. Isabelle [$_I$as you know]$_I$ is an artist.
     c. Isabelle is [$_I$as you know]$_I$ an artist.
     d. Isabelle is an artist [$_I$as you know]$_I$.

Aside from the specific types of constructions that obligatorily form *I*s, the other syntactic notion that is relevant for *I* formation is the root sentence, as defined by Emonds (1976). Specifically, the boundaries of a root sentence delimit an *I*, while those sentences that are not root sentences do not. This is clearly illustrated by the following pair of sentences given by Downing (1970):

(3)   a.   [$_I$Billy thought his father was a merchant]$_I$ [$_I$and his father was a secret agent]$_I$

      b.   [$_I$Billy thought his father was a merchant and his mother was a secret agent]$_I$

It should be noted that there are also cases in which a root sentence does not form a single *I*, and that is when it is interrupted by one of the types of constructions seen above that must obligatorily form an *I* on its own. Such cases have, in fact, already been seen in (1b), (2b), and (2c). Let us consider the case of the root sentence *Isabelle is an artist*, which in (2b) and (2c) is interrupted by the parenthetical element *as you know*. Since the parenthetical must form an *I* by itself, it is no longer possible for *Isabelle is an artist* to form a single *I*. In such cases, any string that is adjacent to the obligatory *I*, and which would not form an *I* for independent reasons, automatically forms another *I* on its own.[4] Thus, the parts of the sentence *Isabelle is an artist* that precede and follow *as you know* form separate *I*s, as seen below, although they are neither the types of constructions that obligatorily form *I*s nor are they root sentences.

(4)   a.   [$_I$Isabelle]$_I$ [$_I$as you know]$_I$ [$_I$is an artist]$_I$
      b.   [$_I$Isabelle is]$_I$ [$_I$as you know]$_I$ [$_I$an artist]$_I$

On the basis of the different criteria seen above for delimiting *I*s, it is possible to formulate the basic definition of *I* as follows:

(5)   *Intonational Phrase Formation*
      I.   *I domain*
           An *I* domain may consist of
           a. all the ϕs in a string that is not structurally attached to the sentence tree at the level of s-structure, or
           b. any remaining sequence of adjacent ϕs in a root sentence.
      II. *I construction*
           Join into an n-ary branching *I* all ϕs included in a string delimited by the definition of the domain of *I*.

It should be noted that while the *I* domain often corresponds to a syntactic constituent, this is not always the case. As expressed in (5), *I* is isomorphic with any of the constituent types that obligatorily form intonational phrases and with a root sentence if it is not interrupted by an obligatory *I*. When a root sentence does have an intervening obligatory *I*, however, it is often the case that the strings on one or both sides of this *I* are not isomorphic to any constituent in syntax. This was seen in the example in (4b), where *Isabelle is* does not form a syntactic constituent,[5] and it is further illustrated in the examples in (6).

(6)   a.   [$_I$They have]$_I$ [$_I$as you know]$_I$ [$_I$been living together for
            years]$_I$
       b.   [$_I$He will never]$_I$ [$_I$as I said]$_I$ [$_I$accept your proposal]$_I$
       c.   [$_I$Charles wouldn't]$_I$ [$_I$I imagine]$_I$ [$_I$have done such a thing]$_I$
       d.   [$_I$That's the tortoise that]$_I$ [$_I$as you know]$_I$ [$_I$inhabits the
            Galapagos Islands]$_I$

In all of these examples, the parenthetical expression forms an obligatory *I* internal to the root sentence within which it is placed, and the strings on either side of this *I* must thus also form *I*s. The result is that the peripheral *I*s delimit strings that are not necessarily isomorphic to any constituent in syntactic structure. While in right recursive languages such as English, it seems that *I*s that are not isomorphic to a syntactic constituent may appear only to the left of the obligatory *I*, it may be that in other types of languages other possibilities also exist. Thus, as in the case of the other prosodic constituents seen so far, *I* makes use of (morpho-)syntactic notions in its definition, though the resulting structures are not necessarily in a one-to-one relation to any constituent found elsewhere in the grammar.

As far as the relative prominence of the ϕs within an *I* is concerned, the position of the strong node cannot be determined for the category as a whole, as it is in the case of the other prosodic constituents. That is, while for any of the constituents below *I* it was possible to specify the position in which the strong sister node was located, at the *I* level we must allow the strong position to vary. Rather than being determined structurally, the strong node under *I* is determined on the basis of semantic factors such as focus and given *vs.* new information. The information needed for determining which is the strong element may be present in the sentence itself, such as the use of an indefinite article (indicating new information) as opposed to a definite article (indicating old information), as illustrated in (7).

(7) a. [$_I$[Leonard]$_{\phi_w}$ [found]$_{\phi_w}$ [a package]$_{\phi_s}$ [on the doorstep]$_{\phi_w}$]$_I$
     b. [$_I$[Leonard]$_{\phi_w}$ [found]$_{\phi_w}$ [the package]$_{\phi_w}$
         [on the doorstep]$_{\phi_s}$]$_I$

In many cases, however, the assignment of stress within an intonational phrase depends on material found in previous utterances or on shared knowledge of a given situation that is not necessarily present in the linguistic context of the utterance in question. On the basis of these observations, a maximally general rule for the relative prominence relations within *I* can be formulated as follows:

(8) *Intonational Phrase Relative Prominence*
     Within *I*, a node is labeled *s* on the basis of its semantic prominence; all other nodes are labeled *w*.

This rule allows for a certain degree of flexibility in stress placement within *I* which is absent at the other levels of the prosodic hierarchy. For example, any of the ϕs in the sentence *My sister sells fresh fruit at the market on Monday* could potentially be labeled *s*, as shown in (9), depending on which element is the most prominent semantically or represents the focused element of the sentence.

(9) a. [$_I$[My sister]$_{\phi_s}$ [sells]$_{\phi_w}$ [fresh fruit]$_{\phi_w}$ [at the market]$_{\phi_w}$
         [on Monday]$_{\phi_w}$]$_I$

     b. [$_I$[My sister]$_{\phi_w}$ [sells]$_{\phi_s}$ [fresh fruit]$_{\phi_w}$ [at the market]$_{\phi_w}$
         [on Monday]$_{\phi_w}$]$_I$

     c. [$_I$[My sister]$_{\phi_w}$ [sells]$_{\phi_w}$ [fresh fruit]$_{\phi_s}$ [at the market]$_{\phi_w}$
         [on Monday]$_{\phi_w}$]$_I$

     d. [$_I$[My sister]$_{\phi_w}$ [sells]$_{\phi_w}$ [fresh fruit]$_{\phi_w}$ [at the market]$_{\phi_s}$
         [on Monday]$_{\phi_w}$]$_I$

     e. [$_I$[My sister]$_{\phi_w}$ [sells]$_{\phi_w}$ [fresh fruit]$_{\phi_w}$ [at the market]$_{\phi_w}$
         [on Monday]$_{\phi_s}$]$_I$

While (8) is formulated in a maximally general way, and all of the pronunciations in (9) are possible, the assignment of relative prominence within *I* is not totally free; there are certain possibilities that are definitely marked with respect to others. For example, of the patterns seen in (9), the first two represent contrastive patterns and thus seem to be marked with respect to the last one, which is the least marked pattern. A more refined version of the *I*-level Relative Prominence rule will undoubtedly also have to account for such differences in markedness.

It should be noted in relation to the flexibility in the position of the strong element within *I*, furthermore, that the n-ary branching prosodic trees proposed in this book offer several advantages over the binary branching trees proposed in earlier work on prosodic phonology (Selkirk, 1978b, 1980a; Nespor and Vogel, 1982). In phonological theories with binary branching trees, the assignment of relative prominence is generally coupled with the geometry of the tree itself. That is, the position of the stressed element in a binary branching tree is determined by the direction of branching of the tree and by a set of principles that specify *a*) whether in a pair of sister nodes $N_1 N_2$, N_1 or N_2 is strong, and *b*) whether or not this choice depends on the branchingness of the nodes. Such principles greatly reduce the number of possible positions for the strong element in a given string; however, in the case of *I*, this is not a desirable result, since there are instances in which the *s* falls on a node that could not be so labeled by any of the generally accepted relative prominence labeling conventions. Consider the abstract sequences of five ϕs grouped into left and right branching *I*s in (10a) and (10b), respectively.

(10)   a.   b.

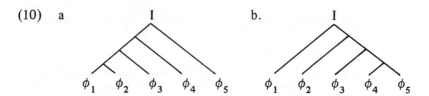

In a left branching tree, the usual labeling conventions can either place *s* on ϕ_1 (i.e., given $N_1 N_2$, N_1 is *s*) or on ϕ_2 (i.e., given $N_1 N_2$, N_1 is *s* iff it branches). In a right branching tree, the labeling conventions will place *s* either on ϕ_5 (i.e., given $N_1 N_2$, N_2 is *s*) or on ϕ_4 (i.e., given $N_1 N_2$, N_2 is *s* iff it branches). There is no way, however, to label ϕ_3 strong. Thus, the labeling conventions would not be able to handle the type of pronunciation in (9c) of the sentence *My sister sells fresh fruit at the market on Monday*. More generally, it would be impossible to assign stress to any node other than the two leftmost or the two rightmost ones. Such a restriction is not built into the relative prominence conventions for n-ary branching trees, and in the case of *I* in particular, this is a desirable outcome since there are clearly cases in which the strong node can occupy a position other than one of the four predictable on the basis of binary tree structures. A further advantage of n-ary branching trees also derives from the fact that there is no theoretical connection between the tree geometry and the s/w assignment rules. It should be noted that the absence of such a connection does not mean that there is no way to restrict the assignment of stress in such trees; in fact, for all of the prosodic constituents below I, it was shown that stress always falls on a specific position within a given type of constituent and is thus restricted structurally. In the case of I, the restrictions are more semantic in nature, but they nevertheless exist, since it is clearly not the case that the position of stress is random. In a system in which the position of stress may follow only from the structure of the tree, however, any placement of stress on a position other than the predicted one would constitute a violation of the principles of the system. In such a system, the fact that the strong node within an I can be in any position and can vary with different pronunciations of the I in question would thus mean that in a large number of cases the relative prominence patterns are in conflict with the basic stress assignment principles. In an n-ary branching system, where the assignment of stress is not necessarily determined strictly on the basis of the tree structure, no such problem arises. Still another advantage of n-ary branching trees will be seen in the next section in relation to the restructuring of I.

7.2. *Restructuring of the intonational phrase*

While constituents of a particular type are always assigned the same structure in syntax regardless of their length or any other linguistic or extra-linguistic factors, the same is not true in phonology. We have already seen in relation to the phonological phrase that, at least in some languages, the length of certain phonological constituents plays a role in determining the ultimate division of a string into ϕs. In particular, we saw that in languages such as Italian a short (i.e. nonbranching) ϕ may, under certain circumstances, be restructured to form a single, larger phonological phrase with an adjacent ϕ. It will be shown in this section that the intonational phrase, too, may undergo a process of restructuring.[6] In the case of I, however, length is only one of several factors that may play a role in determining restructuring. Three other factors we will also examine here are rate of speech, style, and contrastive prominence. Since I restructuring depends in large part on rather global aspects of the speech situation, it is not possible to predict exactly when it will occur. The following discussion is aimed, therefore, at examining the roles the various factors play in increasing or decreasing the probability of restructuring.

Since the basic definition of I specifies that all the ϕs of a root sentence form a single I, if the material dominated by a root sentence is long, the resulting I is automatically long as well. In such cases, I restructuring often occurs to yield somewhat shorter constituents, perhaps for physiological reasons having to do with breath capacity and for reasons related to the optimal chunks for linguistic processing. Thus, in a situation in which no special considerations relating to rate, style, or emphasis must be made, it is possible that a long *I* such as that in (11a) will be broken down into shorter *I*s as in (11b) or (11c).

(11)   a.   [$_I$My friend's baby hamster always looks for food in the corners of its cage]$_I$
       b.   [$_I$My friend's baby hamster]$_I$ [$_I$always looks for food in the corners of its cage]$_I$
       c.   [$_I$My friend's baby hamster]$_I$ [$_I$always looks for food]$_I$ [$_I$in the corners of its cage]$_I$

While it may be structurally possible to break down a given *I* into smaller *I*s, it is clear that the longer the original *I*, the more likely it is to be divided into smaller *I*s. This can be seen by comparing the divisions in (11) with those in (12), where the original *I* is already fairly short.

(12)   a.   [$_I$The hamster eats seeds all day]$_I$
       b.   [$_I$The hamster]$_I$ [$_I$eats seeds all day]$_I$
       c.   [$_I$The hamster]$_I$ [eats seeds]$_I$ [$_I$all day]$_I$

While (12b) and (12c) may represent possible divisions of the sentence into *I*s, they seem much less acceptable than the analogous structures in (11b) and (11c).

The length factor also plays a role in determining how many smaller *I*s are made from a longer one. While it has been suggested that an *I* may in principle be broken down into as many shorter *I*s as there are ϕs in the string (see Selkirk, 1978b), this does not, in fact, seem to be the case. Aside from the syntactic restrictions on *I* restructuring discussed below, there seems to be a tendency to avoid series of very short *I*s and sequences of *I*s of very different lengths. In other words, there is a tendency to establish *I*s of a more or less uniform, 'average' length, although at this point we are not able to characterize this ideal length more precisely. The importance of length can nevertheless be seen in the examples in (13). While the *I* in (13a) could, in principle, be divided into smaller *I*s as in (13b) and (13c), the divisions in (13d) and (13e) are more acceptable.

(13)   a.   [$_I$[Jennifer]$_\phi$ [discovered]$_\phi$ [that her attic]$_\phi$ [had been invaded]$_\phi$ [last winter]$_\phi$ [by a family]$_\phi$ [of squirrels]$_\phi$]$_I$
       b.   [$_I$[Jennifer]$_\phi$]$_I$ [$_I$[discovered]$_\phi$]$_I$ [$_I$[that her attic]$_\phi$]$_I$ [$_I$[had been invaded]$_\phi$]$_I$ [$_I$[last winter]$_\phi$]$_I$ [$_I$[by a family]$_\phi$]$_I$ [$_I$[of squirrels]$_\phi$]$_I$

c. $[_I[\text{Jennifer}]_\phi]_I$ $[_I[\text{discovered}]_\phi$ $[\text{that her attic}]_\phi$ $[\text{had been in-}$ vaded$]_\phi$ $[\text{last winter}]_\phi$ $[\text{by a family}]_\phi$ $[\text{of squirrels}]_\phi]_I$

d. $[_I[\text{Jennifer}]_\phi$ $[\text{discovered}]_\phi]_I$ $[_I[\text{that her attic}]_\phi$ $[\text{had been}$ invaded$]_\phi$ $[\text{last winter}]_\phi]_I$ $[_I[\text{by a family}]_\phi$ $[\text{of squirrels}]_\phi]_I$

e. $[_I[\text{Jennifer}]_\phi$ $[\text{discovered}]_\phi$ $[\text{that her attic}]_\phi]_I$ $[_I[\text{had been in-}$ vaded$]_\phi$ $[\text{last winter}]_\phi$ $[\text{by a family}]_\phi$ $[\text{of squirrels}]_\phi]_I$

Fairly closely associated with the factor of length in determining the restructuring of a given I into smaller Is is the factor of the rate of speech. The more quickly a string is uttered, the less likely it is to be broken down into several intonational phrases. Thus, the faster the rate of speech, the longer the Is of a given utterance tend to be; conversely, the slower the rate of speech, the shorter the Is tend to be. In this way, some more abstract notion of length in terms of timing or rhythm may be respected. That is, in terms of timing, it may be that a quickly uttered long I is in some sense equivalent to a more slowly uttered short I. Thus, for example, if the sentence in (11) above is uttered at a fairly rapid tempo, it will typically contain a single long I, as in (11a). If it is uttered more slowly, however, it is more likely that the same sentence will contain two or three shorter Is, as in (11b) and (11c), respectively.

In addition to length and the rate of speech, the style of speech also plays a role in determining the restructuring of an I into several shorter Is. It is usually the case that the more formal or pedantic the style, the more likely it is for a long I to be divided into a series of shorter Is. This is clearly related to the factor of rate of speech, since more formal styles tend to correspond to a slower rate of utterance. Thus, if the sentence in (14) is uttered in an informal colloquial way, it will most likely consist of a single intonation contour, as in (14a). If, on the other hand, it is uttered as part of a formal presentation, it may consist of two or three contours, as indicated in (14b) and (14c), respectively.

(14) a. $[_I$The adult orangutan constructs a nest every evening out of leaves and twigs$]_I$

b. $[_I$The adult orangutan$]_I$ $[_I$constructs a nest every evening out of leaves and twigs$]_I$

c. $[_I$The adult orangutan$]_I$ $[_I$constructs a nest every evening$]_I$ $[_I$out of leaves and twigs$]_I$

Finally, semantic considerations related to the contrastive prominence of a particular part of an utterance may lead an I to be broken down into smaller ones. In this regard, Bing (1979) distinguishes between contrastive stress, which does not alter the I structure, and contrastive prominence, which leads to the addition of an intonation contour within a string.

For example, (15) can be read with contrastive stress on the word *collect*, as indicated by the italics in the example, but this does not lead to the division of the single *I* into two shorter ones.

(15) [$_I$Our neighbors *collect* antique furniture]$_I$

If, on the other hand, prominence is attributed to a phrase that normally cannot have it, a new intonation contour is created. For example, while pronouns are usually unstressed, under certain circumstances they become semantically prominent and must receive stress. In such cases, the division of *I* constituents must be modified (see Bing, 1979). It should be noted that we are not referring here to contrastive stress, which may appear on pronouns, as on any other type of word, as in *Tell hér to wait*. This is the same type of situation as was seen in (15), where contrastive stress does not require a modification of *I* structure, but instead only determines the position of the strong element within *I*. Contrastive prominence refers to a different type of phenomenon. Consider, for example, the sentence in (16a), which is assigned one *I* since it is dominated by a single root sentence. The sentence in (16b) has the same syntactic structure, and thus is also assigned one *I* by the basic *I* formation rule. The presence of the pronouns, however, requires the listener to interpret this sentence in a specific way, which cannot be the same as the interpretation of (16a). The interpretation of (16b) must be expressed phonologically by placing prominence on the pronouns and this, in turn, causes the single *I* to be restructured as three smaller *I*s, as in (16c).

(16) a. [$_I$Paul called Paula before Carla called Carl]$_I$
      b. [$_I$Paul called Paula before she called him]$_I$
      c. [$_I$Paul called Paula]$_I$ [$_I$before *she*]$_I$ [$_I$called *him*]$_I$

The different possibilities just seen for restructuring intonational phrases all contribute to the flexibility that has been frequently observed in relation to the domains of intonation contours (see, among others, Selkirk, 1978b, 1984b; Bing, 1979). It is clear that as soon as this type of flexibility is required in delimiting a constituent, the constituent cannot be isomorphic with any syntactic constituent since syntax does not allow for the same type of regrouping of the components of a particular string. In this respect, therefore, the phonological hierarchy differs significantly from the syntactic hierarchy.

The flexibility seen in relation to the construction and restructuring of *I* is not, however, completely free. Since the Strict Layer Hypothesis requires that *I* exhaustively dominate one or more ϕs, it follows that whenever *I* restructuring occurs, it must occur at the juncture between two

ϕs. There are, furthermore, certain syntactic constraints on where an *I* may be broken in order to form smaller *I*s. The most important factor seems to be a general tendency to avoid restructuring an *I* in any position other than at the end of a noun phrase. Thus, while the sentence in (17) contains five ϕs, there are only three likely ways of restructuring the original single *I* formed by the basic *I* construction rule, as seen in (18a-c).

(17) $[_I[$The giant panda$]_\phi$ [eats$]_\phi$ [only one type$]_\phi$ [of bamboo$]_\phi$ [in its natural habitat$]_\phi]_I$

(18) a. $[_I[$The giant panda$]_\phi]_I$ $[_I[$eats$]_\phi$ [only one type$]_\phi$ [of bamboo$]_\phi]_I$ $[_I[$in its natural habitat$]_\phi]_I$
      b. $[_I[$The giant panda$]_\phi$ [eats$]_\phi$ [only one type of bamboo$]_\phi]_I$ $[_I[$in its natural habitat$]_\phi]_I$
      c. $[_I[$The giant panda$]_\phi]_I$ $[_I[$eats$]_\phi$ [only one type$]_\phi$ [of bamboo$]_\phi$ [in its natural habitat$]_\phi]_I$

I restructuring is not likely to occur after the verb *eat*, or after the noun *type*, since it is not the end of a noun phrase (i.e. [*only one type of bamboo*]$_{NP}$).

Further support for the proposal that *I* restructuring occurs at the end of an NP, but not after a noun within an NP, comes from embedded possessive constructions such as that in (19a), and its Italian equivalent in (19b).[7]

(19) a. $[_I[$My friend's$]_\phi$ [neighbor's$]_\phi$ [aunt's$]_\phi$ [mother$]_\phi$ [knows$]_\phi$ [a famous writer$]_\phi]_I$
      b. $[_I[$La madre$]_\phi$ [della zia$]_\phi$ [del vicino$]_\phi$ [della mia amica$]_\phi$ [conosce$]_\phi$ [una famosa scrittrice$]_\phi]_I$

The only place in which the long *I*s in these two sentences may be divided is after *mother* in (19a) and after *amica* in (19b). Restructuring after any of the other nouns would interrupt the noun phrase which is the subject of the sentence, and is therefore avoided.

It should be noted that the principle that restructures *I*s after an NP is another source of nonisomorphism between phonological and syntactic constituents in certain cases. That is, restructuring in accordance with the NP restriction may create prosodic structures that are not isomorphic to syntactic structures. Consider the sentence in (20a) and its restructuring in (20b).

(20) a. $[_I$I would never have believed the children of John and Mary to be able to become so ill-mannered$]_I$

b.   [$_I$I would never have believed the children of John and Mary]$_I$
[$_I$to be able to become so ill-mannered]$_I$

Since the first *I* in (20b) does not represent a syntactic constituent, it is clear that in this case, and in cases like it, the prosodic structure must be different from the syntactic structure.

It should be noted, furthermore, that restructuring is not equally likely to apply after all NPs. Rather, there is a further restriction on dividing an *I* into smaller *I*s at the end of an NP that reflects the argument structure of the predicate in question. That is, there seems to be a general tendency to avoid separating an obligatory argument from its verb even if such a division would respect the NP constraint. Optional arguments, on the other hand, seem not to be affected by the same restriction. Thus, the division of the *I* before the optional argument of the verb *buys* in (21b) is more acceptable than the division before the obligatory argument of *gives* in (22b), despite the fact that the syntactic structure of the two sentences is identical.

(21)   a.   [$_I$That kind old lady always buys fresh meat for the stray cats that live in the park]$_I$
     b.   [$_I$That kind old lady always buys fresh meat]$_I$ [$_I$for the stray cats that live in the park]$_I$

(22)   a.   [$_I$That kind old lady always gives fresh meat to the stray cats that live in the park]$_I$
     b.?*[$_I$That kind old lady always gives fresh meat]$_I$ [$_I$to the stray cats that live in the park]$_I$

Thus, it can be concluded that while there is a general preference for breaking an *I* after an NP, this preference may be restricted by the argument structure involved.

In addition to the context following an NP, restructuring of *I* may take place in the context of a new $\bar{S}$. That is, a long *I* may be divided just before the beginning of an $\bar{S}$, but only in cases in which this division does not interrupt an NP. Thus, (23a) may be restructured as (23b), but (24a) may not be restructured as (24b) since doing so would interrupt an NP.

(23)   a.   [$_I$I thought you already knew that Gertrude was moving to southern Italy]$_I$
     b.   [$_I$I thought you already knew]$_I$ [$_I$that Gertrude was moving to southern Italy]$_I$

(24) a. [$_I$I thought you knew the family that was moving to southern Italy]$_I$

  b. *[$_I$I thought you knew the family]$_I$ [$_I$that was moving to southern Italy]$_I$

These examples show that when the two syntactic factors that affect *I* restructuring – the end of NP and the beginning of $\bar{S}$ – are in conflict, it is the NP that 'wins'.

There are also cases in which the beginning of $\bar{S}$ may be in conflict with the restriction against separating an obligatory argument from its verb. As the examples in (25) and (26) show, in such cases it is the beginning of $\bar{S}$ that 'wins'. That is, if necessary, it is possible to override the constraint on restructuring an obligatory argument of a verb, but only if the argument is a sentence. Thus, the division in (25b) is more acceptable than that in (26b).

(25) a. [$_I$Our next door neighbor truly believes that black cats bring bad luck]$_I$
  b. [$_I$Our next door neighbor truly believes]$_I$ [$_I$that black cats bring bad luck]$_I$

(26) a. [$_I$Our next door neighbor truly believes the myth about black cats and bad luck]$_I$
  b.?*[$_I$Our next door neighbor truly believes]$_I$ [$_I$the myth about black cats and bad luck]$_I$

A comparison of the three factors that constrain *I* restructuring reveals a type of hierarchy among these factors. The strongest factor is the NP, which may not be broken by restructuring. The second factor in terms of strength seems to be $\bar{S}$, which allows the creation of a new *I*, except in cases in which this would break an NP. The formation of a new *I* at the beginning of $\bar{S}$ may, however, counteract the effect of the third factor, the restriction against separating an internal argument from its verb.

The fact that *I* restructuring tends to take place only in relation to two syntactic contexts shows that in prosodic phonology the constituents NP and $\bar{S}$ play particularly strong roles in determining the final division of a string into *I*s. That NP and $\bar{S}$ behave in a somewhat special way in relation to prosody is not surprising, however, since these are precisely the two cyclic nodes, at least in languages such as English. Assuming that cyclicity is, in fact, a relevant factor in determining the occurrence of *I* restructuring in languages in which other categories are cyclic, the prediction can be made that it will be this set of constituents that is relevant in constraining *I* restructuring (see Nespor and Vogel, 1982). There are, moreover, addition-

al independent reasons in both syntax and semantics for considering NP and
$\overline{S}$ somewhat special domains (see, among others, Akmajian, 1975; Bach,
1977; Bing, 1979). The fact that the noun phrase seems to have the
stronger effect on *I* restructuring is, furthermore, consistent with observations made by Bing (1979), Gunter (1974), and Ladd (1980), among
others, to the effect that nouns are in some sense the most prominent or
'accentable' part of speech.[8] As far as the role of obligatory arguments in
I restructuring is concerned, the fact that they tend to inhibit division of
a string is a direct reflection of the interaction between argument structure
and phonology at the *I* level of the prosodic hierarchy. The fact that the
constraint against separating an obligatory argument from its verb is the
weakest of the three factors examined here seems to indicate, however,
that the effect of syntax on phonology is stronger than the effect of
argument structure.

While the vast majority of the cases of *I* restructuring seem to follow
the patterns and constraints discussed above, there are some special cases
that cannot be accounted for in the same way. It has often been observed
that lists and complexly embedded constructions have particular intonation patterns. In fact, the *I* divisions in these cases often violate the general
principles proposed above. Consider first the sentences containing lists
in (27a-31a) and their possible restructurings in (27b-31b).

(27)   a.   [$_I$The big fat ugly beast scared away the children]$_I$
       b.   [$_I$The big]$_I$ [$_I$fat]$_I$ [$_I$ugly]$_I$ [$_I$nasty beast]$_I$
            [$_I$scared away the children]$_I$

(28)   a.   [$_I$That mountain road is long narrow windy and bumpy]$_I$
       b.   [$_I$That mountain road is long]$_I$ [$_I$narrow]$_I$ [$_I$windy]$_I$
            [$_I$and bumpy]$_I$

(29)   a.   [$_I$Everyone at the party ate talked sang and danced]$_I$
       b.   [$_I$Everyone at the party ate]$_I$ [$_I$talked]$_I$ [$_I$sang]$_I$
            [$_I$and danced]$_I$

(30)   a.   [$_I$Ducks geese swans and coots inhabit this lake]$_I$
       b.   [$_I$Ducks]$_I$ [$_I$geese]$_I$ [$_I$swans]$_I$ [$_I$and coots]$_I$
            [$_I$inhabit this lake]$_I$

(31)   a.   [$_I$They own two cats three dogs four parakeets and a turtle]$_I$
       b.   [$_I$They own two cats]$_I$ [$_I$three dogs]$_I$ [$_I$four parakeets]$_I$
            [$_I$and a turtle]$_I$

The optional restructuring shown in (27b) violates the NP constraint since it divides the original *I* following APs and not NPs, and in such a way that an NP is broken apart.[9] The restructurings in (28b) and (29b) also violate the NP constraint since they create new *I*s following APs and VPs, respectively. While the restructurings of the lists in (30b) and (31b) do not violate the NP constraint in the sense that they place the *I* divisions after NPs, they do represent violations of the constraint in the sense that they cause a single (complex) NP to be broken down. Since all of the types of lists follow the same prosodic pattern, it is clear that what is relevant is the fact that they are lists, regardless of the type of constituents involved. A special rule for optional restructuring of lists into separate *I*s seems to be needed in addition to the general principles proposed above. Such a rule can be formulated as follows:

(32)   *List Restructuring* (optional)
       In a sequence of more than two constituents of the same type, i.e. $x_1, x_2 \ldots x_n$, an intonation break may be inserted before each repetition of the node X, i.e. before $x_2, x_3 \ldots x_n$.

It should be noted that the word 'repetition' in this rule does not refer to the first X in the sequence but to those subsequent nodes that are the same as X.

A less common type of list pattern arises when the list is separated to a greater extent from the matrix sentence, as typically indicated by a colon in orthography. This pattern is found in sentences like those exemplified in (33) and (34).

(33)   a.   Let's invite: Arnold, Arthur, Archibald, and Zachary.
       b. $[_I$Let's invite$]_I$ $[_I$Arnold$]_I$ $[_I$Arthur$]_I$ $[_I$Archibald$]_I$
            $[_I$and Zachary$]_I$

(34)   a.   We were told to buy the following: milk, eggs, bread, and cheese
       b. $[_I$We were told to buy the following$]_I$ $[_I$milk$]_I$ $[_I$eggs$]_I$
            $[_I$bread$]_I$ $[_I$and cheese$]_I$

To handle these cases, it is only necessary to extend the notion of repetition to cover the first X as well as subsequent Xs. In this way, a new *I* is also formed at the beginning of the first instance of X.

Let us now consider embedded structures, the other area in which *I* restructuring may apply in ways that violate the general constraints. Each of the possible restructurings in (35b-37b) of the respective sentences in (35a-37a) violates the general NP constraint on restructuring.

(35)   a.   [$_I$The book in the bag in the box on the table in the study
            belongs to Albert]$_I$

       b.   [$_I$The book in the bag]$_I$ [$_I$in the box]$_I$ [$_I$on the table]$_I$
            [$_I$in the study]$_I$ [$_I$belongs to Albert]$_I$

(36)   a.   [$_I$This is the cat that ate the rat that ate the cheese]$_I$

       b.   [$_I$This is the cat]$_I$ [$_I$that ate the rat]$_I$ [$_I$that ate the cheese]$_I$

(37)   a.   [$_I$The woman that represents the company that owns the stores
            that sell the machines that brew coffee automatically is a friend
            of mine]$_I$

       b.   [$_I$The woman]$_I$ [$_I$that represents the company]$_I$ [that owns the
            stores]$_I$ [$_I$that sell the machines]$_I$ [$_I$that brew coffee automati-
            cally]$_I$ [$_I$is a friend of mine]$_I$

In each of the restructurings in (35b-37b), an NP is broken into more
than one *I*, contrary to the claim made above that *I* restructuring tends
to avoid interrupting an NP. It is clear, however, that in embedded structures such as those just given, the only way to divide the original long *I*
into shorter *I*s requires that an NP be broken into shorter strings.

Although the embedded structures are syntactically quite different
from the lists in (27)-(31), there is also a way in which the two types of
constructions are related to each other. Just as the lists contain sequences
of the same constituent X, the embedded structures can also be said to
contain sequences of a given node X. In (35), the repeated node is PP
and in (36) and (37), the repeated node is $\bar{S}$, although these cases differ
from the lists in that the repetitions of X begin here before the preceding
X ends. It should be noted that in each of the cases in question there is
not only a particular node label that recurs several times in the string,
but there is also a periodic repetition of the same elements within X.

In some embedded structures, more than one type of node appears in
a repeating pattern, and in such cases it is necessary to have a way to
decide which of the nodes is to be considered the repeating X for the
purposes of *I* restructuring. In the case of (36), in addition to saying that
the repeating node is $\bar{S}$, as in (38), it would also be possible to say that
the repeating node is NP, as in (39).

(38)   This is the cat [$_{\bar{S}}$ that ate the rat [$_{\bar{S}}$ that ate the cheese...

(39)   This is [$_{NP}$the cat that ate [$_{NP}$the rat that ate [$_{NP}$the cheese...

As far as the prosodic structure of such sentences is concerned, however,
there is not a choice. The division into *I*s can only be that seen in (36),

the one that corresponds to the repetition pattern in (38). Once again, the noun seems to play a fundamental role in prosody, since in the cases in which more than one type of X may be taken as the repeating node, the division into shorter Is is always such that the Is end in a noun.

Before concluding our examination of restructuring of embedded constructions, it must be pointed out that not all cases can be handled as repetitions. For example, the sentence in (40) has a complex embedded structure, although the pattern of repeating nodes is not as regular as it is in the embedded structures seen above.

(40) $[_I$ I know the artist that painted the picture of the woman that wrote the book that won the acclaim of many$]_I$

While there are three instances of $\bar{S}$ in this sentence, we cannot count them as a list, as was done in the other embedded structures, since in (40) there is not always a periodic repetition of the same elements in each case. In fact, in such cases, it is much more difficult to decide where the single long I corresponding to the root sentence may be broken down into shorter Is. The results of a division on the basis of the three $\bar{S}$s is quite unacceptable, as can be seen in (41).

(41)   *$[_I$ I know the artist$]_I$ $[_I$ that painted the picture of the woman$]_I$
        $[_I$ that wrote the book$]_I$ $[_I$that won the acclaim of many$]_I$

What lists and embedded structures show is that besides the basic principles that govern I restructuring there are a few specific cases in which additional principles are needed. These additional principles are not, however, totally unrelated to those that account for the rest of the language. That is, in the cases of lists and embedded structures that behave like lists, we have seen that the notion of repetition is crucial. The prosodic effect of this repetition is a series of Is that are of approximately the same length. A similar principle was seen earlier in relation to the division of more typical long Is into several shorter ones, where it was observed that there is a general tendency to restructure Is such that the result is a series of Is of more or less the same length. These principles, along with the interacting factor of speech rate, seem to reflect a general abstract rhythmic organization of speech into chunks of a more or less fixed temporal length. In addition, in the case of embedded constructions, in regular repetitions as well as others, it was observed that the noun plays a central role in determining where intonation breaks may occur. While in embedded constructions we cannot follow the principle used in other cases of restructuring – that is, the introduction of an intonation break at the end of an NP – the category N still seems to be relevant in restructuring, additional evidence of the special role the noun plays in prosody.

Finally, it should be noted that *I* restructuring provides additional motivation for the n-ary branching trees proposed here, as opposed to the binary branching trees proposed in earlier work on prosodic phonology (see also section 1.2.1 above). In a binary branching structure, intermediate nodes are often formed between a given node of level X^n, in the case *I*, and the nodes of level X^{n-1}, in this case ϕ, as seen in (42).

(42)

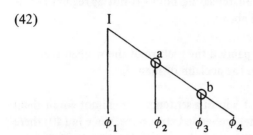

The additional nodes, indicated by the circles in (42), represent additional constituent structure as well. That is, node *a* dominates a constituent consisting of $\phi_2 - \phi_4$, and node *b* dominates a constituent consisting of $\phi_3 - \phi_4$. The presence of such constituents internal to *I* would seem to indicate, further, that this structure should be respected during *I* restructuring. This was in fact proposed in Nespor and Vogel (1982), where it was suggested that *I* restructuring was possible only when the new *Is* that split off from the larger one represented a constituent in the original tree. Only in special cases of emphasis was some other division allowed. The predictions made in relation to (42) by such a claim are that the *I* consisting of $\phi_1 - \phi_4$ could be broken down only as shown in (43).

(43)

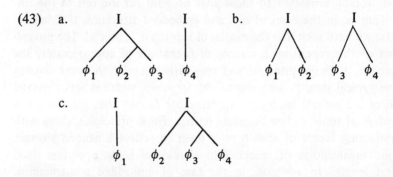

A new *I* could not be created from ϕ_2 and ϕ_3. There are, however, cases in which precisely this combination represents the correct restructuring, as seen in (44).

(44) a. $[_I[\text{European wild cats}]_{\phi_1} [\text{often make}]_{\phi_2} [\text{their winter dens}]_{\phi_3}$
$[\text{in dead tree trunks}]_{\phi_4}]_I$

b. $[_I[\text{European wild cats}]_{\phi_1}]_I \; [_I[\text{often make}]_{\phi_2}$
    $[\text{their winter dens}]_{\phi_3}]_I \; [_I[\text{in dead tree trunks}]_{\phi_4}]_I$

A similar problem also arises with (18a) above, where restructuring of five ϕs creates a new I from $\phi_2 - \phi_4$, a string which would not form a constituent in a binary branching tree. These examples, and many others like them, cannot be accounted for on the grounds that they represent cases of special emphasis, as was originally proposed, since in fact they represent quite neutral pronunciations. It would, of course, be possible to ignore the internal constituent structure in I restructuring, but doing so would destroy one of the functions of precisely this structure.

The use of n-ary branching trees avoids the problems just seen in relation to binary branching trees. That is, since there is no additional constituent structure between I and ϕ, restructuring may group any sequence of ϕs into smaller Is, as long as the division respects the syntactic and argument structure conditions as well as the general timing conditions discussed above. The proposed restructurings in (44) and (18a) respect these conditions.

Thus far, we have only examined the intonational phrase from the point of view of intonation contours, potential pause positions, and relative prominence patterns. While these phenomena would be adequate in themselves as motivation for the I constituent in phonology, there are still other phenomena that operate within I. Specifically, in the following sections, it will be demonstrated that there are also segmental phonological rules that have I as their domain of application.

7.3. Segmental rules in the intonational phrase

For every prosodic constituent we have examined thus far, we have found what we are calling prosodic rules in a variety of languages. The constituent I is no exception, as will be demonstrated below on the basis of several rules in Italian, Spanish, and Greek. Since I is a fairly flexible entity, it follows that the domains of application of I-level rules must also be flexible. That this is in fact the case will also be shown in relation to each of the rules discussed below.

7.3.1. Italian

The first sandhi rule we will examine here is Gorgia Toscana (GT), a rule that is found in the Tuscan variety of Italian. As was mentioned earlier (section 2.3.1), this rule essentially changes the voiceless stops /p, t, k/ into the corresponding fricatives [ϕ, θ, h] between two [−consonantal] segments within and across words.[10] On the basis of our recordings of over 900 sentences read by five speakers of Tuscan Italian from Florence and the immediately surrounding areas, we have found that GT applies throughout the domain corresponding to the intonational phrase as defined by the *I* construction and restructuring rules discussed above, while it does not apply across the boundaries of intonational phrases. This is illustrated by the examples in (45), where '_' indicates that GT applies and '$_{\not{+}}$' indicates that it does not apply. We will limit our attention to the application of GT to /k/, the most common form of the rule.

(45)   a.   [$_I$Hanno catturato sette canguri appena nati]$_I$
             'They have captured seven newly born kangaroos.'
       b.   [$_I$I canarini congolesi costano molto cari in America]$_I$
             'Congolese canaries are very expensive in America.'
       c.   [$_I$Certe tartarughe]$_I$ [$_I$ come si sa]$_I$ [$_I$ vivono fino a duecento anni]$_I$
             'Certain turtles, as you know, live up to two hundred years.'
       d.   [$_I$Almerico]$_I$ [$_I$ quando dorme solo]$_I$ [$_I$ cade spesso dall'amaca]$_I$
             'Almerico, when he sleeps alone, often falls out of the hammock.'

In each of these sentences, the *I* structure is that determined by the basic *I* formation rule given above in (5). It was shown in section 7.2, however, that there are also certain conditions under which the original division of a string into *I*s may be modified by restructuring rules. When this happens, it is the final, restructured *I* structure that determines the domains within which GT applies. Thus, while the sentence in (46) is assigned a single *I* by the basic *I* formation rule, as indicated in (46a), it may also be restructured as two shorter *I*s with a break after an NP, as indicated in (46b).

(46)   a.   [$_I$Il pericolosissimo struzzo nigeriano corre più velocemente di quello siriano]$_I$
             'The extremely dangerous Nigerian ostrich runs faster than the Syrian one.'
       b.   [$_I$Il pericolosissimo struzzo nigeriano]$_I$ [$_I$ corre più velocemente di quello siriano]$_I$

In the first case, the reading with one intonation contour, GT applies to *corre* 'runs' since the initial /k/ of this word is preceded and followed by [−consonantal] segments within the same *I*. In the second case, however, the presence of two intonation contours indicates that restructuring has broken down the longer *I* into two smaller ones such that the [−consonantal] segment preceding /k/ is no longer in the same *I* as the /k/. Since GT only applies when the entire segmental context of the rule is within *I*, it does not apply to *corre* in (46b).

The same pattern can be observed in other types of sentences that undergo restructuring for different reasons as well. For example, if the list in (47) is uttered as a single *I*, GT applies as indicated in (47a); however, if it is restructured and uttered as four *I*s, GT is blocked in certain positions, as indicated in (47b).

(47)   a.   [$_I$Quel giardino ha una gabbia piena di c̲orvi c̲anarini c̲olibrì
e pellicani]$_I$
'That garden has a cage full of crows, canaries, hummingbirds, and pelicans.'

      b.   [$_I$Quel giardino ha una gabbia piena di c̲orvi]$_I$ [$_I$ c̲anarini]$_I$
[$_I$ c̲olibrì]$_I$ [$_I$e pellicani]

Similarly, if embedded constructions are divided into a series of *I*s, GT is blocked when the *I* division falls within the context of the rule. This can be seen by comparing the indicated applications of GT in the sentence in (48a) with those in the restructured form of the same sentence in (48b).

(48)   a.   [$_I$Questo è il gatto c̲he ha mangiato il topo c̲he ha mangiato il
formaggio]$_I$
'This is the cat that ate the mouse that ate the cheese.'

      b.   [$_I$Questo è il gatto]$_I$ [$_I$ c̲he ha mangiato il topo]$_I$ [$_I$ c̲he ha
mangiato il formaggio]$_I$

The fact that GT applies throughout the constituent *I* but not across *I*s means that it is a span rule with the intonational phrase as its domain of application.[11] This can be expressed by means of the following rule, which accounts for the most common changes of /p, t, k/ to [ϕ, θ, h].

(49)   *Gorgia Toscana*

$$\begin{bmatrix} -\text{cont} \\ -\text{voice} \\ -\text{del rel} \end{bmatrix} \rightarrow [+\text{cont}] \; / \; [_I \ldots [-\text{cons}] \_\_\_\_ [-\text{cons}] \ldots]_I$$

The flexibility of the intonational phrase seen above in relation to the positions of intonation breaks and the domains of intonation contours is thus reflected in the *I*-level segmental rule GT as well. That is, we have seen that the various restructuring possibilities for *I* may result in differences in the application of a rule such as GT. It is clear that a purely syntactic specification of the domain of application of GT is not feasible, since there is no way to take into account the different possibilities for the application or lack of application depending on such factors as the length of the original sentence and special situations such as lists. Thus, the problem raised in Chapter 2 (section 2.3) by the fact that a rule such as GT does not apply consistently in relation to a given type of syntactic structure is resolved by the phonological constituent I. That is, it was pointed out that GT often applies between NP and VP, but not always, as seen in (50a) and (50b), respectively.

(50)   a.   [ₗGli uccelli costruiscono i nidi]ₗ
           'Birds construct nests.'
      b.   [ₗCerti tipi di uccelli trovati solo in Australia]ₗ [ᵢ costruiscono
           dei nidi complicatissimi a due piani]ₗ
           'Certain types of birds found only in Australia construct very
           complicated two-story nests.'

It should be noted that although the syntactic complexity of (50b) is greater than that of (50a), this is not the crucial factor in determining the different prosodic constituency in the two cases. That it is indeed length that is the relevant factor can be seen in (51a) and (51b), where the former is syntactically more complex than the latter: the subject NP in (51a) has both a specifier and a complement containing coordination, while the subject NP in (51b) contains only a head. Since (51a) is shorter than (51b), however, the general tendency is for the first sentence, but not the second sentence, to form a single I, as indicated by the application *vs.* nonapplication of GT.

(51)   a.   [ₗLa gru rossa e bianca cade sempre]ₗ
           'The red and white crane always falls.'
      b.   [ₗGiovanbattista Leonardo Confalonieri]ₗ [ᵢ colleziona
           fenicotteri]ₗ
           'Giovanbattista Leonardo Confalonieri collects flamingos.'

It was also pointed out that GT often applies within a VP, but not always, as is illustrated in (51a) and (51b), respectively.

(52)   a.   [ₗOsservano i cardellini col cannocchiale]ₗ
           '(They) observe the goldfinches with the binoculars.'
      b.   [ₗOsservano il rarissimo colibrì peruviano con le penne azzure]ₗ
           [ᵢ con un cannocchiale particolarmente adatto alla situazione]ₗ
           '(They) observe the very rare Peruvian hummingbird with blue
           feathers with binoculars particularly suitable for the situation.'

By formulating GT in terms of the prosodic constituent I, the application *vs.* nonapplication of the rule (50)-(52) is automatically accounted for.

That is, in short sentences (such as (50a) and (51a)) and short VPs (such as (52a)), there is usually a single I and GT thus applies throughout these strings. In longer sentences (e.g. (50b) and (51b)) and longer VPs (e.g. (52b)), however, there is the possibility of restructuring a long I into shorter ones, and in such cases, the context of GT may be interrupted and the rule is consequently blocked.

Another rule of Tuscan Italian exhibits the same behavior as GT. This rule, Intervocalic Spirantization (IS), changes the affricates /tʃ/ and /dʒ/ into the corresponding fricatives [ʃ] and [ʒ], respectively, between [–consonantal] segments within and across words. As the examples in (53) show, this rule applies within I, but it does not apply across Is. ('_' indicates that the rule applies to the segment in question and '$\not{\cdot}$' indicates that it does not apply.)

(53) a. [$_I$Il mio criceto cerca il suo cibo negli angoli della gabbia]$_I$
          'My hamster looks for its food in the corners of the cage.'
      b. [$_I$Temevano che la nuova giraffa ci avrebbe disturbato durante la cena]$_I$
          '(They) were afraid the new giraffe would have disturbed us during dinner.'
      c. [$_I$Eleonora]$_I$ [$_I$ giudice da anni]$_I$ [$_I$ gioca spesso a carte]$_I$
          'Eleonora, a judge for years, often plays cards.'
      d. [$_I$Santo cielo]$_I$ [$_I$ c'è un verme in questa ciliegia]$_I$
          'Good heavens, there's a worm in this cherry.'

The I constituents indicated in these sentences are those assigned by the basic I formation rule. Where I restructuring may apply, we find the same variable application of IS as was seen in relation to GT. That is, if a given string is uttered as a single I, IS applies throughout the entire string. If, however, a long I is broken down into shorter Is, IS applies only within the shorter Is, but not across their boundaries. This can be seen by comparing the application *vs.* nonapplication of IS in the long Is in (54a-57a).

(54) a. [$_I$Il vecchio orso che vive in quella tana gira spesso intorno alle case di notte]$_I$
          'The old bear that lives in that den often wanders around the houses at night.'
      b. [$_I$Il vecchio orso che vive in quella tana]$_I$ [$_I$ gira spesso intorno alle case di notte]$_I$

(55) a. [$_I$Hanno scoperto un rarissimo tipo di tartaruga circa tre anni dopo che era stata dichiarata la sua estinzione]$_I$
          'They discovered an extremely rare type of turtle about three years after it had been declared extinct.'

b. [$_I$Hanno scoperto un rarissimo tipo di tartaruga]$_I$ [$_I$ circa tre
anni dopo che era stata dichiarata la sua estinzione]$_I$

(56) a. [$_I$Hanno citato cinque recensioni cinquanta libri cento articoli
e duecento lavori inediti]$_I$
'They cited five reviews, fifty books, one hundred articles, and
two hundred unpublished works.'

b. [$_I$Hanno citato cinque recensioni]$_I$ [$_I$ cinquanta libri]$_I$ [$_I$ cento
articoli]$_I$ [$_I$e duecento lavori inediti]$_I$

(57) a. [$_I$Gli ho detto ciò che pensavo dell'affare circa il quale
Cinzia mi ha parlato ieri]$_I$
'I told him what I thought about the affair about which Cinzia
spoke to me yesterday.'

b. [$_I$Gli ho detto ciò che pensavo dell'affare]$_I$ [$_I$ circa il quale
Cinzia mi ha parlato ieri]$_I$

In the first two examples, (54) and (55), restructuring can take place
according to the general principles having to do with such factors as
the length of the string and the rate of speech. In both cases, the original
I is divided such that the intonation break falls at the end of an NP. In
the list and embedded construction in (56) and (57), respectively, the
division into shorter *I*s takes place in accordance with the special restructuring rule and the tendency for an *I* to end in a noun. That is, the divisions are placed at the beginning of a repeated node in (56b), and such
that the new *I* division follows a noun in (57b), although it should be
noted that there may be some difficulty in dividing the last sentence since
the embedded constituents do not represent a series of repetitions of the
same structure.

On the basis of the domains within which IS has been found to apply,
it is possible to formulate the following rule that accounts for this
phenomenon:

(58) *Intervocalic Spirantization*

$$\begin{bmatrix} +\text{del. rel.} \\ -\text{ant} \end{bmatrix} \rightarrow [+\text{cont}] \ / \ [_I \ \dots \ [-\text{cons}] \ \underline{\quad} \ [-\text{cons}] \ \dots]_I$$

As this rule shows, IS is a span rule that applies any place in which its
segmental context occurs within an intonational phrase.

As we have seen in this section, the data on GT and IS further con-
firm the proposed definition of *I* as well as the flexible nature of this
constituent. In this way, the rules in question provide motivation for a

separate phonological constituent that is not isomorphic with any syntactic constituent since there are no constituents in the syntactic hierarchy that *a*) provide the necessary domains of application of GT and IS, or *b*) allow for the type of flexibility observed in the application of these rules.

7.3.2. Spanish

As was mentioned in section 2.3.1 above, the rule of Nasal Assimilation (NA) in Spanish exhibits a certain degree of flexibility in its application, similar to the application of the two Italian rules just seen. Since I is the phonological constituent that offers the greatest flexibility as a result of its restructuring possibilities, it would appear that this constituent is the most likely candidate for expressing the domain of application of NA. In fact, the sentences below illustrate that the intonational phrase represents the appropriate domain of application for the rule that assimilates a nasal in point of articulation to a following obstruent within and across words in Spanish.[12] The nasals that assimilate to the following consonant are marked with '$\underline{}$' and those that do not assimilate are marked with '$\underset{+}{}$'.

(59) a. [$_I$Tenían diez canguros en un parque muy cerca de acquí]$_I$
'(They) used to have ten kangaroos in a park very near here.'

  b. [$_I$Las plumas de faisán cuestan tantísimo hoy día]$_I$
'Pheasant feathers are very expensive nowadays.'

  c. [$_I$Un gran balcón]$_I$ [$_I$como saben]$_I$ [$_I$puede ofrecer mucho placer]$_I$
'A large balcony, as they know, can offer much pleasure.'

  d. [$_I$Carmen]$_I$ [$_I$cántanos una nueva canción]$_I$ [$_I$por favor]$_I$
'Carmen, sing us a new song, please.'

In these examples, there are cases of NA within words – for example, *canguros* 'kangaroos', *cántanos* 'sing us' – and across words within an I – for example, *tienen diez* '(they) have ten', *un parque* 'a park', *faisán cuestan* 'pheasant cost'. It can also be seen that NA does not apply across words that are in two different *I*s – for example, *balcón como* 'balcony as', *saben puede* '(they) know can', *canción por favor* 'song please'.

That NA does not always apply in the same way to a given type of constituent but instead may depend on such factors such as the length of the string in question, can be seen, furthermore, in the examples in (60) and (61) below. That is, it is illustrated that NA applies regularly within a VP and between the subject and predicate of a sentence in (60a) and (60b), respectively. The examples in (61a) and (61b), on the other hand, show that the rule does not apply in longer VPs and sentences, respectively, where restructuring has taken place such that the context for NA is interrupted.

(60)   a.   [$_I$Dicen que el delfín es muy inteligente]$_I$
'(They) say that the dolphin is very intelligent.'
   b.   [$_I$Mi faisán come tres veces por día]$_I$
'My pheasant eats three times a day.'

(61)   a.   [$_I$Usa su sombrero carísimo con seis plumas de tucán]$_I$
[$_I$ cuando desea crear la impresión que es una persona muy importante]$_I$
'(She) wears her very expensive hat within six toucan feathers when she wants to create the impression that she is a very important person.'
   b.   [$_I$Muchos estudios sobre el comportamiento del delfín]$_I$ [$_I$concluyen que algunos tipos de delfines son más inteligentes que otros]$_I$
'Many studies about the behavior of dolphins conclude that some types of dolphins are more intelligent than others.'

It should be noted that the divisions of the strings in (61) do not represent the only possibilities. If the same sentences are uttered more quickly and perhaps in a more colloquial style, such restructurings may not take place. In this case, the *I* structure would be that assigned by the basic *I* construction rule. The two sentences in question would thus consist of one *I* each, and NA would apply as indicated in (62).

(62)   a.   [$_I$Usa su sombrero carísimo con seis plumas de tucán cuando desea crear la impresión que es una persona muy importante]$_I$
   b.   [$_I$Muchos estudios sobre el comportamiento del delfín concluyen que algunos tipos de delfines son más inteligentes que otros]$_I$

In addition to the general principles for *I* restructuring which account for the divisions seen above in (61), it is necessary in Spanish, too, to include the same special principles for breaking down lists and embedded structures into shorter *I*s. This can be seen by comparing the application of NA in the unrestructured *I*s in (63a) and (64a) with the lack of application in the restructured forms of these sentences in (63b) and (64b), respectively.

(63)   a.   [$_I$Quería invitar a Juan Carmen Carlos y Beatriz]$_I$
'I would like to invite Juan, Carmen, Carlos and Beatriz.'
   b.   [$_I$Quería invitar a Juan]$_I$ [$_I$Carmen]$_I$ [$_I$Carlos]$_I$ [$_I$y Beatriz]$_I$

(64) a. [₁Eso es el escorpió<u>n</u> que espa<u>n</u>tó al tucá<u>n</u> que espa<u>n</u>tó al faisá<u>n</u> que se paseaba en el jardín]₁
'That is the scorpion that frightened the toucan that frightened the pheasant that was taking a walk in the garden.'

   b. [₁Eso es el escorpión]₁ [₁que espa<u>n</u>tó al tucán]₁ [₁que espa<u>n</u>tó al faisán]₁ [₁que se paseaba en el jardín]₁

The data considered in this section demonstrate that syntactic constituents cannot be taken as the domain of application of NA in Spanish for the same reasons they cannot be taken as the domain of application of GT and IS in Italian. That is, it was seen that the application of Nasal Assimilation is sensitive to such factors as the length of a given string, and as a result, it can apply differently to the same types of constituents of differing lengths. In addition, the possibility of dividing a given string into *I* constituents in more than one way by applying the restructuring rules as well as the basic *I* formation rule allows for a certain degree of variability in the application of NA. That is, depending on such factors as rate and style of speech, as well as the length of a particular string, NA may apply in a given position when the sentence is uttered in one way but not when it is uttered in another way. In syntax, constituents are uniquely defined on the basis of their structural properties, and all constituents of a given type are assigned the same structure regardless of their length and other nonstructural considerations such as speed and style of speech. On these grounds, we propose that the form of the Nasal Assimilation rule in Spanish is as follows:

(65) *Nasal Assimilation*[13]

$$[\text{+nasal}] \;\rightarrow\; \begin{bmatrix} \alpha\text{ant} \\ \beta\text{cor} \end{bmatrix} \; / \; [_{I} \ldots \underline{\quad\quad} \begin{bmatrix} -\text{son} \\ \alpha\text{ant} \\ \beta\text{ cor} \end{bmatrix} \ldots]_{I}$$

7.3.3. Greek

The last language we will consider here is Greek. The rule of *s*-Voicing (SV) in Greek applies both within words and across words, as do the other rules we have examined in this chapter. Specifically, according to SV /s/ is voiced when it is followed by a voiced [+consonantal] segment (see Setatos, 1974), as illustrated in (66), where '‿' in the phonetic transcription (i.e. the second line of each example) indicates an /s/ that assimilates to the voicing of the following segment and '₊' indicates an /s/ that does not assimilate.

(66) a. *κόσμος*
         [kós̱mos]
         'people'
      b. *ασβεστος*
         [ás̱vestos]
         'inextinguishable'
      c. *Θέλεις να πάς;*
         [θélis̱ na pas]
         'Do you want to go?'
      d. *Ο πατέρας μας είχε πολλες δουλειές*
         [o patéras̱ mas íxe polés̱ ðuliés]
         'Our father had many jobs to do.'

SV does not apply across just any two words when its segmental context is present, however, but only across words that are in the same *I*, as illustrated by the sentences in (67), where the square brackets in the second line of each example indicate the *I* structure.

(67) a. *Ο δάσκαλός μας λέει ότι πρέπει να διαβάσεις δύο βιβλία για τις εξετάσεις.*
         [$_I$ o ðáskalos̱ mas̱ léi óti prépi na ðyavásis̱ ðío vivlía yá tis eksetásis]$_I$
         'The teacher tells us that you must read two books for the exams.'
      b. *Ο Πέτρος δεν είναι μαθημένος να τρώει αχινούς με ψωμί.*
         [$_I$ o pétros̱ ðen íne maθiménos̱ na trói axinús̱ me psomí]$_I$
         'Petros is not used to eating sea urchins with bread.'
      c. *Ο άνδρας αυτός, μου φαίνεται, είναι πολύ έξυπνος.*
         [$_I$ o ánðras aftós̱]$_I$ [$_I$mu fénete]$_I$ [$_I$íne polí éksipnos]$_I$
         'This man, it seems to me, is very bright.'
      d. *Εκείνος ο άνδρας, μάρτυς μου ο θεός, δεν θα μπεί ποτέ στο σπίτι μου.*
         [$_I$ekínos o ánðras̱]$_I$ [$_I$mártis̱ mu o θeós̱]$_I$ [$_I$ðen θa bi poté sto spíti mu]$_I$
         'This man, God be my witness, will never enter my house.'

It should be noted that the *I* structure indicated in these examples is that assigned by the basic *I* formation rule proposed earlier. What this shows is that the divisions that are relevant for intonation breaks and contours in English and certain segmental rules in Italian and Spanish are the same divisions that delimit the domains of application of SV in Greek. We can thus formulate the following rule for SV, which shows that it is an *I* span rule, that is, a rule that applies whenever its segmental context is present within an intonational phrase.[14]

(68)   *s-Voicing*

$$\begin{bmatrix} +\text{vce} \\ +\text{strid} \\ +\text{cont} \end{bmatrix} \rightarrow [+\text{vce}] \quad / \quad [_I \ldots \underline{\hspace{1cm}} \begin{bmatrix} +\text{cons} \\ +\text{vce} \end{bmatrix} \ldots]_I$$

As was seen in relation to the other phonological rules examined in the preceding sections of this chapter, rules that apply at the *I* level typically exhibit a certain degree of variability in their application. This is a direct result of the flexible nature of the *I* constituent itself. As the examples in (69) and (70) show, SV is no exception to this pattern. That is, it may apply in a long *I* if the *I* is uttered fairly quickly, but it is blocked when the *I* is restructured in slower speech in such a way that the division interrupts the segmental context of the rule.

(69)   a.   Το σπίτι τις μητέρας της Μαρίας μου αρέσει πολύ.
           [_Ito spíti tis̲ mitéras tis̲ Marías̲ mu arési polí]_I
           'The house of the mother of Mary pleases me a lot.'
       b.   [_Ito spíti tis̲ mitéras tis̲ Marías̲]_I [_Imu arési polí]_I

(70)   a.   Στην Ελλάδα ο κόσμος δεν είναι μαθημένος να πίνει καφέ
           μετά το φαγητό.
           [_Istin eláða o kós̲mos̲ ðen íne maθiménos̲ na píni kafé metá to
           fajitó]_I
           'In Greece people are not used to drinking coffee after meals.'
       b.   [_Istin elaða o kós̲mos̲ ðen íne maθiménos̲]_I [_Ina píni kafé metá
           to fajitó]_I

These two examples illustrate the general *I* restructuring principles. In (69b), the original *I* has been divided following an NP, and in (70b), the original *I* has been divided before the beginning of a new S̄ that is not part of an NP, and thus does not result in the interruption of an NP. As might be expected on the basis of the similarity between the behavior of SV and that of the other rules seen above, the application of SV is also affected by the special cases of *I* restructuring observed in lists and embedded structures. Thus, SV applies in the unrestructured strings in (71a) and (72a), but not in the restructured ones in (71b) and (72b).

(71)   a.   Θα μου άρεξε να αγοράσω αχινούς μπακαλιάρους μπαρμπούνια
           και χταπόδια.
           [_Iθa mu áreze na aγoráso axínus̲ bakaljárus̲ barbúnja ke
           xtapóðja]_I
           'I would like to buy sea urchins, cod, mullets, and octopus.'

b. [ɪθa mu áreze na aγoráso axínus]ɪ [ɪbakaljárus]ɪ [ɪbarbúnya]ɪ
    [ɪke xtapóðja]ɪ

(72) a. Ἔχω δει τους αστακούς μισοφαγωμένους από τους ποντικούς
          δυναστευμένους από τους γάτους διαλυμένους από τους
          σκύλους λιγδιασμένους από το λίπος.
          [ɪéxo ðí tus astakús misofaγoménus apó tus pontikús
          ðinastevménus apó tus γátus ðjaliménus apó tus skílus
          liγðjasménus apó to lípos]ɪ
          'I have seen the lobsters half eaten by the mice destroyed by the
          cats dispersed by the dogs soiled with grease.'
      b. [ɪéxo ðí tus astakús]ɪ [ɪmisofaγoménus apó tus pontikús]ɪ
          [ɪðinastevménus apó tus γátus]ɪ [ɪðjaliménus apó tus skílus]ɪ
          [ɪliγðjasménus apó to lípos]ɪ

The application of SV in certain contexts and its lack of application in
others provides further motivation for the definition of the intonational
phrase proposed earlier in this chapter. That is, it was shown in this section that SV applies within a root sentence, within the types of constructions that form obligatory *I*s, and within the strings that are sisters of such
*I*s, but it does not apply across the juncture between two *I*s. It was demonstrated, furthermore, that SV, like the other *I*-level phenomena examined
in this chapter, is sensitive to such nonsyntactic factors as the length
of a string and its rate of utterance to the extent that they may have an
effect on the restructuring of a given string into shorter *I*s. The special
intonational properties of lists and embedded constructions were also
observed in relation to the application of SV. Finally, the fact that the
division of a string into *I*s by the basic *I* formation rule and the restructuring rules often results in constituents that are not isomorphic to any
constituents found elsewhere in the grammar, as well as the fact that syntactic constituents cannot offer the flexibility needed in order to account
for the domain of application of SV, provides additional evidence for the
intonational phrase as a constituent in the phonological hierarchy.

7.4. Conclusions

In this chapter, another prosodic constituent, the intonational phrase,
was motivated and rules for its construction and possible restructuring
were proposed. The original definition of the domain of *I* was based on the
domains over which intonation contours extend and the positions of
potential rule-governed pauses in English. It was shown, however, that in
addition to accounting for such nonsegmental phenomena, *I* also correctly delimits the domain of application of segmental rules in several

languages: Italian, Spanish, and Greek. As was the case for ϕ, syntactic information must also be referred to in the construction of I. The nature of the syntactic information needed to define the I domain is so general, however, that it was proposed that the I formation rule is, in fact, universal. Furthermore, the two essential syntactic notions, that of structural attachment to the tree and that of root sentence, lend support to the general principle of prosodic constituent formation according to which the higher the constituent is in the hierarchy, the more general the principles are for its definition. It should be recalled that the definition of the domain of ϕ, the constituent immediately under I in the hierarchy, required somewhat more specific syntactic notions, such as the head of a phrase and its recursive side.

It was shown, further, that the intonational phrase may under certain circumstances undergo restructuring, a process seen in relation to the phonological phrase, and one that will be seen again in the next chapter in relation to the phonological utterance. While restructuring in ϕ is quite rigidly determined, restructuring in I is much more flexible. It was shown, in particular, that I restructuring often depends on such nonsyntactic factors as the length of a given I, the rate and style of speech, and special semantic prominence considerations. Syntax is relevant to I restructuring, as is argument structure, only in the sense that the positions in which intonation breaks may occur are restricted by the structure of the string involved. That is, while restructuring may be warranted on the grounds of the length of a particular I, for example, where the breaks may be introduced depends on such factors as whether an NP ends or a new $\bar{S}$ begins at a given point, or whether a given constituent is an obligatory or an optional argument of a given verb. In other words, the relevant notions are that of cyclic node and argument structure. Furthermore, since the end of an NP represents a stronger restriction on restructuring that the beginning of an $\bar{S}$, the other cyclic node, and since the presence of an obligatory argument represents a stronger restriction than the presence of an optional argument, the combination of the two relatively stronger factors yields the strongest type of restriction.

In addition to the general I restructuring phenomena, two special structures, lists and embedded constructions, were examined since they raise problems with respect to the division of a string into intonational phrases. It was proposed to handle these cases with a separate restructuring rule that makes crucial use of the notion of repetition, perhaps as a reflection of a more abstract notion of timing and rhythm. In the special restructuring cases, the noun was shown to play a central role as well. This is not surprising, nor is the fact that the constituents NP and $\bar{S}$ play a central role in the general restructuring rule, since, as was pointed out, the noun has been claimed to be the most 'accentable' part of speech and thus one that is of particular importance to prosodic phenomena. It is also the case that the two syntactic constituents referred to in restructuring (NP and S̄) are somewhat special in other ways in syntax and semantics as well.

The division between a basic constituent construction rule and additional restructuring rules seen in this chapter is similar to the division seen in the chapter on φ and to the division that will be seen in the next chapter, on U. What such a division shows is that phonological constituent formation consists of two qualitatively different rule types. In each case, there is a basic rule that applies obligatorily and in all languages; this gives the fundamental prosodic structure. In addition, there are other rules that may or may not apply, depending on a variety of syntactic and nonsyntactic factors; when they apply, these yield a derived prosodic structure.

Whether basic or derived, all *I*s exhibit internal patterns of relative prominence, as do all the other prosodic constituents. The position of the stressed element within *I* is quite variable, however, a fact that distinguishes *I* from the other constituents. This variability was shown to be the result of the type of criteria that determine the position of stress within *I*. That is, since stress is essentially assigned on the basis of semantic prominence principles such as focus or given *vs*. new information, it follows that a particular string may be uttered with different stress patterns depending on the situation, both linguistic and nonlinguistic. This fact, along with certain facts about restructuring, was shown to provide support for the n-ary branching trees proposed in this book, as opposed to the binary trees proposed in earlier work on prosodic phonology.

Finally, it was shown on several grounds that the phonological constituent *I* is able to account for both the segmental and nonsegmental phenomena examined in this chapter, where syntactic constituents fail to do so. In particular, it was shown that in certain situations the strings that make up an intonational phrase, and thus constitute the domain of application of phonological rules, are not isomorphic to any constituent found in syntax. It was also shown that the flexible nature of *I* is, by definition, incompatible with syntactic constituent structure according to which a given string is assigned a unique analysis on the basis of structural relations among the words in the string. Such factors as the length of the string and the rate of speech, which are essential in determining the ultimate division of a string into *I*s, are beyond the scope of syntax.

NOTES

1. For an analysis of the actual intonation contours, see a number of articles printed in Bolinger (1965) and such works as Crystal (1969), Ladd (1980), Bing (1979), and Pierrehumbert (1980).

2. We are referring here only to grammar-related pauses, as opposed to those that depend solely on performance factors and cannot, therefore, be said to be rule-governed (see Bierwisch, 1966; Downing, 1970; Bing, 1979).

3. Although Selkirk (1984b) accounts for obligatory *I*s in terms of semantic rather than syntactic criteria, her set of constructions is essentially the same as the set identified syntactically.

4. Very similar results are obtained by Bing's (1979) analysis in terms of R constituents.

5. On the analogy of a somewhat similar example in Emonds (1976), it might be possible, although questionable, to consider the sequence *Isabelle is* to be a constituent, i.e. S. It should be noted, however, that even in Emonds's (1976:45) formulation of the parenthetical rule there is no requirement that the string to the left of the parenthetical element be a constituent, as indicated by the variable X in the rule:

$$[_S X - \left\{ \begin{array}{c} NP \\ AP \\ S \\ VP \\ PP \end{array} \right\}]_S - \left\{ \begin{array}{c} S \\ PP \end{array} \right\} \quad \rightarrow \quad 1 \; - \; \emptyset \; - \; 3 \; - \; 2$$

6. While both the notion of length and the process of restructuring are relevant in syntax as well as in phonology, their effects on the final syntactic and phonological structures, respectively, are quite different. In syntax, length plays a role, for example, in Heavy NP Shift, where 'heavy' means 'long'. The role of restructuring in syntax is typically that of joining more than one element into a single longer element, as in the case of verb restructuring in Italian, discussed by Rizzi (1976). In phonology, however, restructuring can also break apart a given element, as will be seen in this section.

7. It should be noted that the genitives to the left of *mother* will first be grouped with the head noun into a single ϕ by the ϕ construction rule seen in Chapter 6 since they are on the nonrecursive side of the head. It seems, however, that in strings of such pre-head modifiers some type of restructuring takes place so that these modifiers may form ϕs on their own, as indicated in (19a).

8. 'Accentable' refers to an inherent property of nouns, and not to the special situation in which heavy stress may be applied for contrastive or emphatic purposes. In such cases, clearly any type of word may bear a strong stress, as in: *Don't invite that unbearable egotist* or *Put the magazine únder the book.*

9. Note that this type of sentence also gives rise to a problem in relation to ϕ since the adjectives to the left of the head of the NP, *beast*, will be joined into a single ϕ with *beast* by the basic ϕ construction rule. This is similar to the problem seen above in relation to the pre-head genitives in (19a) (see also footnote 7). Restructuring will have to take place to assign ϕ status to the adjectives in sentences such as that in (27), as it does to the pre-head genitives.

10. There is actually some variability in the resulting segment. For example, /k/ may be realized as [x], [kx], or even null, as well as [h]. This phonetic variation is not relevant, however, to the present discussion.

11. It should be noted that GT is quite variable in its application and, furthermore, is somewhat stigmatized in Italian (though not in the Florentine dialect). On the basis of additional informal observations, it seems that at least some speakers may allow GT across *I*s as well. In such cases, GT would be a *U*-domain rule rather than an *I*-domain rule and would thus belong with the phenomena discussed in the next chapter. Given the wide variation in the application of GT, in order to do justice to the

rule one would have to control for a number of factors that lie beyond the scope of this book, such as the age, sex, and social status of the speaker and the rate and style of speech. Our discussion of GT is based uniquely on the data described in the text.

12.   While Nasal Assimilation is a widespread phenomenon in all varieties of Spanish, the observations here are made specifically in relation to Porteño, the variety of Spanish spoken in Buenos Aires, since this is the variety spoken by the native speakers we interviewed.

13.   The exact specification of the features may need to be modified slightly in order to account for fine distinctions in point of articulation such as the difference between dental and alveolar articulations (see Harris, 1969). The ultimate choice of features does not affect the point we are making here and we will therefore not discuss it further.

14.   For the distinctive features of Greek, see Malikouti (1970) and Kontou (1973).

Chapter 8

The Phonological Utterance

8.0. Introduction

The last phonological constituent we will consider is the phonological utterance (U), the largest constituent in the prosodic hierarchy. A U consists of one or more intonational phrases, the category just below it in the hierarchy, and usually extends the length of the string dominated by the highest node of a syntactic tree, which we will refer to as X^n. This is not to say, however, that U is simply the phonological counterpart of X^n, a phonological constituent introduced only to avoid making direct reference to syntax in the formulation of phonological rules. In fact, X^n and U are not always the same, as will be demonstrated on the basis of several phonological rules that operate within the U domain, but not within the confines of X^n. It is precisely this type of discrepancy that provides the strongest motivation for the U constituent in phonology since, once again, we are faced with phonological phenomena whose domains of application cannot be formulated strictly in terms of the constituent structure provided by syntax. It will be shown in this chapter that the phonological utterance, like the other prosodic constituents, makes use of syntactic information in its definition, though the end result is not necessarily isomorphic to any syntactic constituent. U will also be shown to undergo a process of restructuring under certain circumstances, in much the same way that the prosodic categories below it in the hierarchy do. What is particularly interesting about U-level restructuring, however, is that it depends not only on phonological and syntactic factors, but also on factors of a logico-semantic nature. Thus, at the highest level of phonological analysis, we find an interaction among several components of the grammar, an interaction which has implications not only for the organization of phonology, but also for the organization of the grammar in general.

8.1. Definition of the phonological utterance domain

In this section we will be concerned with the definition of the basic U constituent. Let us assume for the present discussion that the phonological utterance is delimited by the beginning and end of the syntactic constituent X^n. In other words, let us assume that U consists of those Is that are dominated by the same node X^n in the syntactic tree. That such a unit is relevant in phonology will be demonstrated in the following sections, where several sandhi rules will be examined and shown to operate in a domain so defined. Cases of nonisomorphism between X^n and U will be discussed in section 8.2.

The only syntactic information referred to in the definition of the basic U are the right and left boundaries of the X^n node in question. This is not as trivial a point as it may seem, since a string of Is may or may not be dominated by a single X^n node, or phonological unit. For example, we must be able to group the series of Is in (1) into two separate Us, and this must be done in the way indicated by the brackets in (2a), and not in any other way, such as in (2b) and (2c).

(1)   [My cousin]$_I$ [collects snakes]$_I$ [Gertrude]$_I$ [prefers butterflies]$_I$

(2)   a.   [[My cousin]$_I$ [collects snakes]$_I$]$_U$ [[Gertrude]$_I$
             [prefers butterflies]$_I$]$_U$
        b.   *[[My cousin]$_I$ [collects snakes]$_I$ [Gertrude]$_I$]$_U$
             [[prefers butterflies]$_I$]$_U$
        c.   *[[My cousin]$_I$]$_U$ [[collects snakes]$_I$ [Gertrude]$_I$
             [prefers butterflies]$_I$]$_U$

We can thus formulate the following basic definition of U:

(3)   *Phonological Utterance Formation*
        I.   *U domain*
             The domain of U consists of all the Is corresponding to X^n
             in the syntactic tree.
        II. *U construction*
             Join into an n-ary branching U all Is included in a string
             delimited by the definition of the domain of U.

As far as the assignment of stress is concerned, if relative prominence is taken to mean what it does in smaller units such as the phonological word, where it corresponds to the traditional notion of 'more stress', at the level of the phonological utterance such distinctions seem to make little sense. Except in sentences with special emphasis patterns, such as that in (4), where the italics indicate extra stress, it is generally not possible to say that one I is 'more prominent' than another.[1]

(4)   [$_U$[Clarence]$_{I_w}$ [stop *complaining*]$_{I_s}$]$_U$

Aside from cases of special emphasis, there are nevertheless reasons for assigning values of *w*(eak) and *s*(trong) to the various intonational phrases of a *U*. As Bing (1979:145) suggests, while there is no sentence stress *per se*, there is instead a 'sentence-final intonation which occurs on the final intonation phrase to indicate that the utterance is finished'. This observation, as well as the observation that elements (vowels, syllables, etc.) at the end of a syntactic constituent and in particular at the end of a sentence, tend to be lengthened (see, among others, Klatt, 1975, 1976; Cooper and Paccia-Cooper, 1980), seems to indicate that it is the last *I* of a *U* that is the strong one. The relevant *U* constituency rule is, therefore, as follows:

(5)   *Phonological Utterance: Relative Prominence*
        The rightmost node dominated by *U* is strong; all other nodes are
        weak.

The basic *U* formation and relative prominence rules are illustrated for English and Italian in the sentences in (6) and (7), respectively. It should be noted, however, that the proposal made here is for all languages, since the effects of end intonation contours and final lengthening seem to be universal.

(6) $[_U$[Our next door neighbor$]_{I_w}$ [Mr. Jones$]_{I_w}$ [bought an ocelot last
        week$]_{I_s}]_U$

(7) $[_U$[Due biologici$]_{I_w}$ [finora sconosciuti$]_{I_w}$ [hanno fatto una

        scoperta importantissima$]_{I_s}]_U$

        'Two biologists, unknown up until now, have made an extremely
        important discovery.'

Thus far, we have only assumed, but not demonstrated, that a unit corresponding to the syntactic constituent X^n is relevant in phonology. We will now examine several phonological rules that operate in the *U* domain as defined above, and thus demonstrate the validity of such a constituent.

8.1.1. Flapping in American English
    One phonological rule that applies in the domain of the phonological utterance is Flapping in American English (see Vogel, 1981). Before examining the prosodic domain of this rule, however, we will briefly outline the segmental facts relevant to Flapping.
    Essentially, the Flapping rule applies to both /t/ and /d/ in the same way, changing them to [ɾ] under certain circumstances.[2] Although the

issue of rule ordering is not discussed in detail in this book, we assume that the application of the Aspiration rule, or more accurately, the tensing rule, which operates in foot-initial position in English, occurs before the Flapping rule (see section 3.2.2 above). The *ts* and *ds* in (8a), therefore, are [+tense], while those in (8b) are [−tense].

(8)   a.   [+tense]
            a<u>t</u>one   a<u>d</u>ore   a <u>t</u>issue   I <u>d</u>escribe

      b.   [−tense]
            a<u>t</u>om   a<u>dd</u>er   a<u>t</u> issue   I'<u>d</u> ascribe

We can now state, somewhat informally, the segmental part of the Flapping rule as in (9); the prosodic domain will be discussed below.

(9)   t, d   → ɾ / [−consonantal] _____ V
           [−tense]

This rule accounts for the presence of a flap in the items in (8b), and for no flap in (8a), as shown in (10).

(10) a.   *no flap*
            a[t]one   a[d]ore   a [t]issue   I [d]escribe

      b.   *flap*
            a[ɾ]om   a[ɾ]er   a[ɾ] issue   I'[ɾ] ascribe

It should be noted that the [−consonantal] segment in the rule in (9) allows for Flapping not only in the most obvious environment, between vowels, but also when the segment preceding *t* or *d* is a glide (e.g. *loiter*) or a liquid or nasal with a nonconsonantal articulation (e.g. *hardy, winter*).[3] Since not all varieties of American English exhibit Flapping in these last two contexts, there may be some minor differences in the formulation of the segmental part of the Flapping rule to account for the various regional pronunciations. We will not be concerned with such regional differences here; instead, we will use exclusively the formulation of the environment for Flapping given in (9).

As far as the domain of application of Flapping is concerned, the examples in (11) show that the rule applies in morphologically simple as well as complex words.

(11) a. water   → wa[ɾ]er
      b. rider   → ri[ɾ]er
      c. whitish   → whi[ɾ]ish
      d. headache   → hea[ɾ]ache

Flapping also applies between words in a sentence, or more precisely, a string dominated by X^n, and as the examples in (12) show, it may apply across any type of constituent, syntactic or phonological, regardless of the length of the constituents.[4]

(12) a. a hundred eggs   → a hundre[ɾ] eggs
      b. should ask   → shoul[ɾ] ask
      c. the white owl   → the whi[ɾ] owl
      d. invite Olivia   → invi[ɾ] Olivia
      e. at eleven   → a[ɾ] eleven
      f. My brother bought a parrot last week. →
          ...bough[ɾ] ...
      g. A very dangerous wild cat escaped from the zoo. →
          ...ca[ɾ] escaped...
      h. Some children recently discovered a rare type of newt under-
          neath some rocks in their yard. →
          ...new[ɾ] underneath...
      i. Just the other night a raccoon was spotted in our
          neighborhood. →
          ...nigh[ɾ] a...
      j. Ichabod, our pet crane, usually hides when guests come. →
          Ichabo[ɾ] our...
      k. Although that was not the first camel he rode, it was most
          certainly the last one. →
          ...ro[ɾ] it...

Flapping can apply in all of the positions indicated in these examples. It is blocked only when a pause or other interruption is introduced within the segmental context of the rule. For example, if the last four examples in (12) are read with particular emphasis or in a particularly deliberate style of speech, it is possible that pauses will be introduced after *newt, night, Ichabod,* and *rode,* respectively, leading to the pronunciation of *t* or *d* instead of a flap. Such a pronunciation, however, is by no means necessary, and when the sentences are produced at a normal rate without pauses, it is the form with the flap that is heard. Since we have explicitly limited our attention in this book to phonological phenomena found in speech produced in a colloquial style and at a normal tempo, neither extremely fast nor extremely slow speech, we will not consider further the stylistic and tempo variations that lead to the articulation of stops rather than [ɾ] in cases such as those in the last examples in (12).

The various examples of Flapping in (12) show that this rule can apply, as long as its segmental environment is present, any place within the corresponding X^n constituent, that is, within and across various syntactic constituents and all levels of the prosodic hierarchy. We can conclude, therefore, that the prosodic domain of Flapping is the phonological utterance, since the basic definition given above states that U is coextensive with the maximal projection of X^n. The Flapping rule in (10) can thus be reformulated as in (13) to take the domain into account.

(13)   *Flapping*

   t, d   → ɾ / [...[−consonantal] ____ V ...]$_U$
   [−tense]

As this formulation shows, Flapping is a domain span rule that operates throughout the U constituent. As such, it provides motivation for a phonological unit (at least) the length of X^n in syntax.[5]

8.1.2.   *Two r phenomena in British English*

Further motivation for the phonological utterance as a unit of phonology comes from two phenomena in nonrhotic varieties of British English, that is, those varieties in which post-vocalic *r* is not pronounced (see Wells, 1982). These phenomena, traditionally called the 'Linking-*r*' (LR) and the 'Intrusive-*r*' (IR), both determine the pronunciation of an *r* sound in connected speech in positions where it does not occur when the words involved are produced in isolation, as was mentioned in section 2.3.1 above. In the first case, LR, the *r* in question is actually present in the orthography (e.g. *far* but *fa[r] away*), while in the second case, IR, there is no *r* present in the orthography (e.g. *Anna* but *Anna[r] arrived*). Before examining the prosodic domain of these phenomena, however, we will examine their segmental contexts, and demonstrate that they can both be handled with a single phonological rule.[6] The variety of English discussed here is RP (Received Pronunciation), as described by Jones (1966).

The Intrusive-*r* is found when a word ending in [ɔ], [a], or [ə] is followed by a suffix or another word beginning with a vowel, as seen respectively in (14a-c).

(14)   a.   [ɔ]:   gnaw   *vs.*   gnaw[r]ing
       b.   [a]:   spa   *vs.*   the spa[r] is ...
       c.   [ə]:   Canada *vs.*   Canada[r] is ...

The Linking-*r* is found when a word ending in an orthographic *r* is followed by a suffix or another word beginning with a vowel, as illustrated
in (15), where 'ŕ' stands for an orthographic *r* that is not pronounced.

(15) a. beaŕ   *vs.*   bea[r]ish
       b. otteŕ   *vs.*   the otte[r] is ...

It should be noted that there is no difference, as far as the present
phenomenon is concerned, between those words that actually have as their
last letter an *r* and those that have a 'silent *e*' after the *r* (cf. *hair/hare,
bear/bare, soar/sore, hear/here*, etc.). We will therefore refer to both types
as having a final orthographic *r*.

In order to determine more precisely the segmental context for the
Linking-*r*, it is useful to consider first which vowels may be followed
by an orthographic *r* in final position. As can be seen in (16), a final
r may appear after six vowels and five diphthongs.[7]

(16) a. [i] : deer   b. [ei]: layer
          [ɛ]: bear   [ai]: fire
          [u]: lure   [ɔi]: foyer
          [ɔ]: boar   [au]: sour
          [a]: spar   [ou] : mower
          [ə]: fir

What happens phonetically in the different vocalic environments when
words such as those in (16) are produced in isolation is the following:
a) after [ɔ], [a], and [ə], nothing is heard in the position of the orthographic *r*; *b*) after [i], [ɛ], and [u], including the [i] and [u] closing the
diphthongs, a schwa appears in the position of the orthographic *r*.[8] Thus,
the endings of *deer* and *idea* are the same (i.e. [iə]), and the endings of
mower and *boa* are the same (i.e. [ouə]). The fact that [ə] appears after
[i, ɛ,u] means that the only vowels found in word-final position in words
ending with an orthographic *r* are [ɔ, a,.ə], as summarized in (17).

(17) a. [ɔ], [a], [ə] (unchanged)
       b. [i] → [iə]   [ei] → [eiə]
           [ɛ] → [ɛə]   [ai] → [aiə]
           [u] → [uə]   [ɔi] → [ɔiə]
                                     [au] → [auə]
                                     [ou] → [ouə]

The segmental environment for LR can thus be stated quite simply:
a Linking-*r* appears in the position between [ɔ, a,ə] and another vowel.

It is clear now that the segmental environments for both LR and IR are the same. In fact, the two phenomena can be expressed as a single rule of *r*-Insertion (RI), formulated as in (18).

$$(18) \quad \emptyset \; \rightarrow \; r \; / \left\{ \begin{array}{c} \mathfrak{o} \\ a \\ \mathfrak{e} \end{array} \right\} \underline{\qquad} V$$

This formulation of *r*-Insertion, however, only provides the segmental context of the rule. We will now examine the question of the domain of application of this rule.

It has already been mentioned above that we find an *r* inserted in the proper segmental context when the 'V' in the formulation is the onset of a suffix or another word; the environment does not arise in monomorphemic words. We thus find RI in complex words, both derived and compound, as illustrated in (19).

(19) a. wate*t*   *vs.*   wate[r]y
      b. bea*t*   *vs.*   bea[r]ish
      c. law   *vs.*   law[r] abiding
      d. ea*t*   *vs.*   ea[r] ache

In addition, like Flapping, RI applies between words in a string dominated by X^n regardless of the syntactic relations between the words and the length of the constituents involved, as illustrated in (20).

(20) a. fou*t* ostrich feathers   →   fou[r] ostrich feathers
      b. neve*t* again   →   neve[r] again
      c. some raw oysters   →   some raw[r] oysters
      d. saw Ellen   →   saw[r] Ellen
      e. fo*t* eight   →   fo[r] eight
      f. I'd love to hea*t* a nightingale sing. →
          ...hea[r] a...
      g. A rare type of grasshoppe*t* invaded our yard last year. →
          ...grasshoppe[r] invaded...
      h. We're trying to teach our new Siamese cat not to claw at the
          furniture. →
          ...claw[r] at...
      i. Just last yea*t*, over a hundred dinosaur tracks were discovered
          in the Arizona desert. →
          ...yea[r] over...
      j. The giant panda, as you know, is an endangered species. →
          ...panda[r] as...

    k.   Even though they're protected by law, a lot of migratory birds are killed by hunters every year. →
...law[r] a...

The same observations made above in relation to Flapping hold for RI as far as the introduction of pauses is concerned. That is, *r*-Insertion applies in all the examples in (20), and in any string under X^n, as long as its segmental context is present, when a normal colloquial style of speech is used, and assuming the string can be, and is, uttered in a single breath. Applying the basic definition of the phonological utterance given above, we can conclude that the formulation of the rule is as follows:

(21)   *r-Insertion*

$$\emptyset \;\rightarrow\; r \;/\; [\ldots \begin{Bmatrix} \text{ɔ} \\ a \\ \text{ə} \end{Bmatrix} \underline{\hspace{1cm}} V \ldots]_U$$

This formulation of RI shows that it is a U span rule, like Flapping, and that it therefore applies any place within a phonological utterance where the proper segmental environment occurs.

8.1.3. *U-level phenomena in other languages*

Since most work in phonology has dealt with relatively small units, such as segments and syllables, and has rarely considered phenomena operating above the word level, there is little mention in the phonological literature of rules applying within a domain as large as that defined by X^n, or the phonological utterance, in prosodic terms. Two notable exceptions are a set of rules in Sanskrit discussed by Selkirk (1980a) and a set of rules in Spanish discussed by Harris (1969).

In her analysis of Sanskrit, Selkirk (1980a) mentions a number of rules that operate within the U domain. In particular, Selkirk cites the following five phenomena as U span rules: Glide Formation, Vowel Contraction, Assimilation of *m*, Anusvara of *m*, and Obstruent Cluster Voicing Assimilation. Consider, for example, the last rule, which can be formulated as follows:

(22)   *Obstruent Cluster Voicing Assimilation* (Selkirk's rule (12))

$$[-\text{son}] \;\rightarrow\; [\alpha\text{voice}] \;/\; [\ldots \underline{\hspace{1cm}} \begin{bmatrix} -\text{son} \\ \alpha\text{voice} \end{bmatrix} \ldots]_U$$

This rule accounts for the fact that in a sequence of two obstruents, the voicing of the first obstruent is determined by the voicing of the second one. The examples Selkirk (p.114) provides are repeated in (23).

(23)   ad + si   → atsi   'you throw'
       ad + thas   → atthas   'you eat'
       ap – jaḥ   → ab – jaḥ   'water born'
       dik – gadaḥ   → dig – gadaḥ   'constellation in certain
                                           direction'
       jyok jīva   → jyog jīva   'long-lived'
       parivrāṭ gacchati → parivrāḍ gacchati 'he goes wandering around'

Since Obstruent Cluster Voicing Assimilation, as well as the other rules
mentioned above, are explicitly given by Selkirk as *U* span rules, we interpret this to mean that they behave in the same way that Flapping and *r*-
Insertion behave in English. That is, we assume that the Sanskrit rules
operate throughout a string dominated by X^n, or *U*, whenever their
segmental context is present, and are blocked only when the context is
interrupted by a pause introduced for stylistic or other reasons.

As further motivation for *U* as a unit of phonology, we find a number
of Sanskrit rules that operate at the juncture of two phonological words,
as long as they fall within the *U* domain (see section 4.2.1 above). Selkirk
(p.125) lists the following as ω juncture rules on the *U* domain, although
she does not actually formulate and illustrate all of them: Final Voicing,
Stop to Nasal, *as* > *o*, *s* > ∅, *r*-Deletion, and *a*-Deletion. As an example
of this type of rule, consider Final Voicing, formulated by Selkirk (p.115)
as follows:

(24)   *Final Voicing*   (Selkirk's rule (23))
       [–son] → [+voice] / [...[... ____]ω [[+voice]...]ω...]U

The examples Selkirk (p.115) gives of Final Voicing are listed in (25).

(25)   sat – aha   → sad – aha   'good day'
       samyak uktam   → samyag uktam   'spoken correctly'
       tat namas   → tad namas   'that homage'

Finally, Selkirk mentions Visarga at Pause as a *U* limit rule, that is, one
that applies only at the end of the *U* domain, as seen in the formulation
in (26).

(26)   *Visarga at Pause*   (Selkirk's rule (35))

$$\left\{ \begin{array}{c} s \\ r \end{array} \right\} → ḥ \; / \; [...\_\_\_]_U$$

The examples Selkirk gives of this rule are seen in (27).

(27)   devas → devaḥ   'god'
　　　 punar → punaḥ   'again'

The various examples of Sanskrit we have just seen illustrate three different types of rules that make reference to the domain U in their formulation: U span, ω juncture on U domain, and U limit rules.[9] These rules all
provide further evidence that a domain that extends the length of a string
dominated by X^n is needed in order to account for the application of certain phonological rules.

While the Sanskrit examples were provided by Selkirk with the explicit
intention of motivating U as a domain for phonological rules, we find
further, though less direct, evidence of phonological rules operating in the U
domain in Harris's (1969) analysis of Mexican Spanish phonology.
Although Harris does not discuss the problem of the domain of application of phonological rules in detail, he does make some observations that
are relevant to this issue. Keeping in mind that Harris was working in the
theoretical framework of SPE, which used various boundary symbols
and admitted no phonological units larger than the word, let us examine
Harris's suggestion that at a given point in the application of a series of
phonological rules, all word boundaries or 'termini' are erased and any
subsequent rules apply to the entire string. Specifically, Harris (1969:
59) claims that 'after the removal of termini [and presumably all other
boundary symbols as well], all subsequent rules apply 'across the board':
an entire utterance is scanned and each rule R_i is applied wherever applicable...'. While Harris is cautious in pointing out that the point at which
boundaries are erased depends on the style of speech, he assumes without
further investigation that whenever a rule applies between words it may
automatically apply between any two words in an 'utterance', regardless
of the relationship between the words involved. As we have seen in
previous chapters, there are different types of phonological rules that
operate across words, and a crucial difference among these rules is precisely the fact that they do not all apply within the same domain. While some
do apply throughout a sentence, as do the U-level rules we are examining
in this chapter, others are restricted to smaller domains, such as the
phonological phrase and the intonational phrase.

Of all the rules Harris gives as applying throughout an 'utterance',
there is only one, Voicing Assimilation, for which there is additional
evidence that the domain of application must be the phonological utterance (see section 8.2.1). This is not to say that the others are not also U-
domain rules, but since there is not the necessary information to determine their precise domains of application, we will only list the rules here,
leaving the empirical verification to future research. Specifically, Harris
formulates rules for the following processes with an optional word bound-

ary in their environment, an indication that they not only apply within words, but also across words: Nasal Assimilation (Harris's rule (69f) in the summary of rules), Lateral Assimilation (Harris's rule (69g)), Spirantization (Harris's rule (69h)), Glide/*r* Strengthening, a rule that changes glides into obstruents and the flapped [r] into the trilled [R] (Harris's rule (69j)), Voicing, a rule that voices [p, t, k] under certain circumstances (Harris's rule (69 l)), and Voicing Assimilation, a rule that assimilates the voicing of certain segments (i.e. those with the feature [–heightened subglottal pressure]) to that of the following segment (Harris's rule (69m)).[10] The first three rules apply across words in Allegretto speech, the style described by Harris that seems to correspond best to the style we have taken as the basis for this book, but not in the somewhat more careful Andante style, while the last three rules apply across words in both Andante and Allegretto speech.

As an example of a Spanish rule that operates across words, let us consider Voicing Assimilation (VA), the one rule for which there is additional evidence (to be discussed in section 8.2.1) that the 'utterance' Harris refers to as the domain of application does, in fact, correspond to our notion of phonological utterance. Harris (1969:57) formulates Voicing Assimilation as follows (where h.s. press = heightened subglottal pressure):[11]

(28)
$$\begin{bmatrix} +\text{obstr} \\ -\text{h.s. press} \end{bmatrix} \rightarrow \begin{cases} [\alpha\text{voice}] \,/\, \underline{\quad} (\#) \begin{bmatrix} +\text{cons} \\ \alpha\text{voice} \end{bmatrix} \\ [-\text{voice}] \,/\, \underline{\quad} \parallel \end{cases}$$

The first part of this rule voices [p, t, k, s] when they are followed by certain voiced consonants, and devoices [β, ð, γ] when they are followed by certain voiceless consonants. The second part devoices [β, ð, γ] in absolute final position. The two parts of the rule will be discussed separately.

As the first part of the rule states, VA applies either within a word, that is, in the absence of the optional word boundary, or across (any) two words when the boundary is present. These two cases are illustrated in (29a) and (29b), respectively (from Harris, 1969:38, 40, 44, 60).

(29)   a.   atmosfera   → a[t^d]mosfera   'atmosphere'
            isla   → i[s^Z]la   'island'
            absurdo   → a[β^φ]surdo   'absurd'
            Agfa   → A[γ^X]fa   'Agfa'
       b.   los dos   → lo[s^Z] dos   'both of them'
            Beatriz babea → Beatri[s^Z] babea 'Beatriz slobbers'

The first part of the rule in (28) can now be reformulated as in (30), so that it includes the information that its domain of application is the phonological utterance.

(30) *Voicing Assimilation*

$$
\begin{bmatrix} +\text{obstr} \\ -\text{h.s. press} \end{bmatrix} \rightarrow [\alpha\text{voice}] / \ [... \underline{\quad\quad} \begin{bmatrix} +\text{cons} \\ \alpha\text{voice} \end{bmatrix} ...]_U
$$

It should be noted that this rule no longer makes use of the optional word boundary symbol found in Harris's fromulation. The rule simply applies any place its segmental context is encountered throughout *U*. In fact, the rule in (30) has the same form as the other *U* span rules seen in American and British English and in Sanskrit.

The second part of the Voicing Assimilation rule in (28) represents another type of rule, a domain limit rule in prosodic terms, which is why we are treating it separately here, despite Harris's attempt to collapse it with the first part of VA. Harris uses the symbol '‖' in his formulation to show that the rule applies only when followed by 'silence – that is, total lack of phonation' (p.59). Thus, we can say that the second part of the VA rule, which might more appropriately be called Final Devoicing, applies only at the right limit of a phonological utterance, as does another rule (i.e. the second part of the Glide/*r* Strengthening rule, Harris's rule (69j)). A reformulation of Final Devoicing (FD) in prosodic terms is given in (31).

(31) *Final Devoicing*

$$
\begin{bmatrix} +\text{obstr} \\ -\text{h.s. press} \end{bmatrix} \rightarrow [-\text{voice}] / \ [... \underline{\quad\quad}]_U
$$

Harris does not provide examples of entire sentences at the end of which FD can be observed, but only individual words which would exhibit devoicing when followed by silence. It is not difficult, however, to imagine sentences in which these words appear in the last position. Several such examples are given below (from Harris, 1969:40):

(32) club   → clu[β^ϕ]   'club'
      sed   → se[$\eth^\theta$]   'thirst'
      zigzag   → zigza[γ^x]   'zigzag'

What we can conclude on the basis of our examination of the Spanish data is that they too provide support for *U* as a unit of phonology. That is, despite the fact that Harris's analysis represents a different theoretical framework (and therefore makes use of some different mechanisms, such as boundaries), it is nevertheless possible to interpret his observations in terms that are consistent with the prosodic model described here. That is, we have seen that there are two types of phonological rules in Spanish that make use of the phonological utterance as their domain of application: U span rules and U limit rules. It is worth noting, furthermore, that the reformulation in prosodic terms of the rules we have examined here actually offers several advantages over Harris's SPE-type formulations.

First of all, we have separated the Voicing Assimilation rule into two separate prosodic rules. While this might be considered undesirable in the SPE framework, it reveals more clearly that there are actually two processes involved: one which assimilates the feature [voice] to a following segment throughout the expanse of an utterance, and one which devoices a segment only at the end of an utterance. Claiming that the latter is also a process of assimilation (to silence) does not really increase the generality of the rule, since devoicing before a [−voice] segment applies, as we have seen, any place within an utterance, and devoicing before silence only applies, by definition, in one place, utterance finally. This distinction is clearly captured by the two different types of prosodic rules, since one is a domain span rule and the other a domain limit rule.

Secondly, by reformulating the first part of Harris's VA rules as a U span rule, we are able to simplify the rule somewhat by eliminating the optional boundary symbol '(#)'. This simplification not only represents a savings of symbols, it also resolves a problem raised by Harris precisely in relation to his use of the optional boundary. That is, Harris points out that '(#)' in a rule means that the presence of the boundary is irrelevant, but at the same time, the presence of the symbol does not correctly reflect this situation. '[I]f we write rules with parenthesized boundaries, we do not recognize the fact that the boundaries are irrelevant (since we must mention them in the rules), and their irrelevance does not give us simpler rules' (p.58). Thus, the fact that the optional boundary is not present in the prosodic formulation of VA more accurately represents the fact that the word limits are, indeed, irrelevant to this rule. In the case of Spanish, this advantage must be multiplied by the number of rules given by Harris in which '(#)' appears, since they can all be reformulated as domain span rules, though we will not do so here.

8.2. Nonisomorphism between the maximal domains in the syntactic and phonological hierarchies

On the basis of the phenomena we have examined so far in this chapter, it could be argued that there is really no need for a distinct phonological unit U, since our definition equates U with the string dominated by X^n

in the syntactic tree and all the rules we have considered seem to apply precisely within the confines, or at the end, of such a unit. In other words, it could be argued that, as a unit of linguistic analysis, U is superfluous, since the grammar already contains a constituent of exactly the same dimensions. One could thus posit a single constituent, X^n in syntax, as the domain for the relevant phenomena of both the syntax and the phonology. Not only would such a solution be inelegant, it is also impossible, as will be seen below, since there are cases in which the domain of certain phonological rules does not coincide with that of X^n.

It should be noted that the U domain defined by X^n usually corresponds to what is generally recognized as a 'sentence'. In colloquial speech, however, we often find utterances of the type: *At five* and *Near by*. As the examples in (33) show, when the proper segmental environment is present, the various U-level rules described above apply in these shorter structures as well.

(33) a. At eight   →   A[ɾ] eight
      b. Neaɾ Athens   →   Nea[r] Athens
      c. Law and order   →   Law[r] and order
      d. Los dos   →   Lo[s^z] dos   'Both of them'

While these structures are not generally recognized as sentences, and according to some analyses (see Shopen, 1972) cannot even be derived by deletion rules from sentences, they nevertheless can be handled by the basic definition of U as the string dominated by X^n in the syntactic tree. If we do assume that these structures are derived from an underlying sentence, then X^n represents the highest S node. If we assume, instead, that they are generated as they are, then X^n represents the highest node in the structure in question: $\overline{\overline{P}}$ in (33a) and (33b), $\overline{\overline{N}}$ in (33c) and (33d), etc.

The cases in which the basic definition of U given above is not adequate are those in which a given phonological rule applies across sentences, or more precisely, across strings delimited by different X^n nodes. These cases are, in fact, the ones that provide the crucial evidence that a separate phonological unit, U, is needed in the grammar, as will be seen in the next section.

8.2.1. *Phonological rules operating across sentences*

Although the string dominated by X^n is usually a root sentence (as defined by Emonds, 1976), it may sometimes include more than one root sentence and sometimes less, assuming that the highest node of a syntactic tree may be some category other than S, as suggested above. In this section, we will generally limit ourselves to cases in which X^n is a single (root) sentence, since these are the X^n structures that are most likely to allow the application of phonological rules across their limits. We will therefore refer simply to 'sentences' here, and explicitly point out any cases in which a different structure is used.

While it is difficult to find information in the literature about phonological rules operating between words throughout sentences, it is almost impossible to find reference to rules applying across sentences. In this regard, an observation made by Kahn (1980) about American English and one made by Harris (1969) about Mexican Spanish are particularly interesting.

Kahn (1980:102), in his discussion of Flapping in American English, mentions that the rule may apply between sentences on certain occasions. He cites the following example:

(34)   Have a seat. I'll be right back.   →   ...sea[ɾ] I'll...

According to Kahn, this shows that rules like Flapping are not sensitive to any type of syntactic information. That is, when they apply in discourse, as in the example just seen, they apply in contexts 'in which the strongest imaginable syntactic boundary intervenes' (p.102).

Harris (1969:60) goes into somewhat more detail in his discussion of the application of Voicing Assimilation in Mexican Spanish. He compares the two possible pronunciations of the two-sentence sequence *Los dos. Dámelos.* 'Both of them. Give them to me.' seen in (35), where '‖' represents silence at the end of an utterance, and '↓' the phonetic properties of falling intonation.

(35)   a.   Los dos. Dámelos.   →   [los^Z ðós^Z ↓ dámelos↓]
          b.   Los dos. ‖ Dámelos.→   [los^Z ðós ↓ dámelos↓]

Both (35a) and (35b) have the same intonation patterns, a falling contour at the end of each of the two sentences. The presence of '‖' is not obligatory with a terminal intonation contour, and we see, in fact, that the Voicing Assimilation rule applies across sentences when no pause occurs between them, the case in (35a). The rule is blocked only by the total absence of phonation, the case in (35b).[12] As Harris (1969:60) points out, such examples show 'that the domain of phonological processes such as Voicing Assimilation is not limited to the boundaries of "phonological phrases" or "Phrasierungseinheiten", as has generally been believed'.

Neither Kahn nor Harris addresses the issue of whether such phonological rules may apply across all sentences, nor do they give more than one example of each rule. What is interesting, nevertheless, about their observations is that they show that the domain defined by X^n is not the largest domain of certain phonological rules.

The examples cited by Kahn and Harris are not isolated cases; on further investigation, they turn out to be representative of a systematic phenomenon. Consider, for example, the pairs of sentences in (36a-c), across which we find Flapping, the Linking-*r*, and the Intrusive-*r*, respectively.

(36) a. It's late. I'm leaving. → ...la[ɾ] I'm...
 b. Where's Esthef? I need her. → ...Esthe[r] I...
 c. Call Anna. It's late. → ...Anna[r] It's...

It should be noted that rule application across sentences is not limited to a sequence of only two sentences. In (37), in fact, the Linking-*r* appears between the first and the second sentences, as well as between the second and the third sentences.

(37) I heaf. I heaf. I heaf. → I hea[r] I hea[r] I heaf.

The fact that the same rules found to operate within the *U* defined in terms of the constituent X^n also apply across such constituents means that the definition of *U* given above is not adequate. Since X^n is by definition the largest constituent in X syntax, it is clear that the phonological unit *U* cannot be isomorphic with any syntactic constituent.

Banfield (1973) actually proposed that there is a non-recursive node E ('expression') which would include sentences as well as other material which cannot be embedded in S. While the idea is appealing, it does not resolve the problem at hand, since the types of structures dominated by a single E do not include sequences of $\bar{S}$s such as those seen in (36) and (37). Instead, E is intended mostly to handle such elements as interjections and other material that is in some sense external to a given sentence. Many of these elements have already been handled in the previous chapter, in fact, as constructions that obligatorily form intonational phrases. The problem of joining two separate $\bar{S}$s still remains to be solved.

Finally, since the phonological rules that apply across sentences do not apply across just any two sentences, as will be seen below, it is not possible simply to account for their application in terms of an unspecified series of strings dominated by X^n nodes. Instead, we must define, for the phonology, a distinct unit which represents the domain of application of the type of rules under consideration here.

8.2.2. U restructuring

In order to account for the application of phonological rules across sentences, we need some way to group those sentences in which the rules apply into a single unit. The fact that Flapping normally applies between the two sentences in (38a), but not between those in (38b), shows that it is not possible to group just any sequence of two sentences into a phonological unit.

(38)   a.   Turn up the heat. I'm freezing.   →   ...hea[ɾ] I'm...
       b.   Turn up the heat. I'm Frances.   →   *...hea[ɾ] I'm...[13]

Since the two examples contain the same segmental environments for Flapping and have the same number of syllables and similar syntactic structures, there must be some other explanation for why Flapping applies in one case but not in the other. What is needed is a principled way to determine in which cases a phonological rule applies across sentences and in which cases it does not.

   One possibility is that the application of a rule across sentences depends on the grammatical nature of the sentences themselves. As we have seen in (38), there are at least some cases, however, in which the nature of the sentences involved seems not to be the crucial factor. That is, while in one sequence of an imperative followed by a declarative sentence Flapping is blocked, in another sequence of the same sentence types Flapping is not blocked. A more systematic examination of the various possible combinations of sentences shows that the type of sentences involved is not the relevant criterion. That is, Flapping can apply across all types of sentences, as can *r*-Insertion, as illustrated in items (i) and (ii), respectively, of the examples in (39), where DEC = declarative, INT = interrogative, IMP = imperative and EXC = exclamatory.

(39)   a.   DEC-DEC   i.   It's late. I'm tired.   →
                              ...la[ɾ] I'm...
                       ii.   It's theɾe. I saw it.   →
                              ...the[r] I...
       b.   DEC-IMP   i.   It's Dad. Open the door.   →
                              ...Da[ɾ] Open...
                       ii.   It's Anna. Open the door.   →
                              ...Anna[r] Open...
       c.   DEC-INT   i.   That's a nice cat. Is it yours?   →
                              ...ca[ɾ] Is...
                       ii.   That's a nice caɾ. Is it yours?   →
                              ...ca[r] Is...
       d.   IMP-DEC   i.   Wait a minute. I'm coming.   →
                              ...minu[ɾ] I'm...
                       ii.   Don't staɾe. It's rude.   →
                              ...sta[r] It's...

e.	IMP-IMP	i.	Stop that. Ask nicely.	→
			...tha[ɾ] Ask...	
		ii.	Don't state. Ask him in.	→
			...sta[r] Ask...	
f.	IMP-INT	i.	Leave it shut. Are you crazy?	→
			...shu[ɾ] Are...	
		ii.	Have another. Aren't they good?	→
			...anothe[r] Aren't...	
g.	INT-DEC	i.	Where's Annette? I'm leaving.	→
			...Anne[ɾ] I'm...	
		ii.	Where's the saw? I need it.	→
			...saw[r] I...	
h.	INT-IMP	i.	Why did you wait? Open it.	→
			...wai[ɾ] Open...	
		ii.	What are you waiting for? Open it.	→
			...fo[r] Open...	
i.	INT-INT	i.	Where's Ed? Is he gone?	→
			...E[ɾ] Is...	
		ii.	Where's Paula? Is she late again?	→
			...Paula[r] Is...	
j.	EXC-DEC	i.	What a sight! I'm shocked.	→
			...sigh[ɾ] I'm...	
		ii.	What a boot! I'm shocked.	→
			...boo[r] I'm...	
k.	EXC-IMP	i.	How odd! Ask someone else.	→
			...o[ɾ] Ask...	
		ii.	What a liar! Ask someone else.	→
			...lia[r] Ask...	
l.	EXC-INT[14]	i.	How odd! Are you sure?	→
			...o[ɾ]Are...	
		ii.	What a nice sofa! Is it new?	→
			...sofa[r] Is...	

Rather than the nature of the individual sentences involved, what seems to be crucial in determining whether two (or more) sentences may form a single phonological unit is the nature of the relationship between the sentences. Before considering the relationship between the sentences that may form a single phonological unit, however, it is first necessary to establish several pragmatic and phonological conditions without which *U* restructuring may not occur, regardless of the relationships between the sentences.

In order for *U* restructuring to be possible, the following two conditions of a pragmatic nature must be met:

(40)   *Pragmatic Conditions*
     a.   The two sentences must be uttered by the same speaker.
     b.   The two sentences must be addressed to the same interlocutor(s).

It should be noted that these conditions are relevant only for phonological rules, and more specifically, only for purely phonological rules. There are other types of rules, such as ellipsis and anaphora, that apply just as well across speakers and when directed to different interlocutors (see Williams, 1977). In addition, certain phonological rules that are not, however, purely phonological may violate the conditions in (40). In fact, Liaison in French, in part a morphophonological rule, may apply across speakers when, for example, one speaker hesitates and another speaker resumes his sentence, as illustrated in (41) (Y.–C. Morin, personal communication).

(41)   Speaker 1:   Je cherchais des...
                 'I was looking for some...'
      Speaker 2:   ...[z]allumettes.
                 '...matches.'

In addition to the pragmatic conditions, the following two phonological conditions must be met for *U* restructuring to be possible:

(42)   *Phonological Conditions*
     a.   The two sentences must be relatively short.
     b.   There must not be a pause between the two sentences.

(42a) is rather vague since it is not possible at this time to give more precise indications about the length of the sentence involved. What is clear, however, is that when the sentence are long, phonological restructuring does not occur. As in the case of *I* restructuring seen in the previous chapter, rate of speech appears to play a role here, too, in a type of trade-off relation with length. For both *I* and *U* restructuring, what seems to be crucial is some average length in terms of timing, most probably due ultimately to physiological considerations. The fact that *U* restructuring, and *U*-level rules operating across sentences, are blocked by the presence of a pause is not surprising, since it has often been observed that the introduction of a pause within the context of phonological rules in general tends to destroy the context and thus inhibit the application of the rule. It should be noted, however, that this observation, too, seems to hold only for purely phonological rules, though perhaps not for all such rules. Thus, Liaison may apply across a pause, for example after a hesitation, as illustrated in (43) (Y.–C. Morin, personal communication).

(43)   Le...[z]enfants
       'The children'

It might actually be possible to capture the two pragmatic and the two phonological conditions with a single condition, essentially the second phonological condition, (42b). That is, it may be the case that all of the conditions mentioned above ultimately have the same effect, that of allowing restructuring to apply only when the sentences involved are in some sense temporally adjacent to each other. Any separation due to a change of speakers or interlocutors, pausing for a breath between long sentences, or any other type of pause, is sufficient to impede the restructuring of two sentences into a single phonological utterance, and thus block the application of a *U*-level phonological rule at the point at which the sentences meet.

In addition to the basic conditions on *U* restructuring just seen, the sentences in question must be related to each other in specific ways. On the basis of a series of pairs of sentences submitted to native speakers of American and British (RP) English, we have found that Flapping and *r*-Insertion may apply across sentences only when specific syntactic and/or semantic relations exist between them.[15]

The type of syntactic relationship that must hold between sentences that form a single phonological unit is one in which the interpretation of material in one sentence depends on material in the preceding sentence. In particular, this situation arises in cases of ellipsis and anaphora, illustrated in (44) and (45), respectively, for both Flapping and *r*-Insertion.

(44)   *Ellipsis*
       a.   Martha didn't invite Todd. I did.   → ...To[ɾ] I...
       b.   I can't help heɾ. Arnold can.   → ...he[r] Arnold...

(45)   *Anaphora*
       a.   Where's Pat? I need him.   → ...Pa[ɾ] I...
       b.   What a nice sofa! Is it new?   → ...sofa[r] Is...

In addition to the two syntactic relations, there are three semantic relations that allow a *U*-level rule to apply across sentences. That is, one of the following three logico-semantic connectors must implicitly relate the sentences involved: *and, therefore, because*, as illustrated in (46)-(48), respectively.

(46)   *And*
       a.   You invite Charlotte. I'll invite Joan.   →
            ...Charlo[ɾ] I'll...
       b.   Isabelle's a lawyeɾ. I'm a doctor.   →
            ...lawye[r] I'm...

(47) *Therefore*
    a. It's late. I'm leaving.   →
        ...la[ɾ] I'm...
    b. I'm shorteɾ. I'll go in the back.   →
        ...shorte[r] I'll...

(48) *Because*
    a. Take your coat. It's cold out.   →
        ...coa[ɾ] It's...
    b. Hide the vodka. Alvin's coming.   →
        ...vodka[r] Alvin's...

It is enough if either a syntactic relation or a semantic relation holds between two sentences that form a single phonological unit. It does happen, though, that the sentences involved sometimes exhibit both types of relations, as illustrated below:

(49) a. *Anaphora-And*
      You ask Ed. I'll ask his sister. →
      ...E[ɾ] I'll...
    b. *Anaphora-Therefore*
      This coffee's too bitteɾ. It needs some sugar. →
      ...bitte[r] It...
    c. *Ellipsis-Because*
      Don't call Anna. I want to. →
      ...Anna[r] I...

It should be noted that the connectors *or* and *but* behave differently from *and, therefore*, and *because* with respect to *U* restructuring. That is, *or* and *but* typically do not permit the application of *U*-level rules across sentences. Furthermore, it is extremely difficult to find cases in which *or* and *but* relations are implied between sentences, and when such cases do arise, they are accompanied by complicated intonation patterns. The *or* and *but* relations are therefore illustrated in (50) and (51) with the addition of the words *otherwise* and *though*, respectively, at the end of the second sentence to explicitly signal the relevant relations.

(50) *Or*
    a. Stop that. I'll leave otherwise.   →
      *...tha[ɾ] I'll...
    b. Finish your pasta. I'll eat it otherwise. →
      *...pasta[r] I'll...

(51)   *But*
    a.   It's late. I'm not leaving though.   →
         *...la[ɾ] I'm...
    b.   I didn't invite Peteɾ. I should have though.   →
         *...Pete[r] I...

What these examples show is that if two sentences are related by the notions of *or* or *but*, even if there are relations of anaphora or ellipsis between them, *U* restructuring tends to be blocked, as seen by the lack of application of Flapping and *r*-Insertion across the sentences.

Why only the three connectors *and, therefore*, and *because* allow *U* restructuring is not completely clear. What seems to be the case, however, is that these three connectors can be distinguished from *or* and *but* on the grounds that they can, in some sense, be considered to have a 'positive' value, while *or* and *but* have a 'negative' value. In this regard, an observation made by Cooper and Paccia-Cooper (1980) seems to offer some explanation for the difference in behavior between the two groups of connectors. They report that '[t]here does exist at least one semantic factor – negation – which seems to influence speech timing...'(p.163). Although Cooper and Paccia-Cooper are referring to conjoined adjectives, and not series of sentences, the patterns seem to be quite similar. That is, when adjectives are conjoined by a negative conjunction, *yet* or *but*, it is more likely that a pause will be introduced before the conjunction than when the adjectives are conjoined by a positive conjunction, *and*, as illustrated below with Cooper and Paccia-Cooper's (1980:163) example (1a,b).

(52)   a.   The tall yet frail student flunked chemistry.
      b.   The tall and frail student flunked chemistry.

Since it is precisely the presence of a pause between two sentences that inhibits *U* restructuring, it seems possible that the lack of *U* restructuring with *or* and *but* may, in fact, be due to different timing patterns associated with these negative relations, even if they are not explicitly present in the sentences in question.

On the basis of the various observations made above about when *U*-level phonological rules may apply across sentences and when they may not, we can now modify our definition of the phonological utterance such that it includes, when necessary, more than one sentence. In order to account for these cases, all that is required is that the original *U*, as defined earlier in terms of the string dominated by X^n in the syntactic tree, be allowed to undergo a process of restructuring under certain circumstances. The circumstances under which restructuring occurs are determined by the syntactic and semantic relations just seen. We can thus formulate the following rule for the restructuring of U:

(53)   *U restructuring*
   Adjacent Us may be joined into a single U when the basic pragmatic and phonological conditions are met and when there exists
   a syntactic relation (ellipsis, anaphora) and/or a positive semantic
   relation (*and, therefore, because*) between the Us in question.

It was pointed out above that the pragmatic and phonological conditions may be reducible to a single condition that allows restructuring only when there is no intervening pause. It was also mentioned that the reason that a negative semantic relation between two sentences blocks restructuring may have to do with a tendency to insert a pause in such cases. It might, therefore, be possible to simplify the U restructuring rule and generalize the role of the pause. We will not do so here, however, since the idea is still somewhat speculative and needs more systematic investigation. It should be noted, in any case, that the rule in (53) does not say that Us will necessarily be restructured under the circumstances mentioned, but only that they *may* be restructured. Ultimately, whether U restructuring takes place or not will most likely depend on additional factors as well, such as style and rate of speech. In this respect, the U restructuring phenomenon is quite similar to the I restructuring phenomenon seen in Chapter 7, where it was shown that a number of nonsyntactic considerations are responsible for the final division of a string into intonational phrases.

8.3. Conclusions

We have shown in this chapter that there are certain phonological rules that apply not only *throughout* the largest constituent in syntax, the string dominated by X^n, but also *across* such constituents. Such rules (e.g. Flapping in American English, r-Insertion in RP British English, Voicing Assimilation in Mexican Spanish) provide crucial evidence for the existence of the largest phonological constituent, the phonological utterance. That is, the fact that the domain of application of these rules cannot be identified with any syntactic constituent makes it necessary to establish a distinct prosodic unit, U, as their domain of application. U, like the other prosodic constituents below it in the hierarchy, makes use of syntactic notions in the definition of its domain, though the final result is not necessarily isomorphic with any syntactic constituent.

In the construction and restructuring of U, an interaction was observed between phonology and two other components of the grammar: syntax and semantics. That is, the rules of U formation group phonological constituents, *I*s, into a single n-ary branching tree as long as these *I*s correspond to material dominated by a single node X^n in the syntactic tree. In the case of restructuring, other syntactic information is relevant, specifically, whether the sentences corresponding to the *U*s in question are related by anaphora or ellipsis, such that the interpretation of a given *U* depends on material present in the preceding *U*. The semantic relation between *U*s is also relevant in the case of restructuring, since restructuring may occur only when certain positive relations (*and, therefore, because*) implicitly exist between the *U*s in question. It was seen, furthermore, that for restructuring to be possible, some basic phonological and pragmatic conditions must be met.

What is particularly interesting about the interaction between phonology and the other components of the grammar at the *U* level is the fact that the type of information referred to is of a very general nature. That is, in dealing with the construction of the highest unit in the phonological hierarchy, we only make use of the syntactic notion X^n, and not, for example, whether 'X' stands for S, N, V, etc. We must know whether a certain semantic relation holds between the constituents involved in restructuring, but not, for example, what the meanings or semantic features associated with the individual words are. We must know whether a pause or special intonation pattern is associated with the constituents involved, but we do not need to know the nature of the segments or syllables making up the constituents. The phonological utterance thus provides further evidence that as we go higher in the prosodic hierarchy, we need less specific information in order to define the prosodic constituents, to the point at which only such abstract information as the 'highest node in the syntactic tree' and the nature of the semantic relation between two sentences becomes a relevant factor.

Finally, the fact that semantic information must be taken into consideration in accounting for the domain of application of certain segmental rules raises serious problems for the model of grammar usually assumed in generative theory. What the phonological utterance shows is that the phonological component must have access not only to syntactic information, but also to certain types of semantic information. While some proposals have been made to allow the phonology to 'see' logical form, some of the types of semantic information needed for *U* restructuring are not usually included in the logical form component. It is not a feasible solution to relegate the phonological rules that operate across sentences to a discourse component, or a discourse phonology subcomponent, of the grammar since the same rules that apply across sentences also apply within sentences and even within words. To say that a rule like Flapping is a rule of discourse phonology would obscure the nature of this rule and its very widespread application throughout all levels of the phonology of American English. It would also have the undesirable consequence of requiring a discourse rule to apply before a syllable-domain rule, Glottaliz- ation, since, as was pointed out in section 3.1.2 above, Flapping must be ordered before Glottalization. What is needed, instead, is a somewhat more complex model of grammar that includes more types of interactions among the various components than have typically been allowed, a point we will return to in the last chapter.

NOTES

1. We will not be concerned further with special cases of emphasis or contrast- ive intonation, however, although, as was mentioned, these are probably the cases in which it may, in fact, be possible to say that one I constituent is more stressed than another.
2. There are some minor differences between *t* and *d* with respect to Flapping (see Kahn, 1976), but they are not relevant to the present discussion.
3. See Malécot (1960) and Kahn (1976) for a discussion of nonconsonantal articula- tions of nasals and liquids in American English.
4. We are referring to constituents of 'normal' length. Obviously, a sentence that is too long to be uttered in one breath must have a pause in it, and if the pause falls within the environment for Flapping (or most other phonological rules, for the mat- ter), this will block the application of the rule. This type of phenomenon is beyond the scope of the present work, and will not be considered further here.
5. In Nespor and Vogel (1982), we erroneously proposed that the domain of Flap- ping was *I*. This error was the result of the fact that a number of the test senten- ces we used tended to be uttered with pauses within the context for Flapping, either because they were quite long or because they lent themselves to emphatic or other special types of pronunciations. It is now clear that Flapping applies throughout *U*, across *I* boundaries, on the condition that an unmarked type of pronunciation is used.
6. The following discussion is based on the analysis in Vogel (1986). See also Wells (1982).
7. We do not indicate vowel length here, as Jones (1966) does, to distinguish tense from lax vowels and stressed from unstressed vowels since, in fact, it is not the vowel length that is contrastive. For example, the contrast between *feet* and *fit*, represent- ed by Jones as [fi:t] *vs.* [fit], is represented here is [fit] *vs.* [fɪt], and the difference between the final vowels in *offer* and *fir*, represented by Jones as a contrast between [ə] and [əː], is represented here in terms of a difference in stress. Furthermore, we do not treat separately the cases in which high vowels are shortened to types of glides, [ĭ, ŭ], a distinction made by Jones for certain pronunciations of *happier* [hapiə] vs. *hear* [hiə].
8. In some pronunciations, [ə] may also appear after [ɔ], giving [sɔə] for *sore*. This sequence is not included here since it is much less common than the pronunciation without schwa, which gives [sɔ] for *sore* (see Jones, 1966), and since, in any case, the presence or absence of schwa after [ɔ] does not affect the point under discussion.
9. It should be noted that while *U*-domain rules are not often found in the phonological literature, one does occasionally come across reference to the last type of rule mentioned, the *U* limit rule. In fact, a *U* limit rule is mentioned by Lees (1961)

in his description of Turkish phonology, where we find a rule of Final Liquid Devoicing that devoices /r/ and palatal /l/ in absolute final position.

10. Harris does not name all of his rules; we have supplied descriptive names, where necessary, for the rules under consideration here.

11. It should be noted that Harris (1969) uses the single word boundary as a cover symbol for more complex representations, and does not distinguish between one or more boundaries as is done in SPE and other works in that tradition. Instead, Harris prefers to maintain, for the rules under examination, '...the simplifying fiction that all orthographic word boundaries are correctly represented as #' (p.17).

12. Harris considers the sequence in question to be composed of two sentences, though in fact the first element may be a case of X^n representing a node other than S (i.e. $\bar{N}$), depending on the analysis chosen, or, alternatively, a case of Left Dislocation. Given the falling intonation pattern indicated, however, we assume that Harris means to exclude the last possibility, and consider the two parts of the examples as deriving from separate sentences. In any case, it should be noted that Voicing Assimilation applies quite generally across sentences, as illustrated by the following less controversial examples:

(i)   Quiero los dos. Damelos.   →   ...do[s^z] Damelos
        'I want both of them. Give them to me.'

(ii)   Oigo su voz. Donde está?   →   ...vo[s^z] Donde...
        'I hear his voice. Where is he?'

13. Such a sequence of sentences is possible, for example, in the case of a rapid change of topic or if the speaker is directing the sentences to different addressees.

14. Exclamatory sentences usually begin with *how* or *what*, and therefore do not provide the correct segmental context for Flapping and *r*-Insertion when they are the second sentence in a sequence.

15. In previous work (Vogel, 1981, 1986), a third type of relation was mentioned, a pragmatic one. This no longer seems necessary since the relevant cases can, in fact, be subsumed under the category of semantic relations if we allow shared knowledge of a given situation to play a slightly greater role in interpreting the relation between sentences.

Chapter 9

Prosodic Constituents and Disambiguation

9.0. Introduction

Thus far, our discussion of the various constituents of the prosodic hierarchy has been concerned with strictly phonological phenomena. That is, each phonological constituent was motivated on the basis of the application of specific phonological rules. In this way it was seen that prosodic phonology is a theory of domains in phonology. The definitions of the phonological constituents were shown to incorporate morphological, syntactic, and even semantic notions, and thus it was seen that prosodic phonology is also a theory of interactions between the various components of the grammar and phonology. In this chapter, it will be shown that the constituents of the prosodic hierarchy also provide the relevant structures for the first level of processing in the perception of speech and thus that prosodic theory contributes to a theory of perception of language, as well. That is, it will be shown that prosodic constituents represent more than the domains within which various phonological rules and more subtle phrasing phenomena apply. In addition to delimiting the units of speech production, they also play a role in speech perception, since it is the result of the application of the various phonological and phonetic phenomena that allows a listener to identify the internal structure in the string of speech sounds he hears. The first stage in the processing of the incoming speech signal, the initial parsing of a given string into the various constituents of the prosodic hierarchy, provides the basis for the listener's reconstruction of the syntactic structure of the string and ultimately for his understanding of the message conveyed by the string.

While there does not seem to be any controversy regarding the claim that sequences of speech sounds are not perceived merely as unstructured linear sequences of sounds, or even words, there is some question as to which larger units are relevant in the perception and organization of speech on the part of the listener. There has been much research on speech perception devoted to demonstrating that the relevant units are the constituents of the syntactic hierarchy. This was the scope, in fact, of many early 'click' experiments (e.g. Fodor and Bever, 1965; Garrett, Bever and Fodor, 1966; Fodor, Fodor, Garrett and Lackner, 1975), as well as of more recent work, such as that by Lehiste (1973) and by Cooper and Paccia-Cooper (1980). Other studies were aimed at showing more specifically that certain prosodic phenomena apply in domains determined by syntactic structure and can thus provide the necessary cues for the listener's analysis of a string into its appropriate syntactic structure (e.g. Lehiste, 1972; Lehiste, Olive and Streeter, 1976; Klatt, 1975).

It was suggested by Selkirk (1978b), and argued further by Nespor and Vogel (1983a, 1983b) on the basis of perception data, that it is not syntactic constituents but rather prosodic constituents that provide the relevant information in the first stage of processing of a given string of speech. This is not to say that syntactic structure is irrelevant, but rather that it is relevant only indirectly, since syntactic information is referred to in the construction of the various prosodic constituents above the word level, as seen in the previous chapters.

It follows from the claim that prosodic, rather than syntactic, constituents provide the relevant units for the initial level of processing that any syntactic distinctions that are not reflected in prosodic structure cannot be perceived at this stage of perception. In order to test this claim, we carried out a study of the ability of Italian listeners to disambiguate a set of 78 sentences in which the syntactic differences are reflected in different ways, or not at all, in prosodic structure. In general terms, the prediction was that listeners would be able to distinguish the meanings of only those sentences that have a difference in prosodic structure. In this light, a study of ambiguous sentences in English carried out by Lehiste (1973) will also be discussed. Since Lehiste makes the claim that it is the syntactic constituent structure that is responsible for disambiguation, we will also compare our predictions and results with Lehiste's, and show that prosodic structure makes better predictions about which sentences are disambiguable than does syntactic structure.

Before discussing the predictions and the disambiguation test in detail, however, we will first examine the concept of ambiguity and identify a number of different types of ambiguity. From among this number, those types will be selected which are relevant to the issue under investigation here, that is, the role of prosodic *vs.* syntactic constituents at the first level of processing, the first level at which a listener begins to assign structure to the string of speech he hears, and thus the first stage in which ambiguous sentences may be disambiguated.

9.1. Ambiguity

The study of the phenomenon of ambiguity has a long history, beginning in explicit terms with Aristotle.[2] The term 'ambiguity' has been used to refer to a broad range of phenomena, and is often used generically with the meaning of 'misunderstanding'. A more accurate definition, however, would be that ambiguity, at least in spoken language, is the plurality of meanings for a single sequence of sound segments.

In the most 'classic' case, often called 'homophony' or 'polisemy' (see Ullmann, 1962), ambiguity is the result of the fact that a given word may have more than one meaning, as is illustrated in the Italian example in (1).[3]

(1)   Geltrude l'ha attaccato.
        a.   'Geltrude has attacked it.'
        b.   'Geltrude has attached it.'

The sentence in (1) can be interpreted in two ways because the verb *attaccare* can be interpreted in two ways, that is, in the sense of 'attack' and in the sense of 'attach'. What is important in spoken language, however, is not so much the fact that we have a single word with two meanings, but rather the fact that the sequences of sounds are identical in the two cases.

That ambiguity has to do with sequences of segments, and not other units such as words, can be seen in the comparison of the pronunciations of the two sequences in (2).

(2)   a.   del lago   'of the lake'
        b.   dell'ago   'of the needle'

Despite the fact that the words in (2a) and (2b) are different, the phonetic realization of both expressions is the same. That is, the listener, on hearing only the phonetic form [dellá:go] does not know if the meaning is the one corresponding to the orthographic form in (2a) or to the one in (2b). The problem here is that of the impossibility of assigning a single interpretation to a given string of sound segments.

9.1.1. Types of ambiguity

As has often been observed, there are different types of ambiguity (see Kooij, 1971). Among these, it is possible to distinguish the three types illustrated in (3), on the basis of their structure.

(3)   a.   Non lo conosco.
              'I don't know him.'
        b.   La sua influenza è preoccupante.
              (i)   'His flu is worrisome.'
              (ii)   'His influence is worrisome.'

c.   La vecchia legge la regola.
   (i)   'The old lady is reading the regulation.'
   (ii)   'The old law regulates it.'

It can be said that a sentence like (3a) is ambiguous when it is not clear
to whom the pronoun *lo* 'him' refers. For example, in this case the interpretation may be *Non conosco Michele* 'I don't know Michele' or *Non
conosco Arturo* 'I don't know Arturo', etc. We are dealing here with what
may be called ambiguity at the pragmatic level. In (3b), however, the
ambiguity results from the fact that the word *influenza* has two meanings,
and therefore the sentence may be interpreted either as referring to a
sickness or to a notion of power. This case, like the one seen above in (1),
represents ambiguity at the lexical level. Finally, in the third sentence,
the situation is somewhat more complex, since the syntactic structures
corresponding to the two interpretations are different. In one interpretation of (3c), *vecchia* is a noun ('old lady'), *legge* is a verb ('is reading'),
la is an article ('the'), and *regola* is a noun ('regulation'). In the other
interpretation, however, *vecchia* is an adjective ('old'), *legge* is a noun
('law'), *la* is a clitic ('it'), and *regola* is a verb ('regulates'). In such cases,
we can speak of ambiguity at the syntactic level. It should be noted,
furthermore, that this last type of ambiguity always implies ambiguity
at the lexical level as well. For example, if in the one case *legge* is a noun
and in the other a verb, it follows that the meaning of *legge* must be different in the two cases.

The division of types of ambiguity into the three categories just given
is certainly not the only way of classifying the different types of ambiguity. A slightly different classification is proposed by Ullmann (1962),
and distinguishes among phonetic, lexical, and grammatical ambiguity.
In this classification, the term phonetic ambiguity is used to refer to cases
in which the same sound sequence can be divided into words in more than
one way, giving rise to more than one meaning, as was seen in (2) above,
or as can be seen with the sequence [lakjú:za], which can mean either
'lock' (*la chiusa*) or '(he) has closed it' (*l'ha chiusa*).[4] It should be noted,
however, that most examples of this type would fall into the category
of ambiguity at the syntactic level in the classification presented above,
since different divisions of phonetic material often result in different
syntactic structures. For example, in the case of [lakjú:za], we would
have the following two structures: $[[la]_{ART} [kjú:za]_N]_{NP}$ and $[[l]_{PRO} [a]_{AUX} [kjú:za]_V]_{VP}$.[5] The two other categories cited by Ullmann in
most cases correspond, respectively, to the categories of ambiguity at the
syntactic and lexical levels discussed above.

Another, quite different approach to ambiguity is that of Empson
(1930). Here we find not three, but seven, categories of ambiguity. It

should be noted, however, that this classification is not based on different structures, but rather on different logico-semantic relations that can exist between the different meanings of an ambiguous expression.

In the present work, we will restrict our attention to structural types of ambiguity, and in particular to the types exemplified in (3b) and (3c). That is, we will only consider cases of lexical and syntactic ambiguity, or in other words, those types that can be considered cases of 'linguistic ambiguity' in the strictest sense, as opposed to both pragmatic ambiguity (type (3a)) and the types of ambiguity discussed by Empson that do not depend on structural factors but on various other relations expressed in the sentences in question.

9.1.2. Disambiguation

Under normal communicative circumstances, ambiguity poses problems when a listener, on hearing a string of sounds, could possibly interpret the string in more than one way. Usually, there is some linguistic or nonlinguistic element in the context that helps the listener identify the intended meaning of a potentially ambiguous sentence. For example, the sentence in (4) is understood in one way if the topic of conversation is, explicitly or implicitly, 'drinks', and in another way if the topic has to do with 'ships'.

(4)   Mi piace quel porto.
        'I like that port.'

When the contextual information is inadequate, or totally lacking, disambiguation is sometimes possible nonetheless, though in such cases it must depend on some other type of information. Specifically, it depends on a type of phonological information that goes beyond the individual segments that compose a given expression. Consider, for example, the ambiguous sentence in (5).

(5)   Federico andava solo quando pioveva.
        a.   'Federico went alone when it was raining.'
        b.   'Federico went only when it was raining.'

While the string of segments is identical in the two interpretations corresponding to (5), the prosodic structure is different in the two cases. When the intended meaning is that in (5a), this is usually signalled by a peak in the intonation contour on the word *solo*, while this does not happen with the meaning in (5b).[6] This type of prosodic information helps the listener interpret the sentence in the way the speaker intends it.

Not all ambiguous sentences can be disambiguated prosodically, however, as can be seen in (6).

(6)   Carlotta preferisce le penne rosse.
   a.   'Carlotta prefers the red feathers.'
   b.   'Carlotta prefers the red pens.'

In this case, in the absence of contextual information, there is no way in which a speaker can distinguish prosodically between the meaning of 'feathers' and that of 'pens'. In other words, the prosodic patterns corresponding to both interpretations are the same, and such sentences remain ambiguous to the listener.

In much the same way that we distinguished above between pragmatic ambiguity on the one hand, and linguistic ambiguity in the strict sense, on the other hand, we can distinguish here between pragmatic or contextual disambiguation and linguistic or prosodic disambiguation. Furthermore, just as we restricted our area of investigation to the strictly linguistic types of ambiguity, excluding pragmatic or logico-semantic types, we will concentrate here only on the strictly linguistic means of disambiguation.

9.1.3.   Syntactic structure vs. prosodic structure

It was mentioned above that certain sentences can be disambiguated prosodically while others cannot. The question that arises at this point is what the criteria are that determine whether or not an ambiguous sentence is disambiguable.

According to one proposal, which can be called the 'syntactic proposal', the prosodic structure of a sentence is directly determined by its syntactic structure (see, among others, Lehiste, 1973; Lieberman, 1977; Cooper and Paccia-Cooper, 1980). In other words, different prosodic patterns correspond to different syntactic structures. As far as ambiguous sentences are concerned, this proposal predicts that we will be able to disambiguate those sentences for which the different meanings correspond to different syntactic structures. When, however, the syntactic structures corresponding to the two meanings are the same, the prosodic patterns will also be the same, and such sentences will not be disambiguable for the listener (see Lehiste, 1973).

According to the proposal we are advancing here, the 'prosodic proposal', however, the prosodic structure of a sentence is only indirectly determined by its syntactic structure, as has been seen in the preceding chapters of this book. That is, while the prosodic categories above the word level are constructed in relation to certain syntactic factors, the resulting prosodic structures do not necessarily correspond to the constituent structures of syntax. As far as ambiguity is concerned, the prosodic proposal predicts that the sentences that can be disambiguated are those in which the different meanings correspond to different prosodic structures. By contrast, sentences in which the different meanings have the same pro-

Prosodic Constituents and Disambiguation 255

sodic structure are not disambiguable, regardless of their syntactic structure (see Nespor and Vogel, 1983a, 1983b).

9.2. *Two proposals for disambiguation*

As was seen above, in the absence of adequate contextual information, either linguistic or nonlinguistic, the only indication a listener has as to the meaning of an ambiguous utterance is its prosodic pattern. This prosodic pattern obviously depends on the way in which the string in question is uttered by the speaker. In this section, we will examine the way in which the prosodic pattern of a sentence is determined by the speaker according to the two proposals in question, that is, whether it happens on the basis of syntactic structure or on the basis of phonological (prosodic) structure. In section 9.3 we will discuss the test we carried out in order to empirically evaluate the validity of the two proposals.

9.2.1. *The syntactic proposal*

According to the syntactic proposal, there is a one-to-one relation between the syntactic structure of a sentence and its prosody. It is suggested, specifically, that the ends of syntactic constituents are the sites of a number of prosodic phenomena, such as the lengthening of the final unit (segment, syllable, word), and somewhat less commonly, the presence of a pause and/or laryngealization of the final unit (see Lehiste, 1973; Cooper and Paccia-Cooper, 1980). In other words, it is the position of the syntactic constituent boundaries that determines to a large extent the prosodic pattern of a sentence. It is proposed, furthermore, that the larger the number of boundaries found together in a given position, the more prosodically marked this position will be. Consider the word *fermata* 'stop' in the following two (unambiguous) sentences:

(7)   a.   [La prossima [fermata]$_N$]$_{NP}$ è davanti alla stazione.
           'The next stop is in front of the station.'
    b.   [La [fermata]$_N$ principale]$_{NP}$ è davanti alla stazione.
           'The main stop is in front of the station.'

According to the syntactic proposal, the word *fermata* in (7a) should be lengthened more, and in general contain more constituent-final prosodic information, than its counterpart in (7b). Such a difference would reflect the fact that the end of *fermata* represents the end of two constituents, N and NP, in (7a), but only of N in (7b).

It follows directly from the syntactic proposal that when the two interpretations of an ambiguous sentence have the same constituent structure, it is not possible for a listener to distinguish between the two meanings, regardless of the syntactic labels of the constituents (Lehiste, 1973:112). On the other hand, it should be possible to distinguish between the two meanings in cases in which the syntactic constituents corresponding to the two meanings are different.

On the basis of a test in which 30 subjects were asked to interpret a number of repetitions of 15 ambiguous English sentences, choosing between the paraphrases offered for each sentence, Lehiste claims to have found confirmation for what we are calling the syntactic proposal: 'The set of successfully disambiguated sentences consists of those for which [a] difference in meaning is correlated with a difference in surface constituent structure. The sentences that were generally not disambiguated have only one bracketing, although the constituents may bear different labels' (p.112).

An examination of the data presented in Lehiste's article reveals several inconsistencies which cast some doubt on the conclusions that were drawn on the basis of the test. For example, Lehiste points out that of the 15 test sentences, 10 give results above the chance level (p < .025) and are thus disambiguable. Among the 15 sentences, however, there are only 8 which have different syntactic bracketings for the two interpretations. This means that there should be only 8 disambiguable sentences, if it is true that it is the syntactic structure that directly determines the prosodic pattern of a sentence, which in turn provides the information necessary for the disambiguation of sentences presented orally. It should be noted, furthermore, that of the 10 disambiguated sentences, 7 were among those with only one bracketing. Thus, it is not even the case that all of those (eight) sentences with two bracketings were disambiguated.

In addition, it should be noted that among the test items there are several sentences that behave differently despite the fact that they have the same bracketings. Consider the sentences in (8), which can be bracketed in only one way for the two meanings; the expressions following each sentence are the paraphrases given in the test.

(8) a. The [[shooting] [[of] [the hunters]]] was terrible.
     (Lehiste's (8))
     i.   The hunters shot badly.
     ii. The hunters were shot.
     b. The [[feeding] [[of] [the tigers]]] was expensive.
     (Lehiste's (12))
     i.   The tigers were fed.
     ii. The tigers did the feeding.
     c. The [[screaming] [[of] [the victims]]] was terrible.
     (Lehiste's (Lehiste's (13))
     i.   The victims screamed.
     ii. ?? Somebody screamed 'the victims'.

According to the results of the test, only the first sentence, (8a), is truly ambiguous; the answers to the other two sentences were significantly above the chance level. As Lehiste points out, the highly significant scores for the sentences in (8b) and (8c) are most likely an experimental artifact, a result of the choice of sentences used in the study. That is, while the calculations of ambiguity were based on the assumption that the two meanings of each ambiguous sentence were equally possible, both meanings were not, in fact, always plausible, a consequence of Lehiste's choice to use sentences that had already been discussed and analyzed in the contemporary linguistic literature, rather than sentences constructed in order to test her claims. Specifically, in the cases of (8b) and (8c), the first paraphrase given was the more plausible one, and it is indeed the one that was chosen most frequently. What the results show is not a significant ability on the part of the subjects to disambiguate the sentences in question, but rather a significant preference for one of the two meanings. In this sense, the sentences are not truly ambiguous, although their interpretation reflects semantic considerations rather than syntactic or prosodic structure.

In light of these observations, it no longer seems possible to conclude, as Lehiste did, that the possibility of disambiguating ambiguous sentences depends on their syntactic structure. Instead, the question of whether the ambiguous sentences that can be disambiguated prosodically are those that have different syntactic structures corresponding to their different meanings remains open at this point, and must be further investigated on the basis of more reliable data.

9.2.2. *The prosodic proposal*

Even without controlled experiments, it was observed relatively early in the generative literature that syntax and prosody cannot exist in a one-to-one relation, as is claimed by the syntactic proposal. In fact, as we mentioned above, it was already noted by Chomsky and Halle (1968) that the prosodic pattern in certain sentences, in particular the distribution of pauses, does not always correspond to the constituent structure of the sentences. While the generally accepted syntactic bracketing of the (non-ambiguous) sentence in (9) is that indicated in (9a), this sentence is divided prosodically as in (9b), where the configuration '] [' indicates the position of intonational breaks.

(9)   a.   This is [the cat that caught [the rat that stole [the cheese]]]
       b.   [This is the cat] [that caught the rat] [that stole the cheese]

Minimizing the importance of this type of discrepancy between syntax and prosody, Chomsky and Halle (1968) attribute the problem to a

question of performance. Langendoen (1975), however, gives more importance to the problem, and proposes that there is a distinct component that
is responsible for assigning the appropriate prosodic pattern in cases like
(9), where the prosodic and syntactic structures are not identical.

In the theoretical framework of prosodic phonology, such a discrepancy between syntactic and prosodic structure, instead of constituting a
problem, is one of the fundamental motivations for the internal organization of the phonological component. According to the prosodic proposal
of disambiguation, it is the phonological structures or prosodic constituents (in particular those above the word level), and not the syntactic
constituents, that determine the prosodic pattern of a sentence. In contrast to the syntactic proposal, according to which different prosodic
patterns correspond to different syntactic structures, the prosodic proposal admits the possibility that different syntactic structures can give
rise to the same prosodic pattern. Furthermore, since the prosodic proposal bases the determination of the prosodic pattern of a sentence on its
phonological structure, it follows that there may exist ambiguous sentences with different syntactic structures which are nevertheless not disambiguable because they have the same prosodic structure.

The prosodic approach predicts, therefore, that the only ambiguous
sentences that can be disambiguated linguistically (i.e. prosodically) are
those in which there are different prosodic structures corresponding to
the different meanings. In the next section, we will discuss the experiment
we conducted to evaluate the various predictions made by this proposal
and by the syntactic proposal in relation to a series of ambiguous
sentences in Italian.

9.3. A disambiguation experiment

In order to evaluate the predictions made by the two disambiguation proposals, we devised a perception test to see which ambiguous sentences
listeners were actually able to disambiguate on the basis of their prosody
alone.[7] We will first examine the specific predictions made by the two proposals (section 9.3.1), and then discuss the test itself and its results (section 9.3.2).

9.3.1. Hypotheses

Before formulating the specific hypotheses on the basis of which we
will compare the two disambiguation proposals, it is necessary to analyze
more systematically the different types of ambiguous sentences.

As far as their syntactic structure is concerned, ambiguous sentences
can vary independently on two dimensions: syntactic constituency and

syntactic labels (see Lehiste, 1973). In other words, for any ambiguous sentence with two meanings, the syntactic constituent structures that correspond to the two interpretations may be either the same or different. Similarly, the syntactic labels may also be either the same or different. By varying the values on the two dimensions, we arrive at four logically possible combinations, as seen in Figure 1.

		Syntactic Constituents	
		same	different
Syntactic Labels	same	a	b
	different	c	d

Figure 1. Syntactic labels and constituents in ambiguous sentences

As far as their prosodic structure is concerned, too, ambiguous sentences may vary independently on (at least) two dimensions: the phonological phrase (ϕ) and the intonational phrase (I).[8] Figure 2 represents the four logically possible combinations of the two prosodic dimensions under consideration.

		Phonological Phrases	
		same	different
Intonational Phrases	same	a	b
	different	c	d

Figure 2. Phonological phrases and intonational phrases in ambiguous sentences

The syntactic and prosodic dimensions, however, are not independent of each other, given that the construction of the prosodic constituents depends indirectly on the syntactic structure of a sentence. When the two interpretations of an ambiguous sentence have the same syntactic structure, their prosodic structure must also be the same. In all other cases, however, the ϕ and I structures may vary with respect to the two syntactic factors. The result is that there are ten possible relations between the syntactic and prosodic structures corresponding to the two meanings of an ambiguous sentence, as seen in Figure 3 (from Nespor and Vogel, 1983b:134).

			SYNTAX			
			Constituents Same		Constituents Different	
			Labels Same	Labels Different	Labels Same	Labels Different
P		*I* Same	1	2	3	4
R O	φ Same	*I* Different			5	6
S						
O D		*I* Same			7	8
Y	φ Different	*I* Different			9	10

Figure 3. Relations between the syntactic and prosodic structures of ambiguous sentences

Finally, there is another area in which the two meanings of an ambiguous sentence may differ, and that is at the level of logical form, specifically, where different thematic relations are involved. For example, in the sentence *Volevo farlo suonare* 'I wanted to make him play (an instrument)' and 'I wanted to have it played', *lo* can either serve as the subject of the verb *suonare* 'to play' or as its object. Although it was mentioned earlier that we intended to restrict our attention to different structural types of ambiguity, as opposed to those depending on logico-semantic factors, we did include an additional category in our test, 1', where the only difference between the two meanings was at the level of thematic relations. This was done as a check on the fairly common assumption that such relations do not manifest themselves prosodically. It should be noted that the new category 1' is structurally the same as category 1, since in both cases the syntactic constituents and the syntactic labels, as well as the φ and *I* structures, are the same for both meanings of the ambiguous sentences in question.

The different types of ambiguous sentences used in the test are exemplified in Table 1, where the numbers correspond to those in Figure 3. It should be noted that category 2 is missing from the list; no plausible examples of this type were found in Italian.[9] Instead, category 1' has been included in the list. For each sentence, the labeled prosodic bracketings that correspond to the two meanings are given, and below each meaning the paraphrase used in the test is provided. The English translations are given in Table 2.

Table 1. Examples of different types of ambiguous sentences

Type of sentence	Example
1	a. $[[[\text{Non ho mai visto}]_\phi \ [\text{tanti ricci}]_\phi]_I]_U$
	'Ricci di mare'
	b. $[[[\text{Non ho mai visto}]_\phi \ [\text{tanti ricci}]_\phi]_I]_U$
	'Capelli ricci'
1'	a. $[[[\text{É stato trovato}]_\phi \ [\text{da Antonio}]_\phi]_I]_U$
	'Era a casa di Antonio'
	b. $[[[\text{É stato trovato}]_\phi \ [\text{da Antonio}]_\phi]_I]_U$
	'Antonio l'ha trovato'
3	a. $[[[\text{Marco}]_\phi]_I \ [[\text{ha guardato}]_\phi \ [\text{la ragazza}]_\phi$ $[\text{col canocchiale}]_\phi]_I]_U$
	'La ragazza ha in mano il canocchiale'
	b. $[[[\text{Marco}]_\phi]_I \ [[\text{ha guardato}]_\phi \ [\text{la ragazza}]_\phi$ $[\text{col canocchiale}]_\phi]_I]_U$[10]
	'Marco ha in mano il canocchiale'
4	a. $[[[\text{Luca}]_\phi]_I \ [[\text{fa}]_\phi \ [\text{la foto}]_\phi]_I \ [[\text{e Carlo}]_\phi]_I$ $[[\text{la stampa}]_\phi]_I]_U$
	'Carlo fa la stampa'
	b. $[[[\text{Luca}]_\phi]_I \ [[\text{fa}]_\phi \ [\text{la foto}]_\phi]_I \ [[\text{e Carlo}]_\phi]_I$ $[[\text{la stampa}]_\phi]_I]_U$
	'Carlo stampa la foto'
5	a. $[[[\text{Quando Giorgio}]_\phi]_I \ [[\text{chiama}]_\phi \ [\text{suo fratello}]_\phi]_I$ $[[\text{è sempre nervoso}]_\phi]_I]_U$
	'Giorgio è nervoso'
	b. $[[[\text{Quando Giorgio}]_\phi]_I \ [[\text{chiama}]_\phi]_I \ [[\text{suo fratello}]_\phi]_I$ $[[\text{è sempre nervoso}]_\phi]_I]_U$
	'Suo fratello nervoso'
6	a. $[[[\text{Quando Giorgio}]_\phi]_I \ [[\text{va}]_\phi \ [\text{al ristorante}]_\phi]_I \ [[\text{con Luisa}]_\phi$ $[\text{e Manuela}]_\phi]_I \ [[\text{è sempre felice}]_\phi]_I]_U$
	'Giorgio è felice'
	b. $[[[\text{Quando Giorgio}]_\phi]_I \ [[\text{va}]_\phi \ [\text{al ristorante}]_\phi]_I \ [[\text{con Luisa}]_\phi]_I$ $[[\text{Emanuela}]_\phi]_I \ [[\text{è sempre felice}]_\phi]_I]_U$
	'Emanuela è felice'[11]

7   a. [[[Ho visto]$_\phi$ [in svendita]$_\phi$]$_I$ [[degli sgabelli]$_\phi$
[per pianoforti]$_\phi$ [antichi]$_\phi$]$_I$]$_U$
'Gli sgabelli sono antichi'

    b. [[[Ho visto]$_\phi$ [in svendita]$_\phi$]$_I$ [[degli sgabelli]$_\phi$
[per pianoforti antichi]$_\phi$]$_I$]$_U$[12]
'I pianoforti sono antichi'

8   a. [[[Ho visto Marco]$_\phi$ [dal monaco]$_\phi$]$_I$]$_U$
'É a casa del monaco che l'ho visto'

    b. [[[Ho visto]$_\phi$ [Marco Dal Monaco]$_\phi$]$_I$]$_U$
'Il cognome di Marco è Dal Monaco'

9   a. [[[Ha parlato naturalmente]$_\phi$]$_I$]$_U$
'É ovvio che ha parlato'

    b. [[[Ha parlato naturalmente]$_\phi$]$_I$]$_U$
'Ha parlato in modo naturale'

10   a. [[[Lì]$_\phi$]$_I$ [[[suonano insieme]$_\phi$]$_I$]$_U$
'Laggiù stanno suonando'

    b. [[[Li suonano insieme]$_\phi$]$_I$]$_U$
'Suonano gli strumenti'

Table 2. Translation of disambiguation test examples

Type of Sentence	Example
1	a. I have never seen so many sea urchins. 'Sea urchins'
	b. I have never seen so many curls. 'Curly hair'
1'	a. It was found at Antonio's. 'It was at Antonio's house'
	b. It was found by Antonio. 'Antonio found it'
3	a. Marco looked at the girl with the binoculars. 'The girl is holding the binoculars'
	b. Marco looked at the girl with the binoculars. 'Marco is holding the binoculars'

4   a. Luca makes the picture and Carlo the print.
            'Carlo makes the print'
      b. Luca takes the picture and Carlo prints it.
            'Carlo prints the picture'

5   a. When Giorgio calls his brother he is always nervous.
            'Giorgio is nervous'
      b. When Giorgio calls his brother is always nervous.
            'His brother is nervous'

6   a. When Giorgio goes to the restaurant with Luisa and Manuela he is always happy.
            'Giorgio is happy'
      b. When Giorgio goes to the restaurant with Luisa Emanuela is always happy.
            'Emanuela is happy'

7   a. I saw on sale some antique piano stools.
            'The stools are antique'
      b. I saw on sale some stools for antique pianos.
            'The pianos are antique'

8   a. I saw Marco at the monk's.
            'It was at the monk's place'
      b. I saw Marco Dal Monaco.
            'Marco's last name is Dal Monaco'

9   a. He spoke naturally.
            'It's obvious that he spoke'
      b. He spoke naturally.
            'He spoke in a natural way'

10   a. There they are playing together.
            'Over there they are playing'
      b. They are playing them together.
            'They are playing the instruments'

Let us now return to the specific predictions made by the two disambiguation proposals. The syntactic proposal predicts disambiguation in those cases in which the syntactic structures corresponding to the different meanings are different, thus in types 3-10. The prosodic proposal, on the other hand, predicts disambiguation in those cases in which the prosodic structures are different, thus in types 5-10. The predictions are therefore different in two cases, in types 3 and 4, where the syntactic structures of the two meanings are different but where the prosodic structures are the same.

Another difference between the two disambiguation proposals is that the syntactic proposal allows for only two possible types of results, while the prosodic proposal allows for more. That is, according to the syntactic proposal, the two possibilities are: (*i*) different syntactic structures and therefore disambiguation, and (*ii*) the same syntactic structures and therefore no disambiguation. The prosodic proposal, on the other hand, allows for the following possibilities: (*i*) different prosodic structures at both the ϕ and I levels and therefore complete disambiguation, (*ii*) the same prosodic structures at both the ϕ and I levels and therefore no disambiguation, (*iii*) different prosodic structures at one of the levels (ϕ or I) and therefore partial disambiguation. In relation to possibility (iii), although there is no *a priori* reason for distinguishing between those cases in which the difference is at the ϕ level and those in which it is at the I level, the hypothesis can be made that a difference at the I level is more 'audible', since the end of an I automatically represents a difference at the ϕ level as well, while the boundary of a ϕ does not necessarily coincide with an I boundary. In other words, we can expect there to be more prosodic boundary markers at the end of an I (and ϕ) than at the end of only a ϕ, thus making disambiguation more likely when there is a difference at the I level. Thus, possibility (iii) can actually be divided into two separate cases: (*iii* ') different prosodic structures only at the ϕ level and therefore some disambiguation, and (*iv*) different prosodic structures only at the I level and therefore somewhat more disambiguation.

Taking as a starting point the proposal that makes more specific predictions, the prosodic proposal, we formulated the following hypotheses, which were then tested on the basis of the perception test described in the next section (see Nespor and Vogel, 1983b:135):

(16)   *Disambiguation Hypotheses*
   a.   Sentences in which both the ϕ and I structures are the same for both interpretations are not disambiguable even when the syntactic structures are different.
   b.   Disambiguation is most likely when both the ϕ and I structures are different for the two interpretations.
   c.   Disambiguation is more likely when the I structures are different for the two interpretations (and ϕ structures are the same) than when the ϕ structures are different (and I structures are the same).
   d.   Sentences in which the two interpretations differ only in thematic relations are not disambiguable.

It is Hypothesis *a* that distinguishes most clearly between the two disambiguation proposals. Hypotheses *b* and *c* also distinguish between the two proposals, though somewhat less directly. In other words, since it is only the prosodic proposal that makes the type of prediction found in *b* and *c*, a difference in listener responses along these lines would provide support for the prosodic proposal. Finally, although Hypothesis *d* does not distinguish between the two disambiguation proposals, it was included as verification of the assumption that thematic roles do not affect the prosody of a sentence.

9.3.2. Disambiguation test

Subjects

The disambiguation test was presented to 36 adults, all of whom were from northern Italy. The subjects were all speakers of standard Italian and were either university graduates or students at the time of testing.

Material

The test consisted of a series of 78 ambiguous sentences, representing the 10 types described above. They were recorded by M. Nespor, a speaker of a standard northern variety of Italian, and presented to the subjects on a Uher 2000 tape recorder. Two versions of the test were prepared (Test I and Test II), and of the 36 subjects, half heard one version and half the other version.

In the preparation of the two versions of the test, each sentence was read with the intention of presenting one of the two possible meanings of a sentence in one version, and the other meaning in the other version. Thus, only the combination of the two tests gave all of the 156 possible meanings of the 78 sentences. To ensure the correct reading of the test sentences in the preparation of the tapes, each ambiguous sentence was preceded by a nonambiguous sentence with the same construction as that of the desired meaning of the ambiguous sentence. The nonambiguous sentence was not recorded; it was only used to 'program' the pronunciation of the ambiguous sentence. The number of syllables and position of stresses in the primer sentence were kept as close as possible to those in the target sentence, as is illustrated in (17).

(17) a. Test I
        primer: Marco ha guardato la ragazza col neo grande.
                'Marco looked at the girl with the large mole.'
        target: Marco ha guardato la ragazza col canocchiale.
                'Marco looked at the girl with the binoculars.'
    b. Test II
        primer: Marco ha guardato la ragazza con interesse.
                'Marco looked at the girl with interest.'
        target: Marco ha guardato la ragazza col canocchiale.
                'Marco looked at the girl with the binoculars.'

The subjects indicated their responses on answer sheets that contained lists of the two possible paraphrases for each sentence. Two versions of the answer sheet were used as well. The pair of paraphrases for each sentence were given in one order in one version, and in the opposite order in the other version. Thus, for each test (I and II), half of the subjects received one order of presentation of the paraphrases and the other half received the other order. This was done to avoid potential effects due to a tendency on the part of the subjects to consistently choose either the first or the second answer, or to follow any other nonlinguistic strategy in selecting their answers. For example, the paraphrases provided on the answer sheet for the example in (17) are those in (18); as was just mentioned, half of the subjects received an answer sheet with the expressions in the order given in (18), and half received an answer sheet in which the expressions were given in the opposite order.

(18)   a.   La ragazza ha in mano il canocchiale.
            'The girl is holding the binoculars.'
       b.   Marco ha in mano il canocchiale.
            'Marco is holding the binoculars.'

Procedure

Each subject heard only one version of the test, and thus only one form of each of the 78 sentences. Each sentence was played twice. The first time, the subject was supposed to listen to the sentence and think of what it meant, and only afterwards read the two paraphrases given on the answer sheet. At this point, the sentence was presented again and the subject had to indicate which of the two paraphrases best corresponded to what was recorded on the tape. The subjects were encouraged to respond 'spontaneously', without thinking too much about the sentences. If they were totally unable to choose one of the two possible meanings, the subjects were instructed to write 'A', for ambiguous, next to the item in question.

Results

Before we discuss the actual results of our experiment, it should be noted that our analysis, like Lehiste's, rests on the assumption that the two interpretations of each ambiguous sentence were equally plausible. Since we did not verify this assumption on the basis of an independent evaluation of our test sentences, our study is potentially open to the same criticism we made earlier of Lehiste's study. There is, however, an important difference between Lehiste's experiment and ours: the number of stimuli used. Since Lehiste tested only 15 sentences, the effect of several examples with a large discrepancy between the plausibility of the two meanings is relatively large. In our experiment, on the other hand, in which 78 sentences were tested, the presence of a small number of unrepresentative examples does not have a significant effect on the overall results.

In the analysis of the results, the answers corresponding to the meaning intended by the speaker on the tape were marked '+' and those corresponding to the other meaning were marked '−'. The cases in which a subject indicated that both answers were equally possible by writing 'A' were divided between the two values '+' and '−'. There were, in fact, very few such cases.

Table 3 presents the percentages of the '+' answers for each of the types of sentences investigated. In addition, the predictions made by the two disambiguation proposals are indicated for each type of sentence ('+' = disambiguation predicted, '−' = disambiguation not predicted).

Table 3. Per cent responses corresponding to intended meaning of ambiguous sentences

Type of Sentence	% Choice of Intended Meaning	Predicted Disambiguation	
		Syntactic Proposal	Prosodic Proposal
1	50.0	−	−
1'	51.4	−	−
3	59.1	+	−
4	52.6	+	−
5	86.1	+	+
6	94.9	+	+
7	67.8	+	+
8	75.8	+	+
9	90.2	+	+
10	90.2	+	+

Ideally, a nondisambiguable sentence should result in the choice of the intended meaning 50% of the time, while a totally disambiguable sentence should result in the choice of the intended meaning 100% of the time. With these patterns in mind, let us now examine the actual results obtained in the test, and their implications with respect to the hypotheses formulated above in (16).

It should be noted, first of all, that for the two categories 1 and 1', for which both disambiguation proposals predict nondisambiguation, the results are, in fact, very close to the ideal of 50% choice of the intended meaning.

As far as the first hypothesis is concerned, the one which most directly distinguishes between the two proposals, we see that the sentence categories 3 and 4, in which the prosodic structures are the same for the two meanings despite different syntactic structures, behave fairly similarly to the first two (nondisambiguable) categories. That is, while the percentages for categories 3 and 4 are somewhat higher than those for categories 1 and 1', they are nevertheless very far from the ideal of 100% that would indicate disambiguability.

We can conclude, therefore, that Hypothesis a (see (16)) is confirmed, and thus that ambiguous sentences with the same prosodic structures for the two interpretations are essentially not disambiguable, even when their syntactic structures are different.

Hypothesis b, however, is only partially confirmed. It is true that the highest percentages of disambiguation, ±90%, are observed in those categories 9 and 10, where both the ϕ and I structures are different for the two meanings. It is also true, however, that very similar results are observed for the cases in which only the I structures are different, categories 5 and 6. What this means is that Hypothesis b is confirmed in so far as there is no category of sentences that is more disambiguable than those in which both ϕ and I are different, but it is not confirmed to the extent that there are other categories which appear equally disambiguable.

The comparison of the scores for categories 5 and 6 on the one hand, and 7 and 8 on the other, provides confirmation of Hypothesis c. That is, the percentage of disambiguation in the first two categories, in which only the I sturctures are different, is considerably higher than that in the other two categories, where only the ϕ structures are different.

Finally, Hypothesis d was also confirmed. Specifically, the fact that category 1' is not disambiguable, as can be seen from the score of 51.4% selection of the intended meaning, shows that a difference only at the level of thematic relations does not contribute to the prosodic patterns of sentences such that the intended meaning can be identified by the listener.

9.4.   Conclusions

On the basis of the results of the perception test just described, we can conclude that the possibility of disambiguating ambiguous sentences depends on the prosodic structures rather than on the syntactic structures corresponding to the different interpretations of a given sentence. It is the prosodic proposal, therefore, that accounts more accurately for the results.

Specifically, the prosodic proposal accounts for the observed patterns better than the syntactic proposal in two areas. First of all, we saw that the first hypothesis was confirmed, showing that it is the presence or absence of a difference at the prosodic level of analysis that predicts whether or not an ambiguous sentence can be disambiguated. A difference at the syntactic level cannot determine the disambiguation of a sentence if the prosodic structures are the same. Secondly, the fact that the prosodic, but not the syntactic, proposal allows for the distinction among various degrees of disambiguation is another point in favor of the prosodic proposal, since the test results provided evidence for three degrees of disambiguation. That is, it was found that the cases in which the prosodic structures were different at the I level were the most disambiguable, with an average of close to 90% choice of the intended meaning. Cases in which only the ϕ structures were different were systematically less disambiguable, while those cases in which the prosodic structures were the same at the ϕ and I levels were not disambiguable, regardless of their syntactic structure. The syntactic proposal allows for only two possiblities: disambiguable or not disambiguable.

Finally, the confirmation of the last hypothesis shows that sentences with only a difference at the level of thematic relations are not disambiguable. Thus, the only relevant differences in determining the possibility of disambiguation are phonological differences, and in particular, differences in the prosodic structures corresponding to the different interpretations of an ambiguous sentence.

In addition to providing an answer to the specific question raised in this chapter as to whether it is syntactic or prosodic constituent structure that accounts for the ability of listeners to disambiguate ambiguous sentences, the results of the disambiguation test have implications for the theory of perception in general. That is, the results show that listeners rely on phonological units that are not necessarily isomorphic to syntactic constituents in the first stage in their processing of a string of speech sounds. These phonological units, the prosodic constituents that have been argued for on independent grounds in the previous chapters of this book, in particular the phonological phrase and the intonational phrase, can thus be seen as a bridge between the sounds of a language and the interpretation of the meaning of a string of such sounds. That is, they provide the listener with the link needed to proceed from the perception of a sequence of segments to the final syntactic analysis of the sequence in question. This follows, in fact, from the nature of the prosodic constituents themselves. That is, since the domains of these constituents are constructed on the basis of syntactic notions, once a listener has identified the prosodic structure of a given sentence, this structure can be associated with the appropriate syntactic structure by a procedure that works in the opposite direction of the mapping procedure that is originally responsible for the creation of the prosodic constituents. Thus, only those syntactic structures that are directly reflected in prosodic structure are perceived by a listener and, as a consequence, only those ambiguous sentences that have different prosodic structures corresponding to their different meanings can be disambiguated. Syntactic differences corresponding to the different meanings that are not reflected in prosodic structure cannot contribute to the disambiguation of ambiguous sentences. Our conclusion is, therefore, that it is prosodic structure, not syntactic structure, that provides the clues to the first stage in the analysis of incoming speech. This is not to say that syntax is not relevant at the first stage of processing in speech perception, but rather it is only indirectly relevant, mediated through the prosodic structure of a given utterance.

NOTES

1. The perception test discussed here represents the product of earlier work described in Nespor and Vogel (1983b), and the data comprise the results of tests carried out expressly for this book as well as those carried out somewhat earlier, as will be made clear below. Sections 9.1. and 9.2, furthermore, have previously been published in Italian in Vogel (1984b).

2. See Kooij (1971) for a historical summary of the study of ambiguity.

3. Since the disambiguation test we carried out was in Italian, we will use Italian examples throughout the present discussion of the types of ambiguity as well.

4. We are dealing with a northern variety of Italian here, where intervocalic *s* is pronounced [z], and where Raddoppiamento Sintattico does not apply after the auxiliary *ha* 'has'.

5. In the present study, we have not explicitly taken into account the subcategory of phonetic ambiguity mentioned by Ullmann within our category of syntactic ambiguity. It would undoubtedly be interesting to investigate such 'juncture' phenomena, which have received much attention in the past, in particular from American structuralists (e.g. Bloomfield, 1933; Moulton, 1947; Trager and Smith, 1951), within the framework of prosodic phonology as well.

6. There are also other prosodic differences between the pronunciations corresponding to the two meanings of the sentence, but the difference mentioned here seems to be the most noticeable one.

7. The test discussed here is an extention of the one reported in Nespor and Vogel (1983b). The same sentences have been used, but the number of subjects tested has been increased from 20 to 36. A comparison of the results in Nespor and Vogel (1983b) with those presented here shows that we are, in fact, dealing with a general phenomenon, since the patterns observed in both cases are very similar.

8. There are clearly also other syntactic dimensions (e.g. depth of embedding) as well as other prosodic dimensions (e.g. clitic group) along which one can say that (ambiguous) sentences may vary. We will restrict our attention here to the two syntactic and prosodic dimensions mentioned, since they are the ones that bear most directly on the issues at hand.

9. This type of sentence is fairly common in English, however, as illustrated by sentences like *The French teachers met in the morning*.

10. The fact that the prosodic structures are the same for the two meanings of this sentence is a result of the application of the restructuring rule discussed in Chapter 7

that affects short Is. Before the restructuring, in fact, the prosodic structure of the meaning in b is different: $[[[Marco]_\phi]_I \ [[ha\ guardato]_\phi \ [la\ ragazza]_\phi]_I \ [[col\ canoc-chiale]_\phi]_I]_U$. It should be noted, however, that the normal pronunciation of this sentence is with the restructuring.

11. It should be noted that occasionally there are orthographic differences between the two versions of the test sentences. The segmental sequences are nevertheless the same, and this is what is relevant to our test.

12. The fact that the two prosodic structures for this sentence are different depends on the fact that in type $7b$ the restructuring rule discussed in Chapter 6 has applied to create a new ϕ. It should be noted, in addition, that a similar situation arises in sentences of type 9, where ϕ restructuring applies for the meaning of $9b$, but not $9a$.

Chapter 10

Prosodic Domains and the Meter of the Commedia

10.0 Introduction

The language of poetry differs from ordinary spoken language in that in addition to the linguistic level there is an abstract pattern with its own rhythmic alternations. Meter can be viewed as an entity in between these two levels or, put in other words, as the 'encoding of a simple abstract pattern into a sequence of words' (Halle and Keyser, 1971:140).[1] Such an intermediate entity is accounted for by a set of correspondence rules operating between the linguistic level on the one hand and the abstract pattern on the other.[2]

The abstract pattern is observed more or less rigorously by different poets and in different poetic traditions. There are poems in which the abstract pattern is rigidly respected and the linguistic level must thus be constrained in various ways. Certain words are excluded *a priori* because they cannot match the abstract pattern; for example, a dactylic pattern cannot be matched with a word such as *ràraménte* 'seldom', whose rhythm is trochaic. Most other words, though not excluded, can occur only in certain positions; for example, a word such as *cittá* 'city' can only be matched with a dactylic pattern in such a way that the first syllable corresponds to the last position of a dactylic foot and the second syllable to the first position of the next foot. In more complex poetic compositions, such as the *Commedia* (also known as *Divina Commedia*), however, it is not always the language that gives in under the strength of the abstract pattern, but it is sometimes the pattern itself that undergoes certain modifications that are imposed on it by the natural rhythm of language.

The types of correspondence rules that may apply to match the two levels so as to ultimately yield a metrical line of verse are constrained in various ways. One of the tasks of a theory of meter is to specify these constraints.

The abstract pattern of verse is best represented in a hierarchical fashion (see Kiparsky, 1977; Piera, 1982). Let us call the terminal nodes of such a hierarchy metrical positions. In poetry, where the number of syllables contained in a line of verse is a crucial aspect of meter, the metrical positions of a verse are put in correspondence with units on the linguistic level: syllables. The matching between the two levels is not always straightforward, however, in that metrical positions and syllables do not always stand in a one-to-one relation. A theory of meter must specify how this type of disparity is resolved. Proceeding to higher levels, the question arises as to which linguistic structure can be most fruitfully used to account for the way in which conflicts between language and abstract metrical patterns are resolved.

It has often been proposed that syntactic structure must be taken into consideration in order to account for certain metrical regularities (see, among others, Elwert, 1968; Kiparsky, 1975, 1977; Di Girolamo, 1976; Beltrami, 1981). For example, Elwert (1968) observes that Italian verse must be read in a way that takes into account the syntactic value of the words in a given context. Kiparsky (1975, 1977), on the other hand, proposes more specifically that the division into constituents of the surface syntactic structure must be taken into account in order to specify the context of certain metrical phenomena. While syntax certainly plays a role in the organization of meter, we believe that the only syntactic notions that may be relevant in determining metrical regularities are those incorporated in prosodic structure. Direct reference to syntactic structure as suggested by Kiparsky is excluded. In fact, it is a prediction of the organization of the grammar proposed in the present book that rules that account for phenomena as phonological in nature as meter cannot see anything deeper than the phonological deep structure, that is, the division into prosodic constituents.

In this chapter, we will show that it is indeed the prosodic structure and not the syntactic structure that accounts for several regularities found in the most common type of verse in the Italian poetic tradition, that is, the hendecasyllable. Our results are in agreement with Hayes (to appear), who first recognized the relevance of prosodic structure for meter. While Hayes's analysis of English verse makes crucial use of all categories above the word level, we will concentrate here on the phonological phrase.

The data which form the empirical basis of the following discussion are taken from the *Inferno*, the first of the three canticles of Dante Alighieri's *Commedia*. Occasionally, however, lines taken from one of the other two canticles, *Purgatorio* and *Paradiso*, are also used in the examples.

10.1.   *The metrical hierarchy of the hendecasyllable*

The abstract pattern of poetic meter is organized in an architectonic fashion, independently of the linguistic level with which it is associated. In music, tones are grouped into motives, motives into phrases, phrases into periods (see Cooper and Meyer, 1960:2); similarly, in the abstract metrical pattern, metrical feet are grouped into cola, cola into lines, lines into tercets, etc. (see among others, Piera, 1982). Let us call this hierarchy the metrical hierarchy.

In the particular case of the hendecasyllable, each line contains ten metrically relevant positions. The tenth position is always stressed, and it is optionally followed by one or two extrametrical syllables. The metrical positions constitute the terminal nodes of the metrical hierarchy. The reason for considering the syllables to the right of the tenth as extrametrical is that they do not in fact count for the purposes of the basic rhythm of a line of verse. Their presence or absence depends solely on the location of the main stress of the last word of the line. That is, if the last word has final stress, the line contains no extrametrical syllables. If, instead, the last word is stressed on the penultimate or antepenultimate syllable, then the line contains one or two extrametrical syllables, respectively. Thus, the three lines ending in the ways illustrated in (1) are metrically equivalent (see Piera, 1982), although the extrametrical syllables do have a certain influence on the actual rhythm of a line of verse.

(1) a.   .....il cár   syllables
          9 10   positions

     b.   .....il cáro   syllables
          9 10   positions

     c.   .....il cárico   syllables
          9 10   positions

A verse has a basic pattern which characterizes its underlying rhythm (see Kiparsky, 1975). In the case of the hendecasyllable, we assume that the ten metrically relevant positions are grouped into metrical feet (see Fussel, 1965; Keyser, 1969) with iambic rhythm, that is, feet that dominate two nodes, of which the left is labeled *weak* and the right is labeled *strong*.[3] The advantage of assuming such an underlying pattern is that several characteristics of the hendecasyllable are accounted for if we make this assumption. First of all, a large proportion of hendecasyllabic lines is uniformly iambic. Secondly, by assuming an underlying iambic pattern, the tendency for metrical stresses to fall on even positions observed in the rest of the lines is automatically accounted for. Thirdly, the fact that the syllables following the last stressed one are extrametrical also finds an explanation in the iambic pattern. That is, if the abstract pattern is iambic, there are no metrical positions after the last stressed position.

The level above the foot in the metrical hierarchy is the colon. Piera (1982) has proposed that a colon may contain either two or three metrical feet, and that in the hendecasyllable the rightmost position of each colon contains the designated terminal element, that is, it has metrical stress. While Piera has uniformly binary branching cola, as shown in the abstract patterns for the hendecasyllable in (2), we do not know of any motivation for the extra (circled) constituents between the metrical foot (MF) and the colon. That is, the positions 3 through 6 in the first case and 7 through 10 in the second case do not form a metrically relevant unit. We therefore choose to represent the two basic patterns for the hendecasyllable as in (3) (see also Hayes, to appear). The geometry of the metrical trees is thus the same as the geometry of the prosodic trees.

(2) binary branching hendecasyllables

a.

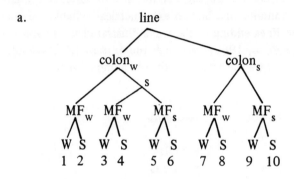

b.

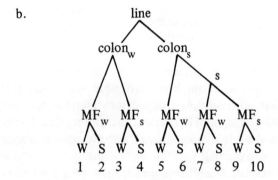

(3) n-ary branching hendecasyllables

a.

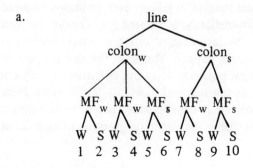

b.

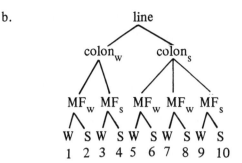

One of the fundamental – and to our knowledge still unexplained – characteristics of the hendecasyllable has been shown by Piera to follow from the postulation of the colon constituent: the existence in the majority of hendecasyllables of a major stress either on the sixth or on the fourth position – the two possible rightmost (i.e. strong) nodes of the first colon – and a major stress on the tenth position, which always occupies the rightmost node of the second colon.

As may be seen in (3), the uppermost constituent in the hendecasyllable is the line, which groups together the two cola. Of these, the right one is labeled *strong* and the left one is labeled *weak*, which accounts for the fact that the tenth position is perceived as more heavily stressed than any of the preceding ones.

10.2 The basic correspondence rules of the hendecasyllable and prosodic categories

Before we begin our discussion of the location of stress prominence in the hendecasyllable of the *Commedia*, a few comments are in order with regard to the nature of the data. It should be noted, first of all, that one can never be sure when discussing the rythmic patterns of the *Commedia* that the work referred to is actually that created by Dante. The *Commedia* is a poem consisting of three canticles and a total of 14,233 lines, written at the beginning of the fourteenth century. The original manuscript does not exist, and as scribes copied the work over the years, the original may have undergone modifications in a number of areas including rhythm. As Bertinetto (1973:56) observes, it might very well be that the influence of the well-established examples of Petrarch has had a 'normalizing' effect on the rhythmic patterns of the *Commedia*. In the present analysis, we make use of Petrocchi's 1966/67 critical edition of the *Commedia*.

As far as the hendecasyllable itself is concerned, it should be noted that it is characterized by a specific rhythmic pattern. In this pattern there are more prominent positions, that is, positions that receive a metrical stress, and less prominent, or unstressed, positions. A metrical stress in a line is referred to as an ictus. It is well known that in the recitation of the *Commedia*, as in that of most poems, there is a certain freedom as to how many and which ictuses are actually pronounced (see also Bertinetto, 1973; Di Girolamo, 1976). Various factors play a role in determining the actual recitation of a line of verse, including the rate of speech. We will not enter into a discussion of these performance factors here, however, since we are interested in poetic competence. It should be noted, though, that the extent to which two recitations of the same line may vary is very large. At one extreme, there is what Kiparsky (1975:585) calls 'the school-boy manner of imposing a mechanical alternating rhythm on the verse, i.e. reciting according to the underlying metrical pattern'. At the other extreme, there is a style of recitation that respects almost completely the rhythmic alternations of ordinary language, that is, a style of recitation more similar to that of prose. In this chapter, we will not account for the different performances of the *Commedia*, but rather for its metrical organization (see, among others, Jakobson, 1960; Bierwisch, 1966; Halle and Keyser, 1966; Kiparsky, 1975). As Halle and Keyser (1966:372) clearly put it, '[t]he meter of a poem determines to a great extent the manner in which a poem is performed. It never determines the performance completely, however, any more than a score of a sonata completely determines the way in which the sonata should be performed.' Just as the goal of linguistic theory is the characterization of linguistic competence, the goal of a theory of poetic meter is the characterization of poetic competence. With this in mind, we will now proceed to see how the basic pattern of the hendecasyllable described in section 10.1 above is coupled with the linguistic level.

As we said above, the hendecasyllable has ten metrically relevant positions, the tenth of which always has metrical stress. This positiom is matched with a syllable that bears primary word stress.[4] Since the vast majority of words in Italian have penultimate stress, the vast majority of the lines of the *Commedia* have one extrametrical syllable, as exemplified in (4), where the numbers under the lines indicate the positions. If the last word of the line has antepenultimate stress, there are two extrametrical syllables, and if the last word has final stress, there are no extrametrical syllables, as shown in (5) and (6), respectively.[5]

(4)   a.   Stavvi Minòs orribilmente e rìnghia: Inferno, V, 4
             1   2   34 5 67 8   9 10
             'There stands Minos, horrible and snarling:'
      b.   essamina le colpe ne l'intráta;   Inferno, V, 5
             1 2 3 4 5   6 7   8   9 10
             'upon the entrance he examines their offenses;'

    c.   giudica e manda secondo ch'avvínghia.   Inferno, V, 6
        1 2 3   4 5 67 8   9 10
       'judges and dispatches (them) according as he entwines.'

(5)   Seguendo 'l cielo sempre fu durábile   Paradiso, XXVI, 129
       1 2   3   45 6   7 8 9 10
       'durable forever... following the heavens'

(6)   fuor vivi e però son fessi cosí   Inferno, XXVIII, 36
       1 2 3   45 6 7 8 9 10
       '...in their lifetime...and therefore are thus cleft'

In these examples,[6] it can also be seen that the metrical positions preceding the tenth are not always in a one-to-one correspondence with syllables. In (6), for example, the third position is matched with two syllables: *vi* and *e*. A necessary condition for the occurrence of this phenomenon, traditionally called synaloepha, is that the first syllable must end in a vowel and the second must begin with a vowel. The adjacency of vowels is not, however, a sufficient condition for synaloepha in Italian, as may be seen in the eighth and ninth positions of the line in (7), where the opposite phenomenon, traditionally called dialoepha, occurs instead.

(7)   come bevesti di Letè ancoi;   Purgatorio, XXXIII, 96
       1 2 3 4 5 6 789 10
       'how you have drunk of Lethe this very day'

It is important to observe that when synaloepha occurs, there is no phonetic modification of the two syllables involved: they count as one metrical position, but they remain fully pronounced. We will not enter into a detailed discussion of synaloepha and related phenomena here, since doing so would bring us too far from our main concern. (See, however, among others, Elwert, 1968; Beccaria, 1970; Di Girolamo, 1976, for a discussion of these phenomena in Italian verse.)

What we have seen thus far is how the lowest constituent of the metrical hierarchy, the metrical position, is matched with the lowest constituent of the prosodic hierarchy, the syllable. We proceed now to the second level of the metrical hierarchy: the metrical foot. We propose that the metrical foot (MF) is matched with the second level of the prosodic hierarchy: the prosodic foot. The optimal matching between the two is one in which the strong node of the MF corresponds to the strong syllable of a Σ. (It should be recalled that at the Σ level no distinction is made between primary and secondary word stresses; this can only be seen in relation to the word itself.) Let us call the foot level of stress in the line of verse secondary ictus. The optimal matching of the two hierarchies at the foot level produces a uniformly iambic rhythm, as in the following lines. The accent marks in examples (8)-(16) indicate primary and secondary stress. All foot level ictuses are marked with an *x* above the metrical position that bears it. Metrical prominence at higher levels is not marked.

(8)

               x   x   x   x   x
a. Nel mézzo del cammín di nóstra víta   Inferno, I, 1
     1   2 3 4   5   6   7 8 9 10
     'Midway in the journey of our life'

            x   x   x   x   x
b. mi rìtrovái per úna sélva oscúra   Inferno, 1, 2
     1 2 3 4 5 6 7 8   9 10
     'I found myself in a dark wood'

              x   x   x   x   x
c. Lo giórno se n'andáva e l'áere brúno   Inferno, II, 1
     1   2 3   4   5 6 7   8 9 10
     'Day was departing and the dark air'

     x   x   x   x   x
d. togliéva gli ànimái che sóno in térra   Inferno, II, 2
     1 2 3   4 5 6   7 8 9   10
     'was taking the creatures on earth'

These examples also show another characteristic of the hendecasyllable of the *Commedia*, that is, that monosyllabic words may be either stressed or unstressed, depending on their location in the abstract metrical pattern. Thus the preposition (plus article) *del* 'of the' in (8a) bears a secondary ictus, while the preposition *per* 'for' in (8b) does not. This is a characteristic of all monosyllables, even clitics, as may be seen in (8c), where the clitic *se* bears a secondary ictus.

The different behavior of monosyllabic and polysyllabic words with respect to the location of ictuses is not a peculiarity of Italian verse. Jakobson (1960) observes that one of the invariant characteristics of Russian verse is that a word stress can coincide with a weak position in the abstract pattern only if it belongs to a monosyllable. Kiparsky (1975, 1977) has shown that in English iambic pentameter a weak position in the basic pattern may correspond to any stress at the linguistic level only if it is in a monosyllabic word.

The rhythmic alternation of the basic pattern given so far does not fully account for the rhythm of the hendecasyllable, since the five ictuses are not all equally prominent; that is, some are stronger than others. In the metrical hierarchy, the strong node of the constituent that dominates the MF, the colon, has a higher degree of stress than its weak sister nodes. The problem now is to determine how this strong metrical position is matched with a syllable at the linguistic level. Specifically, we must determine which linguistic constituent is relevant for this matching. We propose that the DTE of a colon is matched with the DTE of a phonological phrase to yield a primary ictus. Examples of this optimal matching, or basic pattern, are given in (9) and (10), where a primary ictus is marked with an x above the secondary ictus level.

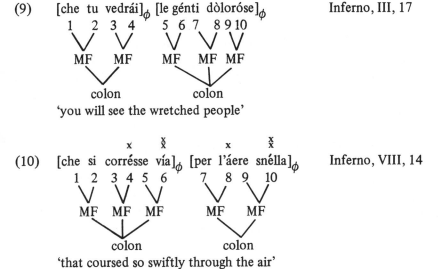

(9)   [che tu vedrái]$_\phi$ [le génti dòloróse]$_\phi$ Inferno, III, 17

'you will see the wretched people'

(10)   [che si corrésse vía]$_\phi$ [per l'áere snélla]$_\phi$ Inferno, VIII, 14

'that coursed so swiftly through the air'

The line in (9) is an example of what is traditionally called the *a minore* hendecasyllable and that in (10) of the *a minore* hendecasyllable. Within the framework presented here, a justification is given to this traditional division as well as to the fact that these two types of hendecasyllable are the most frequent, since they correspond to the two basic patterns. Within an account of the hendecasyllable that does not make use of the metrical hierarchy, the distinction between *a minore* hendecasyllables and *a maiore* hendecasyllables is not an interesting one since, as Elwert (1968) observes, it is not based on anything essential but is only a way to classify the most frequent types of lines (see also Leonetti, 1934-38). It should be noted that while in (9) and (10) the cola are perfectly matched with phonological phrases, this is not a condition on the well-formedness of the hendecasyllable. The matching is between the DTEs of the constituents of the two hierarchies, not between the constituents themselves. Thus, the line in (11) is an example of the basic pattern, even though the second colon contains a position that corresponds to the last syllable of the phonological phrase whose DTE is matched with the DTE of the first colon.

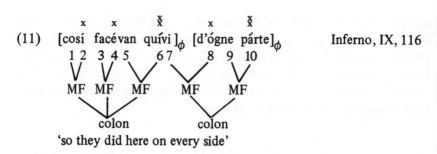

(11)   [cosí facévan quívi]$_\phi$ [d'ógne párte]$_\phi$ Inferno, IX, 116

'so they did here on every side'

The rhythmic pattern created by the primary ictuses is such that in each case there is never less than one, or more than two, weak positions between two strong positions, or between one strong position and the end of the line. This is in agreement with a very general principle of rhythmic alternation (see, among others, Sesini, 1938, 1939; Chatman, 1965, 1972; Savoia, 1974-75; Selkirk, 1984b) that accounts for the fact that there is a tendency to establish binary patterns, that is, a tendency to establish a regular alternation of strong and weak elements. Ternary patterns are a variant of binary patterns (see, among others, Liberman, 1975; Kiparsky, 1975; Hayes, 1980). Quaternary patterns, instead, are perceived as two adjacent binary patterns. Similarly, patterns with more than four elements are perceived as a succession of binary and ternary patterns. Given the basic pattern of the *a maiore* hendecasyllable, repeated in (12a) below, and the principle of rhythmic alternation, an even more rhythmic result is obtained by adding a primary ictus on the second position, as in (12b).[7] Consequently, such a line of verse has three cola instead of two, which accounts for the observation that a hendecasyllabic line does not necessarily have one metrical break, but might in certain cases have two (see, among others, Sesini, 1939; Elwert, 1968).

(12)   a.   x   x   b.   x   x   x
             x   x   x   x   x   x   x   x   x   x
             •   •   •   •   •   •   •   •   •   •

A number of the *a maiore* hendecasyllables in the *Commedia* are, in fact, instances of this pattern, as illustrated in (13).[8]

(13)   a.   x̆   x   x̆   x   x̆
             [Nel mézzo]$_\phi$ [del cammín]$_\phi$ [di nóstra víta]$_\phi$

                                                                                Inferno, I, 1

             'Midway in the journey of our life'

                          x̆   x   x̆   x   x̆
       b.   [Temp'éra]$_\phi$ [dal princípio]$_\phi$ [del mattíno]$_\phi$
                                                                          Inferno, I, 37

             'It was the beginning of the morning'

$$\overset{\overset{x}{x}}{}\qquad x\qquad \overset{\overset{x}{x}}{}\qquad x\qquad \overset{\overset{x}{x}}{}$$

c. [e'l sol]$_\phi$ [montáva'n su]$_\phi$ [con quélle stélle]$_\phi$

Inferno, I, 39

'and the sun was mounting with the stars'

It should be noted that the primary ictus on the second position, too, is matched with the strong node of a phonological phrase. In such cases, a line contains three phonological phrases instead of two.

To sum up thus far, we have proposed that in the basic pattern of the hendecasyllable, the secondary ictuses correspond to the DTE of the prosodic category foot and the primary ictuses correspond to the DTE of the phonological phrase. No distinction is made between primary and secondary word stresses, which amounts to saying that the word plays no role in the basic assignment of ictuses.

The secondary stresses we have seen so far were all located to the left of primary stresses. Whether secondary stresses also exist to the right of primary stresses within a word is an issue on which there is no agreement (see, among others, Camilli, 1965; Di Girolamo, 1976; Bertinetto, 1979; Vogel and Scalise, 1982). For metrical purposes, we will assume only that, when occurring to the right of the primary word stress, alternating syllables – starting from the rightmost one – may be matched with strong nodes of a metrical foot. That is, they may receive a secondary ictus in the line, as exemplified in (14), where the word *vergine* 'virgin', has primary stress on the first syllable, but receives a secondary ictus also on the last syllable.

(14)
$$\qquad x\qquad \overset{\overset{x}{x}}{}\qquad x\qquad x\qquad \overset{\overset{x}{x}}{}$$

Per cui morí la vérgine Camílla   Inferno, I, 107
'for which the virgin Camilla ... died'

Alternating syllables to the right of the primary stress (always starting from the rightmost one) receive a secondary ictus not only within a word, but also in the larger prosodic category clitic group, as exemplified in (15), where the clitic *li* has some degree of stress.

(15)
$$\overset{\overset{x}{x}}{}\ x\qquad \overset{\overset{x}{x}}{}\qquad x\qquad \overset{\overset{x}{x}}{}$$

e vídili le gámbe in su tenére   Inferno, XXXIV, 90
'and saw him with his legs held upwards'

As far as the primary ictus and the role of the phonological phrase in its assignment are concerned, we will now show that it is, in fact, the phonological phrase of the prosodic hierarchy, and not a syntactic constituent, that allows us to account for the location of the primary ictuses in what we have proposed to be the basic pattern of the hendecasyllable. It should be recalled that one of the crucial differences between the domain of the phonological phrase and syntactic structure is that a ϕ may undergo certain restructurings that a syntactic phrase may not undergo. That is, ϕ may be restructured in Italian to include the first nonbranching complement of a head, while it may never include either the first complement if it is branching or any other complement. These distinctions between different types of complements cannot be captured in terms of syntactic constituents. From an analysis of the *Inferno*, it turns out that in the case of a head plus a nonbranching first complement, the primary ictus only falls on the complement, while in the case of a head plus a branching complement there are two primary ictuses, one on the head and one on the right branch of the complement. Two lines that exemplify this contrast are given in (16), where only the relevant ϕ s and ictuses are marked.

(16)

           x   x̆
                    x̆

a.   Genti [che l'áura néra]$_\phi$ si gastiga?   Inferno, V, 51

      'People that are so lashed by the black air?'

           x   x̆   x   x̆

b.   Dico [che quándo l'ánima]$_\phi$ [mal náta]$_\phi$ Inferno, V, 7

      'I mean that when the ill-begotten soul'

In (16a), *nera* 'black', a nonbranching adjectival complement of the noun *aura* 'air', is restructured into one ϕ with the head noun, as indicated by the presence of only one primary ictus. In (16b), instead, *mal nata* 'ill-begotten', a branching complement of the head noun *anima* 'soul', may not be restructured, as indicated by the presence of two primary ictuses, one on *anima* and one on *nata*. These facts are easily accounted for in terms of the prosodic category phonological phrase by assuming that in the *Commedia* ϕ restructuring tends to apply maximally. They are impossible to account for in terms of syntactic constituency, however, since, as was discussed in Chapter 2, the distinction between branching and nonbranching complements cannot be captured in terms of syntactic constituents.

To sum up, we have made a proposal in this section that accounts for the basic patterns of the *Commedia*. These patterns are the result of a matching between the abstract metrical hierarchy on the one hand and prosodic structure on the other. The basic patterns are established, according to our proposal, when the DTEs of two categories of the metrical hierarchy, the metrical foot and the colon, match the DTEs of two categories of the prosodic hierarchy, the foot and the phonological phrase.

These are by no means the only patterns found in the *Commedia*, as will become clear in the next section, where we will discuss a number of derived patterns, that is, patterns that are generated through the application of additional correspondence rules.

10.3. Additional correspondence rules

In this section, we will discuss some of the rules that take as input one of the basic patterns discussed in section 10.2 and give as ouput what we will call derived patterns (see Kiparsky, 1975). The application of additional correspondence rules is necessary when there is a mismatch between the prominence relations of the metrical hierarchy and those of the linguistic material that is coupled with the metrical hierarchy to form a line of verse. The degree to which a line of verse deviates from the basic pattern of that verse gives the degree of complexity of the verse (see Halle and Keyser, 1971; Piera, 1982), also called tension (see Kiparsky, 1975; Di Girolamo, 1976). Thus the lines of verse we will consider in this section are all more complex than the ones seen so far.

There are two types of correspondence rules that may apply to create a derived pattern: those that make a modification in the metrical hierarchy and those that make a modification in the prosodic hierarchy. These rules will accordingly be called metrical and prosodic rules. We will not attempt to give a complete account of the derived metrical patterns found in the *Commedia* here; that is, we will not give an exhaustive treatment of the correspondence rules of Dante's hendecasyllable. Instead, we will limit our discussion to examples of the two types of rules that demonstrate the crucial role played by the prosodic hierarchy in the delimitation of the domains in which these rules may apply within a line of verse.

While one is inclined to view the derived patterns as deviations from the basic patterns, it must be kept in mind that no negative judgment is implied with respect to the quality of their rhythm. To clarify this point, Jakobson (1960:364) makes a very illustrative comparison between deviations from basic meter and attempts of *coups d'état*. If a coup is successful, the conspirators become the representatives of the law. Similarly, '[i]f the violences against the meter take root, they themselves become metrical rules'.

10.3.1. Metrical rules
The hendecasyllable is characterized by a set of metrical rules that modify its basic metrical pattern under the pressure of linguistic structure. That is, the linguistic level imposes its own rhythmic alternations in a number of cases. The particular phenomenon we will analyze here is Inversion (see Fussel, 1965; Kiparsky, 1975; Piera, 1982; Hayes, to appear), the oc-

currence of a sequence of a stressed and an unstressed syllable in an iambic metrical foot. This phenomenon may be accounted for by a metrical rule that inverts the weak and strong nodes in a metrical foot, as illustrated in (17).

(17)   *Inversion*

If in a line of verse there is a single case of Inversion, and if it does not take place in the first MF of the line, this rule has the effect of creating a clash of ictuses, as shown in (18). This constitutes a violation of the principle of rhythmic alternation.

(18)   ... . x . x ... → ... . x x . ...

It should be recalled from Chapter 6 that primary stresses on adjacent syllables in ordinary spoken language may be found only across two phonological phrases in Italian. Within a phonological phrase, several rules ensure that stress clashes are eliminated. One of these rules is Stress Retraction. From an analysis of the lines with a single case of Inversion in the *Inferno*, it turns out that here, too, the two adjacent strong elements are always in two separate ϕs. In other words, the rule of Inversion takes place only at the beginning of a phonological phrase. This is not a peculiarity of the Italian hendecasyllable; Hayes (to appear) has shown that Inversion is ϕ initial in iambic pentameter in English as well, in particular in the verse of Shakespeare, Milton, and Shelley. Hayes also demonstrates that a syntactic definition of the domain of Inversion, as proposed by Kiparsky (1975), cannot account for all the facts, since Inversion appears to make a crucial distinction between branching and non-branching complements. As we have pointed out, this distinction is incorporated in the definition of the phonological phrase; the same distinction cannot be made in terms of syntactic constituents. Similarly, in the *Inferno*, cases of Inversion are found in the first word of a branching complement that immediately follows the head, as illustrated in (19), where Inversion occurs in the word *degno*, which occupies the first branch of the complement of *alcun*, that is, *degno di nota*. No cases of Inversion, however, are found in similar cases in the only word of a nonbranching complement.

(19)
          x   x   x̆   x̆   x
     Se tu ne vedi alcun *degno* di nota   Inferno, XX, 104
     'If you see any that are worthy of note'

Inversion in the hendecasyllable in Italian, as well as in iambic pentameter in English, is thus an example of a metrical rule that needs to make reference to a category of the prosodic hierarchy.

From what we have said thus far, it might seem that clashes across ϕs are tolerated both in ordinary language and in poetry, in violation of the more general principle of rhythmic alternation. This is not, however, the case. As far as ordinary language is concerned, the ϕ limit rule of Final Lengthening (see Chapter 6) may, in fact, be interpreted as a way of introducing enough distance between the two stresses to make their adjacency tolerable to the ear. In verse, a clash would seem even more offensive than in ordinary language and, in fact, a phenomenon discovered by Sesini (1939) applies to reestablish rhythmic alternation at the phonetic level. In his analysis of the hendecasyllable of Petrarch, Sesini notes that a sequence of two strong syllables is always followed by a sequence of two weak syllables. In fact, this also follows from our metrical hierarchy, unless Inversion takes place in the last metrical foot of a hendecasyllable which does not contain any extrametrical syllables. (It should be recalled that we are only analyzing lines with a single application of the rule.) The configuration of the environment in which Inversion has applied is illustrated in (20), where the relevant portion of the line is underlined.

(20)

$$\begin{array}{ccc} MF & MF & MF \\ \Lambda & \Lambda & \Lambda \end{array}$$

$$\cdots \ \cdot \ \underline{x}]_\phi \ [\ \underline{x} \ \cdot \ \cdot \ \underline{x} \ \cdots$$

Sesini notes that at the phonetic level, rhythmic alternation is reestablished. First of all, a small pause is inserted between the two ictuses. This pause, which Sesini calls 'silenzio musicale' ('musical silence'), is perceived as having the same length as one position in the verse. Second, the two unstressed positions that follow the two stressed ones are somehow contracted to occupy together a single metrical position. A hendecasyllable like the one in (21) thus has a rhythmic pattern with the temporal values indicated by the musical notes in (22) (from Sesini, 1939:562).

(21)

$$\begin{array}{ccccc} x & x & \overset{\times}{x} & x & \overset{\times}{x} \end{array}$$

e li parenti miei furon lombardi   Inferno, I, 68
1 2 34 5   6 78   9   10
'and my parents were Lombards'

(22)

$$\begin{array}{cccccccc} & & & & x & x & \cdot & \cdot \end{array}$$

1 2 3 4 5 6 7 8 9 10 11

It should be noted that here too we are concerned with poetic rhythmic competence rather than the performance of a line of verse, as is Sesini, who analyzes 'quello che avviene nel nostro istinto ritmico' ('that which happens in our rhythmic instinct').

In the terminology of prosodic phonology, the phenomena just described may be accounted for by two rules that make reference to the phonological phrase. The first rule, Silent Position Insertion, inserts a silent position in the line of verse between two phonological phrases.[9] The second rule, Reduction, reduces to one position two metrical positions that correspond to the weak nodes of a phonological phrase. Both rules operate when needed to reestablish the fundamental iambic pattern.

Sesini (1939) also observes that an argument in favor of his proposal is that the position inserted between the two otherwise clashing ictuses does not need to be silent. In many cases, one of the two positions where the clash occurs corresponds to two syllables at the linguistic level; that is, there is synaloepha. The additional position is thus, in a way, already available. An example of this situation is given in (23),[10] where the seventh metrical position corresponds to the two syllables *mo* and *o* on the linguistic level.

(23)

$$. \quad \overset{x}{\underset{x}{}} \quad . \quad x \quad . \quad \overset{x}{\underset{x}{}} \quad \overset{x}{\underset{x}{}} \quad . \quad . \quad \overset{x}{\underset{x}{}}$$

Rispuosemi: 'Non omo,]$_\phi$ [omo già   fui   Inferno, I, 67
1   2 3 4   5 6   7   8 9   10
' "No, not a living man, though once I was" he answered me'

It has been observed by Pennings (1985) that synaloepha between two adjacent ictuses is just one of the ways used by Dante to increase the distance between two ictuses; alternative ways to alleviate the clash are synaeresis and vowel deletion. Synaeresis has an effect similar to synaloepha, differing only in that it takes place without a word. Vowel deletion, instead, deletes a word-final vowel and thus the syllable node that dominates it. The consonants that were the onset of this syllable become part of the coda of the preceding syllable. This syllable, and thus the metrical position associated with it, therefore contains more segments than it did before the deletion of the following syllabic node. These three phenomena, synaloepha, synaeresis, and vowel deletion, have the common effect of creating extra phonetic material between the two ictuses, thus making the insertion of an extra metrical position more natural.

In this section, we have given an example of how the application of metrical rules – that is, rules that modify the basic metrical pattern of a line of verse – is constrained by the organization of the corresponding linguistic material into phonological phrases. In the next section, we will show that in the case of prosodic rules too, the relevant linguistic level above the foot for the matching between the abstract metrical pattern and the linguistic structure is the phonological phrase.

10.3.2. Prosodic rules

Prosodic rules become operative in the derivation of a line of verse when, in cases of tension between meter and language, meter 'wins'. The language then undergoes certain modifications that are not typical of ordinary spoken language, but must be seen in relation to the abstract metrical pattern. In a sense, then, the language of poetry is more elastic than ordinary language. We will not give a complete account of the prosodic rules of the *Commedia*, that is, of all the adjustments that the language of Dante may undergo to fit the hendecasyllabic metrical pattern. Rather, we will limit our discussion to the occurrence of stress clashes and the ways in which they are resolved, thus reestablishing the desired rhythmic alternation. It will be shown that in the determination of which solution is chosen to eliminate adjacent ictuses in a given line of verse, the prosodic category phonological phrase plays a crucial role.

We will begin our analysis of clashes with the cases of adjacent ictuses created by the metrical rule of Inversion, described in section 10.3 above. Since Inversion is ϕ initial, it can never create a stress clash within a ϕ. Instead, it will always be the case that the clashing ictuses are at the end of one ϕ and at the beginning of the next ϕ. These clashes are not, however, always equally strong; while the ictus in ϕ-final position corresponds in all cases to the DTE of ϕ, the next ictus may either correspond to the main stress of a following nonbranching ϕ or to a weak node of a branching ϕ. This node must in any case bear the DTE of a foot. These two configurations are illustrated in (24a) and (24b), respectively.

(24)   a.

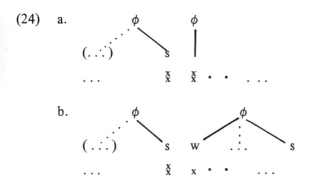

   b.

In both cases it can be seen that these clashes, created by Inversion, are followed by two weak positions on the metrical level (see section 10.3).

In order to account for the ways in which these stress clashes are resolved, we propose the general condition on prosodic rules of the hendeca-syllable given in (25).

(25)   *Condition on prosodic rules* (hendecasyllable)
A prosodic rule may never affect a primary ictus.

The clash illustrated in (24a), which contains two primary ictuses, may thus not be resolved at the linguistic level and, in fact, it is the configuration that triggers the two metrical rules given in section 10.3.1: Silent Position Insertion and Reduction. The clash illustrated in (24b), on the other hand, is such that only the first ictus may not be affected by a prosodic rule. The second ictus may, in principle, be moved rightward to the next position. It thus has the possibility of reestablishing the desired iambic pattern, as illustrated in (26). This is in fact what happens. We will call the rule that accounts for this stress movement Stress Postposing.

(26)   *Stress Postposing*

$$
\begin{array}{c}
\text{x} \\
\ldots \text{x x} \ . \ _\bullet \ \ldots
\end{array}
\rightarrow
\begin{array}{c}
\text{x} \\
\ldots \text{x} \ _\bullet \ \text{x} \ _\bullet \ \ldots
\end{array}
$$

It should be noted that the configuration to the left of the arrow in (26) is also one that triggers the two metrical rules mentioned above. We propose that both the prosodic and the metrical solutions are possible and that the choice depends on one's interpretation of the verse. As Sesini (1939:559) notes, the line of Petrarch's sonnet *Quand'io son tutto vol-to...* (When I am all turned...)[11], given in (27), may have either of the two metrical patterns given in (27b) and (27c).

(27)   a.   Tacito vo ché le parole morte
b.   Tacito vó ché le paróle morte

c.   Tacito vó che lé paróle morte

'I go silent; for my dead words'

The same two rhythmic patterns may also be attributed to similar cases in the *Commedia* as shown in (28) and (29).

(28)   a.

e volser contra lui tutt'i runcigli   Inferno, XXI, 71

        x   x   x̆̄   x   x̆̄

b.   e volser contra lui tutt'i runcigli   Inferno, XXI, 71

     . . .   ♩ ♩ ♩ ♩ . . .

'and turned all their hooks against him'

(29)   a.   x̆̄   x   x̆̄   x   x̆̄

          La bocca mi basció]$_\phi$ [tutto tremante]$_\phi$ Inferno, V, 136

     . . .   ♩ ♪   ♩ ♩ ♩   . . .

         b.   x̆̄   x   x̆̄   x   x̆̄

         b.   La bocca mi basció]$_\phi$ [tutto tremante]$_\phi$

     . . .   ♩   ♩ ♩ ♩   . . .

     '. . . kissed my mouth all trembling'

The role played by the prosodic category ϕ in the determination of the environment in which the two metrical rules of Insertion and Reduction may apply has been discussed in the previous section. Here, it must be noted that the prosodic rule of Stress Postposing applies only to the weak node of a ϕ and moves its stress rightward to the next position in the line, if the last position of the preceding ϕ bears a primary ictus. In the terminology of the theory of phonology presented in this book, it is thus a ϕ juncture rule. Stress Postposing is therefore the first example of a prosodic rule that operates to avoid clashes of ictuses in a line of verse and that makes crucial use of the prosodic category phonological phrase.

     Let us now turn our attention to clashes that, unlike the ones just discussed, are not created by the phenomenon of Inversion. While the clashes created by Inversion are characterized by being situated across two phonological phrases, this is not the case for other types of clashes. That is, we may find other clashes both within ϕs and across ϕs. The second characteristic that distinguishes the clashes created by Inversion is that they are followed by two weak positions in the line. This is not the case for other clashes, which are, instead, most often preceded by two weak positions, as schematized in (30).[12] It should be noted that within a ϕ, clashes by definition may not occur between two primary ictuses. Instead, these clashes are due to the adjacency of a secondary and a primary ictus, as illustrated in the configuration in (30).

                   x

(30)   . . . [. . . ..xx . . .]$_\phi$ . . .

In this case, the secondary ictus is suppressed from its original position (see also Beltrami, 1981) and is retracted to the previous position, as illustrated in (31), thus reestablishing an iambic pattern.

(31)   a.

ch'attende [ciascun uom]$_\phi$ che Dio non teme

Inferno, III, 108

'that awaits every man who fears not God'

b.   che drizzan [ciascun seme]$_\phi$ [ad alcun fine]$_\phi$

Purgatorio, XXX, 110

'which direct every seed to some end'

This rule is reminiscent of the rule of Stress Retraction that takes place in ordinary spoken language, also to avoid a clash within a phonological phrase (see section 6.3). While in ordinary language a clash may be retracted only to another syllable within the same word, this restriction does not apply to verse, as seen in (32), where the clashing ictus is on a monosyllabic word but the stress moves to the word to its left within a phonological phrase, as shown in (32).

(32)   a.

Peró giri Fortuna]$_\phi$ [la sua rota]$_\phi$ Inferno, XV, 95

'therefore let Fortune whirl her wheel'

b.   perch'i fu' ribellante]$_\phi$ [a la sua legge]$_\phi$ Inferno, I, 125

'because I was rebellious to His law'

Let us now consider the cases of clashes that take place between two phonological phrases and that are not created by Inversion. Here too, the clash may arise either from two primary ictuses or from one primary ictus and an adjacent secondary ictus. In the first case, no prosodic rule may apply, since any modification of the ictuses would violate the condition on prosodic rules given in (25) above. The configuration of the environment around the clash is also not such as to permit the application of the two metrical rules seen in section 10.3.1 since, as we already noted, the clash is not generally followed by two weak positions. We have seen above that in these cases the clash is most often preceded by two weak positions. It has been suggested by Pennings (1985) that in these cases a metrical rule applies which is essentially the mirror image of that discovered by Sesini (1939). That is, the two weak positions preceding the clash are reduced and a silent position is inserted between the two primary ictuses. The final effect in this case, too, is the reestablishment of the iambic rhythm on the phonetic level. The application of these metrical rules is illustrated in (33).

$$\overset{x}{\underset{x}{}} \quad \overset{x}{\underset{x}{}} \quad \overset{x}{\underset{x}{}}$$

(33)   Di subito drizzato gridó: 'Come?   Inferno, X, 67

    ...   𝄞 𝄞𝄞 ❭ 𝄞 ...

'Suddenly straightening up he cried "How?" '

We will now turn to cases of clashes between one primary stress and one secondary stress across phonological phrases. These clashes may in principle be resolved by a prosodic rule. The particular rule that applies in these cases is Destressing, as exemplified in (34).

$$\overset{x}{\underset{x}{}} \qquad \overset{\emptyset}{\underset{x}{\uparrow}} \; . \; \overset{x}{\underset{x}{}}$$

(34)   Noi veggiam,]$_\phi$ [come quei]$_\phi$ ch'ha mala luce

                                                  Inferno, X, 100

'Like one who has had light, we see'

Since, as was mentioned above, these clashes are not followed by two weak positions in the line, Destressing eliminates the clash but does not create a lapse of more than two unstressed positions. The principle of rhythmic alternation is thus respected in this case too. In the terminology of prosodic phonology, this is one more example of a prosodic rule that acts in order to eliminate a clash in a line of verse and that must refer to the phonological phrase. Specifically, Destressing represents another case of a ϕ juncture rule.

We have shown above that the domain of application of a number of prosodic rules is adequately formulated in terms of the ϕ constituent of the prosodic hierarchy. We will now demonstrate, on the basis of several lines of the *Commedia*, that a constituent of the syntactic hierarchy cannot accomplish the same task. The two prosodic rules on the basis of which we will illustrate this point are Stress Retraction and Stress Postposing. Both rules may apply within a domain that includes a phrasal head and its first nonbranching complement. In the case of a head whose first complement branches, however, the rule does not apply even if the local environment is met. This distinction, as we have said above, is incorporated in the definition of the phonological phrase, while it cannot be made on the basis of syntactic constituents. The line in (35) indicates that Stress Retraction cannot apply when the clash is between the last position of a phrasal head and the first position of a branching complement.

(35)   Lasciáte ógni speranza, voi ch'intrate   Inferno, III, 9

        'Abandon every hope, you who enter'

The clash, underlined in the example, is between the stress of the verbal head *lasciate* and that of the first word of the complement *ogni* since there is synaloepha between the last syllable of the verb (*te*) and the first syllable of *ogni* (*o*). Stress Retraction, however, cannot apply and the clash must thus be resolved in another way. If we describe the domain of Stress Retraction in terms of ϕ, the reason the rule does not apply is clear: the two clashing ictuses are in different ϕs. If we refer to syntactic constituents, however, we cannot account for this fact, since the same type of syntactic node (in this case $\overline{V}$) dominates a head plus its complement, whether this is branching or not. If the complement is nonbranching, however, Stress Retraction may apply, as shown in (36).

(36)   a.   io non ti verró diétro di gualoppo   Inferno, XXII, 114
           'I won't follow you at a gallop'

       b.   Cagnazzo a cotal motto levó 'l múso   Inferno, XXII, 106
           'Cagnazzo at these words raised his muzzle'

A similar asymmetry in the behavior of branching and nonbranching first complements of a head can be seen in relation to Stress Postposing. This rule, as we have pointed out above, may move an ictus from a weak node of ϕ rightward if necessary to avoid a clash. In (37), a possible environment for Stress Postposing is exemplified. It should be recalled that Stress Postposing is only one of the rules available in the hendecasyllable to eliminate this clash.

(37)   di ch'ío]$_\phi$ [réndo ragióne]$_\phi$ in questo caldo.'   Inferno, XXII, 54
       'for which I render reckoning in this heat.'

The ictus on *rendo* may be moved rightward according to our proposal because *rendo*, a verbal head, and *ragione*, its nonbranching direct object, form a phonological phrase. The ictus on *rendo* is therefore secondary, that is, it is in correspondence with a weak node of ϕ. In (38), however, the clash between *andar* and *suso* cannot be eliminated in the same way.

(38)   li occhi nostri n'andár]$_\phi$ [súso]$_\phi$ [a la cima   Inferno, VIII,3
       'our eyes went upward to its summit'

According to our proposal, the reason Stress Postposing may not apply in this case is that the adverbial head *suso* cannot form a ϕ with its first complement, since the complement is branching. *Suso* therefore forms a ϕ on its own and thus bears a primary ictus that may not be affected by

Stress Postposing. Once more, syntactic constituents cannot account for the difference in behavior illustrated on the basis of the lines in (37) and (38).

To sum up, we have shown in this section that certain rhythmic phenomena in the hendecasyllable of the *Commedia* can be accounted for by means of one condition on prosodic rules and three prosodic rules. All of these need to refer to both the metrical hierarchy and the prosodic hierarchy, specifically the phonological phrase. This indicates that the prosodic hierarchy, rather than the syntactic hierarchy, is the linguistic level relevant for the description of the prosodic rules of the hendecasyllable of the *Commedia*.

10.4. Conclusions

Verse is the result of the matching between an abstract metrical pattern and language. In this chapter, we have shown that the linguistic level involved in this matching is the phonological deep structure or prosodic structure. In particular, it has been proposed that the basic patterns of the hendecasyllable of Dante's *Inferno* are those in which the prominent nodes of the metrical hierarchy, specifically the strong nodes of metrical feet and cola, match the prominent nodes of the prosodic hierarchy, specifically those of feet and phonological phrases. Since we have proposed that the hendecasyllable is basically iambic, this amounts to saying that there is a tendency for secondary stresses – that is, the DTEs of feet – to fall on even positions in the line, and for the DTEs of phonological phrases to coincide with the rightmost node of the cola.

No respectable poet, of course, will write a poem in which all lines conform to the basic pattern, since the result would be a tedious and impersonal rhythm. Instead, there is in most lines a certain amount of tension between the metrical pattern and language. The solution of this tension may be seen as the attempt to compromise on the part of the two levels. As in all compromises, every party must give in to a certain extent. When the meter gives in, the result is a modification of the basic iambic pattern. The possible deviations from the basic pattern are described in terms of metrical rules. When, on the other hand, the language gives in, the result is a modification of the rythmic alternations of ordinary language. The possible modifications of this rhythm are described by means of prosodic rules.

We have argued that in these cases too, it is the prosodic structure that accounts for what are possible and what are impossible applications of the rules. That is, both the metrical and the prosodic rules we have analyzed are constrained in their application by the phrasing determined by the prosodic hierarchy. Just as is the case for phonological rules of ordinary spoken language, so also in poetry we find, for example, that some rules may modify the metrical pattern only at the beginning of a prosodic constituent, or only at the juncture of two prosodic constituents. Similarly, certain prosodic rules of the hendecasyllable are bound to one particular prosodic domain, or to one of its limits.

As was mentioned above, it has been demonstrated by Hayes (to appear) that the prosodic hierarchy is the linguistic level that must be referred to in order to account for a number of correspondence rules in English verse; in particular, the iambic pentameter of Shakespeare, Milton, and Shelley and the acatalectic trochaic tetrameter of Longfellow's *Song of Hiawatha*. Hayes also proposes this to be a more general characteristic of meter, that is, he hypothesizes that 'syntax has effect in metrics only insofar as it determines the phrasings of the [p]rosodic [h]ierarchy', which amounts to saying that metrics is a purely phonological phenomenon. Hayes therefore calls this hypothesis the Hypothesis of Phonological Metrics. The analysis of the hendecasyllable of the *Inferno* presented here is further confirmation of this hypotbesis.

Since we have shown in this book that prosodic rules of ordinary spoken language have direct access only to prosodic structure and not to syntactic structure, it follows from the theory developed here that another purely phonological phenomenon – meter – should not have access to any structure deeper than the prosodic one. The confirmation of the Hypothesis of Phonological Metrics thus offers additional support for the theory of prosodic phonology in general.

NOTES

1. It should be noted that within grid theory – as proposed, among others, by Liberman (1975), Liberman and Prince (1977), Prince (1983), and Selkirk (1984b) – there is an abstract pattern, the grid, which represents the rhythmic alternation of natural language. The basic difference between this grid and the abstract level we will posit here for poetry is that while the precise nature of the rhythmic patterns is not inherent in the grid, it *is* inherent in the abstract level posited for verse.
2. While a distinction can be made between metrical pattern (the number of positions in a verse) and rhythmical pattern (the distribution of strong elements in the metrical pattern), we will not make this distinction here. See Baratta (1981).
3. A similar assumption is made by Piera (1982) for the hendecasyllable in Spanish. A basic iambic pattern for the Italian hendecasyllable has been assumed, among others, by Sesini (1939) and Elwert (1968).
4. There are a few exceptions to this generalization (see Di Girolamo, 1976), that is, cases in which a syllable that occupies the tenth position does not bear primary word stress but is nonetheless metrically prominent. Since lines of this type are very restricted in number and are clearly perceived as metrically complex, they do not invalidate the generalization.
5. All the translations of lines of the *Commedia* are taken from Singleton (1970, 1973, 1975).

6. In these and all following examples, only the ictuses relevant to the discussion are marked.

7. A rule that has a similar effect, Beat Addition, has been proposed by Selkirk (1984b) to account for certain rhythmic patterns of natural language. See also Prince's (1983) rule of Perfect Grid Construction.

8. It should be noted that by adding a primary ictus on the second position, this ictus becomes adjacent on the second level to the last primary ictus of the preceding line of verse. The slight pause that separates one line of verse from the next, however, prevents these ictuses from being perceived as clashing.

9. Rules that insert silent positions have also been proposed to account for certain aspects of the rhythm of natural language (see, among others, Liberman, 1975; Selkirk, 1984b).

10. In this as well as other lines that will be used in the rest of this chapter, a primary ictus falls on a position different from that allowed by the basic pattern. In this case, for example, the metrical pattern has a primary ictus on the eigth position, which is moved by Inversion to the seventh position. This is an indication that a metrical rule has applied to adjust the metrical pattern to fit the linguistic material. Here too, the linguistic constituent needed to describe the domain of application of the rule is the phonological phrase.

11. The English translations of Petrarch are taken from Durling's (1976) translation.

12. The fact that in those cases in which two weak positions do not follow a clash there are two weak positions preceding it has been brought to our attention by Karijn Helsloot.

Chapter 11

Conclusions

A fundamental characteristic of spoken language is the relation between the continuous flow of sounds on the one hand, and the existence of structured patterns within this continuum on the other hand. In this respect, spoken language is related to many other natural and man-made phenomena around us, such as the movement of the ocean and musical compositions, which are characterized not only by their typically flowing nature but also by the fact that they are structured into distinct units such as waves and measures.

Prosodic phonology is a theory of the way in which the flow of speech is organized into a finite set of phonological units. It is also, however, a theory of interactions between phonology and the other components of the grammar. The interactions, in the form of mapping rules that build phonological structure on the basis of morphological, syntactic, and semantic notions, provide the set of phonological units necessary to characterize the domains of application of a large number of phonological rules. While the division of the speech chain into various phonological units makes reference to structures found in the other components of the grammar, a fundamental aspect of prosodic theory is that the phonological constituents themselves are not necessarily isomorphic to any constituents found elsewhere in the grammar.

Although the specification of the domains within which phonological rules are bound is the main goal of prosodic phonology, it turns out that the same units are relevant in other areas of the organization of language as well. For example, even in the absence of phonological rules, the prosodic units of grammar are relevant at the first level of speech processing in the disambiguation of ambiguous sentences. In addition, the constituents provided by prosodic phonology account for a number of rhythmic patterns and metrical conventions observed in works of poetry.

The organization of phonology into prosodic units encompasses seven hierarchically structured levels, going from the syllable to the phonological utterance. While the two smallest units, the syllable and the foot, are essentially constructed on the basis of phonological criteria, the remaining units represent each in its own way the interface between phonology and the other components of the grammar. The pattern that emerges from the various types of interactions is one in which the degree of abstractness and generality of the nonphonological information required correlates with the height of a prosodic constituent in the hierarchy. In particular, the mapping rules that construct the phonological word and the clitic group must make reference to such specific notions as the position in which affixes and clitics are attached to their host. Phonological phrase construction makes reference to such general syntactic notions as the head of a phrase and the direction of embedding. The two highest prosodic constituents, the intonational phrase and the phonological utterance, make use of even more general notions, such as the root sentence and the highest node in the syntactic tree, respectively.

At the three uppermost levels of the prosodic hierarchy, restructuring rules are needed under certain circumstances to readjust the prosodic structures built by the mapping rules. While the mapping rules make reference only to morphological and syntactic structure, the restructuring rules also make reference to semantic notions and to factors such as the length of the string in question and the rate and style of speech. The restructuring rules, like the basic mapping rules, exhibit a correlation between the height of a constituent in the hierarchy and the generality and abstractness of the criteria on which restructuring is based. That is, in the case of the phonological phrase, the crucial notions are that of phrasal complement and the length of the complement as defined by its branchingness. As far as the intonational phrase is concerned, however, the relevant criteria for restructuring include the notion of cyclic node and a somewhat abstract notion of temporal length, as defined on the basis of a combination of such factors as the length of a given string and the rate of speech. Finally, in the case of the phonological utterance, restructuring depends on the existence of certain syntactic relations and implicit semantic connections between adjacent sentences. The fact that most restructurings are optional allows for a certain degree of variability at the highest levels of the prosodic hierarchy. Given that syntax does not permit any variability in its constituent structure, it is even clearer in the case of restructured strings that the prosodic and syntactic hierarchies represent independent and often nonisomorphic structures.

Since the mapping rules that create the prosodic constituents above the word level make crucial use of specific syntactic notions and thus reflect certain aspects of syntactic structure, once the prosodic constituents are established, the application or lack of application of a particular phonological rule can be used in the diagnosis of problematic syntactic constructions. That is, in cases in which more than one analysis of a given construction is possible on syntactic grounds, whether or not a phonological rule applies between two words can be taken as evidence that the words are members of the same or different phonological constituents.

This, in turn, can be taken as evidence that the words must be in one or another type of syntactic relation to each other.

While the mapping rules represent the phonological interpretation of those aspects of the other components of the grammar that are relevant for the sound pattern of a language, the output of the mapping rules provides the deep structure of the purely phonological component. It is this phonological deep structure that contains the representation of the domains of application of the purely phonological rules of a language, that is, those rules that make reference only to phonological entities: the phonological structures that are modified by the rule and the prosodic domain within which the rule applies. The theory of prosodic phonology is thus a stronger theory than one in which phonological rules make direct reference to morphological and syntactic notions in addition to phonological notions, in that it allows us to impose restrictions on the domains in which sandhi rules apply. That is, it allows us to capture the generalization that the vast majority of these rules do not apply in domains other than those present in phonological deep structure.

Thus, even if the mapping rules that define the prosodic constituents need to make reference to a number of nonphonological concepts, prosodic theory represents a substantial simplification of phonology in general in that the mapping rules apply only in order to create the deep structure. It is not necessary, therefore, for each phonological rule to repeat the set of nonphonological notions in its formulation; it is sufficient to make reference only to the appropriate constituent(s) in the specification of the domain of application of a rule.

Given that there are subsystems of phonology other than prosodic theory, such as grid theory and autosegmental phonology, the prediction is made on the basis of the fact that prosodic phonology represents a theory of domains, that the phonological component of the grammar must be internally organized in a modular fashion. It follows from such a position that rules whose structural change is best accounted for within another subsystem of the phonological component will make reference to prosodic phonology for the specification of their domain of application. This is the case, for example, of rhythm rules that represent the interaction between grid theory and prosodic phonology and of harmony rules that represent the interaction between autosegmental and prosodic phonology.

The interactions among the different subsystems of the phonological component, along with the interactions between the phonological component and the other components of the grammar, require a somewhat more complex model of grammar than has thus far been assumed within generative theory. The standard T-model, in particular, turns out to be both too strong and too weak. It is too strong in the sense that s-structure, the input to the phonological component, contains a type of information (i.e. phonetically empty syntactic constituents) whose presence makes incorrect predictions as to the application of phonological rules. The T-model is too weak, on the other hand, in that s-structure is the only input to the phonology and thus does not allow for any direct interaction between the phonological component and the other components of the grammar. Such interactions, however, have been shown to be necessary. The different types of interactions that are required by the model of prosodic phonology advanced in this study on the basis of the phonological rules of a number of different languages can be represented schematically as in Figure 1.

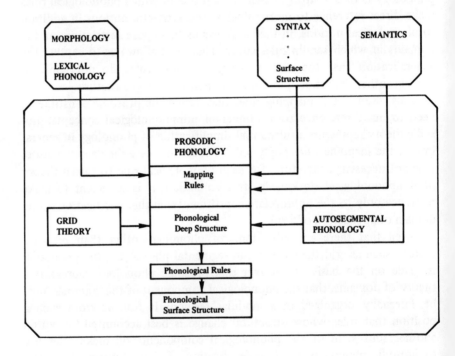

Fig. 1. Model of the interactions between prosodic phonology and the other subsystems of the grammar

The problems that arise in relation to the T-model are eliminated in the model in Figure 1. As can be seen, first of all, a part of each of the three components, syntax, morphology, and semantics, provides direct input to the mapping rules of the phonological component. In addition, the problem created by taking s-structure and thus also syntactic constituents without phonetic content to be the input to the phonology is resolved by the fact that in Figure 1 the part of the syntactic component that interacts with the phonology is the surface structure, that is, a structure with labeled bracketings but without empty constituents.

In conclusion, the relation between the continuous flow of speech sounds and the structure internal to this flow is the relationship that exists between the final phonetic production of a given string and the analysis of this string in terms of the set of interactions among the subsystems of the phonology and among the components of the grammar. A fuller understanding of the sound pattern of human language will not be attained, however, until a deeper understanding is reached of the interaction of grammar with other cognitive systems as well as with human motor capacities and perception.

Bibliography

Akmajian, A. (1975) More evidence for an NP cycle. *Linguistic Inquiry* 6, 115-129.

Alighieri, Dante, *La Commedia*. Secondo l'antica Vulgata. Ed. by G. Petrocchi (1966-67).

Alighieri, Dante. *The Divine Comedy*. Translated by C.S. Singleton. (1970) *Inferno*; (1973) *Purgatorio*; (1975) *Paradiso*. Princeton: Princeton University Press.

Allen, M.R. (1978) *Morphological Investigations*. Ph.D. diss.: University of Connecticut.

Anderson, S. (1982) Differences in rule type and their structural basis. In H. van der Hulst and N. Smith (eds.), *The Structure of Phonological Representations*. Part II. Dordrecht: Foris. 1-25.

Aronoff, M. (1976) *Word Formation in Generative Grammar*. Linguistic Inquiry Monograph 1. Cambridge, Mass.: MIT Press.

Bach, E. (1977) Montague grammar and classical transformational grammar. Paper presented at the Conference on Montague Grammar, Philosophy and Linguistics. Albany: SUNY.

Banfield, A. (1973) Narrative style and the grammar of direct and indirect speech. *Foundations of Language* 10, 1-39.

Baratta, G. (1981) Ritmo. *Enciclopedia*. Torino: Einaudi.

Basbøll, H. (1978) Boundaries and ranking rules in French phonology. In B. de Cornulier and F. Dell (eds.), *Études de Phonologie Française*. Paris: Éditions du Centre de la Recherche Scientifique.

Beccaria, G.L. (1970) Dialefe. *Encyclopedia Dantesca*. Rome: Enciclopedia Italiana Treccani.

Bell, A. and J.B. Hooper (eds.) (1978) *Syllables and Segments*. Amsterdam: North-Holland.

Beltrami, P.G. (1981) *Metrica, Poetica, Metrica Dantesca*. Pisa: Pacini.

Bertinetto, P.M. (1973) *Ritmo e Modelli Ritmici*. Torino: Rosemberg and Sellier.

Bertinetto, P.M. (1979) *Aspetti Prosodici della Lingua Italiana*. Padova: CLESP.

Bierwisch, M. (1965) Poetik und Linguistik. In H. Kreuzer and R. Gunzenhäuser (eds.), *Mathematik und Dichtung*. München: Nymphenburger

Verslagshandlung. 49-65. Also published in English as: Poetics and linguistics. In D.C. Freeman (ed.) (1970) *Linguistics and Literary Style*. New York: Holt, Rinehart and Winston. 96-118.

Bierwisch, M. (1966) Regeln für die Intonation deutscher Sätze. *Studia Grammatica 7: Untersuchungen über Akzent und Intonation im Deutschen*. Berlin: Akademie-Verlag. 99-201.

Bing, J. (1979) *Aspects of English Prosody*. Ph.D. diss.: University of Massachusetts, Amherst. IULC, 1980.

Bloomfield, L. (1933) *Language*. New York: Holt.

Bolinger, D. (1965) *Forms of English: Accent, Morpheme, Order*. Cambridge, Mass.: Harvard University Press.

Booij, G. (1977) *Dutch Morphology*. Dordrecht: Foris.

Booij, G. (1981) *Generatieve Fonologie van het Nederlands*. Utrecht: Het Spectrum.

Booij, G. (1983) Principles and parameters in prosodic phonology. *Linguistics* 21, 249-280.

Booij, G. (1984) Neutral vowels and the autosegmental analysis of Hungarian vowel harmony. *Linguistics* 22, 629-641.

Booij, G. (1985) Coordination reduction in complex words: a case for prosodic phonology. In H. van der Hulst and N. Smith (eds.), *Advances in Non-Liner Phonology*. Dordrecht: Foris.

Booij, G. (to appear) Lexical phonology and the organization of the morphological component. In E. Gussmann (ed.), *Rules and the Lexicon*. Lublin: Katolicki Uniwersytet.

Booij, G. and J. Rubach (1984) Morphological and prosodic domains in lexical phonology. *Phonology Yearbook* 1, 1-27.

Camilli, A. (1941) I rafforzamenti iniziali. *Lingua Nostra* 3, 170-174.

Camilli, A. (1965) *Pronuncia e grafia dell'italiano*. Firenze: Sansoni.

Chatman, S. (1965) *A Theory of Meter*. The Hague: Mouton.

Chatman, S. (1972) Ritmo, metro, esecuzione. In R. Cremante and M. Pazzaglia (eds.), *La Metrica*. Bologna: Il Mulino.

Chomsky, N. (1965) *Aspects of the Theory of Syntax*. Cambridge, Mass.: MIT Press.

Chomsky, N. (1970) Remarks on Nominalization. In R.A. Jacobs and P.S. Rosenbaum (eds.), *Readings in English Transformational Grammar*. Waltham, Mass.: Ginn and Co. 184-221.

Chomsky, N. (1981) *Lectures on Government and Binding*. Dordrecht: Foris.

Chomsky, N. and M. Halle (1968) *The Sound Pattern of English*. New York: Harper and Row.

Chomsky, N. and H. Lasnik (1977) Filters and control. *Linguistic Inquiry* 8, 425-504.

Clements, G.N. (1978) Tone and syntax in Ewe. In D.J. Napoli (ed.),

Elements of Tone, Stress and Intonation. Washington, D.C.: Georgetown University Press.

Clements, G.N. and S.J. Keyser (1983) *CV Phonology. A Generative Theory of the Syllable*. Cambridge, Mass.: MIT Press.

Clements, G.N. and E. Sezer (1982) Vowel and consonant disharmony in Turkish. In H. van der Hulst and N. Smith (eds.), *The Structure of Phonological Representations*. Part II. Dordrecht: Foris. 213-255.

Cooper, G. and L. Meyer (1960) *The Rhythmic Structure of Music*. Chicago: University Press.

Cooper, W.E. and J. Paccia-Cooper (1980) *Syntax and Speech*. Cambridge, Mass.: Harvard University Press.

Crystal, D. (1969) *Prosodic Systems and Intonation in English*. Cambridge: Cambridge University Press.

Crystal, D. (1980) *A First Dictionary of Linguistics and Phonetics*. London: André Deutsch.

Cupaiolo, F. (1959) *Grammatica Latina*. Milano: Principato.

Di Girolamo, C. (1976) *Teoria e Prassi della Versificazione*. Bologna: Il Mulino.

Dixon, R.M.W. (1970) Olgolo syllable structure and what they are doing about it. *Linguistic Inquiry* 1, 273-276.

Dixon, R.M.W. (1977a) Some phonological rules of Yidin^y. *Linguistic Inquiry* 8, 1-34.

Dixon, R.M.W. (1977b) *A Grammar of Yidin^y*. Cambridge: Cambridge University Press.

Downing, B. (1970) *Syntactic Structure and Phonological Phrasing in English*. Ph.D. diss.: University of Texas, Austin.

Durling, R.M. (trans.) (1976) *Petrarch's Lyric Poems*. Cambridge, Mass.: Harvard University Press.

Elwert, W.T. (1968) *Italienische Metrik*. München: Max Hueber. Also published in Italian as: W.T. Elwert (1973) *Versificazione italiana, dalle origini ai giorni nostri*. Firenze: Le Monnier.

Emonds, J. (1976) *A Transformational Approach to English Syntax. Root, Structure-Preserving and Local Transformations*. New York: Academic Press.

Emonds, J. (1980) Word order in generative grammar. *Journal of Linguistic Research* 1, 33-54.

Empson, W. (1930) *Seven Types of Ambiguity*. London: Chatto and Windus.

Encrevé, P. (1983) Liaison sans enchaînement. *Actes de la Recherche en Sciences Sociales* 43, 39-66.

Farmer, A.K. (1980) *On the Interaction of Morphology and Syntax*. Ph.D. diss.: MIT.

Fiorelli, P. (1958) Del raddoppiamento da parola a parola. *Lingua Nostra* 19, 122-127.

308   *Prosodic phonology*

Fodor, J.A. and T. Bever (1965) The psychological reality of linguistic segments. *Journal of Verbal Learning and Verbal Behavior* 4, 414-420.

Fodor, J.A., J.D. Fodor, M.F. Garrett and J.R. Lackner (1975) Effects of surface and underlying clausal structure on click location. *Quarterly Progress Report of the MIT Research Laboratory of Electronics*.

Fudge, E.C. (1969) Syllables. *Journal of Linguistics* 5, 253-286.

Fussel, P., Jr. (1965) *Poetic Meter and Poetic Form*. New York: Random House.

Garcia-Bellido, P. (1979) Trilled vs. flapped /r/: some remarks on the syllable structure of Spanish. Paper presented at NELS 10, Ottawa, Ontario.

Garrett, M.F., T. Bever and J.A. Fodor (1966) The active use of grammar in speech perception. *Perception and Psychophysics* 1, 30-32.

Giannelli, L. (1976) *Toscana, Profilo dei Dialetti Italiani*. 9. Pisa.

Gianelli, L. and L. Savoia (1979-1980) L'indebolimento consonantico in Toscana. *Rivista Italiana di Dialettologia* 2, 23-58; 4, 39-101.

Gimson, A. (1970) *An Introduction to the Pronunciation of English*. 2nd. ed. London: Edward Arnold.

Graffi, G. (1980) Universali di Greenberg e grammatica generativa. *Lingua e Stile* XV. 3, 371-390.

Guitart, J.M. (1979) On the true environment for weakening and deletion in consonant-weak Spanish dialects. Paper presented at the Conference on Non-English Language Variation in the Western Hemisphere, University of Louisville, Kentucky.

Guitart, J.M. (1980) Entorno a la sílaba como entidad fonemática en los dialectos del Caribe hispánico. Paper presented at the V Simposio de Dialectología del Caribe Hispánico, Caracas, Venezuela.

Gunter, R. (1974) *Sentences in Dialog*. Columbia, S.C.: Hornbeam Press.

Hale, K. (1980) Remarks on Japanese phrase structure: Comments on the papers on Japanese syntax. In Y. Otsu and A. Farmer (eds.), *MIT Working Papers in Linguistics* II. 185-203.

Hale, K. (1981) On the position of Walbiri in a typology of the base. IULC.

Hall, R. (1944) *Hungarian Grammar*. Language Monographs 21. Baltimore: LSA.

Halle, M. (1973) Prolegomena to a theory of word formation. *Linguistic Inquiry* 4, 3-16.

Halle, M. and S.J. Keyser (1966) Chaucer and the study of prosody. In D.C. Freeman (ed.), *Linguistics and Literary Style*. New York: Holt, Rinehart and Winston. 366-426.

Halle, M. and S.J. Keyser (1971) *English Stress: Its Form, Its Growth, and Its Role in Verse*. New York: Harper and Row.

Harris, J. (1969) *Spanish Phonology*. Cambridge, Mass.: MIT Press.

Harris, J. (1983) *Syllable Structure and Stress in Spanish*. Cambridge, Mass.: MIT Press.

Hayes, B. (1981) *A Metrical Theory of Stress Rules*. Ph.D. diss.: MIT. IULC, 1980.

Hayes, B. (1982) Metrical structure as the organizing principle of Yidin^y phonology. In H. van der Hulst and N. Smith (eds.), *The Structure of Phonological Representations*. Part I. Dordrecht: Foris. 97-110.

Hayes, B. (to appear) The prosodic hierarchy in meter. In P. Kiparsky and G. Youmans (eds.), *Proceedings of the 1984 Stanford Conference on Meter*. Cambridge, Mass.: MIT Press.

Hoji, H. (1982) X-schema in Japanese and the * parameter. Ms. University of Washington.

Hooper, J.B. (1972) The syllable in phonological theory. *Language* 48, 525-540.

Hooper, J.B. (1976) *An Introduction to Natural Generative Phonology*. New York: Academic Press.

Hoorn, H. van (1983) Cancellazione della vocale finale prima di consonante. Ms. University of Amsterdam.

Householder, F. (1964) Three dreams of Modern Greek phonology. *Word* 20.3. Special Publication 5, 17-27.

Hulst, H. van der (1984) *Syllable Structure and Stress in Dutch*. Dordrecht: Foris.

Hulst, H. van der (in preparation) Verkleuring van lange vocalen voor *r*: een woorddomein regel.

Hulst, H. van der and N. Smith (1982) Prosodic domains and opaque segments in autosegmental phonology. In H. van der Hulst and N. Smith (eds.), *The Structure of Phonological Representations*. Part II. Dordrecht: Foris. 311-336.

Hyman, L. (1977) On the nature of linguistic stress. In L. Hyman (ed.), *Studies in Stress and Accent*. SCOPIL 4. Los Angeles: USC Linguistics Department. 37-82.

Jackendoff, R. (1974) Introduction to the $\overline{\text{X}}$ Convention. IULC.

Jaeggli, O. (1980) Remarks on *to* contraction. *Linguistic Inquiry* 11, 239-245.

Jakobson, R. (1960) Linguistics and poetics. In T. Sebeok (ed.), *Style in Language*. Cambridge, Mass.: MIT Press. 350-385.

Jones, D. (1986) *The Pronunciation of English*. Cambridge: Cambridge University Press.

Kahn, D. (1976) *Syllable-based Generalizations in English Phonology*. Ph.D. diss.: MIT. IULC.

Kahn, D. (1980) Syllable-structure specifications in phonological rules. In M. Aronoff and M.-L. Kean (eds.), *Juncture*. Saratoga, Calif.: Anma Libri.

Kaisse, E.M. (1977) On the syntactic environment of a phonological rule. In W.A. Beach, S.E. Fox and S. Philosoph (eds.), *CLS* 13. 173-185.

Kaisse, E.M. (1983) The syntax of Auxiliary Reduction in English. *Language* 59, 93-122.

Kaisse, E.M. (1985) *Connected Speech. The Interaction of Syntax and Phonology*. New York: Academic Press.

Kean, M.-L. (1980) Grammatical representations and the description of language processing. In D. Caplan (ed.), *Biological Studies of Mental Processing*, Cambridge, Mass.: MIT Press. 239-268.

Kenstowicz, M. and C. Kisseberth (1977). *Topics in Phonological Theory*. New York: Academic Press.

Keyser, S.J. (1969) The linguistic basis of English prosody. In D.A. Reibel and S.A. Schane (eds.), *Modern Studies in English Grammar*. Englewood Cliffs, New Jersey: Prentice-Hall. 379-394.

Keyser, S.J. and P. Kiparsky (1984) Syllable structure in Finnish phonology. In M. Aronoff and R.T. Oehrle (eds.), *Language Sound Structure*. Cambridge, Mass.: MIT Press. 7-31.

King, H.V. (1970) On blocking the rules for contraction in English. *Linguistic Inquiry* 1, 134-136.

Kiparsky, P. (1975) Stress, syntax and meter. *Language* 51, 576-616.

Kiparsky, P. (1977) The rythmic structure of English verse. *Linguistic Inquiry* 8, 189-247.

Kiparsky, P. (1979) Metrical structure assignment is cyclic. *Linguistic Inquiry* 10, 421-442.

Kiparsky, P. (1982) From cyclic phonology to lexical phonology. In H. van der Hulst and N. Smith (eds.), *The Structure of Phonological Representations*. Part I. Dordrecht: Foris. 131-175.

Kisseberth, C. and M. Abasheikh (1974) Vowel length in Chimwi:ni. A case study of the role of grammar in phonology. In A. Bruck, R. Fox and M. LaGaly (eds.), *Papers from the Parasession on Natural Phonology*. Chicago: CLS. 193-209.

Klatt, D. (1975) Vowel lengthening is syntactically determined in a connected discourse. *Journal of Phonetics* 3, 129-140.

Klatt, D. (1976) Linguistic uses of segmental duration in English: acoustic and perceptual evidence. *Journal of the Acoustic Society of America* 59, 1208-1221.

Klavans, J. (1982) *Some Problems in a Theory of Clitics*. Ph.D. diss.: University College London, 1980. IULC.

Klavans, J. (1985) The independence of syntax and phonology in cliticization. *Language* 61, 95-120.

Kohler, K.J. (1966) Is the syllable a phonologocal universal? *Journal of Linguistics* 2, 207-208.

Kontou, D.T. (1973) Fast speech rules and some phonological processes of Modern Greek: a preliminary investigation. Athens: University of Athens, School of Philosophy Publications.

Kooij, J. (1971) *Ambiguity in Natural Language*. Amsterdam: North-Holland.

Kuryłowicz, J. (1948) Contribution à la théorie de la syllabe. *Biuletyn Polskiego Towarzystwa Jezykoznawaczego* 8, 80-114.

Ladd, D.R. (1980) *The Structure of Intonational Meaning*. Bloomington: Indiana University Press.

Lakoff, G. (1970) Global rules. *Language* 46, 627-639.

Langendoen, D.T. (1975) Finite-state parsing of phrase-structure languages and the status of readjustment rules in the grammar. *Linguistic Inquiry* 6, 533-554.

Lapointe, S.G. and M.H. Feinstein (1982) The role of vowel deletion and epenthesis in the assignment of syllable structure. In H. van der Hulst and N. Smith (eds.), *The Structure of Phonological Representations*. Part II. Dordrecht: Foris. 69-120.

Leben, W. (1973) *Suprasegmental Phonology*. Ph.D. diss.: MIT.

Leben, W. (1982) Metrical or Autosegmental. In H. van der Hulst and N. Smith (eds.), *The Structure of Phonological Representations*. Part II. 177-190.

Lees, R.B. (1961) *The Phonology of Modern Standard Turkish*. The Hague: Mouton.

Lehiste, I. (1972) Timing of utterance and linguistic boundaries. *Journal of the Acoustical Society of America* 51, 2018-2024.

Lehiste, I. (1973) Phonetic disambiguation of syntactic ambiguity. *Glossa* 7, 107-122.

Lehiste, I., J.P. Olive and L.A. Streeter (1976) Role of duration in disambiguating syntactically ambiguous sentences. *Journal of the Acoustical Society of America* 60, 1199-1202.

Leone, A. (1962) A proposito del raddoppiamento sintattico. *Bollettino del Centro di Studi Filologici e Linguistici Siciliani* 7, 163-170.

Leonetti, P. (1934-1938) *Storia della Tecnica del Verso Italiano*. Napoli: Morano.

Lepschy, A.L. and G. Lepschy (1977) *The Italian Language Today*. London: Hutchinson.

Lewis, G.L. (1967) *Turkish Grammar*. Oxford: Clarendon Press.

Liberman, M. (1975) *The Intonational System of English*. Ph.D. diss.: MIT. IULC.

Liberman, M. and A. Prince (1977) On stress and linguistic rhythm. *Linguistic Inquiry* 8, 249-336.

Lieberman, P. (1967) *Intonation, Perception, and Language*. Cambridge, Mass.: MIT Press.

Longobardi, G. (1980) Remarks on infinitives: a case for a filter. *Journal of Italian Linguistics* 5, 101-156.

Lowenstamm, J. (1979) *Topics in Syllabic Phonology*. Ph.D. diss.: University of Massachusetts, Amherst.

Lowenstamm, J. (1981) On the maximal cluster approach to syllable structure. *Linguistic Inquiry* 12, 575-604.

Malécot, A. (1960) Vowel nasality as a distinctive feature in American English. *Language* 36, 222-229.

Malikouti, A. (1970) Μετασχηματιστική μορφολογία του νεοελληνικού ονόματος. Ph.D. diss.: University of Athens.

Malikouti-Drachman, A. and G. Drachman (1981) Slogan chanting and speech rhythm in Greek. In W. Dressler (ed.), *Phonologica 1980*. Innsbruck: IBS. 283-292.

Marotta, G. (to appear) Rhythmical Constraints on 'Syntactic Doubling'. *Journal of Italian Linguistics*.

McCarthy, J. (1979) On stress and syllabification. *Linguistic Inquiry* 10, 443-466.

Miyara, S. (1981) Phonological Phrase and Phonological Reduction. *University of Massachusetts Occasional Papers in Linguistics* 7. 154-183.

Mohanan, K.P. (1981) *Lexical Phonology*. Ph.D. diss.: MIT. IULC, 1982.

Morin, Y.-C. and J. Kaye (1982). The syntactic bases for French liaison. *Journal of Linguistics* 18, 291-330.

Moulton, W. (1947) Juncture in Modern Standard German. *Languague* 23, 212-226.

Muysken, P.C. (1977) *Syntactic Developments in the Verb Phrase of Ecuadorian Quechua*. Dordrecht: Foris.

Napoli, D.J. and M. Nespor (1979) The syntax of word initial consonant gemination in Italian. *Language* 55, 812-841.

Navarro Tomás, T. (1957) *Manual de Pronunciación Española*. New York: Hafner.

Nespor, M. (1977) *Some Syntactic Structures of Italian and Their Relationship to the Phenomenon of Raddoppiamento Sintattico*. Ph.d. diss.: University of North Carolina, Chapel Hill.

Nespor, M. (1983) Formele eigenschappen in fonologie en syntaxis. *TTT* 3.3/4, 260-276. Also published in English as: M. Nespor (1983) Formal properties in phonology and syntax. *Lingua e Stile* 18, 343-360.

Nespor, M. (1984) The phonological word in Italian. In H. van der Hulst and N. Smith (eds.), *Advances in Non-Linear Phonology*. Dordrecht: Foris.

Nespor, M. (1986) The phonological word in Greek and Italian. In H. Andersen and J. Gvozdanović (eds.), *Proceedings of the Working Group on Sandhi Phenomena in the Languages of Europe*.

Nespor, M. and M. Scoreretti (1985) Empty elements and phonological form. In J. Guéron and J.-Y. Pollock (eds.), *Grammatical Representation*. Dordrecht: Foris.

Nespor, M. and I. Vogel (1979) Clash avoidance in Italian. *Linguistic Inquiry* 10, 467-482.

Nespor, M. and I. Vogel (1982) Prosodic domains of external sandhi rules. In H. van der Hulst and N. Smith (eds.), *The Structure of Phonological Representations*. Part I. Dordrecht: Foris. 225-255.

Nespor M. and I. Vogel (1983a) Prosodic hierarchy and speech perception. In *La Percezione del Linguaggio*, Atti del Seminario, 1980. Firenze: Accademia della Crusca. 339-362.

Nespor, M. and I. Vogel (1983b) Prosodic structure above the word. In A. Cutler and D.R. Ladd (eds.), *Prosody: Models and Measurements*. Berlin: Springer, 123-140.

Newman, P. (1972) Syllable weight as a phonological variable: the nature and function of the contrast between 'heavy' and 'light' syllables. *Studies in African Linguistics* 3, 301-323.

Niedermann, M. (1953) *Précise de Phonétique Historique du Latin*. Paris: Librairie C. Klinckieck.

Noske, R. (1982) Syllabification and syllable changing rules in French. In H. van der Hulst and N. Smith (eds.), *The Structure of Phonological Representations*. Dordrecht: Foris. 257-310.

Odden, D. (1980) The phrasal phonology of Kimatuumbi. Ms. Yale University.

Pennings, L. (1985) Scontro di due ictus nel verso di Dante. Ms. University of Amsterdam.

Petrarca, F. *Canzoniere*. Ed. by G. Contini. Torino: Einaudi. (1968)

Petrarch, F. *Petrarch's Lyric Poems*. Translated by R.M. Durling (1976). Cambridge, Mass.: Harvard University Press.

Petrocchi, G. (ed.) (1966-67) *La Commedia*. Secondo l'antica Vulgata. By Dante Alighieri.

Piera, C. (1982). The hendecasyllable in Spanish. Ms. Cornell University.

Pierrehumbert, J. (1980) *The Phonology and Phonetics of English Intonation*. Ph.D. diss.: MIT.

Pike, K. (1947) Grammatical prerequisites to phonemic analysis. *Word* 3, 155-172.

Pike, K. and E. Pike (1947) Immediate constituents of Mazateco syllables. *International Journal of American Linguistics* 13, 78-91.

Platzak, C. (1979) *The Semantic Interpretation of Aspect and Aktionsarten*. Dordrecht: Foris.

Pratelli, R. (1970) Le renforcement syntactique des consonnes en italien. *La Linguistique* 6, 39-50.

Prince, A. (1983). Relating to the grid. *Linguistic Inquiry* 14, 19-100.

314   *Prosodic phonology*

Prince, A. (1984) Phonology with tiers. In M. Aronoff and R. Oehrle (eds.), *Language Sound Structure*. Cambridge, Mass.: MIT Press. 234-244.

Pulgram, E. (1970) *Syllable, Word, Nexus, Cursus*. The Hague: Mouton.

Riemsdijk, H. van (1978) *A Case Study in Syntactic Markedness*. Dordrecht: Foris.

Riemsdijk, H. van and E. Williams (1981) NP-structure. *The Linguistic Review* 1, 171-218.

Rizzi, L. (1976) Ristrutturazione. *Rivista di Grammatica Generativa* 1, 1-54.

Rizzi, L. (1979) La teoria della traccia e processi fonosintattici. *Rivista di Grammatica Generativa* 4, 165-181.

Rischel, J. (1982) On unit accentuation in Danish and the distinction between deep and surface phonology. ARIPUC 16, 191-239. Also published in *Folia Linguistica XVII* (1983).

Rohlfs, G. (1949) *Historische Grammatik der Italienischen Sprache und ihrer Mundarten*. Bern: A. Francke A.G.

Rotenberg, J. (1975) French Liaison, phrase structure, and semicyclical rules. Ms. MIT.

Rotenberg, J. (1978) *The Syntax of Phonology*. Ph.D. diss.: MIT.

Rubach, J. (1984) *Cyclic and Lexical Phonology: The Structure of Polish*. Dordrecht: Foris.

Safir, K. (1985) Binding in relatives and LF. *Glow Newsletter* 14, 77-79.

Saib, J. (1978) Segment organization and the syllable in Tamazight Berber. In A. Bell and J.B. Hooper (eds.), *Syllables and Segments*. Amsterdam: North-Holland, 93-104.

Saito, M. and H. Hoji (1983) Weak crossover and move α in Japanese. *Natural Language & Linguistic Theory* 1, 245-259.

Sapir, E. (1930) Southern Paiute, a Shoshonean language. *Proceedings of the American Academy of Arts and Sciences* 65.1.

Sassen, A. (1979) Morfeem- en syllabegrens. *TABU*, 25-28.

Savoia, L.M. (1974-1975) Condizioni fonetiche nel fiorentino comune e alcune proposte per una teoria fonologica concreta. *Studi di Grammatica Italiana* 4, 209-330.

Scalise, S. (1983) *Morfologia Lessicale*. Padova: Clesp.

Scalise, S. (1984) *Generative Morphology*. Dordrecht: Foris.

Schane, S.A. (1968) *French Phonology and Morphology*. Cambridge, Mass.: MIT Press.

Selkirk, E.O. (1972) *The Phrase Phonology of English and French*. Ph.D. diss.: MIT. IULC, 1982.

Selkirk, E.O. (1978a) The French foot: on the status of French 'mute' e. *Studies in French Linguistics* 1, 141-150.

Selkirk, E.O. (1978b) On prosodic structure and its relation to syntactic structure. Paper presented at the Conference on Mental Representation in Phonology. IULC, 1980. Published in T. Fretheim (ed.) (1981) *Nordic Prosody II*. Trondheim: TAPIR. 111-140.

Selkirk, E.O. (1980a) Prosodic domains in phonology: Sanskrit revisited. In M. Aronoff and M.-L. Kean (eds.), *Juncture*. Saratoga, Calif.: Anma Libri. 107-129.

Selkirk, E.O. (1980b) The role of prosodic categories in English word stress. *Linguistic Inquiry* 11, 563-605.

Selkirk, E.O. (1982) *The Syntax of Words*. Cambridge, Mass.: MIT Press.

Selkirk, E.O. (1984a) On the major class features and syllable theory. In M. Aronoff and R.T. Oehrle (eds.), *Language Sound Structure*. Cambridge, Mass.: MIT Press. 107-136.

Selkirk, E.O. (1984b) *Phonology and Syntax: The Relation between Sound and Structure*. Cambridge, Mass.: MIT Press.

Sesini, U. (1938) Il verso neolatino nella ritmica musicale. *Convivium* 5, 481-502.

Sesini, U. (1939) L'endecasillabo: struttura e peculiaritá. *Convivium* 11, 545-570.

Setatos, M. (1974) Φωνολογίαϛτῆς Κοιν῀ης Νεοελληνικῆς. Αϑήνα: Παπαζήσης.

Shopen, T. (1972) *A Generative Theory of Ellipsis*. Ph.D. diss.: UCLA.

Siegel, D. (1974) *Topics in English Morphology*. Ph.D. diss.: MIT.

Siegel, D. (1977) The adjacency condition and the theory of morphology. *NELS* 8, 189-197.

Singleton, C.S. (trans.) (1970, 1973, 1975) *The Divine Comedy*. By Dante Alighieri. (1970) *Inferno*; (1973) *Purgatorio*; (1975) *Paradiso*.

Smith, N. (in preparation) Evidence for the foot as a hierarchical unit in Žuǀ'hõasi.

Snyman, J.W. (1975) *Žuǀ'hõasi: Fonologie en Woordenboek*. Kaapstad: A.A. Balkema.

Steriade, D. (1982) *Greek Prosodies and the Nature of Syllabification*. Ph.D. diss.: MIT.

Stowell, T. (1981) *Origins of Phrase Structure*. Ph.D. diss.: MIT.

Strauss, S. (1982) *Lexicalist Phonology of English and German*. Dordrecht: Foris.

Ternes, E. (1973) *The Phonemic Analysis of Scottish Gaelic*. Hamburg: Helmut Buske Verlag.

Tompa, J. (1972) *Kleine ungarische Grammatik*. Budapest: Akadémiai Kiadó.

Trager, G. and H. Smith (1951) An outline of English structure. *Studies in Linguistics, Occasional Papers 3*. Norman, Oklahoma: Battenberg Press.

Traina A. and G. Bernardi Perini (1977) *Propedeutica al Latino Universitario*. Bologna: Pátron.

316   *Prosodic phonology*

Trommelen, M. (1983) *The Syllable in Dutch*. Dordrecht: Foris.

Ullman, S. (1962). *Semantics: An Introduction to the Science of Meaning*. Oxford: Basil Blackwell and Mott.

Vago, R. (1976) Theoretical implications of Hungarian vowel harmony. *Linguistic Inquiry* 7, 243-264.

Vago, R. (1980) *The Sound Pattern of Hungarian*. Washington, D.C.: Georgetown University Press.

Vanelli, L. (1979) Una forma supplettiva dell'articolo e la sua fonosintassi. *Rivista di Grammatica Generativa* 4, 183-206.

Vennemann, T. (1971) The phonology of Gothic vowels. *Language* 47, 90-132.

Vennemann, T. (1972) On the theory of syllabic phonology. *Linguistische Berichte* 18, 1-18.

Vennemann, T. (1974) Words and syllables in natural generative grammar. In A. Bruck, R.A. Fox and M.W. LaGaly (eds.), *Papers from the Parasession on Natural Phonology*. Chicago: CLS. 346-374.

Vergnaud, J.-R. and M. Halle (1978) Metrical structure in phonology. Ms. MIT.

Vogel, I. (1977) *The Syllable in Phonological Theory; with Special Reference to Italian*. Ph.D. diss.: Stanford University.

Vogel, I. (1981) Structure prosodiche dell'Inglese. *Rivista di Grammatica Generativa* 6, 181-205.

Vogel, I, (1982) *La Sillaba come Unitá Fonologica*. Bologna: Zanichelli.

Vogel, I. (1984a) On constraining phonological rules. In H. van der Hulst and N. Smith (eds.), *Advances in Non-Linear Phonology*. Dordrecht: Foris.

Vogel, I. (1984b) Sintassi, prosodia e disambiguazione. *Quaderni Patavini di Linguistica* 4, 21-50.

Vogel, I. (1985) Review of J. Harris, *Syllable Structure and Stress in Spanish*. *Journal of Linguistics* 21, 195-208.

Vogel, I. (1986) External sandhi rules operating across sentences. In H. Andersen and J. Gvozdanović (eds.), *Proceedings of the Working Group on Sandhi Phenomena in the Languages of Europe*.

Vogel, I., M. Drigo, A. Moser and I. Zannier (1983) La cancellazione di vocale in Italiano. *Studi di Grammatica Italiana*, 191-230.

Vogel, I. and S. Scalise (1982) Secondary stress in Italian. *Lingua* 58, 213-242.

Wanner, D. (1980) Romance and the rhythmical nature of stress. In F.H. Nuessel Jr. (ed.), *Contemporary Studies in Romance Languages*. IULC.

Warburton, I.P. (1970) Rules of accentuation in classical and modern Greek. *Glotta* 48, 107-121.

Wells, J.C. (1982) *Accents of English. Vol. 1: Introduction*. Cambridge: Cambridge University Press.

Welmers, W.E. (1973) Igbo tonology. *Studies in African Linguistics* 1, 255-278.

Welmers, W.E. and B.F. Welmers (1969) Noun modifiers in Igbo. *International Journal of American Linguistics* 35, 315-322.

Wheeler, D.W. (1981) *Aspects of a Categorial Theory of Phonology*. Ph.D. diss.: University of Massachusetts, Amherst.

Whitman, J. (1982) Configurationality parameter. Ms. Harvard University.

Whitney, W.D. (1889) *Sanskrit Grammar*. Cambridge, Mass.: Harvard University Press.

Williams, E. (1977) Discourse and logical form. *Linguistic Inquiry* 8, 101-139.

Woitsetschlaeger, E.F. (1976) *A Semantic Theory of the English Auxiliary System*. IULC.

Yip, M. (1980) *The Tonal Phonology of Chinese*. Ph.D. diss.: MIT. IULC.

Zanoni, L. (1948) *Grammatica Latina. Morfologia e Sintassi*. Milano: Mondadori.

Zwicky, A. (1970) Auxiliary reduction in English. *Linguistic Inquiry* 1, 323-336.

Zwicky, A. (1977) On clitics. Paper presented at the 3rd International Phonologie-Tagung, University of Vienna, 1976. IULC.

Zwicky, A. (1984) Clitics and particles. In A. Zwicky and R. Wallace (eds.), *Ohio State Working Papers in Linguistics* 29, 148-173.

Subject Index

Language and Rule Index

Name Index